JN415819

Yonsei Korean Studies Series No. 1

Koryŏsa chŏryo
Ia
Essentials of Koryŏ History

Translated by

Sem Vermeersch

Yonsei University Press

Koryŏsa chŏryo Ia
Essentials of Koryŏ History

Translated by Sem Vermeersch

Copyright©2021 by 연세대학교 국학연구원

All rights reserved. No part of this publication may be reproduced, stored in a retrieval system or transmitted in any form or by any means, whether electronic, mechanical, photocopying, recording or otherwise, without the prior written permission of the author.

Published and Printed in the Republic of Korea by Yonsei University Press.
50 Yonsei-ro, Seodaemun-gu, Seoul, 03722, Republic of Korea

Tel: 82-2–2123–3378~80
Fax: 82-2–2123–8673
E-mail: ysup@yonsei.ac.kr
http://press.yonsei.ac.kr

ISBN 978–89–6850–550-8 (93910)

₩ 25,000

Preface

Yonsei University has long been a center for the study of Korea. Through the establishment of its Kukhak yŏn'guwŏn (Institute of Korean Studies) in 1977, it further systematized and optimized the existing research capacity that centered on Korea's role in East Asian history, literature, religion, and philosophy. The Institute of Korean Studies inherited and continues the academic achievements of the Tongbanghak yŏn'guso (Institute of East Asian Studies) in researching Korean culture and history from the perspective of its interrelatedness with East Asian culture. The Institute has also reproduced and published a number of classics including the *Siyong hyangak po* 時用鄕樂譜, *Wŏrin Sŏkpo* 月印釋譜, *Soaron* 小兒論, *Tongmun yuhae* 同文類解, *P'alsea* 八歲兒, *Samyŏk ch'onghae* 三譯總解, *Han-Han ch'ŏngmungam* 韓漢淸文鑑, and *Koryŏsa* 高麗史. Moreover, besides publishing the *Koryŏsa* (History of Koryŏ) in 1953, on two occasions—in 1961 and 1996—it published an index to the *Koryŏsa*, thereby contributing to a broad understanding of traditional Korean literature, thought, and society.

In tune with the Institute's efforts to promote Korean Studies through the *Koryŏsa*, it is also striving to internationalize Korean Studies by preparing an English translation of the *Koryŏsa chŏryo* 高麗史節要 (Essentials of Koryŏ History), which can be regarded as an abbreviation of the *Koryŏsa*. With increasing internationalization and globalization, there is also an increased need for mutual understanding and cultural exchange. In response to Korea's socio-economic development, internationally interest in Korean studies has increased. The establishment of university centers and departments dedicated to the study of Korea in the US and Europe has led to the introduction of more courses and programs on Korea. In many cases, in-depth research on pre-modern Korean society is being carried out at major US universities in particular, but although knowledge of the Korean language is a prerequisite for such research, Korea can and should play an active role too in the internationalization of Korean studies through the translation into English of its classics. Thus, the translation of a key work such as the *Essentials of Koryŏ History* can contribute greatly to research on not only Korean history but also literature, philosophy, and society.

This English translation of the *Essentials of Koryŏ History* is the outcome of a special project of Yonsei's "Globalization of Korean Studies" program (Sep. 2005–Feb. 2007) under the direction of Professor Do Hyeonchul. The first instalment, Edward J. Shultz and Hugh H.W. Kang's translation of the sections dealing with the Military Period, appeared in December 2014. Here in the second instalment is Sem Vermeersch's translation of the opening chapters of the *Essentials of Koryŏ History*. I hope that publication of this book may provide an opportunity for understanding Korea's traditional culture, and contribute to the development of Korean Studies as a well-established global discipline.

Finally I would like to thank Professor Do Hyeonchul for making publication of this book possible by initiating the research project and providing the institutional support. Also, I would like to thank the editorial team of Yonsei University Press under the directorship of Ha Kyungsim for taking care of publication of the Institute's books in spite of the difficult situation the publishing world is facing.

Kim Seongbo
Director, Institute of Korean Studies
Yonsei University
February 2021

Introduction

Following publication of Edward (Ned) Shultz and Hugh Kang's translation of chapters (*kwŏn*) 11 to 17 of the *Koryŏsa chŏryo* (Essentials of Koryŏ history) in 2014, here finally I am able to present the beginning of this panoramic history of the Koryŏ dynasty. However, since the number of pages covered by chapters 1 to 10 is almost double that of 11 to 17, I decided to split it into two volumes, starting with chapters 1 to 5 translated here. At the time of publication, I have barely started translating the remaining chapters, so it may be a while before the second part is published.

Ned Shultz has already provided a good introduction to the characteristics and background of the *Koryŏsa chŏryo* in his translation, but since that volume is not exactly widely available,[1] and since I would like to add some different angles to the story, I think it is well worth providing my own introduction to this translation.

On the whole, I have tried to follow the model set in the translation of chapters 11 to 17, which cover the reign of King Ŭijong (1146–1170) and the military period (1170–1259)—first of all because that model is sound, and second to provide continuity in style if not in voice. The layout of the chapter structure is the same, as is the translation of most key terms. The excellent glossary of official terminology found in volume II has served as a guide to my translation; however, the bureaucracy of Koryŏ took a long

1 Edward J. Shultz and Hugh H. W. Kang, trans., *Essentials of Koryŏ History* II (Paju: Jimoondang, 2014).

time to mature, and since the early Koryŏ official system is quite different from that of the twelfth century, it was necessary to add my own list of terminology; this will be explained in more detail below, in the section on conventions.

Whether or not the translation of a work of official historiography such as this one is successful, hinges to a large degree on how the terminology is handled. This is not a narrative history, but something more akin to an official report: it is written by bureaucrats for bureaucrats, and is full of their jargon, i.e. official titles, types of communication, institutions etc. Since they perfectly understood what these terms stood for, it is never explained what a certain institution did or how it functioned. Korean scholars have devoted a lot of research on the bureaucratic system, but even so figuring out what duties a particular office entailed and what kind of authority it gave its incumbent remains an arduous task.

I have to confess that this is an issue that remains to be resolved: there is as yet no handbook of official titles such as the one produced for the classical Chinese bureaucracy by Charles Hucker.[2] A draft glossary produced by Ned Shultz proved immensely helpful, as it is the first step towards producing standard translations of key terms, something sorely needed to raise the level of scholarship on Koryŏ. Of course, given the similarities with the Chinese bureaucratic system, I have made extensive use of Hucker's dictionary to translate office titles. In the case of early Koryŏ, which had developed its own system and terms, in many cases I had to simply devise new terms. Without knowing the exact remit of these early Koryŏ institutions, translating them is often no more than an educated guess. But even if an office title is borrowed from China and has a clearly defined function, one cannot simply assume that in Koryŏ it functioned exactly in the same way as in China.

A case in point is the Royal Secretariat (Chungsŏ-sŏng 中書省). As one of the Three Departments (Samsŏng 三省), it formed the core structure of the

2 Charles O. Hucker, *A Dictionary of Official Titles in Imperial China* (Stanford: Stanford University Press, 1985).

Tang government system: The Royal Secretariat, which assisted the ruler in his exercise of power through formulating and promulgating edicts and decrees; the Chancellery (Munha-sŏng 門下省), which acted as an overseer of this process; and the Department of Ministries (Sangsŏ-sŏng 尙書省), the executive branch, which comprised the six ministries that executed policies in six important areas (personnel, taxation, military, rites, punishment, public works).[3] Although the Three Departments are first mentioned in the first year of T'aejo's reign (918) it is clear that they did not exist in that form until much later.

Exactly when they emerged, and under what form, is however very difficult to determine. It is generally agreed that it was King Sŏngjong (r. 981–997) who first tried to introduce the Tang system. The *Koryŏsa chŏryo* writes that in 982 he changed the existing Advisory Council (Naeŭi-sŏng 內議省) into the Department of Royal Secretaries-Chancellery (Naesa Munha-sŏng 內史門下省). Note the different name for the Royal Secretariat, and also the fact that it was combined with the Chancellery. It was only in 1061, under the reign of King Munjong, that the Naesa-sŏng finally changed its name into Chungsŏ-sŏng. Hence the general understanding that the Koryŏ bureaucratic system was only finalized under Munjong (r. 1046–1083). However, such statements do not reveal much about the actual working of the system. The term Naesa is attested before 982 (see an entry for 976, where mention is made of the minister of the Royal Secretaries), and also sometimes occurs after 1061. It does seem to have its origins in China where it was used as an alternative term for the Chungsŏ-sŏng,[4] but most of all it appears to be emblematic of the early Koryŏ system, itself based on the structure put in place by the preceding

3 Of course, the structure was vastly more complex than this. A good summary of the Tang system (and that of later dynasties) can be found as appendix to Hucker's *Dictionary*. A good introduction to the Koryŏ system can be found in John Duncan, "The Formation of the Central Aristocracy in Early Koryŏ," *Korean Studies* 12 (1988): 39–61, especially 43–45. In Korean the most accessible introduction remains Han Yongun's chapter in vol. 13 of the National Institute of Korean History's *Han'guksa* (Kwach'ŏn: Kuksa p'yŏnch'an wiwŏnhoe, 1993), 9–155.

4 Hucker, *Dictionary*, no. 4250.

state, known from 911 as T'aebong (see Table 1, in appendix). Rather than an intricate hierarchical system of checks and balances, it seems to have been a horizontal system where responsibilities were evenly distributed. Moreover, given that the sources invariably mention the minister(s) of the department (e.g. Naesaryŏng 內史令), never the department, it is possible that it was not a full-fledged institution.

This example should help to illustrate the difficulty of accurately grasping the Koryŏ system: gradually pushed into the straightjacket of the "ideal" Chinese model, it never quite fitted that model. Indeed, this model probably obscured the underlying operation of the bureaucracy. Arguably even more difficult to grasp is the system of regional administration. Usually referred to as the "kun-hyŏn" 郡縣 system after the main constituent local administrative units, in fact there were many more categories. In general the main prefectures (*chu* 州) were most important, followed by districts (*pu* 府), prefectures (*kun* 郡), and counties (*hyŏn* 縣). However, this apparently neat hierarchy is deceptive. Localities could change in status depending on their loyalty or whether they were the residence of influential court or military figures. Counties were further differentiated into control counties, where a centrally appointed magistrate governed, and subordinate counties (*sokhyŏn* 屬縣) controlled by them. Furthermore there were many other localities such as *pugok* 部曲 and *so* 所, reserved for special classes of disenfranchised people. Since they do not occur frequently, I have left these untranslated, but provided a short explanatory footnote at first mention.[5]

Besides understanding the jargon, another important condition for a successful translation is a correct understanding of the text and the context in which it was produced. As is well known, the *Koryŏsa chŏryo* was presented to the throne in 1452 by Kim Chongsŏ 金宗瑞 (1383–1453).[6] Just a year earlier the same Kim Chongsŏ had presented the *Koryŏsa* to

5 The best introduction in English to the problem of Koryŏ local administration is Yokeun Jeong, "The Management of Koryŏ: Local Administration (Kunhyŏn) and its Operation," *Korean Studies* 41 (2017): 99–127.

6 *Munjong sillok* 12 (2/2/20).

the throne.[7] These works are thus very much complementary: whereas the former uses a chronological system (*p'yŏnnyŏn* 編年), the latter uses a thematic system (*kijŏn* 紀傳, lit. annals–biography), consisting of annals, treatises, and biographies. The *Koryŏsa* is by far the bigger work at 132 chapters against the *Koryŏsa chŏryo*'s 35. However, the *Essentials of Koryŏ history* is not merely a condensed and reorganized version of the *History of Koryŏ*. Although ultimately there are no great discrepancies in content, it is highly likely that they were ultimately redacted based on the same sources but as separate projects. And due to their different iterations of the same events, their discrepancies offer different possible interpretations of these events. Also, the *Koryŏsa chŏryo* has many "commentaries" inserted by historians, usually to disparage what they regarded as degenerate Koryŏ customs.[8]

Of course, this by itself does not make much difference in terms of interpreting the text. However, comparison of difficult passages often proves helpful in resolving difficulties. The *Koryŏsa chŏryo* often condenses information, or leaves out an event that helps to shed light on other passages. For example, since this work does not have a biography section, biographical information about an important official is usually inserted after the notice of his death, albeit in a much more condensed format than the biographies of the *Koryŏsa*; thus, in such cases it is often helpful to check the full biography for a better understanding of very terse passages about the person at hand. But more importantly, slight divergences between the two works show that they are themselves redacted versions of earlier sources. While it has long been held that historiographers were bound by rules of absolute fidelity to their sources (*suribujak* 述而不作), i.e. that they wrought their texts by quoting verbatim from the source texts, recent research by Ro Myoungho has shown that in certain cases the texts were edited, for example when Koryŏ practices were deemed to go against what

7 *Munjong sillok* 9 (1/8/25).

8 Pyŏn T'aesŏp, Koryŏsa *ŭi yŏn'gu* (Seoul: Samyŏngsa, 1982), 189–193.

was deemed proper for a kingdom.[9]

This should perhaps be anything but a surprise: we know that the composition of the official history of Koryŏ was an arduous process. The first attempt was undertaken by Chŏng Tojŏn and others immediately following the founding of Chosŏn in 1392, and presented to the throne in 1395. This was the *Koryŏ kuksa* 高麗國史 in 37 chapters. However, it was never accepted: allegedly because of omissions and because it was too biased towards the new ruling dynasty and critical of Koryŏ actors, thus lacking objectivity.[10] Attempts by early Chosŏn kings to interfere with the process were likely another factor behind the abortion of the early efforts at Koryŏ historiography,[11] so that when Kim Chongsŏ and his colleagues finally managed to present a version that was acceptable to the king and officialdom at large, this must have been a compromise.

Since the veritable records of Koryŏ, the main source for compiling these histories, were likely destroyed after the finalization of the project, we shall never know how the early Chosŏn historiographers rewrote history. Further complicating the matter is the fact that the veritable records of Koryŏ themselves had been subject to vicissitudes and tampering. The Khitan invasion of 1010 seems to have destroyed all the early Koryŏ *sillok*, and later Koryŏ records were sometimes compiled decades after the death of a king.[12] Thus the *sillok* for the first century or so of Koryŏ's existence had to be rewritten from scratch; but in what state they reached the early Chosŏn period is far from certain. A note at the end of Ch'oe Sŭngno's famous memorial which we find under the year 982 explains that "the remaining six points were lost in the military conflict of the *kyŏngsul* year (1010)." Yet Ch'oe's memorial still covers several pages, in fact more than

9 See No Myŏngho, "*Koryŏsa* ŭi 'ch'amŭi chi sa' wa 'taesa ch'ŏnha' ŭi 'isil chiksŏ:' Haeksim i sakche toen Koryŏ ŭi hwangje chedo" ["Straight copying of facts" and the "overstepping the limits" of the "great pardon of the Under-Heaven" in the *Koryŏsa*: Deleting the core of the Koryŏ imperial system], *Han'guksaron* 60 (2014): 1–56.

10 Pyŏn T'aesŏp, Koryŏsa *ŭi yŏn'gu*, 9.

11 See Graeme Reynolds, "Culling Archival Collections in the Koryŏ–Chosŏn Transition," *Journal of Korean Studies* 24, no. 2 (2019): 225–253.

12 Ibid., 230.

the whole reign of King Kwangjong (r. 945–975). Kwangjong's reign is particularly hard done by, since it is by far the sparsest chronicle of all reigns. In how far this is due to the fact that records were lost, or that Koryŏ annalists were deliberately silent, or that Chosŏn historiographers culled material is unfortunately impossible to determine. But we should at least be attuned to this fact, and hopefully future research will pay more attention to the lacunae, imbalances, and different voices in the *Essentials of Koryŏ History*.[13]

Given these problems, how has this translation tried to resolve them? In all honesty, given the tight schedule under which I had to finish this translation, it was not possible to give satisfactory explanations for the peculiarities of the text. Therefore, in case of difficult or problematic terminology, I have simply added a footnote to explain it as best as possible but also to try and pinpoint what the problem is. As for the bias imposed by the compilers, here there is of course no easy way out. The problem is that the bias is not expressed by what is written, but mostly by what is omitted: following the convention of Chinese historiography, blame is apportioned by simply stating facts, it is up to the reader to determine whether this is proper action or not. Hence the importance of the "historian's comments" (*sasin wal* 史臣曰) to indicate that frequent temple visits or temple construction is a dereliction of royal duty. Given the terseness of the original, I have simply tried to infer the general tone or intention of certain passages and translated accordingly. Dialogues for example are invariably introduced by the verb "*wal* 曰" but rather than simply translating "the king said…" "the council said…" depending on the context I have also translated as "argued" "rebuked," etc. Another example: every time the Censorate critiques a decision of the king or an official makes a policy proposal, when the king agrees it is simply noted "*chong chi* 從之" or "[the king] agreed with this."

13 For example, in early Koryŏ royal proclamations are almost invariably indicated with the term *kyo* 教, "instruction," but from Hyŏnjong's reign onwards the term *che* 制 is used. Both can be interpreted as a kind of decree, executive orders to the officialdom. The term *cho* 詔 "edict" is used only rarely: see e.g. Munjong 11 (1057), fourth month. It is not certain whether there was a change in practice, whether the terms were later corrected, or whether they represented different purposes.

Depending on the context however, I have translated "the king put this into effect" or "the king agreed with this proposal" or other expressions. This will hopefully aid readability; after all, the intended reader of this text was far more knowledgeable about the court procedures, and could fill in this information for himself. This is not the case for modern readers however.

Let me emphasize once again that this translation is not as polished as I had wished. When Prof. Do Hyeonchul, then director of the Institute of Korean Studies at Yonsei University, contacted me late in 2014 to undertake the translation of the first 10 chapters, I promised to finish this in five years. This proved overly optimistic, but rather than dragging this further out, I thought it best to simply release what I have managed to translate so far as it is. Though falling short of the standards of academic translation of Hanmun (Classical Chinese) texts set by sinologists, at least I hope that this translation has struck a balance between readability and accuracy, so that at long last the story of Koryŏ's founding is made available to a readership outside the Korean peninsula. Finally, I would be remiss if I failed to mention my indebtedness to the pioneering work of Korean translators of this text; notably the version made available through the website of the National Institute of Korean History was extremely helpful.[14] I would also like to thank Prof. Do for entrusting me with this task, and Ned Shultz for reading through the whole draft translation and catching numerous errors.

Conventions

As mentioned above, like volume II this volume also includes a separate glossary of important terms, mainly offices and titles. However, I have omitted the run-of-the mill terms of the Chinese-style bureaucracy, such as Director of the Chancellery or Vice-minister at one of the ministries in the Department of Ministries. Instead, these terms can be found in tables 3 to 4, which make it easier to grasp the relative position of these posts within

14 http://db.history.go.kr/KOREA/item/level.do?itemId=kj&types=r The source text I used is a reprint of the 1453 edition (Hosa bunkō, Nagoya) published by Asea munhwasa in 1972.

a particular office. Likewise, offices and rank titles from the early Koryŏ period can be found in tables 1 and 2. Not much is known about this early system, however, since the monograph on officialdom in the *Koryŏsa* does not include a description of this bureaucratic system; hence the tables should be seen merely as a guide, not as a definitive description of the system.

As much as possible I have tried to translate terms. This is the case for offices and titles as described above, but also for the generic part in proper nouns: thus rather than writing Hoegyŏng-jŏn 會慶殿, I have rendered it Hoegyŏng Hall. Likewise -chŏng 亭 is translated "pavilion," -chin 鎭 "garrison," -kang 江 "river," and -yŏk 驛 "station." As for the main administrative divisions, -to 道 is rendered as province, -mok 牧 as department, -no 路 as circuit, and -kye 界 as "border circuit." The most commonly used divisions, however, are -chu 州 "greater prefecture," -kun 郡 "prefecture," -pu 府 "district," and -hyŏn 縣 "county." For some cases however where it was difficult to find a suitable equivalent I have left it untranslated, notably for *pugok* 部曲 and *so* 所. Also -wŏn 院, -sa 寺 are left as such: the former is used for either monastic or palace compounds, while the latter denotes Buddhist monasteries. Finally, -nŭng 陵 for royal tombs has also been left untranslated.

Weights and measures have also been left untranslated, since any Western equivalent is tenuous at best; the reader is referred to a separate glossary of weights and measures in appendix.

I have tried to keep explanatory footnotes to a minimum; most allusions to classics are very briefly explained because without such context it would be difficult to understand what is being argued. If no specific edition to a classic is mentioned, it means that the text has been retrieved from the Chinese Text Project website (ctext.org). For the rest, the footnotes are fairly haphazard, since I inserted them where I felt a historical place name of particular office needed some explanation, or where a problem needed to be flagged. Most offices and titles are however left without further explanation in English translation, since they can be checked in the tables, the glossary, in Hucker's dictionary, or in Vol. II.

Likewise, I have inserted characters where it was felt they are needed to aid understanding rather than systematically for each and every name or title. Also, they have been inserted in cases where interpretation was difficult. For example, sometimes Japanese names are mentioned, but since it is not clear how they should be Romanized according to Japanese pronunciation, I have Romanized them following the Korean pronunciation, and inserted characters. For Korean names McCune-Reischauer system is used; Chinese names follow the Pinyin system. How to treat Khitan and Jurchen names was a headache; because we do not know how they should be Romanized following the Khitan or Jurchen language, I have chosen to Romanize the Khitan (Liao) names in Pinyin and the Jurchen names in McCune-Reischauer. My reasoning for this is that throughout this volume, Jurchen peoples are invariably treated as subordinate to Koryŏ, either as "barbarian" others or (quasi) vassals, but mostly within the orbit of Koryŏ.

Sem Vermeersch
Seoul, December 21, 2020

Contents

Memorandum on presenting the *Essentials of Koryŏ History* [to the throne]

Kim Chongsŏ, Third State Councilor of the State Council, rank 1A, in charge of the Hall of Worthies and Royal Lecture mat, director of the Office of Historiography, Mentor to the Heir Apparent, and others respectfully submit a refined copy of the newly composed *Essentials of Koryŏ History*. Truly trembling in apprehension, your subject Kim Chongsŏ and others prostrate themselves and venture the following words to your majesty.

We humbly observe that the chronological style [of historiography] originated with the Zuo Commentary of the *Spring and Autumn Annals*, while the annals-essays style [of historiography] started with Sima Qian's *Records of the Historian*. Starting with Ban Gu's [*History of the Former Han*], all court historians have taken Sima Qian's *Records of the Historian* to be their model, and none have not used it. This is due to its vast scale, its contents covering everything comprehensively. However, we cannot escape the problem that it has many superfluous parts and is difficult to consult. Therefore historians cannot discard either [of these historiographical models] because both have strong and weak points.

Now Koryŏ emerged at the end of the Tang dynasty, eliminating evil forces through military might and capturing people's minds through magnanimity. Thus a dynasty was founded and passed on to later generations. Eventually shrines were founded and law statutes decided; schools were raised and the civil service examinations were established; the Department of Royal Secretariat was founded to manage all affairs and establish the core of the ruling structure; royal inspectors of local government were dispatched to investigate prefectures and counties, and the greedy and corrupt could not get their way; the garrison militia system allowed for a settled army that relied on farming [in peace time]; the stipend land system allowed officials to enjoy a salary across generations; punishment was used to govern and officialdom was equipped with a hierarchy of ranks, and the country was at peace; the people had enough to eat, so this way government established an era of unprecedented peace.

After the middle of the Koryŏ period the rulers could no longer overcome the burdens placed on their government, and in their court they were entrapped by the seducement of love and favoritism, while on the outside they were controlled by powerful or perfidious ministers. Several powerful enemies invaded brandishing their weapons. Everything was topsy-turvy to the point that a fake royal stole the throne. The sacrifices to the Wang lineage were interrupted and there was no one to succeed their throne. King Kongyang went against what was correct, and eventually his foolishness and depravity caused the ruin of the dynasty. Then Heaven gave birth to a true sovereign[1] so that our people could live peacefully again; this is definitely not something that could be accomplished by human power.

King T'aejo [Yi Sŏnggye, r. 1392–1398], posthumous title Kanghŏn taewang, first ordered his state councilors to compose a history of Koryŏ. King T'aejong [r. 1400–1418], posthumous title Kongjŏng taewang, then ordered that the mistakes [in this history] be corrected but in the end it could not be successfully accomplished. King Sejong, posthumous title Changhŏn taewang, with the assistance of numinous sages, set forth a civilizational transformation, and ordered your subject and others to

1 In the original woodblock editions of the text, before every mention of Chosŏn sovereigns there is a line break so that the sovereign's title appears at the top of the next line. I have not attempted to replicate this in the layout of this translation.

select a number of officials and establish a bureau so as to compile and edit [a history of Koryŏ], instructing "First write a comprehensive history and next a chronological history." Your subject and the other officials received this order with trembling and did not dare to be even slightly idle. Unfortunately before the book could be presented to the king, suddenly we were abandoned [due to the king's death]. Your majesty then respectively continued the will of the previous monarch and ordered us to finish the project.

Looking back, having received this order in the past from the previous king, we lacked the courage to firmly decline on account of our rusticity, and years later in the autumn of the *sinmi* year (1451) managed to finish the book [i.e., the *Koryŏsa*]. Thus we gathered all those events that are worth instructing the world about, and all those situations that can be a source of pride as well as model, deleted the superfluous and summarized [the essential], ordering everything chronologically by year for easy referencing. As such, the events related to 475 years [of history] and thirty-two kings are covered comprehensively without omission, both detailed affairs and outline ones, all are included. In terms of historical craft, originally we are poorly equipped, but even though the phrasing may be rustic and the account of events unrefined, it may be of some modest assistance towards instructing the way by encouraging good and guarding against evil.

May you favor us by perusing it in a moment of leisure and quiet, and endeavor to investigate the flourishing virtue of old, and by recovering the way of governing the world through this, pass on the benefit to the people; this would be an unsurpassed blessing. The *Essentials of Koryŏ history* that we compiled in thirty-five fascicles follows this memorandum, respectfully for your information; we are greatly perturbed and fearful by this impudence. Your subject Kim Chongsŏ and others, filled with apprehension prostrate ourselves, and prostrate ourselves again, respectfully inform you.

On a day in the second month of the third year of the Jingtai era (1452), Kim Chongsŏ, Third State Councilor of the State Council, rank 1A, in charge of the Hall of Worthies and Royal Lecture mat, director of the Office of Historiography, Mentor to the Heir Apparent, and others respectfully submit this memorandum.

Conventions of the *Essentials of Koryŏ History*

(1). In the present endeavor of compilation, we have selected the essential affairs that are relevant to government, insurrection, rising and falling; all that one should be careful to avoid has been carefully selected and recorded, the rest can be found in the regular history and has thus been omitted.

(2). In the nomenclature, even though using terms such as "royal ancestor" (*chong* 宗), "your majesty" (*p'yeha* 陛下), or "heir apparent" (*t'aeja* 太子) is presumptuous and a transgression of the role [of a vassal country], they have been written exactly as in the old [sources] to preserve the true [nature of Koryŏ]. As for frequent events such as court audiences or sacrifices, they have been recorded only if there is sufficient reason to do so. If the king personally participated in the sacrifice, then it is [invariably] written down. As for the king's traveling to temples or receiving bodhisattva precepts, or holding a Buddhist ceremony, since the kings did this so frequently, it would be excessive to write them all down; therefore for each king the first occurrence of an event only is written down. As for giving food to monks, for huge events where up to a 100,000 monks are fed, such waste of money needs to be recorded. As for the exchange of envoys with the suzerain country, even though this is a frequent event it needs to be written down as a mark of respect for China. Disasters or uncanny events that are experienced, however small, need to be recorded because Heaven's censure needs to be taken seriously. Carousing in the fields with banquets and music, even though a frequent event, needs to be written down as a warning against idle pleasure. The appointment, retirement, dismissal, and banishment of important officials, and the employment of the worthy in all its aspects, all need to be written down. Memorials and other proposals that were implemented or were otherwise important also need to be written down as precedents to be referred to.

(3). Following the precedent of Wang Mang [in the History of the Han], for Sin U's reign no regnal dates are used, only the cyclical dates to correct the crime of insolence.

(4). In [Sima Guang's] *Universal Mirror for the Aid of Government*, the chronological record [for Wang Mang's last year] is determined through the [chronology] of the succeeding [Emperor Guangwu]. According to this precedent, what comes before the tenth month of the first year of King Kongyang, even though it is the reign of King Sin Ch'ang, it is also recorded as the first year of King Kongyang.

Historian-officials[2]

Kim Chongsŏ, Chŏng Inji, Hŏ Ik, Yi Sŏnje, Yi Kyejŏn, Sin Sŏkcho, Sin Sukchu, Pak P'aengnyŏn, Kim Yemong, Kim Maenghŏn, Yang Sŏngji, Yi Ye, Kim Chigyŏng, Kim Yunbok, Kim Han'gye, Yu Sŏngwŏn, Yi Kŭkkam, Yun Kigyŏn, Pak Wŏnjŏng, Kim Chil, Hong Yakch'i, Yi Hyojang, Yi Ik, Chŏn Hyou, Yi Yunin, Kim Yong, Han Sŏbong, Yun Chayŏng.

2 In this list I have omitted the office titles of these officials.

1. T'aejo

T'aejo, Divine Sage Grand Ruler[1]

His given name was Kŏn 建, and his courtesy name Yakch'ŏn 若天.[2] His surname was Wang, and he came from Song'ak Prefecture in Hanju.[3] He was the eldest son of the prefect of Kŭmsŏng 金城, [Wang] Yung 隆. On the 14th *pyŏngsul* day of the first month of the *chŏngyu* year—the fourth year of the Qianfu era of Emperor Xizong of Tang, and the third year of King Hŏngang of Silla [877]—his mother Lady Han gave birth to T'aejo in their residence south of Song'ak. A divine light of purple essence pervaded the room, filling up the courtyard for the whole day, and forming a coiling and twisting shape that resembled a dragon.

When young he was clever and bright; his august forehead showed a sun-shaped protuberance,[4] his jaws were square and his forehead wide. His reserve of *ki* was as deep as that of a hero, and his voice was resounding. He

1 These are the posthumous titles of the Koryŏ founder Wang Kŏn (877–943), which were bestowed after his death. The first, "grand progenitor" (T'aejo) is the standard temple name (*myoho* 廟號) for dynastic founders, whereas the second is an honorific title (*si* 謚).

2 The names meaning "the builder" and "like Heaven" respectively.

3 Hanju was the name of modern-day Seoul in Unified Silla, while Song'ak referred to Kaesŏng, then a prefecture subordinate to Hanju.

4 I.e., a sign of greatness, perhaps inspired by the *ūrṇā*, the jewel (originally a tuft of hair) in the forehead of a Buddha.

was generous of spirit, to the degree that he wanted to save the world. He was on the throne for twenty-six years and reached the age of sixty-seven.

T'aejo First Year [918]

Fourth year of the Zhenming era of the last emperor of Later Liang, the third year of the Shence era of the grand progenitor (Taizu) of the Khitan.

Summer, sixth month, *pyŏngjin* [15th] day. T'aejo ascended the throne in the P'ojŏng (Implementing policy) Hall [of the palace]. [He declared] that the country's name was to be Koryŏ, and changed the original [era name] to Ch'ŏnsu 天授 (Heaven bestowed).

Formerly, Sejo[5] had constructed a house south of Song'ak. The monk Tosŏn 道詵[6] came to rest under a tree that stood outside the house gate. He sighed, "This earth should bring forth a sage ruler." When Sejo heard this, he stumbled outside in a hurry to welcome him. Together they went up to Song'ak. Tosŏn investigated [the earth] below, and scrutinized [the mountains] above, and then wrote a letter. Handing it over to Sejo, he said "Sir, next year you will obtain a precious son, and after he has grown up you can give him the letter. The letter is secret and should not be revealed to the world."

When T'aejo was seventeen, Tosŏn came again, and asked to see him, saying "You have encountered an era with countless number of misfortunes,

---

5 Sejo 世祖, "epochal progenitor" is the temple name given to Wang Kŏn's father, Wang Yung. For more details on his life, see the *P'yŏnnyŏn t'ongnok*, the chronologically arranged record of Wang Kŏn's ancestors that can be found at the beginning of the *Koryŏsa*.

6 Tosŏn (827–898), known as the father of Korean geomancy, was a Sŏn monk of the Tongni-san mountain school. He is especially famous for predicting and aiding the rise of T'aejo, but is also said to have devised new geomantic principles in which Buddhism could improve a deficient site. Yet in the Ten Injunctions (see the twenty-sixth year of T'aejo), his rules of geomancy are invoked to limit the number of temples, since temples established on spots not selected by him could damage the energy of the terrain and thus harm its inhabitants.

and the people of the Three Dynasties[7] have waited for you to save them. Therefore, I will instruct you on the method of leading an army and making a battle formation, and how to make use of the land and the time; and also on the principles of observing the geomantic features and securing supernatural protection."

At the time the Silla polity was weakened, and a host of bandits rivaled each other in setting up [their own polities]. Kyŏn Hwŏn 甄萱[8] rebelled and occupied the southern prefectures, calling them Later Paekche. Kungye 弓裔[9] availed himself of the territory of Koguryŏ, installed his capital at Ch'ŏrwŏn, and called the country T'aebong 泰封. Sejo was then the *sach'an* 沙飡[10] of Song'ak Prefecture, and pledged allegiance to Kungye's state. Kungye was pleased and made him prefect of Kŭmsŏng 金城.[11] Sejo therefore told Kungye, "Great king, if you want to rule over the territory of Chosŏn, Suksin, and Pyŏn Han,[12] the best thing to do is to make Song'ak into a fortified city and appoint my eldest son as its lord." Kungye followed

---

7 This refers to the Xia, Shang, and Zhou Dynasties of Chinese antiquity, but is here used simply to indicate a very long period of time.

8 He was the son of Ajagae, castle lord of Sangju, and according to some sources a descendant of Queen Sado of Silla. He may have declared himself king as early as 892, and was finally vanquished by Wang Kŏn in 936. See Iryŏn, "Hu Paekche Kyŏn Hwŏn," *Samguk yusa* 2. Although his name is mostly romanized as Kyŏnhwŏn, as if it were his first name only, both *Samguk yusa* and *Samguk sagi* clearly state that his original surname was Yi, but that he later changed it to Kyŏn; hence my decision to romanize as Kyŏn Hwŏn

9 Kungye, whose surname was Kim, was allegedly an illegitimate son of a Silla king. Although he was ordered to be killed, his wet nurse took pity and saved him. He then grew up in a Buddhist monastery, but seems to have been convinced he was destined to rule the country. He first set up a rebel base in the Kangnŭng area in 894, and soon after launched a new state, which frequently changed name. Kim Pusik, "Kungye chŏn," *Samguk sagi* 50.

10 *Sach'an* is originally the title of the 8th level in the office rank system of Silla, open to those of head-rank six in the Silla bone-rank system. However, by this time it had likely become a kind of merit title bestowed on military leaders or simply taken by them.

11 I.e. Kyŏngju, the capital of Silla. Since Kyŏngju was then still ruled by the Silla dynasty, this was no more than a nominal title. According to *Koryŏsa* 1.1b, this happened in 896.

12 Chosŏn and Suksin were states located in the northern half of the peninsula, while Pyŏn Han was located somewhere along the middle reaches of the southern coast. While we know that Old Chosŏn came to an end in the early 2nd century BC, no firm dates can be attached to the other states.

this advice and ordered T'aejo to construct Paröch'am fortress,[13] and indeed made him castle lord.

At the time T'aejo was twenty. Later he subjugated Kwangju, Ch'ungju, Tangsŏng, Ch'ŏngju, and Koeyang,[14] and pacified them. For this meritorious act he was given the title of *ach'an* 阿粲[15] He also led a naval force to attack Kŭmsŏng, which was taken. He also attacked and took more than ten prefectures and counties [around Kŭmsŏng], and changed the name of Kŭmsŏng 錦城 to Naju 羅州.[16]

Yangju 良州[17] then declared an emergency, and Kungye ordered him to relieve them. As soon as he returned he proposed a policy to pacify the border and extend the territory. All those at court took note of him, and Kungye also marveled, and promoted him to the rank of *alch'an* 閼粲.[18] He attacked Sahwa 沙火 Garrison in Sangju 尙州[19] and after numerous battles with Kyŏn Hwŏn managed to subjugate it.

T'aejo noticed that Kungye was arrogant and cruel, and thus frequently he had his sights on escaping the palace. Fortuitously, Kungye was worried about Naju, and therefore ordered T'aejo to go there and garrison it. He was promoted to the rank of *hanch'an* 韓粲[20] and made a navy general.

---

13 This is generally thought to correspond to what became the royal enclosure in the city of Kaesŏng, the northwestern part of the capital city of Koryŏ.

14 Tangsŏng is now Namyang-myŏn in Hwasŏng city, in the southern part of Kyŏnggi Province; Koeyang is now Koesan in North Ch'ungch'ŏng Province. The other cities still carry the same name. This would imply that T'aejo had conquered the whole northern part of Later Paekche, corresponding to modern Kyŏnggi and North Ch'ungch'ŏng Province.

15 The sixth office rank in the Silla office system, originally the highest rank attainable to someone of the head-rank six group.

16 This is still the current name; Kŭmsŏng "the brocade city" not to be confused with Kŭmsŏng "the golden city," modern Kyŏngju.

17 Modern Yangsan, located between Pusan and Ulsan in South Kyŏngsang Province. Located close to the Silla capital Kyŏngju, this would imply that Silla's authority was by then reduced to the capital region only.

18 Despite its resemblance to Silla office ranks, this appears to be a title newly created by T'aebong under Kungye. It seems to have given access to the second rank in a government office. See the table in Cho Insŏng, "T'aebong," *Han'guksa* 11: 150.

19 According to *Koryŏsa*, this took place in 906.

20 Again, an office rank title created under T'aebong. This rank apparently entitled the holders to be leaders of important government offices. See Cho Insŏng, "T'aebong," *Han'guksa* 11: 150. According to *Koryŏsa*, all this took place in 909.

He promoted sincerity and supported the scholars, so that military authority and benevolence went hand in hand. To attack and subjugate the enemy's territory, Kungye ordered the *alch'an* Chonghŭi 宗希[21] and Kim Ŏn 金言 to assist T'aejo in preparing warships and attacking Chindo 珍島 Prefecture in Kwangju, as well as Koido 皐夷島 Fortress.[22] After progressing on these places, they next went to Tŏkchinp'o 德津浦.[23] Kyŏn Hwŏn lined up his battleships between Mokp'o and Tŏkchin. Each ship's bow was attached to the next ship's stern. Land and water soldiers thus formed an unbroken force,[24] which looked daunting.

The generals [of T'aebong] were worried about this, but T'aejo said "An army's overcoming [of its foe] lies in its unity, not in its numbers." Then he led his army in a sudden attack on the enemy ships. Withdrawing slightly, taking avail of the wind he spread fire across [the enemy line]. More than half of the ships burned and sank, and more than 500 enemy soldiers were killed. Kyŏn Hwŏn escaped in a small skiff.

Before this, within the jurisdiction of Naju, various counties had become isolated from our forces, since bandit troops had cut them off. None would help the other, all were worried and suspicious. At the time, everyone's mind was occupied by this. Kim Ŏn and others, because in spite of their merit they had not received any rewards, were rather set on dissolving [their

---

21 In this period of Korean history, many people carried names that were not or barely sinicized; also, many people may not yet have had a surname. In this case too, while this may be taken as a person named Chong Hŭi, i.e., whose surname was Chong, this is in fact not a surname. The *Koryŏsa* and *Koryŏsa chŏryo* compilers seem to have taken it as such, as can be seen in the convention of naming a person by his given name after first mention: thus, a passage on Kyŏn Hwŏn calls him simply Hwŏn later on. However, it is likely that the *Koryŏsa* compilers, working in the fifteenth century, tried to fit these names into the system of surname-name that was alien to the period. I have assumed that these are simple names, and have therefore not split unless the person has an established Sinitic surname.

22 An island off the coast of modern Muan County in South Chŏlla Province. Chindo is still called thus; island on the southwestern tip of the peninsula.

23 Located to the north of modern Yŏngam Prefecture.

24 If Tŏkchin was indeed located in the present Tŏkchin-myŏn north of Yŏngam, it would mean that Kyŏn Hwŏn's warships occupied the Yŏngsang River between Tŏkchin and Mokp'o. This maneuver may have been intended to prevent T'aejo from returning upriver to his stronghold in Naju.

alliance with Kungye]. T'aejo however said "Be careful, and do not neglect your duties. Only if we unite forces and have undivided loyalties will we be able to obtain good fortune. The present ruler kills many who did not commit crimes, yet those who flatter see their ambitions fulfilled. Those inside the palace have no way to protect themselves. It is better to serve away from the center in campaigns [against the enemies], and thereby to assist the king with all our might." The generals agreed, and subsequently they went to Pannam 潘南 County[25] harbor to free their hands in planning against the enemies.

At the time there was a bandit leader who held sway over Aphae 壓海 County[26] called Nŭngch'ang 能昌. He hailed from the sea islands and was skilled at naval warfare, and was therefore nicknamed "sea otter." He gathered together refugees and small bandits from Kalch'o 葛草 island[27] with whom he formed a single force. When T'aejo arrived [in the area], they wanted to harm him. T'aejo told his generals: "Nŭngch'ang already knows that I arrived, and surely is planning a move together with the island brigands. Although their number is small, if they join forces and gather their strength, block the front and cut off the rear, the outcome of the battle will be far from certain. If ten or more people who are familiar with the water don their armor and grab their spears, and on a light ship cross over to Kalch'o island harbor at nightfall, if they grab whoever goes back and forth there to lay plans, so that their plans are blocked, then we have a chance." All the generals agreed, and effectively they caught a small skiff, and Nŭngch'ang was on board. They captured him and sent him to Kungye, who executed him.

Kungye bestowed the [rank of] *p'ajinch'an* 波珍飡 [and office of] Chancellor on T'aejo so as to summon him [back to the capital]. At that time all the nobility and officials suppressed their feelings and exercised extreme caution; every time they witnessed someone get slandered, they abruptly

---

25 Located south of Naju on the Samp'o river, a tributary of the Yŏngsang.

26 An island located off the coast of Mokp'o.

27 Located southwest of Yŏnggwang Prefecture, the island now seems to have become integrated into the mainland.

and to a man refused to help. The court officials and military officials were all self-satisfied and loyal [to Kungye]. T'aejo was very apprehensive of this, and again requested an outside posting. Kungye also regarded the leadership of his navy as weak and insufficient to deter the enemy, thus he relieved T'aejo of the position of chancellor and again put him in charge of the navy at Naju.

When Paekche and the various water bandits heard that T'aejo was returning, they were paralyzed with fear and did not dare to make a move. T'aejo upon his return reported on the success of his ships and the measures he took against various situations. Kungye was pleased and told those around him "Among all our generals, who can compare with him?" At the time Kungye falsely accused many of treason. Daily he killed more than a hundred. One day he urgently summoned T'aejo. Eyes blazing with anger he looked at him for a long time, and then said "Yesterday you gathered a group of people and plotted treason; what do you say to that?" T'aejo laughed and said "Nothing of that is true." Kungye used to regard himself as Maitreya, and said "Don't try to trick me, I can look into your mind and therefore I know. I will now enter a samādhi to look [into your mind]." Then he closed his eyes and folded his hands, and looked up towards Heaven for a long time. Then Ch'oe Ŭng, the Keeper of Memorials, feigned dropping his brush to T'aejo's side and left his seat to retrieve it. When passing T'aejo he told him quietly "If you don't give in you will be in danger." T'aejo understood, and immediately said "I indeed planned treason, and for this I deserve to die." Kungye laughed loudly and said "you sir are really honest." He immediately rewarded him with gold, silver, and decorated saddles.

T'aejo once dreamt of climbing to the top of a nine-story golden pagoda that stood in the middle of the sea. That year in the third month there was a merchant whose name was Wang Changjin. Coming from China, he stayed at the market place. Suddenly he saw a man of imposing appearance in the middle of the market; he had a snow-white beard and whiskers, and wore an old-style cap and the clothes of a Buddhist layman. In his left hand he was holding a bowl, and in his right hand an old mirror. He addressed Changjin as follows: "Would you like to buy my mirror?" Changjin traded the mirror for rice, and hung it on the wall of his market [stand]. When the sunlight struck the mirror, there vaguely appeared tiny characters that were readable. The contents was roughly as follows: "In the three water, under the four knots, the emperor sends his son down to Chin and Ma. First Kye[rim] is controlled and next Ap[nok] struggled with. In a snake year, one of two dragons sees the other and buries his body; in the blue wood, one takes the appearance of black metal. In the east one can see either flourishing or declining. Flourishing or declining will exterminate the evil and dirty dregs."

Changjin initially did not know there was any writing, but when he saw it he thought it out of the ordinary, and presented it to Kungye. Kungye ordered him to describe the man [who had sold him the mirror] so as to seek him, but he could not be found. However in the Palsap-sa 勃颯寺 temple of Tongju there was an old statue of the star-suppressor who resembled him, and who also held a bowl in his left and a mirror in his right hand. Changjin was happy that a resemblance could be established. Kungye marveled at this and ordered his scholars Song Sahong, Paek T'ak, Hŏ Wŏn, and others, to explain the text. They said [among themselves] "as for 'In the three water, under the four knots, the emperor sends his son down to Chin and Ma,' this refers to Chin Han and Ma Han. As for 'In a snake year, one of two dragons sees the other and buries his body; in the blue wood, one takes the appearance of black metal,' the 'blue wood' refers to pine trees, or in other words a descendant of an inhabitant of Song'ak [pine peak] with the 'dragon' character in his name will become the sovereign. Chancellor Wang [Kŏn] has the marks of a ruler or noble, could it be him who is meant? 'Black metal' refers to the iron in the name of the present capital of Ch'ŏrwŏn. The present ruler came to power in this place, could it be that he will also perish there? As for 'First Kye[rim] is controlled and next Ap[nok] struggled with,' this means that after Chancellor Wang becomes ruler, he will first obtain Kyerim [Silla] and later the Amnok River." The three men told each other, "If we tell him the truth the ruler will guess that we want to kill him, and

Chancellor Wang will meet with a sticky end, and we too will not be able to escape such a fate." Thus they made up a story and reported that to Kungye.

On the *ŭlmyo* (14th) day of the sixth month, the marshals[28] Hong Yu, Pae Hyŏn'gyŏng, Sin Sunggyŏm, and Pok Chigyŏm hatched a secret plan to visit T'aejo's house at night so as to urge him to take the throne; however he had no intention [of listening to them]. They then made sure that his wife Lady Yu knew about the plan. They told her "Would there perhaps be a newly ripened fruit in the garden? Could you go and pick it?" Lady Yu understood their intention and went out through the north door, hiding in a tent.

Thereupon the marshals told him, "Now the king's government impudently metes out punishment and randomly kills wives and murders sons,[29] and kills officials indiscriminately; the people have fallen into dire poverty. We are afflicted as people once were by Jie and Zhou,[30] there is nothing to add to that. Doing away with the dark and ushering in the light, this is the great plan of the under-Heaven. We beseech you to implement the transition of dynasties just as Zhou replaced Yin [Shang]." T'aejo blushed and refused their request, saying "I have pledged myself with loyalty and righteousness. Even though the king may be cruel, how can I harbor two minds? If a subject punishes a ruler, it is called breaking the mandate. I am effectively not virtuous enough to follow in the footsteps of Tang and Wu.[31] I fear that later generations will think that [using the cruelty of Kungye] was just an excuse. The ancients used to say 'one can be a prince for a day, but one is a sovereign for life.' Viscount Ji of Yanling 延陵季子[32] said "having the country is not my capability." Then he went away and tilled the land.

28 Kijang 騎將: lit. 'horse-riding general.'

29 A reference to the fact that he killed his wife for criticizing him as well as her two sons.

30 The last rulers of the Xia and Shang dynasties respectively; regarded as the archetypal tyrants of Chinese history.

31 The founders of Shang and Zhou respectively.

32 This refers to Ji Zha (ca. 590–ca. 510 BC), the fourth son of King Shoumeng of Wu. See David R. Knechtges, "Southern Metal and Feather Fan," in *Southern Identity and Southern Estrangement*, eds. Ping Wang and Nicholas Morrow Williams (Hong Kong University Press, 2015), 25.

How would I surpass Jizi's capability?"

The marshals said: "In times of calamity it is easy to lose [the mandate of] Heaven, if together we do not choose revolt, then we have to undergo his destruction. As for those ordinary people in the country who suffer severe pain, day and night we think on how to restore [their lives] to them. Furthermore, all those of authority and position have been eliminated. Among the men of virtue, none is equal to you. All our hopes therefore rest with you. If you do not follow [this plea], we are sure to die within a day. All the more so given what is said in the text on the mirror of Wang Changjin, how could you go against Heaven and die at the hands of a someone who stands all alone [under heaven]?"

Lady Yu emerged and told T'aejo "Raising righteousness to replace cruelty, this is the way it has been from old. I have heard what you discussed with your marshals. As your wife I am greatly angered, all the more so since you are a stout and brave man." She then took up his armor and put it on him. All the marshals supported him, and sat a large number of lights on top of stacked up [sacks of] grain, and performed the ritual of ruler and subject. They made people run outside while shouting "Lord Wang has raised the righteous banner!" The people of the country came running, and those that came outside could not be counted. First they went to the palace gates to knock and make a noise; already 10,000 people were waiting there. When Kungye heard this he no longer knew what to do. Wearing plain clothes he left the north gate and hid under rocks in a valley. There he was found by the Puyang 斧壤 people who inflicted harm on him.[33]

On the *chŏngsa* [16th] day a proclamation read: "The ruler of T'aebong, when the four prefectures[34] collapsed he eliminated the bandits and gradually expanded the territory. But before achieving unification, he ruled the people with cruelty, and elevated treachery to the highest art form, and slander and abuse became essential skills [at court]. Corvée labor was onerous and taxes heavy, and lands lay fallow due to a lack in farmers.

---

33 Modern P'yŏnggang 平康, just north of Ch'ŏrwŏn.

34 It is not certain which four this alludes to.

But the palaces were of exorbitant scale and mobilization of construction workers did not stop. As a result, resentment grew. Then he arrogated for himself all kinds of titles of respect, and killed his wife and children. Heaven and earth cannot tolerate this, and gods and people alike resented this; with such dereliction and despair, wasn't this sufficient as a warning! Now we have without due merit received the throne, and aspire to elevate the worthy and remain close to the people. We should take care not to 'follow in the tracks of an overturned cart,' and set clear standards that anyone can follow. With the people I want to make a new beginning, reforming and improving customs; with my officials I want to have the 'enjoyment of a fish in the water;' like the sea and all the rivers leading to it peaceful and clear, everyone in the center and in the outlying regions should be at ease; this is our cherished aim." The ministers all bowed in gratitude, saying "We the subjects experienced the rule of T'aebong, which harmed the good and brutalized the innocent. Old and young were wailing in despair, there was none who did not harbor a grudge. Now we have encountered a sagacious and enlightened [rule], and obtained protection of our lives. How can we not repay this by exerting all out strength!"

The king told the *hanch'an* Ch'ongil from Ch'ŏngju: "The ruler of T'aebong, because the soil of Ch'ŏngju is fertile and there are many people of influence and power, feared they would insurrect, and therefore wanted to exterminate them. He then summoned the soldiers Yun Chŏn and Aegyŏn to assemble eighty soldiers, and put many innocent people in shackles and sent them on the road [to Ch'ŏrwŏn]. You should hurry and release them so that they can return to their fields and villages."

The cavalry man T'ae P'yŏng was made office chief in the Ministry of Police and Provost Marshal. He was talented in writing and history, and was very skilled at clerical work. Originally he was a house scribe to the Yŏmju brigand leader Yu Kŭmsun, but when Kungye defeated Kŭmsun, T'ae P'yŏng surrendered himself. However, Kungye was angry that he had not submitted for a long time, and he ordered him to become a soldier in one of the five divisions that followed T'aejo. When the country was founded he was given a lot of power.

The cavalry general Hwan Sŏn'gil planned to ambush and kill [T'aejo]. Originally Sŏn'gil and his younger brother Hyangje had merit in assisting [T'aejo] to ascend the throne. The king had complete confidence in him. Often he made him lead the crack troops of his personal guards. His wife told him: "your talent and power surpass that of everyone else; with officials and soldiers you submitted [to T'aejo] and thereby obtained great merit. However, the reins of government are with others, isn't this depressing!" Sŏn'gil in his heart agreed with this. Then secretly he gathered a group of soldiers and waited for an opportune time to revolt. Pok Chigyŏm knew of this and secretly told the king. However, as there were still no traces [of a plot], he did not act. One day the king was sitting in the [throne] hall discussing politics with several scholars. Sŏn'gil and more than fifty of his henchmen suddenly entered the palace courtyard holding weapons, they went directly to harm him. The king assessed the situation and stood up. With a sharp voice he upbraided him, saying "Even though your might has brought you this far, how could the fact that I stand here be anything but heaven's [will]. The Heavenly Mandate has already been settled, and you dare to take it?" When Sŏn'gil saw the king his confidence was shaken and he seemed to doubt. He withdrew his armor and with his followers ran away. The guardsmen pursued and killed them. Hyangje arrived later and knowing the situation was lost ran away too, but the pursuing troops killed him.

An edict read "Establishing offices and distributing official positions is primordial for the country; in transforming the customs and pacifying the people the use of sagaciousness is urgent. To be honest, it has been a long time that we lacked [proper] officials, so how could it be possible to rule the chaos? I am not bright when it comes to knowing people, and have lost sleep in considering people for office. If we would merely employ the deficient because they cherish office, both in the center and the provinces all the officials would simply nominate themselves for office. Only if we straighten things out now will future generations be able to have peace. Now for their selection and deployment, it is fitting that all the gentry pass through tests, so that we do our utmost to select the best and make all the officials get along well. From the center to the provinces, it should all be thus, this my wish." Then he made Kim Haengdo chancellor of the State Council, Kŏmgang minister of the Department of Administration, Im Myŏngp'il minister of Police and Provost Marshal, Im Hŭi minister of the Ministry of Defense, Chin Wŏn minister of the Ministry of Finance, Yŏmchang minister of the Ministry of Justice, Kwip'yŏng minister of the Ministry of the Navy, Son Hyŏng minister of the Ministry of Royal Treasures and Craft, Chin Kyŏng minister of the Court Treasury, and Chin Chŏng minister of the Department of the Royal Treasury. These were all people of sound character and straight morality, who were even-handed in dealing with affairs; the first and foremost thing in establishing the [dynastic] enterprise is to promote those with merit. Im Chŏgyŏ was made vice-chancellor of the State Council, Nŭngjun and Kwŏn Sik were both made vice-ministers of the Department of Administration, Kim In and Yŏngjun both vice-minister of the Ministry of Defense, Ch'oe Min and Kyŏnsul both vice-minister of the Ministry of Finance, Pak Inwŏn and Kim Ŏn'gyu both vice-minister of the Ministry of Education, Im Sanghwŏn vice-minister of the Ministry of the Navy, Yo Inhwi and Hyangnam both vice-minister of the Ministry of Royal Treasures and Crafts, Nŭnghye and Hwip'il both vice-minister of the Honor Guard. They were all good at achieving their tasks and serve the public without indolence, skillful at solving problems they satisfy people's minds. Kang Yunhyŏng was made director at the Department of Administration, Sin Il and Im Sik both director at the State Council, Kukhyŏn vice-director [at the State Council], Ye Ŏn assistant director at the Department of Administration, Kok Kŭmhoe assistant chief [at the Department of Administration], Yu Kilkwŏn office chief [at the Department of Administration]. At all the other offices and departments office chiefs or other junior administrative positions were filled. At the foundation of a new country, talent should be judiciously employed so that all the administrative tasks are harmonized.

Pak Chiryŏng was made chancellor [of the State Council].

The *sop'an* Chonggan and the general of the Honor Guard Chŏkpu were executed. Through treachery and deceit they had found fortune under Kungye, and did harm to the good people.[35] As soon as he ascended the throne Wang Kŏn had them executed.

The hermit Pak Yu came to see the king, who received him with decorum, and asked him: "The way of establishing principle can only be found in seeking sages. Now that you have come, it is like obtaining Fu Yan[36] or the scholar of the Wei river bank.[37]" Thus he bestowed a cap and belt on him, put him in charge of vital affairs and also bestowed the surname Wang on him. Yu's character was upright and he was completely versed in classics and histories. Originally he had served Kungye as vice-director of a department, and was later transferred to the secretariat of the crown prince. Seeing that Kungye's government was dissolute he left his home and hid in mountain valleys. When he heard that the new king had been enthroned he came.

A proclamation said, "A country should be frugal in its affairs, and thus the people will be prosperous and the storehouses full. Even if there are calamities like floods, drought, or famine, one should still be prepared. All the palace estates and the stipend villages of the crown prince have amassed grain, but much of it has rotted." To save them, he appointed the office chief at the Department of Administration, Nŭngbŏm, as emissary for grain inspection.

When the bureaucratic system was established, a proclamation said: "We have heard that in reforming a system handed down from the previous polity, the mistakes should be rectified and the details settled. To lead the profane and educate the people, one should be very careful about the terminology. Under the previous system, the T'aebong ruler considered the Silla nomenclature for ranks and offices and the names of prefectures and villages vulgar, and replaced them with a new system. Although it was in

35 According to the *Koryŏsa* (1.11a), Chonggan had been a monk in his youth.

36 Fu Shuo, of the Shang Dynasty.

37 This refers to Jiang Taigong, aka. Lü Shang, a minister of King Wen of Zhou. Having retired, one day he met King Wen while fishing on the Wei River. See *Shiji* 32.

force for several years, the people never managed to become proficient in it, causing confusion. Now we will follow the Silla system; however, those terms of the new system whose meaning is clear and easy to understand will be retained."

The *ilgilch'an* Nŭngyun presented an auspicious fungus he had found in his garden, with nine stems and three caps. The king granted him grain from the palace storehouse.

The cavalry general Ihŭnam was executed in the market place. Ihŭnam was originally a mounted archer, who presented his services when that brought him profit. He served Kungye in the desire of obtaining an official appointment. In the last year of Kungye, he seized Ungju[38] and thus occupied it. When he heard that the king had ascended the throne, he secretly harbored a malicious plan. Without being summoned, he went to the court of the new king. Many of his soldiers fled, and Ungju was again taken by Later Paekche. The acting minister of justice Yŏmchang was close to Ihŭnam and knew about his secret plan. He therefore alerted the king as follows: "Ihŭnam has abandoned the garrison and came here of his own accord to damage the border. His crime is real and critical. Originally we stood shoulder to shoulder, yet as I serve the king I now have to set aside my feelings. Still, I cannot bear to see him executed; moreover, the exact contents of his treason has not yet been revealed. He surely has something put together."

Yŏmchang then requested that he be secretly observed, and the king sent a man from the palace to Yŏmchang's house.[39] From a tent he waited for him. Ihŭnam's wife Lady Hwan went to the outhouse, and talked to herself at length, saying "if my husband's plans fail then great calamity will befall me." As soon as she had spoken he went to the palace to relate what had transpired. Ihŭnam was thrown in jail, and the king ordered all officials to debate on the punishment to be meted out; all agreed he deserved execution. The king personally deferred to this judgment, saying "You habitually

38 Modern Kongju in S. Ch'ungch'ŏng Province,

39 Perhaps Ihŭnam was staying there after coming to the capital from Ungju.

harbored an evil intent and thereby brought yourself down like this. As for escaping punishment [on the recommendation of your friend], the law is equal for everybody, there cannot be any curbing of the law on private grounds." Ihŭnam merely shed tears. The king ordered him to be beheaded in the marketplace. His family and associates were not punished.

Seventh month, autumn. A proclamation read "The ruler of T'aebong, in dealing with people merely followed his desires, using them as a means to gather wealth and not following the old regulations. On one *kyŏng*[40] of land six *sŏk*[41] of rent was collected; households living at postal stations were levied three bundles of silk. This led the people to abandoning the plough and discarding the loom; everyone just left [the land] and roamed around. From now on, for land rent tax and other taxes, the general law of the world will be followed as a rule.

The vice-chancellor of the State Council, Sunp'il, was excused from his position on account of his illness and replaced by the vice-minister of Defense Yŏlp'yŏng.

The general of the Ch'ŏngju regiment,[42] Kyŏn'gŭm, and the vice generals Yŏnik and Hŭnghyŏn came to see [the king]. Each was granted a horse and silk was dispatched [to their homes]. From the beginning, since there had been much rebelliousness and deceit among Ch'ŏngju people, the king considered that unless early measure were taken, later on he would surely regret it. Thus he sent the locals Nŭngdal, Munsik, and Myŏnggil to appraise the situation. Nŭngdal returned and reported: "There is nothing going on." Munsik and Myŏnggil privately told [the king about] the Ch'ŏngju people Kim Kŭn'gyŏm and Kwanjun: "Although Nŭngdal reported that nothing is going on, by the time the new grains ripen, I'm afraid there will be a rebellion. Kyŏn'gŭm and others say that the people of Ch'ŏngju together with locals who reside in the capital such as Kim Kŭn'gyŏm, Kwanjun, and Kim Ŏngyu are disloyal, and should be removed together. We cannot be

40 One *kyŏng* = 100 mu, unit of area. See table of weights and measures.

41 One *sŏk*: picul, about 60 kilograms in weight.

42 Yŏnggun 領軍: probably not a regular army, but a local militia.

indolent about this."

The king said "my mind is set on stopping the killing. I want to pardon even those who are guilty, and all the more these people, who all have merit in my gaining power and supporting righteousness. To obtain one prefecture, should I kill those who are loyal and wise? I don't think so." Kyŏn'gŭm grew afraid and withdrew.

Kim Hŭnggyŏm, Kim Ŏngyu, and others heard about this, and reported to the king: "The other day, Nŭngdal reported again that there was nothing going on, but we firmly believe that this is not the case. Now looking at what Kyŏn'gŭm and others have said, we cannot guarantee that all is safe. Please detain them [in the capital][43] to observe the changes [they have instigated]." The king followed this advice, and told Kyŏn'gŭm and others, "What you have told me today, although I cannot follow through on this advice, I greatly esteem your loyalty, you can return early and set at ease the people's minds." Kyŏn'gŭm and the others replied "We have braved numerous calamities and all kinds of slander and praise, but do not care for recrimination or reward. There is nothing greater than pledging wholehearted support for the country until our bones are returned [to their homeplace]. However, among the people of the prefecture, each has his own mind, so once a disturbance begins, we fear that it will be difficult to control. Please send an official army as a show of support." The king agreed to this, and send the cavalry generals Hong Yu, Yu Kŭmp'il[44] and others to lead 1500 troops to garrison and defend the prefecture.

Afterward Toan Prefecture reported that Ch'ŏngju was secretly colluding with Paekche and planning to betray the king. He then sent cavalry general Nŭngsik leading troops to further assist the garrison. Thus a revolt did not take place.

Chigye was appointed vice-chancellor of the State Council.

Eighth month. The king told his assembled ministers: "Thinking about

---

43 This presumably refers to Kim Hŭnggyŏm and Kim Ŏngyu.

44 Yu Kŭmp'il 庾黔弼: the second character could also be pronounced "Kŏm," hence some interpret his name as Yu Kŏmp'il.

the problem of bandits plaguing all our circuits, I noticed how after my accession some fell between the borders [of Koryŏ and Silla] and were a cause for concern. I separately dispatched envoys to all of them with heavy presents and light words to show my benevolence and my intention of pursuing peaceful relations. Effectively, many attached themselves to Koryŏ. Only Kyŏn Hwŏn of Later Paekche did not exchange envoys."

The leader of Koram-sŏng[45] in the northern territories, Yun Sŏn, came to submit. Yun Sŏn was brave and good at military strategy. Towards the end of Kungye's reign he fled the troubles and went to the northern border. Together with more than 2,000 followers he resided at Koram-sŏng, invoking the fact that the Black Water barbarians were raiding the northern borders.[46] At that time he heard that the king was sending envoys with a royal proclamation, so he came to submit, and the northern border became peaceful.

A proclamation read: "The ruler of T'aebong believed in prophecies, rejected Song'ak and returned to Puyang,[47] where he constructed a new palace. The people were greatly troubled by the construction labor, and the three seasons [of spring, summer and autumn] were lost for agriculture. The situation was further aggravated by famine and repeated epidemics. All families were afflicted by death, and the roads were lined with corpses. One bolt of fine cloth went for a price of five *sŭng*[48] of rice. It came to the point that people sold themselves or their children as slaves. I take great pity on them." Thereupon he ordered that records be made of their whereabouts and that this be reported to him. Then he managed to redeem more than 1,000 of them by using cloth and silk from the palace storehouses.

A proclamation read "When King Wu of Zhou overthrew the Shang dynasty, he issued grain and distributed wealth. When Gaozu of the Han

---

45 The present location of this fortress is not known.

46 I.e., to protect the border from these raids he occupied the castle as part of a defensive strategy. Another possible reading for this sentence is that he "called upon the Black Water barbarians to raid the northern borders," but this seems less likely. Hŭksu 黑水, literally 'black water' refers to a branch of the Malgal (Ch. Mohe) people that had lived in NE Asia, including the northern part of the Korean peninsula, since ancient times.

47 Although located north of Ch'ŏrwŏn, here it appears to refer to Ch'ŏrwŏn.

48 One *sŭng* (pint) equals approximately 0.5 liters.

destroyed Xiang Yu, he let all the people who had fled to mountains and marshes return to their fields and villages. I[49] am ashamed of my virtue, so insignificant [in comparison]. Having gained control over this great heritage, although aided by the helping grace of Heaven, I also relied on the force of the people carrying me forward. Now it is time to let the ordinary folks settle down and 'let the rooms be sealed' [for happiness as in the new year ceremony]. However, I inherited a ruined system; if we do not exempt from rent and taxes and encourage agriculture and sericulture, how will all the families have enough?" Thereupon he exempted the people from taxes and corvée duties for three years. Those who had fled to the four directions, he let them return to their fields and villages. Furthermore, a general amnesty was declared to give everyone respite.

A proclamation read: "The interplay of ordering and assisting between ruler and ministers is a magnificent design of the times. To establish it, those with high merit in the world should be bestowed so that they are endowed with reeds [i.e., wetland] and fields; they should be rewarded with lofty titles and high office. This is the constant statute of a hundred generations, the vast principle since time immemorial. I am originally of insignificant talent and inferior knowledge. [Therefore] I rely on the eminence of the various [ministers] so as to establish a broad foundation. At the time of the deposed tyrant, loyalty was depleted. Those among the ministers who are principled, should thus be rewarded with merit status. Among those of the first class, there are Hong Yu, Pae Hyŏn'gyŏng, Sin Sunggyŏm, and Pok Chigyŏm. Among the second class there are Kyŏnkwŏn, Nŭngsik, Kwŏn Sin, Yŏm Sang, Kim Rak, Yŏnju, and Manan. Every one of them has been granted gold and silver vessels, brocade-embroidered bedding, damask and silk. More than 2,000 people were granted third class [merit status]. Each of them has been given damask and silk, as well as grain. I want to save lives and the people together with you, yet could not guard my ministers' integrity to the end. [Despite this,] having performed merit such as this, how could I

49 For the sake of convenience I have translated *chim* 朕, the "royal I" simple as "I" rather than using the *pluralis majestatis* as used by Western kings.

not feel ashamed about my lack of virtue [in giving such meager reward]! However, if there is merit and no reward, there is no way to motivate people in the future. Therefore there are the rewards given such as this today to you all. Please understand my intentions."

Kyŏn Hwŏn sent the *ilgilch'an* Min Hap to congratulate T'aejo on his accession. The king went to the Taejung Hall to receive these congratulations, and sent Min Hap off with lavish gifts.

Vice-minister at the Department of Defense Hwŏnsik was transferred to the position of vice-minister at the Department of Administration.

More than ten major prefectures and counties including Ungju and Unju[50] rebelled and attached themselves to Paekche. The king ordered the former Chancellor Kim Haengdo to take up the position of special envoy to pacify the southeast province, and gave him charge of all military affairs in Aju[51] so as to help him prepare.

Yu Munyul was appointed director at the State Council.

Ninth month. The Cavalry general Pok Chigyŏm reported: "The officer at the Ministry of Police and Provost Marshal, Im Ch'un'gil, together with his fellow Ch'ŏngju man Pae Ch'onggyu and the Kyech'ŏn men Kanggil and Ach'agwi,[52] and the Maegok[53] man Kyŏngjong are plotting against the king. They should be apprehended and questioned." They were all brought to submit at court, and the king ordered their execution. Only Pae Ch'onggyu escaped.

The Ch'ŏngju man Hyŏnyul was made a director at the Ministry of Police and Provost Marshal. But the cavalry generals Hyŏn'gyŏng, Sunggyŏm and others said, "Previously, Im Ch'un'gil was made an officer at the Ministry of Police and Provost Marshal, but he had rebellious intentions and was later found out to be guilty. This was all done with the intention of taking control of military power so as to assist Ch'ŏngju. Now that Hyŏnyul is made a director

---

50 Modern Hongsŏng, South Ch'ungch'ŏng Province.

51 Modern Asan, South Ch'ungch'ŏng Province.

52 Or: Kanggira, Ch'agwi? Kyech'ŏn is a Paekche-era name; it was renamed Changt'aek County in early Koryŏ and attached to Changhŭng (S. Chŏlla Province)

53 Silla-era name of Hoein County (Ch'ungch'ŏng Province).

at the Ministry of Police and Provost Marshal, we are very worried."

The king agreed with their protests, and made him instead a director at the Ministry of Defense.[54]

The former chancellor Ku Chin was made chancellor of the branch department of the State Council in Naju Prefecture.[55] Ku Chin refused to go on the grounds of the long period of time he had exerted himself for T'aebong. The king was not pleased, and told Yu Kwŏn: "For ages I have been through numerous trials and dangers, yet never referred to them as 'exertions.' In truth, I am in awe of authority [that comes with office]. Now Ku Chin adamantly refuses to take up his position, is this acceptable?" Yu Kwŏn replied: "Rewards are made to recompense good actions, and punishments to censor evil actions. He should be given the highest punishment to set an example for all the lower officials." The king approved of this advice. Ku Chin was terrified, apologized for his crime, and left to take up his position.

The Sangju leader Ajagae[56] sent a messenger to report his submission to Koryŏ. The king ordered a ceremony to receive him. During the rehearsal of the ceremony on the polo court, the civil and military branches of the officialdom lined up according to rank. Director at the State Council Yu Munyul and auxiliary at the same council Chu Sŏn squabbled over their places.[57] When the king heard this he said: "Yielding one's place is the origin of etiquette, respect is the root of virtue; now that we are about to receive a guest with etiquette, it will become obvious whether or not the etiquette is accomplished. Now that I hear that these two have squabbled

---

54 Most likely this was an administrative position, whereas the previous one was more hands-on. In this position he would likely not be able to seize arms or resources.

55 Taehaengdae 大行臺: according to Hucker (no. 5056), this is an abbreviation of the term Shangshu daxingtai 尙書大行臺, a kind of local branches of the Department of State Affairs established in semi-independent local governments. Since Koryŏ did not yet have a Department of State Affairs, I assume it was a branch of the State Council.

56 According to the biography of Kyŏn Hwŏn, his father's name was Ajagae. See *Samguk sagi* 50.

57 Chu Sŏn's position is given as auxiliary (*chik* 直), which means "someone assigned to an agency without having nominal status at that agency" (Hucker, no. 933). Hence the confusion over their respective places.

over places, how can they be said to take heed of respect? They should be sent to the border to set an example for this kind of transgression."

The king told his assembled ministers: "The old capital P'yŏngyang has fallen to ruins a long time ago. It is now covered in thorny bushes and lush verdure, and barbarians come there to hunt, also taking the opportunity to pillage. We should move people there to resettle the place and provide them with a strong protective screen.[58]" Then households from Hwangju, Pongju, Haeju, Paekchu, and Yŏmju were chosen to be resettled in P'yŏngyang. The king's cousin, Wang Siryŏn, was appointed grand protector and dispatched there together with the vice-chancellor of the State Council Yŏlp'yŏng to assist him. Also, four or five administrative posts were also established.

The vice-minister of the Department of the Royal Treasury, Yu Ch'ŏngnyang, was made vice-chancellor of the State Council. At the time of the change of the Heavenly Mandate, the soldiers and officials in charge of storehouses all ran away, Yu Ch'ŏngnyang was the only one to stay at his post, so that nothing from the storehouses in his charge was lost. Therefore he was given this position.

Winter, tenth month. Nŭngyul was made vice-chancellor of the State Council, and Chigye recorder at the Department of Administration.

The Ch'ŏngju [region] leader, the *p'ajinch'an* Chin Sŏn and his younger brother Chin Sŏnjang planned a rebellion; they were brought to court and executed.

Eleventh month. The P'algwanhoe was instituted. An official said: "the former kings every year in the second month of winter organized the fast of the eight commandments[59] to pray for blessings. I beg you to honor this

---

58 Here it is not clear whether the people are meant to act as a screen or whether they would be given a protective screen (=walls). The following year, however, a city wall would be built.

59 P'algwan literally means "eight commandments" or "eight precepts." Buddhist laypeople are supposed to follow the five precepts (do not steal, lie, take intoxicants, take life, or have illicit relations), but on certain days of the month they had to take three additional ones because their behavior was scrutinized by the gods. Such days are known as posadha, and the custom spread from India to China and Korea. However, evidently in the course of time

institution." The king said, "I lack in virtue, and therefore to protect this great enterprise [i.e., the dynasty], I rely on the Buddha to pacify the realm." Thereupon in the polo court a circle of lamps was made, flanked by rows of incense burners, so that the whole place was as brightly lit as if it were day. Also, two colored tents were made, each more than 50 feet high. They were constructed as a lotus platform, it was dazzling to behold. A hundred plays, songs and dances were held there, including the music troupe of the four immortals, cart-ships of dragons, phoenixes, elephants and horses, all old stories of Silla. All the officials paraded in their full official dress, carrying their insignia of rank. The whole capital came to look, and feasted day and night. The king watched from the Wibong pavilion. It was nominally a gathering to offer to the Buddha and please the spirits. After this it became an annual event.

T'aejo, second year [919]

Fifth year of the Zhenming era of the Later Liang, fourth year of the Shence era of Khitan

Spring, first month. The capital was established to the south of Mt. Song'ak, and the prefecture was promoted to the status of Kaeju.[60] Markets and shops were established, and wards and neighborhoods were differentiated. Also, the new capital was divided into five districts and six garrisons were established.

Third month. The king founded ten temples, including Pŏbwang-sa and Wangnyun-sa,[61] in the capital, and all the derelict pagodas, shrines, and images of the two capitals were repaired.

---

it became in Korea associated with a single day of the year (usually the 15th of the eleventh month), developing into a festival that incorporated native traditions.

60 A *chu* 州 is sometimes translated as province, but it is really a more important prefecture than a *kun* 郡; it is usually the center or one of the most important localities in a province or circuit.

61 A list of the remaining ten temples can be found in *Samguk yusa*, wangnyŏk, "Koryŏ T'aejo."

Historian's note: "Barely a year after he had established the new dynasty, he constructed ten temples in the capital and repaired pagodas and shrines in the two capitals. How lamentable! Was he confused regarding the relative importance and urgency of matters? Or was he enticed by theories of fortunetellers or Buddhists? At the time the two strong countries [Khitan and China] had not yet been pacified, and among the various towns [of the peninsula], those who had not yet submitted to Koryŏ were numerous.

The wars were not yet finished, and the people had not yet recovered from natural and man-made disasters. Why then spend so much effort on useless projects such as these? Furthermore, there was opulent and lavish expenditure to the extreme. It even went so far that the king personally wrote commentaries [on Buddhist sūtras] and held great convocations of monks to celebrate their completion. This is grave indeed; it is the Buddha enticing the minds of the people. Everywhere everybody rushed to make donations [to temples] and worried that it would not suffice because of the brilliance and opulence of T'aejo's [donations]. This could not but create confusion among the masses. All the more so for those on the lowest rungs of society; and even more so for the ministers and people who modeled themselves on the ruler.

What a pity! The warning delivered by the fact that Silla's fall was precipitated by the construction of temples, how could it be merely an instruction for one's later years [rather than something to be taken care of immediately]? Thus the deleterious effects of these policies were passed on to the next generations, who worshiped and believed them. It even went as far as giving as much as 70,000 [*sŏk*] of rice in one day, and feeding as many as 30,000 monks in a year.[62] Among the images in the temples, there is none that is not decorated with gold or silver; among the thousands of boxes and ten-thousands of scrolls [of Buddhist texts] there is none that is not made of gold or silver letters. The palace halls became places for Buddhist chanting, and bonzes occupied the quarters of the instructors. Yet

---

62 For the former event, see the first year of King Hyejong's reign; for the latter, see e.g. the tenth month of 1031 (22nd year of Hyŏnjong).

they too couldn't save the country from chaos and destruction. Buddhism is a calamity for the country and damaging people. How tragic. We should take this as a warning."

Three generations of the king's ancestors were given posthumous titles. His great-grandfather was given the title Wŏndŏk taewang, and the temple name Kukcho (national progenitor); his spouse was given the title Chŏnghwa wanghu. His grandfather was given the title Kyŏnggang taewang and the temple name Ŭijo (beautiful progenitor); his spouse was given the title Wŏnch'ang wanghu. His deceased father was given the title Wimu taewang, and the temple name Sejo (epochal progenitor); his spouse was given the title Wisuk wanghu.

Autumn, eighth month. The king went to Ch'ŏngju. At the time the city was still recalcitrant, and many rumors were circulating. He went there to personally reassure the people and build a city wall. He then returned to the capital.

Osan fortress was changed into Yesan County. The king dispatched the great councilors Aesŏn and Hong Yu to pacify and gather more than 500 dispersed households [to settle there].

Ninth month. The literatus Qiu Yangui [K. Ch'u Ŏngyu] from the country of Wu-Yue came to submit to Koryŏ.

Winter, tenth month. A fortress was built for P'yŏngyang.

In this year a fortress was built for Yonggang County.

T'aejo Third year [920]

Sixth year of the Zhenming era of Later Liang, fifth year of the Shence era of Khitan

Spring, first month. Silla for the first time sent an envoy with presents.

The general of Kangju,[63] Yunung, sent his son Ilkang as hostage.

---

63 One of the nine chief prefectures of Silla, it received this name in 747. Modern Chinju, in South Kyŏngsang Province.

Ilkang was made *ach'an*, and betrothed to the sister of vice-minister Haenghun. Director Ch'unyang was dispatched to inform and comfort Kangju.

Third month. Koram Garrison on the northern border suffered from numerous invasions by the northern barbarians. T'aejo gathered all his generals and spoke: "Now the evil of the south [Later Paekche] has not yet been destroyed and the northern barbarians cause us much concern. I am constantly worried, and would like to send Yu Kŭmp'il to stop them. What do you think?" They agreed, and Yu Kŭmp'il was dispatched with an expeditionary force[64] of 3,000. They built a big fortress and guarded it, and afterwards the border became secure.

Autumn, ninth month. Kyŏn Hwŏn sent the *ach'an* Kungdal to offer peacock feather fans and bamboo arrows.

Hamjong and Anbuk fortresses were built.[65]

Winter, tenth month. Kyŏn Hwŏn invaded Silla and seized the two prefectures of Taeryang and Ch'usa[66] and marched on towards Chillye Prefecture.[67] Silla dispatched the *ach'an* Kim Yul to request assistance, and the king sent troops to relieve them. When Kyŏn Hwŏn heard this, he retreated [from Chillye]. This was the first time a conflict arose with us.

In this year the king made an inspection tour of the northern border and returned.

T'aejo Fourth year [921]

First year of the Longde era of Later Liang, sixth year of the Shence era of Khitan

---

64 The original text has Kaejŏng Army 開定軍: This could refer to "an army from Kaejŏng," but since no such place name is attested, it is probably a term for a special expeditionary force.

65 Hamjong is located in Kangsŏ prefecture, South P'yŏngan Province; Anbuk, also in South P'yŏngan, was located on the Ch'ŏngch'ŏn river, and corresponds with the current Anju.

66 Taeryang corresponds to modern Hapch'ŏn in South Kyŏngsang Province, Kusa to Ch'angwŏn in the same province.

67 Modern Kŭmsan in South Ch'ungch'ŏng Province.

Spring, second month. The chief of the Black Water [Malgal], Kojara, together with 170 people submitted.

Hundred-and seventy-one of the Talgo barbarians of the north invaded Silla via the Tŭngju[68] route. General Kyŏnkwŏn engaged and defeated them, not even a single horse returned [to their homeland]. The king ordered that those with merit should be granted 50 *sŏk* of grain each. When the Silla kind heard about this he was happy and sent an envoy to express gratitude.

Summer, fourth month. The Black Water [Malgal] Aŏgan submitted together with 200 people.

Autumn, ninth month. Director Sŏnhaeng was sent to inspect the frontier districts and reassure the local people.

Winter, tenth month. Taehŭng-sa was constructed on Ogwan-san, and the monk Iŏn was invited there to serve as its master.[69]

The king went to the Western Capital.

Twelfth month. The king invested his son Mu as the right heir, by which the heir apparent is meant. Although he was only seven, T'aejo knew that he had the virtue to continue his rulership. Fearing that his mother of the O clan would be deemed unworthy and thus prevent him from taking the throne, he took a yellow robe from an old box and gave it to Queen O. She showed it to *taegwang*[70] Pak Surhŭi, who understood its meaning and requested him to be installed as right heir.

Kungch'ang, Myŏnggwŏn, and others from Paekche surrendered. They were given land and houses.

During this year Unnam County[71] was provided with a city wall.

---

68 Anbyŏn in North Hamgyŏng Province.

69 According to his stele, he was called Iŏm 利嚴 (869-936) rather than Iŏn 利言. He served as the first preceptor to King T'aejo. See Sem Vermeersch, *The Power of the Buddhas: The Politics of Buddhism During the Koryŏ Dynasty* (Harvard University Asia Center, 2008), 127.

70 In contrast to rank titles such as *ach'an* or *pajinch'an*, which are of Silla origin, this is the first mention of what are clearly Koryŏ ranks. See table 2.

71 Musan in Yŏngbyŏn County, North P'yŏng'an Province.

T'aejo Fifth year [922]

Second year of the Longde era of Later Liang, first year of the Tianchan era of Khitan

Spring, second month. The Khitan presented camels and left.

Summer, fourth month. Irwŏl-sa was built northwest of the palace compound.

Sixth month. General Wŏnbong of Haji County[72] submitted.

Autumn, seventh month. General Sunsik of Myŏngju[73] submitted. Originally the king was worried that Sunsik would not submit, but the vice-chancellor Kwŏn Sŏl said, "the father appeals to the son, the older brother instructs the younger, this is the principle of Heaven. Sunsik's father, Hŏ Wŏl, is now a monk in the palace temple, so we should send someone to instruct him [to tell his son to submit]. The king agreed, and Sunsik sent his eldest son Suwŏn as a pledge. He was granted the surname Wang and given fields and houses.

Winter, eleventh month. Hong Sul, the lord of Chinbo castle, sent an envoy to request submission, and the king sent the *wŏnyun* Wang Yu and the vice-minister Sap'il and others to comfort and instruct him.

During this year, he resettled the *taesŭng* Chiryŏng, Haengp'a and others, together with their whole families and sons of good houses of various prefectures and counties in the Western Capital.

The king went to the Western Capital to newly instate its officials.

After six years, the walls for the Western Capital were completed.

The king personally settled the people at Asŏn Fortress.[74]

T'aejo Sixth year [923]

First year of the Tonggwang era of King Zhuangzong of Later Tang, second year of the Tianchan era of Khitan

72 This refers to modern P'ungsan County in Andong, North Kyŏngsang Province.

73 Modern Kangnŭng, Kangwŏn Province.

74 Located in Hamjong, in Kangsŏ Prefecture, South P'yŏngan Province.

Spring, third month. The general of Haji County, Wŏnbong, was made *wŏnyun*, and his county was [renamed and] elevated to Sunju head prefecture.

The general of Myŏngji fortress,[75] Sŏngdal, together with his younger brothers Idal and Sŏrim came to attach themselves to Koryŏ.

Summer, fourth month. *Taegwang* Yu Kŭmp'il was sent with a royal instruction to the northern border tribes, and more than 1500 attached themselves to Koryŏ. Also, the northern tribes returned more than 3,000 people who had been captured in battle.

Sixth month. Piao Yan [K. Pak Am], a scholar-official from Wu-Yue, came to submit.

Autumn, eighth month. General Yangmun of Pyŏkchin Prefecture[76] sent his son-in-law Kyuhwan to submit. Kyuhwan was made *wŏnyun*.

Winter, eleventh month. Hong Sul, the lord of Chinbo castle, sent his son Wang Rip to offer thirty suits of armor. Wang Rip was offered the title of *wŏnyun*.

T'aejo Seventh year [924]

Second year of the Tongguang era of Later Tang, third year of the Tianchan era of Khitan

Autumn, seventh month. Kyŏn Hwŏn sent his sons Sumigang and Yanggŏm to attack Chomul Prefecture.[77] The king sent his generals Aesŏn and Wang Ch'ung to relieve them. Aesŏn died in battle but the people of Chomul Prefecture held fast. Sumigang and his brother, sensing they had lost the advantage, retreated.

Ninth month. Silla king Sŭngyŏng died, and his younger brother Wiŭng ascended the throne.[78] When his demise was announced the king expressed

75 Probably in P'och'ŏn, Kyŏnggi Province.

76 Pyŏkchin Prefecture 碧珍郡: Modern Sŏngju in North Kyŏngsang Province.

77 The location of this place name could not be identified.

78 Sŭngyŏng is the personal name of King Kyŏngmyŏng (r. 917–924), and Wiŭng that of King Kyŏng'ae (r. 924–927). See Kim Pusik, *Samguk sagi*, fasc. 11.

his condolence and established a maigre feast to procure posthumous blessings, and sent envoys of condolence.

This year, Oejesŏg-wŏn, Kuyo-dang, and Sinjung-wŏn were built.

T'aejo Eighth year [925]

Third year of the Tongguang era of Later Tang, fourth year of the Tianchan era of Khitan

Spring, third month. Worms that measured seventy feet in length emerged to the east of the palace walls. At the time, this was interpreted as a sign that Parhae was about to submit.

The king went to the Western capital.

Autumn, ninth month. General Nŭnghyŏn of Maejo castle sent an envoy to request submission.

Winter, tenth month. General Nŭngmun of Koul District[79] came to submit, leading his officials and soldiers. Because his castle was close to the Silla capital, the king comforted him and then sent him back, only retaining his subordinates the director Paegŭn and the *taegam* Myŏngjae, Sangsul, and Kungsik.[80]

The great general to subdue the west, Yu Kŭmp'il, was sent to attack Yŏnsan Garrison[81] in Paekche, and he killed their general Kilhwan. He also attacked Imjon Prefecture, killing or capturing more than three thousand.

The king went to fight Kyŏn Hwŏn in Chomul Prefecture, but Kyŏn Hwŏn's troops were very fierce, and the battle was indecisive. The king wanted to continue the battle with the aim of exhausting the enemy soldiers, and Yu Kŭmp'il led his soldiers to join in. Kyŏn Hwŏn was surprised by Koryŏ's military power, and wanted to settle for peace. He sent his son-in-law Chinho as hostage, and the king exchanged his cousin Wang Sin as

---

79 Modern Yŏngch'ŏn, North Kyŏngsang Province.

80 Names that literally mean "bright talent," "dialogue," and "shape of the bow;" hence, this likely refers to his most talented advisers.

81 Yŏnsan is also the name of the prefecture in which the garrison was presumably situated. It was located in the territory of what is now Ch'ŏngwŏn, North Ch'ungch'ŏng Province.

hostage. Since Kyŏn Hwŏn was his senior by ten years, he addressed him as uncle, and wanted to call him to his camp to discuss the situation. But Yu Kŭmp'il admonished him, saying "man's mind is hard to know, how can you be so imprudent as to be intimate with the enemy?" The king then desisted. When the Silla king heard this, he sent an envoy to report "Kyŏn Hwŏn has deceived again and again, one cannot be familiar with him." The king agreed.

Eleventh month. T'amna sent tribute.

Twelfth month. The Khitan destroyed Parhae. Parhae is originally Songmal Malgal. At the time of Empress Wu (r. 690-705), Tae Choyŏng of Koguryŏ protected the Liaodong area, and Emperor Ruizong (r. 710–712) invested him as king of Parhae-gun. Therefore they called themselves Parhae, but also comprised Puyŏ, Suksin, etc., ten countries. They had writing, ritual and music, a bureaucracy, five capitals, fifteen provinces, sixty-two prefectures over an area extending over 5,000 *li*. Their population numbered several hundred thousand, and they bordered on our country. They were enemies with the Khitan, and when the Khitan leader mounted a massive attack on Parhae and besieged Horhan fortress, he destroyed the country and renamed it East Khitan. Its heir Tae Kwanghyŏn together with General Sin Tŏk, Minister at the Ministry of Rites Tae Hwagyun, Equalizer of the Old and Steward of Government Tae Wŏngyun,[82] Minister at the Ministry of Public Works Tae Pongmo, General of the Left and Right Guard Tae Simno, Junior General Modugan, Honorary Merit Subject Pak Ŏ, and Minister at the Ministry of Public Works O Hŭng, together with several ten-thousand households fled; the king was generous, bestowed the surname Wang and personal name Kye on him and made him member of the royal household. He found him a consort and ennobled his loyal aides.

---

82 The passage 均老司政大元鈞 does not make sense; the first four characters normally should designate an office, but it does not remotely resemble any known type of office. I have therefore rendered it literally; it might be a mistake, or a Parhae office not documented in any other source.

T'aejo Ninth year [926]

First year of the Tiancheng era of Emperor Mingzong of Later Tang, first year of the Tianxian era of Emperor Taizong of Khitan

Summer, fourth month. Kyŏn Hwŏn's hostage Chinho died of illness, and the king sent the executive Ikhwŏn to dispatch the body for funeral. Kyŏn Hwŏn accused us of killing him, and killed Wang Sin, [the Koryŏ hostage]. He advanced with his army to Ungjin. The king ordered all cities to fortify their walls and not leave them. The Silla king sent an envoy with the following message: "Kyŏn Hwŏn has gone against the treaty and raised troops, yet Heaven will certainly not assist him. If you, great king, raise an impressive force just once, he will surely seal his own fate." The king replied to the envoy "It is not that I fear Kyŏn Hwŏn, but when the evil reaches its peak, he will bring defeat upon himself."

Before this, Kyŏn Hwŏn had offered a white horse with blue mane and tail from Chŏryŏng Island.[83] Later he heard a prophesy saying that a famous horse from Chŏryŏng Island would flee to Paekche, he regretted it. An envoy came to ask the horse back. The king laughed and agreed to do so.

Winter, twelfth month. The king went to the Western Capital to inspect various prefectures and garrisons, and then returned to Kaegyŏng.

This year, Chang Pin was sent to Tang [as an envoy].

T'aejo Tenth year [927]

Second year of the Tiancheng era of Later Tang, second year of the Tianxian era of Khitan

Spring, first month. The king personally attacked Yongju Prefecture[84] of Paekche and conquered it. By that time, Kyŏn Hwŏn had broken the treaty and invaded the border numerous times. The king had endured this for a

83 This is thought to refer to Yŏng island south of Pusan.

84 Modern Yonggung in Yech'ŏn, North Kyŏngsang Province.

long time, but since Kyŏn Hwŏn clearly intended to flaunt his power and sleight him, the king attacked. The Silla king sent a number of troops to assist him.

Kyŏn Hwŏn dispatched the body of Wang Sin for funeral.

Third month. The king defeated the Unju castle lord Kŭngjun below the walls of his city. After this he attacked Kŭnp'um castle[85] and conquered it.

Summer, fourth month. The king sent the navy generals Yŏngch'ang and Nŭngsik together with ship navigators to attack Mt. Hadol[86] and three other places in Kangju.

The king attacked Ungju but could not conquer it.

Autumn, seventh month. The king sent the *wŏnbo* Chaech'ung and Kim Rak to attack Taeryang castle. They took hostage the general Ch'uhŏjo and more than thirty others, destroyed the walls and returned.

Eighth month. The king went on an inspection tour to Kangju and passed by the Kosagari castle.[87] The castle lord Hŭngdal had prior to this dispatched his son Kwigwan [as a mark of submission]. Thereupon all the administrators that Paekche had installed to govern the castle also submitted. The king praised them and bestowed a salary from Ch'ŏngju upon Hŭngdal and a salary from Chinju on his eldest son Chundal, a salary of Hansu on his second son Ungdal, and a salary of Changch'ŏn on his third son Oktal.[88] He also bestowed land and houses.

---

85 Also known as Kŭn'am Castle, a Silla fortress located in the Sangbuk district of Mun'gyŏng.

86 It is not known where exactly this place can be located. As seen earlier, Kangju (modern Chinju) had submitted to Wang Kŏn, but evidently, some smaller counties nominally under jurisdiction of Kangju had not done so.

87 This corresponds to modern Mun'gyŏng, which occupies a strategic position as it controls a mountain pass (now known as Mun'gyŏng saejae) which connects Silla territory with that of Koryŏ.

88 Chinju 珍州 refers to a place in modern Kŭmsan, South Ch'ungch'ŏng Province; Hansu probably refers to the modern Hansu district in Chech'ŏn, North Ch'ŭngch'ŏng Province; and Changch'ŏn to modern Changdan, close to the capital Kaesŏng. What exactly is meant by salary (*nok* 祿) here is not clear; it is unlikely that the whole locality was assigned as a kind of fief or stipend village, so it probably refers to a part of the tax money from those places.

The king repaired Paesan Castle[89] and ordered the *chŏngjo* Chesŏn to take command of two divisions to guard it.

The general of Myŏngju, Sunsik, dispatched his son Changmyŏng with 600 soldiers to make them part of the regular army in Kaesŏng.

Ninth month. Kyŏn Hwŏn attacked Kŭnp'um fortress and burnt it. Then he proceeded with a raid on Silla's Koul District. When he threatened the outer limits [of Silla's capital area], the Silla king sent Yŏnsik with an urgent message requesting help. The Koryŏ king told the chancellor Konghwŏn, the *taesang* Son Haeng, and the *chŏngjo* Yŏnju: "Silla has been our ally for a long time. Now that they are in distress, we simply have to aid them." He dispatched Konghwŏn and others with a 10,000-man strong force thence. Before they reached [Kyŏngju]. Kyŏn Hwŏn had gotten wind of their advance, and suddenly entered the Silla capital. At the time, the king and queen, together with his concubines and relatives had gone to the Posŏk Pavilion[90] to amuse themselves with drinking [games]. Suddenly they heard that the [enemy's] troops had arrived, and all of a sudden they were in complete disarray. The king and queen fled to the detached palace south of the city. All his ministers and officials of the court, together with palace women and musicians, were all slaughtered. Kyŏn Hwŏn gave free rein to his soldiers to loot everywhere, including the royal palace. He ordered his staff to search for the king. He placed the king amidst the troops and forced him to take his own life, and then violated the queen. He also let his underlings ravish the concubines.

He then installed the king's nephew Kim Pu as king, and took his younger brother Hyoyŏm and the minister of state Yŏnggyŏng as hostage. They took as many boys and girls as they could, hundreds of artisans and soldiers, as well as countless treasures, and returned [to Paekche].

When T'aejo heard about this, he sent an envoy to express his condolences, and personally led 5,000 of his crack cavalry; he intercepted

89 In Hogye County of Mungyŏng. This is the Silla name.

90 The famous "Abalone rock" pavilion in Kyŏngju. The stone water drain supposedly used for floating wine cups in drinking games can still be seen in Kyŏngju.

Kyŏn Hwŏn near Tonghwa temple on P'algong-san.[91] The battle was fierce but turned to Koryŏ's disadvantage. Kyŏn Hwŏn's troops had surrounded the king who was in grave danger, but his great generals Sin Sunggyŏm and Kim Rak fought with all their might and died for him.[92] All his troops had been routed, and the king barely managed to escape with his life. Kyŏn Hwŏn took advantage of this victory to seize Taemok Prefecture[93] and burned all its fields and the accumulated harvest.

The king deeply mourned the death of the two generals, and made Kim Rak's younger brother Ch'ŏl and Sin Sunggyŏm's younger brother Nŭnggil and son Po *wŏnyun*. He also founded Chimyo-sa for the repose of their souls. Sin Sunggyŏm hailed from Kwanghae-ju, and was very brave and strong. In many battles he gained merit, and was posthumously given the title Changjŏl [sturdy and loyal]. He was also enshrined together with T'aejo in the royal ancestral shrine.

Winter, tenth month. Kyŏn Hwŏn dispatched a general to invade Pyŏkchin Prefecture and cut down the grain in the two prefectures of Somok and Taemok. In the eleventh month, he burned the grains at Pyŏkchin Prefecture. The *chŏngjo* Saeksang engaged him in battle but died.

Twelfth month. Kyŏn Hwŏn sent a letter to Koryŏ with the following contents: "Recently the Silla minister of state (*kuksang*) Kim Kwanyŏm and others went to invite you to enter their capital. This is like the freshwater turtle responding to the call of the sea turtle;[94] it is like a quail donning the plumes of a hawk. This will merely lead to the destitution of people's livelihoods and the destruction of the shrine for the earth and grain deities. Therefore I took preemptive measures like Liu Kun who didn't want to

---

91 This is to the north of the city of Taegu. Kyŏn Hwŏn had to pass here on his way back to Paekche after his loot of Kyŏngju.

92 It is widely thought that Sin Sunggyŏm saved the king by donning his armor and pretending to be him, giving T'aejo time to flee the battle. There is still a shrine and grave mound dedicated to Sin near the battle site.

93 Modern Yakmok district, Ch'ilgok Prefecture, North Kyŏngsang Province.

94 Comparing someone to a turtle has long been a heinous insult in Chinese tradition. Since turtles were thought to be promiscuous, the expression "turle's egg" in particular challenges someone's parentage, and is thus the equivalent of calling someone a "bastard."

risk getting struck by Zu Ti's whip,[95] and wielded the axe of Han Qinhu.[96] I swore to the hundred officials a pledge as bright as the sun, and instructed the six ministries with righteousness. Unexpectedly, treacherous ministers fled the country and the king died. Then a cousin of King Kyŏngmyŏng (r. 917–924) and a non-agnatic grandson of King Hŏn'gang (r. 875–886) was recommended for the throne.[97] This again threw the country into turmoil; for the mourned ruler was a ruler but in name. Yet you did not seriously think about the pledge of loyalty, and merely listening to rumors you made a hundred schemes and spied on all localities. But when you invaded others' territories, you could not even get a glimpse of my horse's head or manage to pull a hair from my oxen. At the beginning of winter, the general leader Saeksang's hands were tied at his Sŏngsan camp, and within the next month the *chwasang* Kim Rak's bones were exposed in front of Miri-sa. We killed and captured numerous [of your soldiers], and put to flight quite a few more. It being so clear who is the strongest, you surely know who is going to win. What I am now looking forward to is hanging my bow in the pavilions of P'yŏngyang, and watering my horses in the P'ae River.

However, on the third day of the last month, the envoy from the state of Wu-Yue, vice-minister Ban, came to transmit a royal decree, which read: 'I know that your country and Koryŏ have enjoyed cordial relations for a long time, and have concluded an alliance as neighboring countries. However, recently because of the death of both sides' hostages, the goodwill of old was lost and you started invading each other's borders; so far the arms have

---

95 This refers to a story from the Chinese Jin dynasty, when Liu Kun wrote to a friend that he slept with a spear under his pillow upon hearing that Zu Ti had received an appointment, because he feared that Zu Ti wanted to strike him.

96 Han Qinhu was a general from the Sui Dynasty who helped defeat the Chen dynasty's armies.

97 This refers to King Kyŏng'ae (r. 924–927), the king whom Kyŏn Hwŏn had forced to commit suicide. In fact, according to the *Samguk sagi* (k. 11, Kyŏng'ae wang) he was a brother to King Kyŏngmyŏng, who were both sons of King Sindŏk (r. 912–917), and whose mother was a daughter to King Hŏn'gang. Their father was supposedly a distant descendent of Adalla Isagŭm, and they thus had the surname Pak, which had not ruled over Silla for nearly eight centuries! Since the *Samguk sagi* says that they were "brothers through the same mother" it is possible that they had a different father.

not yet been laid down. Now I especially send this envoy to your circuit, and expect that you will transfer the text to Koryŏ: you should renew friendly relations and forever bury the hatchet.' I value righteousness, and am deeply respectful of the king, as I am firmly intent on serving the great. As soon as I was appraised of this edict, I immediately wanted to uphold its instructions. However, I considered that even if you would want to stop [fighting], you would not be able to do so; even when beaten into a corner you would still fight on. Now I have copied the words of the edict and send them to you, please consider the words carefully and take them to heart. Moreover, when a hare and hound take turns [running to see who is the fastest], they wear each other out, and become the object of ridicule. When the snipe and the mussel grapple with each other, it would make them a laughing stock.[98] Take your repeated misguided attempts [at war] as a warning, and be sure to take this advice to avoid any later regrets."[99]

In this year Im Ŏn was sent to [Later] Tang.

T'aejo Eleventh year [928]

Third year of the Tiancheng era of Later Tang, third year of the Tianxian era of Khitan

Spring, first month. The king answered as follows: "Prostrate, I received the edict transmitted by the peace envoy from Wu-Yue, the vice minister Ban, and also humbly took note of your long description of the state of affairs. I humbly accept the good words from the missive delivered by the ornate palanquin of the great envoy and your letter, and also accept their instruction. Upon reading these exalted words, even though my feelings surged, upon opening your precious letter I could not suppress feelings of doubt. Now I entrust a reply letter [to the envoy] to swiftly convey what is

98 According to the proverb, if the mussel and snipe grip each other, the fisherman gets the profit. I.e. a prolonged war of attrition would benefit a third party. Despite Kyŏn Hwŏn's bluster at the beginning of his letter, here he seems to concede that in the case of continued conflict, he would not so easily conquer Koryŏ.

99 According to the *Tongguk t'onggam* (k. 12, 25a), this letter was written by Ch'oe Sŭngu.

on my mind. Above I have received Heaven's grace, and below have been pushed forward by the people, and thus have presumed to avail myself of the power of a general, and obtained the chance to rule this country. At the time the Three Han were in grave peril, and the nine territories[100] lay waste. Among the ordinary people, many had tied yellow headscarves [and became bandits], and among the fields, there was none which did not lie fallow. These are all stark warnings that there is a need for putting a stop to the chaos and infighting. If there is something with which the country's disasters can be remedied, it is surely by establishing friendly relations with neighboring countries. As a result of establishing friendly ties, across several thousand *li* farmers and silk cultivators could be seen to enjoy their work, and for seven or eight years the soldiers were idle. Then in the tenth month of the *ŭlyu* year [925] suddenly a conflict erupted, which led to armed clashes. You initially underestimated the enemy and drove straight in like a prayer mantis into a cart track [unaware of the oncoming cart]. In the end you realized the difficult situation you were in and valiantly withdrew, like a mosquito carrying a mountain. With clasped hands you declared a ceasing of hostilities, and pointing to heaven made an oath: from today onwards, forever let's live in joy and peace—and if someone breaks this covenant, let the gods strike him death! I, too, wanted to put a stop to the war, and looked forward to the benevolence of non-killing.[101] Then I broke up the encirclements to give the exhausted troops a rest, and consented to the exchange of hostages; all I wanted was to give the people repose. This is my great virtue towards the people of the south! How could you, even before the blood drawn for the oath had dried, violently spread your poison like bees or scorpions and attack innocent people; how could you like a crazy wolf or tiger cause such distress to the capital region of Silla, terrorize the capital Kŭmsŏng, and shake the royal house to its very foundations? Who resembles the authority

---

100 *Kut'o* 九土: this is traditionally a reference to the nine divisions of China under the mythical Emperor Yu, which are more commonly referred to as *kuju* 九州. Here it is probably used metaphorically for all prefectures and counties.

101 Here the Confucian virtue of humanity (*in*) is equated with the Buddhist precept against killing.

of Duke Huan of Qi or Duke Wen of Jin in relying on righteousness to honor the Zhou?[102] In preying on an opportune time to plot against the Han, you display the treachery of Wang Mang and Dong Zhuo.[103] Instead of displaying the utmost esteem towards the king, you vainly had him refer to you as 'your son.' This is upsetting the order of worthy and vile, treating upper and lower as equal, and amounts to a subverting of the loyalty and purity of the king's mainstay. How can there again be peace at the altar for grain and earth deities! In my heart there is no hidden hatred, my mind is set straight on honoring the king, so that I did not hesitate to assist his position at court and go and support him when his country was in crisis. But as for you, when you perceive the slightest chance of gain, you forget the munificence of heaven and earth, execute the king and burn the palace halls, slaughter ministers and ordinary people alike, and cart off court women together with all kinds of valuables that you looted. Your original evil surpasses even Jie and Zhou,[104] your inhumanity is worse than wild animals and birds. My resentment could bring down heaven, and my sincerity could obliterate the sun. I swore with the tenacity of an eagle pursuing a bird, and with the zest of dogs and horses again raised an army after two years behind palisades.[105] The battles on land were like thunder strikes and lightning flashes, the attacks on water were like tigers grappling and dragons soaring. Every time we made a move, without fail we scored a success. When Yun Pin was pursued on the coast, the suits of armor were stacked mountain high; when Ch'uhŏjo was captured at the border castle, the corpses lay spread out across the fields; at Yŏnsan Prefecture Kilhwan was beheaded in front of his troops; near Mari fortress

102 Duke Huan of Qi (d. 643 BC) and Duke Wen of Jin (697–628 BC) were both leaders of states in the Spring and Autumn period of Chinese history, but showed strong loyalty to the Zhou dynasty.

103 Wang Mang usurped the throne of the Western Han dynasty, established the Xin dynasty and ruled from 9 to 23 AD, after which the Han dynasty resumed. Dong Zhuo grabbed power towards the end of the Eastern Han dynasty, deposing the emperor in 190 AD and installing another one; he was assassinated in 192 AD.

104 Arch villains in Chinese history; King Jie was the last ruler of the Xia dynasty, and King Zhou the last ruler of the Shang dynasty.

105 The meaning of this part is not clear, but seems to refer to the period of two years following the conclusion of a treaty to the resumption of hostilities in 927.

Suo was executed beneath the flag; the day Imjon was taken Hyŏngjŏk and hundreds of others lost their lives; when Ch'ŏngju was breached, Chiksim and four or five others offered their heads; at Tonghwa Temple, when the enemy merely saw our flag they fled in all directions. At Kyŏngsan they performed the ceremony of 'putting in a coin' [in the mouth of a dead person] to show their willingness to surrender. At Kangju they came from the south to submit, and at Naju they moved from the west to attach themselves to us. With conquests like these, how could the recovery of territory [lost to Later Paekche] be far off? We ought to look forward to washing away the many grudges of Zhang Er at the Zhu River camp,[106] and to accomplishing a resounding victory like the Han monarch at the Wu River pavilion.[107] Finally the wind-swept waves will become calm and both the realm and the seas will be eternally calm. With the aid of Heaven, where else could the mandate go? All the more so since we have received from the august monarch of Wu-Yue a virtue that is so vast it embraces even the wild outlands, and whose humanity is so deep as to care for the ordinary people. He especially prepared an edict for us in his palace, instructing to put an end to the troubles in this country of green hills. Since we have now received such instruction, would we dare disobey it? If you choose to accept this instruction and put away all your weaponry, not only will you have responded to the humanity and grace of the upper country, you will also continue the threads that have been interrupted.[108] If you fail to correct your ways, then even if you regret it later it will be too late."

Sunsik from Myŏngju led his followers to court, and was granted the surname Wang and given the title of *taegwang*. His son Changmyŏng was granted the name Yŏm and given the title of *wŏnbo*. The minor general Kwangyŏng was also granted the surname Wang and given the title of

106 Zhang Er (d. 202 BC) was a warlord during the Warring States period and the Qin dynasty. At the break-up of the Qin, he first was loyal to Xiang Yu, but later switched sides to Liu Bang, the founder of the Han dynasties. The grudges mentioned here likely refer to the deceit of his colleague Chen Yu.

107 This refers to the defeat of Xiang Yu, who committed suicide here.

108 Presumably referring to the genealogy; thus, the lineage of rulers.

taesŭng.

The *wŏnyun* Kim Sang and the *chŏngjo* Chingnyang and others wanted to go and relieve Kangju. They had to pass by Ch'op'al fortress and were defeated by castle lord Hŭngjong. Kim Sang died there.

Second month. The king dispatched the *taesang* Yŏm Sang, the minister Nŭnggang and others to build a wall for Anbuk Prefecture. The *wŏnyun* Pak Kwŏn was made garrison head commander, leading a force of 700 men; they were also given arms.

Summer, fourth month. The king went to T'angjŏng Prefecture.[109]

A castle was built on Ok-san in Unju and manned by an armed garrison.

Fifth month. The *wŏnbo* Chin'gyŏng and others from Kangju were transporting grain to Koja Prefecture when Kyŏn Hwŏn took avail of this opportunity to lay siege to Kangju. Chin'gyŏng returned to fight them but was defeated and more than three hundred soldiers died. The general Yumun submitted to Kyŏn Hwŏn.

Sixth month, *kapsul* [1st] day. There was an earthquake in Pyŏkchin Prefecture.

The *ich'an* Chin'gyŏng died. He was posthumously made *taegwang*.

Seventh month. The king personally took charge of the attack against Samnyŏn fortress,[110] but could not conquer it. He then went to Ch'ŏngju. Later Paekche dispatched a general to attack Ch'ŏngju. At the time, Yu Kŭmp'il had received orders to build walls for T'angjŏng Prefecture. He had a dream in which a giant told him "tomorrow there will be an insurrection in the western plane, you should go there quickly." Yu Kŭmp'il woke up alarmed, and hurried to Ch'ŏngju to fight the Paekche force and defeated it. He pursued them to Tokki Garrison and killed or captured more than three hundred.

Eight month. Kyŏn Hwŏn ordered his general Kwanhŭn to fortify Yangsan. The king dispatched a command regarding the fortress. The *wŏnbo* Wang Ch'ung led his troops to attack and drive them away. Kwanhŭn

109 Now Onyang, in Asan, South Ch'ungch'ŏng Province.

110 Samnyŏn-sŏng 三年城: in modern Poŭn-gun, North Ch'ungch'ŏng Province.

retreated and strengthened the Taeryang fortress. He gave his troops permission to seize the grains from Taemok Prefecture. After that he divided his troops so that some were stationed along Kokchuk Pass, thus blocking the roads. Then the king ordered Wang Ch'ung and others to lay in waiting at Chomul fortress.

The king went to Ch'ungju and returned.

The Silla monk Honggyŏng returned from Min commandery in Tang, his boat carrying a set of the complete Buddhist canon. When he reached the Yesŏng River, the king personally came out to welcome him, and the canon was placed in the Chesŏg-wŏn.

Ninth month. The *taesang* Kwŏn Sin died.

Ŭn Kyejong, who hailed from Parhae, came to see the king at the Ch'ŏndŏk Hall, and bowed three times. People said that this was a breach of courtesy, yet the *taesang* Hamhong said: "Bowing three times is a custom of ancient times for people who have lost their country."

Winter, eleventh month. Kyŏn Hwŏn selected crack troops to attack Oŏgok fortress. They killed a thousand armed soldiers, and the generals Yangji, Myŏngsik and others, six altogether, submitted. The king had their wives and sons executed in front of the troops and their bodies displayed publicly.

This year the king inspected the northern border, and moved the construction site of Chinguk fortress, changing the name to T'ongdŏk Garrison. The *wŏnyun* Ch'ungin was made head of the garrison.

T'aejo Twelfth year [929]

Fourth year of the Tiancheng era of Later Tang, fourth year of the Tianxian era of Khitan

Spring, third month. The king dispatched the *taesang* Yŏm Sang to fortify Ansil Garrison, and tasked the *wŏnyun* Ŏmsu with inspecting and garrisoning it. He also had Yŏngch'ŏng County fortified.

Summer, fourth month. The king went to the Western Capital to inspect the prefectures and garrisons, and returned.

Sixth month. He made the *wŏnbo* Changp'il a *taesang*.

The tripitaka from India, the dharma master Mahura, came. The king welcomed him with due decorum.

Autumn, seventh month. The king went to Kiju[111] to inspect the prefecture and its garrisons, and returned.

Kyŏn Hwŏn invaded Ŭisŏng Prefecture with a force of 5,000 armored soldiers. The castle lord, the general Hong Sul, died in the battle. The king cried for him, and mourned for him, saying: today I lost my right and left hands.

Kyŏn Hwŏn also invaded Sunju, and the general Wŏnbong fled.

Ninth month. The king went to Kangju.

The king dispatched the *taesang* Sigyŏm to build walls for Ansu Garrison,[112] and made the *wŏnyun* Hŭnp'yŏng garrison commander. He also had walls built for Hŭngdŏk Garrison[113] and made the *wŏnyun* Ajasŏng garrison commander.

Winter, tenth month. The *ilgilgan* Yŏmhŭn from Paekche came to submit.

Kyŏn Hwŏn was planning to attack Kosagari castle, but the castle lord Hŭngdal heard about it in advance. He wanted to give battle but first took a bath. Suddenly he noticed the character 'extinction' on his right shoulder, and within ten days he died of illness. Kyŏn Hwŏn surrounded Kaŭn County but could not take it.

Twelfth month. Kyŏn Hwŏn surrounded Koch'ang Prefecture,[114] and the king went to relieve it. When he passed by Yean Garrison, he consulted with his generals: "When we have to fight under adverse conditions, what can we do about it?" The *taesang* Konghwŏn and Hong Yu said: "If the situation is not advantageous for us, we should take a shortcut, we cannot go via the Bamboo pass." But Yu Kŭmp'il said, "I have heard that if the

---

111 Kiju 基州: located in the area of modern P'unggi, North Kyŏngsang Province.

112 Ansu 安水: probably located in Kaech'ŏn Prefecture, South P'yŏngan Province.

113 Hŭngdŏk-chin 興德鎭: This may refer to Hŭngdŏk Prefecture, now corresponding to Sunch'ŏn in South P'yŏngan Province.

114 Koch'ang 古昌: modern Andong, North Kyŏngsang Province.

weapons are inferior and the battle dangerous, with a mind set on death and without the plan to survive, one can surely gain victory. Now that we face the enemy, if we don't engage in battle but merely think about possible defeat, what will happen? If we do not immediately relieve them, the more than three thousand troops at Koch'ang will join forces with the enemy. How disastrous that would be! I wish to advance with the army to strike at them rapidly." The king approved of this, and Yu Kŭmp'il then engaged the enemy from Chŏsu-bong (Pig's head peak), and scored a major victory. The king entered the prefecture, and told Yu Kŭmp'il, "Today's victory is all on account of your strength."

T'aejo Thirteenth year [930]

First year of the Changxing era of Later Tang, fifth year of the Tianxian era of Khitan

Spring, first month. The general from Taeam castle, Sŏnp'il, came to submit. Earlier, the king once wanted to go to Silla but bandits had rendered the roads dangerous, so he was greatly worried. Sŏnp'il then guided him with a marvelous plan, so that he could pass through safely. Thus, when he eventually came to court, the king treated him lavishly. Because his age was already advanced, he called him uncle.

The king himself led the troops in Koch'ang Prefecture, where they faced off on Pyŏng-san (Vase hill) against Kyŏn Hwŏn's army, which was stationed at Sŏk-san (Stone hill), just 500 paces across. Then they gave battle; Kyŏn Hwŏn lost and retreated. They captured the executive Kim Ak, but those who were killed numbered more than 8,000. Koch'ang Prefecture reported that Kyŏn Hwŏn had dispatched a general to attack and subdue Sunju, capturing people and households and taking them away. The king immediately went to Sunju and repaired its walls, and also punished its general, Wŏnbong. Sunju was lowered to a county and renamed Haji.[115]

115 Note that it thus reverted back to its original status and name; it had been elevated in status and name following Wŏnbong's submission to Koryŏ.

The Koch'ang castle lord, Kim Sŏnp'yŏng, was made *taegwang*, and Kwŏn Haeng and Chang Kil were made *taesang*. The prefecture (*kun* 郡) was elevated to Andong District (*pu* 府). After this, Yŏng'an, Hagok, Chingmyŏng, Songsaeng, and other counties and prefectures, more than thirty altogether, submitted one after the other.

Second month. The king dispatched an envoy to Silla to report this victory. The Silla king sent an envoy with return presents and a letter inviting the king for a meeting. At the time, all the prefectures, districts and villages from the eastern part of Silla, more than 110 fortified places from Myŏngju to Hŭngnye District,[116] submitted to Koryŏ.

The king went to Iro Garrison[117] and fortified it; he then renamed it Singwang Garrison, and moved people to sustain it. The two castles of South and North Mijilbu[118] both submitted.

Summer, fifth month, *imjin* [29th] day. The king went to the Western Capital, but returned from there [to Kaesŏng] by the *kyŏngja* (7th] day of the sixth month.

Autumn, eighth month. The king went to Taemok Prefecture,[119] merged it with East and West Tosol into Ch'ŏnan District, and installed a commander-in-chief. He made the *taesŭng* Chegung commissioner and the *wŏnbo* Ŏmsik vice-commissioner.

The king dispatched the *taesang* Yŏm Sang to construct a fortress at Masan, calling it Ansu Garrison. The *chŏngjo* Hŭnhaeng was made garrison commander.

The king went to Ch'ŏngju and had a city wall constructed.

Ullŭng-do sent envoys to offer local products. The envoy Paekkil was

116 Also known as Hŭngnyŏ, modern Ulsan. In other words, virtually the entire southern half of the eastern coastline of the peninsula.

117 Near Kyŏngju; in 1018 Hyŏnjong would merge it administratively into Kyŏngju.

118 Present Ŭich'ang-ŭp in Yŏng'il, north Kyŏngsang Province. In 940 T'aejo would merge these into Hŭnghae Prefecture.

119 As Jeong Yo-keun points out, this Taemok Prefecture 大木郡 should not be confused with the one with the same name seen first in the ninth month of 927. It was originally called Taemog'ak Prefecture 大木岳郡 in Paekche and Taerok Prefecture 大麓郡 in Silla, and corresponds to modern Mokch'ŏn-myŏn in Ch'ŏn'an. Chŏng Yo'gŭn, "Hu Samguk sidae Koryŏ ŭi Nambang chinch'ullo punsŏk," *Han'guk munhwa* 44 (2008), 15.

made *chŏngwi*, and the envoy T'odu was made *chŏngjo*.

Ninth month. Kaejibyŏn[120] sent an envoy to request submission.

Winter, twelfth month. The king went to the Western Capital and established a school. Before that, there had been no academic learning in the Western Capital. The king ordered the man of refined talent,[121] Kŏn'ak, to remain there and act as academician and doctor of letters. He separately established academies and gathered students from the six wards of the Western Capital as well as professors. Later, when the king learnt how he had promoted learning, he bestowed fine silk to encourage him, and also established the vocations of medicine and prognostication. He also bestowed 100 *sŏk* of grain to establish an educational treasury. "Treasury" is a dialect word [for an endowment]. Following a donation of cash or grains, interest is collected from the principal. Since its benefits spread far and wide and for a long time, it is called "treasury."[122]

In this year, a wall was built for Yŏnju.[123]

T'aejo Fourteenth year [931]

Second year of the Changxing era of Later Tang, sixth year of the Tianxian era of Khitan [931]

Spring, second month, *chŏngyu* [9th] day. The Silla king dispatched the prefect Kyŏmyong to announce Silla's allegiance to Koryŏ.

On the *sinhae* [23rd] day of the same month, the king led more than fifty mounted soldiers to Silla. The Silla king ordered all officials to welcome him in the suburbs, and he was feasted in the Imhae Hall of the palace.

---

120 According to the *Han'guk yŏksa chimyŏng sajŏn* (accessed through krpia.co.kr), this is also refers to Ulsan. However, as seen above, Ulsan (then known as Hŭngnye or Hŭngnyŏ) had then already submitted, so perhaps this is another locality near Ulsan.

121 *Xiucai* 秀才: in China, this term referred to someone who had passed the lower (county-) level examination, but here it may simply have been used as a term of respect.

122 The term used is *po* 寶, which was widely used in Koryŏ, especially for Buddhist endowments or foundations.

123 Modern Kaech'ŏn, North P'yŏng'an Province.

Drunken from wine, the Silla king said, "Because I have wronged Heaven, Kyŏn Hwŏn has pummeled me into submission and bereaved me. What pain could be greater than this!" Then he shed tears like rain, and all those around him wailed. T'aejo also shed tears and tried to comfort him. He stayed in the Silla capital for several weeks and then returned. The Silla king saw him off to Hyŏl Castle, and gave his cousin Yugyŏm as hostage.

From the moment the king had arrived, his troops behaved in a dignified way without harming anyone in the least, and therefore the people of the Silla capital congratulated each other, saying "formerly, when Kyŏn Hwŏn came, it was like encountering a wild dog or tiger; now when Lord Wang came, it was like meeting a parent."

Third month. Yu Kŭmp'il was slandered and hid himself on Kok island.

Autumn, eighth month. The king dispatched the *poyun* Sŏn'gyu to give the Silla king a saddle as well as damask, gauze, colored silk, and brocade; officials were given colored silk and undyed silk, and soldiers tea and caps, all gifts commensurate with rank.

Winter, eleventh month. The king went to the Western Capital to inspect prefectures and garrisons and then returned.

This year, Anbuk District was established, and the *wŏnyun* P'yŏnghwan was made garrison commander of Kangdŏk Garrison. The king told his officials: "The people of the northern border have the face of humans but the heart of beasts. When hungry they come, but when full they leave; when it is to their advantage, they will forget any sense of shame. Although they have submitted for now, we never know when they might turn their backs on us again. Thus, when they pass by our prefectures and garrisons, make sure to construct hostels outside of our walls to receive them."

T'aejo Fifteenth year [932]

Third year of the Changxing era of Later Tang, seventh year of the Tianxian era of Khitan

Summer, fourth month. In the house of a resident of the Western capital, a hen turned into a rooster.

Fifth month, *kapsin* [3rd] day. A storm blew over the Western Capital, blowing all the tiles off the roofs. When the king heard this, he told his officials, "Recently, I have finished reconstruction of the Western capital, and have moved people to resettle it. Relying on the mysterious power of the earth, I pacified the Three Han and was planning to make this the capital. Then, how come we have disasters such as these? Formerly, during the Jin dynasty there was an evil official who harbored devious plans. In his house a hen transformed into a rooster. Yet he did not change his evil ways, and in the end was executed. Then during the time of Prince Liu Pi of Wu, a fierce wind destroyed gates and uprooted trees, yet the king did not heed this warning, and in the end met with disaster.[124] What these omens are saying is that the corvée labor is not executed equally, and that tributes and taxes are too onerous. Below the people resent those above, and therefore there are such heavenly responses. With the experiences of the ancients in mind, how could we now ignore these appeals [to the ruler's consciousness]. Now all over the country the drafting of laborers for construction does not cease; also expenditure remains large, and we cannot cut on taxes. Privately, I think that it is this which has led to Heaven's castigation. Day and night I worry about this, and do not dare to be idle or rest even for a minute. Now the army and the country need the taxes, so we cannot reduce them. Yet I have also contemplated that you, ministers, may not be entirely fair-minded in terms of the public good, leading to public discontent. Or perhaps it is your reluctance to share that has led to these strange happenings. Either way, each of you must correct your mind, so that no calamity arises."

Sixth month. The Paekche general Kongjik came and submitted.

Autumn, seventh month. The king attacked Ilmosan fortress to the south and sent Chŏngyun to inspect the northern borders.

Ninth month. Paekche dispatched the *ilgilch'an* Sanggwi with ships and troops to invade the Yesŏng River and burn a hundred ships in Yŏmju,

---

124 Liu Pi (216-154 BC) was a nephew of Emperor Gaozu of Han. He instigated the so-called rebellion of the seven states, but was defeated and executed.

Paekchu, and Chŏngju. He also seized 300 horses that had been grazing on Chŏsan island[125] and returned.

Winter, tenth month. The navy admiral Sang'ae of Paekche attacked and looted Taeu island.[126] The king dispatched the *taegwang* Manse and others to relieve them. But the situation was not advantageous for our army, and the king was worried. Then Yu Kŭmp'il sent a letter from Kok Island, saying "Although I am burdened by guilt and demoted, I heard that Paekche has invaded our maritime counties. I wish to select myself conscripts and fit out warships to control them. Please, your highness, do not worry." When the king saw the letter, he cried and said "I believed the slander and drove away a wise person, this is my lack of insight." He then dispatched an envoy to call him back and comfort him with the following words: "You, sir, are truly innocent. Without harboring any anger, you merely thought about helping the country. I am truly ashamed and regretful. I will reward you for your loyalty so that it will be known to all [that you are without guilt]."

Eleventh month. The former vice-minister at the Department of Administration, Ch'oe Ŭng, died. He was from T'osan in Hwangju. When his mother was pregnant with him, there was a yellow cucumber plant in the garden of their house, but when the fruits ripened, they were oriental melons. Someone from their village informed Kungye of this. Kungye made a divination, which said that "[this is a sign that] a boy will be born, but he will not be auspicious for the county. Be careful, do not employ him!" His parents then raised the boy in hiding. When he grew up, he mastered the Five Classics, and was good at composing. He worked at the Hallim Academy for Kungye, who cherished him greatly. When T'aejo became king, he was thus working for the Academy of Letters,[127] but T'aejo soon made him a director at the State Council. Ch'oe Ŭng was intelligent and

---

125 Chŏ-san 猪山: literally "pig's mountain." Although a fortress with that name was located west of Ch'ŏngju, this is clearly a different locality, probably referring to one of the islands off the coast near Kaesŏng.

126 Taeu-do 大牛島: Greater ox island: location unknown.

127 Wŏnbong-sŏng 元鳳省: Since this office later became the Hallim Academy, it must have been a kind of predecessor: its officers specialized in the composition of important documents.

very proficient in administrative affairs. At the time, his reputation was widespread. T'aejo once told him "You are both very learned and talented, and you also know how to govern the country. You exert yourself for the country and uphold the public good, disregarding your own self you remain upright. Comparing you to the reputation of the ancients is surely no exaggeration." He then made him vice-minister at the Department of Administration, and shortly afterwards transferred him to the post of vice-Chancellor of the State Council. However, Ch'oe declined, saying "My colleague Yun Pong is my senior by ten years, please appoint him first." T'aejo said "Before I had heard the saying 'If one can give way for the sake of propriety, then how could ruling the country be difficult?',[128] and now I can witness someone who puts it into practice." Thereupon he made Yun Pong vice-Chancellor.

Ch'oe was a strict vegetarian. Once he was ill, and the king sent the crown prince to visit the sick, urging him to make sure that Ch'oe had some meat. However, Ch'oe adamantly refused. Then the king himself went to his residence, and told him "In not eating meat, you commit two mistakes. First, by not protecting your body, you cannot look after your mother to the end, this is unfilial. Second, you will not live long; this will mean that I will mourn a pillar of state too early. This is disloyalty." Ch'oe then forced himself to follow this advice, and for the first time ate meat, and consequently recovered. Until now, when he died of disease at the age of thirty-five. T'aejo mourned him deeply, and gave him the posthumous title of *wŏnbo*, and was also very generous in his assistance to the funerals. He was successively given the titles of *taegwang*, grand guardian to the heir apparent. He was also posthumously styled Hŭigae, and later his memorial tablet was enshrined together with T'aejo in the same chamber of the Royal Ancestor Shrine.[129]

This year, Koryŏ again attacked the fortress of Ilmosan, and this time destroyed it. Also, this year the *taesang* Wang Chung'yu was sent to Later

---

[128] From the *Analects* 4.13.

[129] This happened in the 18th year of King Hyŏnjong (1027).

Tang to offer local products.

T'aejo Sixteenth year [933]

Fourth year of the Changxing era of Later Tang, eighth year of the Tianxian era of Khitan

Spring, third month. [Later] Tang dispatched the imperial groom, Wang Qiong, of the chief minister rank, and the grand treasurer, Yang Shaoye, of vice-minister rank, to invest the king as "specially promoted acting grand guardian, area commander in chief of the Hyŏnt'o Commandery with special powers, pillar of state, acting envoy of the grand righteous army." They also enfoeffed him as king of the country of Koryŏ, and bestowed the calendar, silver utensils, and silk. They also transmitted a decree enfeoffing his spouse née Yu as Lady of Hadong Prefecture, and also a decree informing the generals and administrators of the three armies that Wang Kŏn had been enfeoffed as king of Koryŏ. Then the Tang calendar was for the first time proclaimed, and Tang era names started being used.

Summer, fifth month. The great general for conquering the south, Yu Kŭmp'il, was guarding Ŭisŏng District. The king sent an envoy with the following words: "Considering that Silla has so often been attacked by Paekche, I dispatched a general to prevent such invasions. Now I heard that Paekche has destroyed and looted Hyesan fortress, Abul Garrison, and other places. If they should invade further as far as the Silla capital, you should go and help them." Yu Kŭmp'il then chose eighty strong men to join him. When they reached the place to ferry over the river, he told his troops: "If we meet enemy troops here, I will not be able to return alive. But when I consider that all of you will also suffer from the sword blades, you are free to make your own plans." His soldiers spoke: "We are ready to die. How could we let our general die alone?" Then they made a pact to attack the enemy with all their might. Then they crossed the river and encountered the Paekche general commander Singŏm and his troops. When they saw how dangerous Yu Kŭmp'il and his troops looked, he did not engage them but retreated.

When Yu Kŭmp'il reached [the capital of] Silla, young and old came out of the city to welcome him. Crying, they said "We did not expect that today we would see you, *taegwang*. If it were not for the *taegwang* Yu, we would be mincemeat." Yu Kŭmp'il stayed for seven days, and then returned to give battle with Singŏm at Chado. He scored a great victory, and captured seven of his generals, killing or capturing many [soldiers]. When news of the victory reached the king, he said "if it were not for Yu Kŭmp'il, who could have pulled this off?" When he returned to the palace, the king came out of his throne hall to personally welcome him. Taking his hands, he said "A merit such as yours, sir, is rare even among ancients. You are carved in my heart; never will I forget you." Yu Kŭmp'il thanked him, saying "I only did my job. Why, your highness, do you have to put it like that?" The king approved of this.

This year the king introduced palace ranks for the army.

T'aejo Seventeenth year [934]

First year of the Qingtai era of King Lu of Later Tang, ninth year of the Tianxian era of Khitan

Spring, first month. The king went to the Western Capital to inspect the northern garrisons and returned.

Summer, fifth month. The king went to Yesan Garrison, and issued the following order: "The poison of the T'aebong ruler spread to the ordinary people and turned the gods of earth and grain upside down. I inherited his authority and continued to construct this new country. A people oppressed by harsh corvée labor, how could that be my intention? However, the weapons have not yet been laid to rest. Braving wind and rain, I have inspected the garrisons in all provinces and prefectures, and repaired and completed their defenses. As a result, all males have been conscripted, and women have been forced to be drafted for labor. Not able to endure the hardship, some have fled to mountains and forests, and some have taken to accusing officials. It is unknown how many have done so. Families of power and influence have added to this with additional abuses. How could I, with just a single body, go to each household to verify this? The ordinary people, having no further recourse, are thus crying out [to heaven] for help. All you notables who live on the grain stipends given as salary should take heed from my embracing the people as my own children. You should take pity on the people who work the land of your stipend villages. Those in the local yamen[130] who are ignorant, are made to administer the stipend villages, and give in to their greed and exploit the people. But how could you know that? And even if you knew, how could you stop it? As for those who appeal, the officials local and central cover up and assist each other, and the cause of the people's anger and enmity lies here. I have already taken heed of this, and wish that those who are aware of this, exert themselves even more; those who do not know, take this as a warning. Those who transgress my order will be issued a separate, tainted record.[131] If after issuing such tainted record one still takes the crime of hiding [the faults of people] as a wise action and does not raise this issue; in such a case, how would we hear about the reality of good and evil? Wouldn't it be better to have people who uphold loyalty and redress crimes? You all should heed my instructions and listen to my words on rewards and punishments. Those who have committed a crime, whether they are elite or base, they will be punished up to their sons and grandsons. If their merit is big and crime small, this will be taken into account when meting out reward and punishment. If they do not correct their ways, I will go after their salaries, and for the rest of their lives they will not receive anything. If their will is sincere and they serve the public, and throughout their career there is no blemish, for their whole life they will enjoy a lavish salary. Later they will be referred to as an eminent family, and until their sons and grandsons will receive reward. This is not something that I am

---

130 Note that the *Koryŏsa* has, for the same passage "family retainers" (*kasin* 家臣) rather than yamen (*a* 衙), which is an official institution at the local level.

131 *Yŏmkwŏn* 染卷: probably refers to a "negative evaluation" on a personnel record, which would hinder promotion.

just declaring today; it will be transmitted for ten thousand generations as a model order. If someone is accused of a crime by the people and summoned, if he does not appear this order will apply. If they fail to appear after a second summons, they will first be caned ten times to set an example for the crime of not following this order. Only then will their crime be assessed. If officials and *hyangni* do not follow this order, and intentionally obstruct it, the days [they hold up the order] will be counted and they will be punished accordingly. Furthermore, if there are those who remain untouched by this order by relying on authority and influence, their names will be made public."

Autumn, ninth month, *chŏngsa* [20th] day. The old man [of the South Pole] star[132] was visible.

The king personally led an attack on Unju. When Kyŏn Hwŏn heard this he organized a force of 5000 armored soldiers, and told [T'aejo]. "When our two armies clash, given our respective forces, nobody will be safe. I fear that an untold number of soldiers will be killed or wounded; we should conclude peace and maintain our respective borders." The king consulted with his generals. The general of the right Yu Kŭmp'il spoke: "As things stand now, it is unacceptable not to fight. I wish that our king will observe how I and others destroy the enemy; do not worry." Thus when the enemy had not yet formed a battle formation, he suddenly struck them with a crack force of a few thousand. He killed or captured more than 3,000 enemy soldiers. He also captured the diviner Chonghun, the medical doctor Hun'gyŏm, and the generals Sangbong and Ch'oe P'il. When they heard this news, more than thirty fortifications north of Ungjin all surrendered.

This year the king sent the *taesang* Yŏm Sang to fortify T'onghae Garrison; the *wŏnbo* Chaehwŏn was made garrison commander.

The Western Capital was afflicted by drought and locusts.

---

132 *Namgŭk noinsŏng* 南極老人星: one of the 28 traditional constellations, it was thought to be visible only in times of peace. Equivalent to the virgin constellation.

T'aejo Eighteenth year [935]

Second year of the Qingtai era of Later Tang, tenth year of the Tianxian era of Khitan

Spring, third month. Kyŏn Hwŏn's son Singŏm hid his father in the Kŭmsan Buddhist temple and killed his younger brother Kŭmgang. Kyŏn Hwŏn had more than ten sons. His fourth son Kŭmgang was tall and wise, and Kyŏn Hwŏn loved him the most. He wanted to pass the throne to him. But his elder brothers Singŏm, Yanggŏm, and Yonggŏm[133] knew this, and were worried. At the time Yanggŏm and Yonggŏm were on military duty outside the capital of Later Paekche, leaving Singŏm alone. At his side was the *ich'an* Nŭnghwan. He made people conspire with Yanggŏm and Yonggŏm, and urged Singŏm to start a revolt.

Summer, fourth month. The king told his ministers, "Naju and more than forty prefectures have been within our borders for a long time and are completely loyal. Recently they have been either taken away or plundered by Later Paekche. For the past six years the sea roads there have also been blocked. Who can assist them for me?" All the notables recommended Yu Kŭmp'il, but the king said: "I also thought of him, but recently the roads to Silla have been dangerous, yet he has gone there and made them safe. Considering his efforts, it is difficult to order him yet again." Yu Kŭmp'il then submitted that "although I am advanced in years, how can I not give my all for the important tasks besetting the country?" The king happily accepted, and crying said "If you accept this mission, nothing would make me happier than that." He appointed Yu Kŭmp'il great general commander-in-chief. He sent him off all the way to the Yesŏng River and bestowed a royal ship before dispatching him. Yu Kŭmp'il went to Naju, and after setting it in order returned. Again the king went to the Yesŏng River to receive and comfort him.

Sixth month. Kyŏn Hwŏn and his youngest son Nŭngye, his daughter Aebok, his favorite concubine Kobi and others fled to Naju, and requested to become part of the Koryŏ dynasty. The king sent his general Yu Kŭmp'il,

---

133 Their names meaning divine sword, good sword, and dragon sword respectively.

the *taegwang* Manse, and the *wŏnbo* Hyangye, O Tam, Nŭngsŏn, and Ch'ungjil via the sea road to Naju to welcome him. When he arrived in Kaesŏng, the king again addressed him as uncle, bestowed as residence the southern palace and granted a position at the top of the official hierarchy. He also granted Yangju as stipend village, and furthermore gold and silk, forty male and forty female slaves, and fourteen horses. Singang, a former Paekche man who had submitted, was tasked with managing his estate (*agwan* 衙官).

Autumn, ninth month. The king went to the Western Capital to inspect Hwanghae Prefecture and returned.

Winter, tenth month, *imsul* [1st] day. The Silla king Kim Pu dispatched Vice-chancellor Kim Ponghyu to request becoming part of Koryŏ. The king dispatched the acting chancellor Wang Ch'ŏl and the vice-chancellor Han Hŏn'ong to deliver a reply.

On the *kabo* [3rd] day of the eleventh month, the Silla king, at the head of all his officials, set out from the royal capital of Silla. Both nobles and ordinary people followed them. The fragrant carriages and ornate horses stretched for more than 30 *li*. The roads were filled with throngs of onlookers, who lined the roads like dikes. The prefectures and counties [they passed through] gave as much as they could to those on the road, and the king sent people to make sure everyone was fine. On the *kyemyo* [12th] day the Silla king together with Wang Ch'ŏl and the rest arrived in Kaegyŏng. The king made sure the guard of honor was ready and went out to the suburbs to greet the Silla king and his retinue. He ordered the crown prince and all the high officials to escort him as he took residence in the Willow Flower Palace. On the *kyech'uk* [22nd] day the king went to the main hall of the palace and gathered all the officials, both of the civil and of the military branches. On this occasion they celebrated the wedding ceremony of the king's oldest daughter, the princess of Nangnang, to the Silla king. On the *kimi* [28th] day the Silla king sent a letter stating "My country has gone through dangerous situations and chaos for a long time, and its days are numbered. I do not expect to be able to strengthen its dynastic foundations in the future. I would like to perform the ceremony of making myself a subject to Koryŏ." The king did not grant this request.

On the *sinyu* [1st] day of the twelfth month, all the ministers submitted a memorial saying "Just as Heaven does not have two suns, earth does not support two kings. With two sovereigns in one country, how can the people bear this? We request that you accept the Silla king's plea." On the *imsin* [12th] day the king went to the Ch'ŏndŏk Hall and gathered all the high officials and rank and file. He addressed them as follows: "I have sworn a blood oath with Silla, and for a long time both our countries have protected our altars of the earth and grain deities, and for eternity would be on good terms. Now the Silla king has firmly requested to become a vassal, and you all approve of this. Although in my mind I am ashamed, it is difficult to refuse." Then he received Kim Pu in the courtyard, and they held the ceremony [of submission]. All the assembled officials cheered loudly, their voices shaking the palace. Kim Pu was made a merit subject "Contemplating brightness, following the transformation, protecting the country," pillar of state and king of Nangnang, and given the title of *chŏngsŭng*. His stipend village measured 8,000 households, and his position was higher than that of the crown prince. He received an annual emolument of one thousand *sŏk* of grain. The country of Silla was renamed Kyŏngju, and was granted to Kim Pu as a stipend village.[134] His followers were all re-employed and granted field emoluments that were superior to the old system. The king also built the Sillan Palace[135] and granted it to Kim Pu. Also, he made him local inspector for Kyŏngju, which meant that he was in charge of all local officials below the level of village head and vice-village head. Then this system was also put into effect for all the merit subjects. Each was made local inspector of his prefecture; this is the beginning of the system of local

134 It is not clear if that is in addition to the one previously mentioned, or if that stipend village of 8,000 households actually refers to Kyŏngju. On the problem of these stipend villages granted to the former rulers of Silla and Paekche, see Pak Ch'unsik, "Namal Yŏch'o ŭi sigŭp e taehan ilkoch'al." *Sach'ong* 32 (1987): 33-96.

135 Sillan 新鸞: "divine phoenix." Perhaps a wordplay on the name Silla?

inspectors.[136]

Originally when Kim Ponghyu came to request submission, the king treated him with utmost decorum, and before sending him off, told him "Now the king of Silla has given his country to me, this is a great gift indeed! I would like to conclude marriage ties with the house of Silla so as to create an ever-lasting family relation such as between maternal uncles and cousins. When Kim Pu heard this, he reported back "My paternal uncle, the *chapkan* Ŏngnyŏm, has a daughter who is beautiful in virtue and appearance, she is the only one fit to be your bride." The king then married her. She became known as Queen Sinsŏng, and gave birth to Wang Uk, later styled Anjong.[137]

Yi Chehyŏn commented: "According to Kim Pusik's commentary,[138] 'As to the fact that King Kyŏngsun gave the mandate of his dynasty to our T'aejo, although he failed to hold on to it himself, it is still an act worthy of praise. If he had held out and fought with all his might against the Koryŏ army, his family would have been annihilated and the innocent people would have suffered greatly. Because he did not hesitate to declare fealty, sealed the granaries and kept the census records of prefectures and counties, which he all offered when he submitted, his merit to the dynasty, and his virtue toward the people, are great indeed. Formerly, the Qian family offered their country of Wu-Yue to the Song, and Song Zizhan praised their loyalty.[139] Now the merit and virtue of Silla vastly exceeds that of Wu-Yue. Our T'aejo had

---

136 *Sasim* 事審: a term that only occurred in early Koryŏ; in the absence of a system of centrally appointed magistrates, it seems to be an attempt to put an administrative gloss on a situation where local magnates (*hojok*) had effective control over local society anyway. See Hong Sŭnggi, "Koryŏ chŏn'gi ŭi *sasim* kwa *hyangni*," *Yŏksa hakpo* 166 (2000): 37–65.

137 He would become father to King Hyŏnjong.

138 Yi Chehyŏn (1287–1367) was one of the most famous intellectuals and politicians of the late Koryŏ period; he was tasked with writing a national history (*Kuksa* 國史), which has not been transmitted, but his assessment of each Koryŏ king has been preserved and is included in the *Koryŏsa chŏryo*. Kim Pusik (1075–1151): author of the *Samguk sagi*. The following quotation is found at the end of chapter 12 of that work, the last chapter of the Silla Annals.

139 The Qian family ruled Wu-Yue (roughly modern Zhejiang) from ca. 900 to 978, when they submitted peacefully to the Song dynasty. Song Zizhan is the style of Su Shi (1037–1101).

many spouses and concubines, and his sons and grandsons were numerous. But it was a maternal grandson of a Silla royal, Hyŏnjong, who gained the throne [as the eighth ruler of Koryŏ], and after that all kings descended from him. Isn't this what can be called the retribution of this passive virtue?' Kim Kwanŭi, Im Kyŏngsuk, and Min Chi all wrote that the lady of the Taeryang court, née Yi, was a daughter of the *t'aewi* Yi Chŏng'ŏn, and gave birth to King An, but it is not known on what basis this claim is made."[140]

This year the vice-minister of the Department of Rites, Hyŏng Sun, was set to Tang.

Ihol and Sukchu were fortified.

T'aejo Nineteenth year [936]

First year of the Tianfu era of Emperor Gaozu of Later Jin, eleventh year of the Tianxian era of Khitan

Spring, second month. The son-in-law of Kyŏn Hwŏn, General Pak Yŏnggyu, requested submission. Earlier, he had secretly told his wife: "Our great king has labored for over forty years to lay the foundation for a hereditary dynasty, but because of a family feud has lost his territory and sought refuge in Koryŏ. Now a faithful wife does not serve two husbands, and a loyal subject does not serve two lords. So, if we abandon our lord to serve the rebellious son, then how could I face the righteous gentlemen of the world? Moreover, I have heard that the King of Koryŏ is magnanimous and upright. Having obtained the minds of the people, he is about to obtain Heaven's favor, and will surely become king of the Three Han. Now, what if I would draft a letter to comfort my king, and at the same time enquire covertly

---

140 The Lady of the Taeryang court seems to refer here to one of T'aejo's spouses, and is here mentioned likely because she was also of Silla descent. However, "Prince of the Taeryang Court" is also the title of Hyŏnjong before he became king. "King An" might refer to Wang Uk, later given the temple name Anjong, or to Hyŏnjong himself, whose courtesy name was Anse 安世. As Hyŏnjong was prince of the Taeryang court, perhaps the title was also applied to his mother and grandmother retroactively.

with T'aejo as to his plans for us in the future?" His wife wholeheartedly agreed, and thus they sent a messenger to convey their intention. Moreover he said [to T'aejo], "If we [?] raise a righteous army, please meet it from the palace, so that they are received by the king's army."[141] The king was greatly pleased, and bestowed generous presents on the envoy. When he returned he reported to Pak Yŏnggyu "If you humbly receive the lord's beneficence, the roads will be without obstruction. Then you can first see the king; the general can ascend the throne hall; your wife will be treated with the respect of an older sister and aunt. In the end there will necessarily be a lavish reward, heaven and earth and spirits have all heard these words."[142]

Summer, sixth month. Kyŏn Hwŏn made the following request. "Your subject is old and crossed the waves over a long distance to submit to your highness. Now I wish there be raised soldiers and authority granted to execute my bandit son." The king first wanted to bide his time, but was moved by this firm request and granted it. Then he first sent the *chŏngyun* and military general Pak Surhŭi to command infantry and cavalry numbering 10,000 and go to Ch'ŏn'an.

Autumn, ninth month. The king led the three armies to Ch'ŏn'an, where they joined the other troops and marched on towards Ilsŏn.[143] Sin'gŏm moved from the opposite direction and they faced off across the Illi river. The king and Kyŏn Hwŏn went to inspect the troops. Kyŏn Hwŏn together with the *taesang* Kyŏnkwŏn, Pak Surhŭi, and Hwangbo Kŭmsan, and the *wŏnyun* Kang Yuyŏng led a cavalry of 10,000 called the Heaven-supporting army. The great general and *wŏnyun* Nŭngdal, Kiŏn, Han Sunmyŏng, and Hŭnak, and the *chŏngjo* Yŏngjik and Kwangse, led an infantry of 10,000. For the left force, the *taesang* Kim Ch'ŏl, Hong Yu, and Pak Sugyŏng, the *wŏnbo* Yŏnju, and the *wŏnyun* Hwŏllyang led a cavalry army of 10,000 called

141 I am not sure of the meaning here, but when moving north to submit to T'aejo, Pak Yŏnggyu probably wanted to avoid the army of local leaders; though loyal to T'aejo, they might not be convinced he was going to be loyal.

142 Here the meaning is even more obscure; it could still be the reported speech of the envoy, but it could also be simply a statement of what happened.

143 This refers to Sŏnsan, part of Kumi city in N. Kyŏngsang Province.

the complementing Heaven army. The great general and *wŏnyun* Samsun and Chullyang, and the *chŏngjo* Yŏngyugil, Kangch'ung, and Hŭn'gye commanded an infantry of 10,000. For the right force, the *taegwang* Wang Sunsik of Myŏngju, the *taesang* Kŭngjun, Wang Yŏm, and Wang Ch'a, and the *wŏnbo* In'il led a cavalry force of 20,000. The *taesang* Yu Kŭmp'il and the *wŏnyun* Kwanmu and Kwanhŏn led a force of Black Water [Malgal], Talgo, Ch'ŏllŭk and other barbarian crack cavalry of 9,500 called the aiding Heaven army. The great general the *wŏnyun* Chŏngsun and the *chŏngjo* Aejin led an infantry force of 1,000 called the Heavenly Valor army. The great general the *wŏnyun* Chŏnghŭi and the *chŏngjo* Kyŏnhwŏn[144] led an infantry force of 1,000 called the Shielding Heaven Army. The great general Kim Kŭkchong and the *wŏnbo* Chugan led an infantry of 1,000 called the Central Army. Furthermore the great general and *taesang* Konghwŏn, the *wŏnyun* Nŭngp'il, and the general Wang Sayun led a cavalry force of 300. The armies of the various castles numbered 14,700 and acted as an auxiliary force to the three armies.[145] Then the drums rolled and the three armies marched on, but suddenly in front of them there appeared a white cloud shaped like a sword and halberd. It hovered over our troops and moved towards the enemy lines together with them. The Paekche left generals Hyobong, Tŏksuk, Aesul, and Myŏnggil saw that the Koryŏ army was vastly superior in numbers and better equipped, and threw away their weapons and surrendered to the left wing army. The enemy soldiers were dispirited and did not dare to move. The king comforted Hyobong and his fellow generals and asked about Singŏm's location. Hyobong said, "Singŏm is with the central army. Please, king, gather your left and right army and strike at him, and you shall be victorious." The king ordered Konghwŏn to strike straight at the central army. All three armies advanced together, and took the enemy in a pincer movement. The enemy army collapsed and fled. They took as prisoners of war the generals Hŭn'gang, Kyŏndal,

144 Kyŏnhwŏn 見萱: not to be confused with the former Paekche ruler Kyŏn Hwŏn 甄萱.

145 In all, the troops at his disposal would thus number a staggering 87,500 soldiers! Especially the fact that nearly 50,000 are said to have been mounted is difficult to take at face value.

Ŭmsul, Yŏngsik, Ubong, and others, altogether 3200; they furthermore killed 5,700 soldiers. The enemy fled in defeat, and our army pursued them until Hwangsan Prefecture.[146] They fled past T'an pass and set up camp at Ma fortress. Then Singŏm, Yanggŏm, and Yonggŏm together with all their officials surrendered. The king comforted them, and ordered that the 3200 Paekche generals and elites be sent back to their homes. Only Hŭn'gang, Pudal, Ubong, Kyŏndal and others, forty people together with their wives and children, were sent to the capital. The king scolded Nŭnghwan to his face, saying "The one who first plotted together with Singŏm to imprison his father the king is you. Is this how you behave as a righteous subject?" Nŭnghwan hung his head in shame and did not respond. He was then ordered to be executed. [The king] furthermore said "The fact that Singŏm seized the throne was because he was threatened [by Nŭnghwan], not because it was originally his intention. Furthermore, since he has sought refuge [in Buddhism] to atone he will be forgiven." Because of all the accumulated worries Kyŏn Hwŏn developed an illness and within a few days died in a Buddhist temple in Hwangsan.

The king went to the Paekche capital and issued the following order: "Since your leaders have already submitted, and you have not violated us, we will listen to you as our people. Generals and officials of talent will be employed; the army will not even harass you in the slightest, and leave all prefectures and counties in peace." The people rejoiced greatly. Singŏm was granted an aristocratic title and Yanggŏm and Yonggŏm were banished to Chinju, and subsequently killed.

To Yŏnggyu he said "Since Kyŏn Hwŏn lost his country and came to us from afar, not one of his ministers or sons comforted him. Only you and your wife came from afar to harmonize with your ruler in utmost sincerity, and at the same time submitted to us; this righteousness cannot be forgotten." He then granted him the position of *chwasŭng* and also bestowed 1,000 *kyŏng* of fields, and gave permission to use up to thirty-five horses at

146 Hwangsan Prefecture 黃山郡: modern Yŏnsan, Nonsan city, South Ch'ungch'ŏng Province.

post stations to receive his family members. He also gave official posts to his two sons.

When the king returned from Paekche, he went to the Wibong Pavilion to receive the congratulations of all officials and the people. Since the king had now unified the Three Han, he wanted to urge his subjects to be loyal and righteous. Then he himself composed a book of "Admonitions for Government" in one fascicle to warn his officials. He personally wrote eight copies and distributed them to officials in the capital and the provinces.

Winter, twelfth month. The *taegwang* Pae Hyŏn'gyŏng died. Pae Hyŏn'gyŏng hailed from Kyŏngju, and his physical power far surpassed that of other people. He rose through the ranks and was with T'aejo on all his campaigns. Because his merit was so great, the king personally went to his house when his illness was severe. Holding his hand he said "Alas! Fate! Since your sons and grandsons are present, I venture to make myself scarce." The king went outside and Pae Hyŏn'gyŏng died. The king stopped his carriage and ordered his officials to take care of the funeral. Later he returned to bestow the posthumous title Muyŏl. He was later enshrined together with T'aejo in the royal ancestor shrine.

This year the king constructed Kwanghŭng, Hyŏnsŏng, Mirŭk, and Nae Ch'ŏnwang temples. He also constructed Kaet'ae temple in Yŏnsan.

T'aejo Twentieth year [937]

Second year of the Tianfu era of Later Jin, twelfth year of the Tianxian era of Khitan

Summer, fifth month. The *chŏngsŭng* Kim Pu offered a jade belt which could surround the waist ten times and had sixty-two links. The king received it and ordered that it be stored in the Ministry of Royal Treasures and Crafts. What happened before: the Silla envoy Kim Yuk came to Kaesŏng, and the king asked: "Silla has three great treasures: the sixteen foot golden statue [of the Buddha], the nine-story pagoda [of Hwangnyong-sa], and the holy belt. As long as the three treasures exist, the country also will not perish. The statue and the pagoda still exist, but I wonder about the whereabouts of the holy belt?" Kim Yul answered "your subject has never heard about a holy belt." The king laughed and said "How can a cherished statesman like yourself not know about a great treasure of the country?" Kim Yul felt ashamed and upon his return told the Silla king about this. The Silla king asked his ministers but nobody knew. Then there was an old monk of Hwangnyong-sa who said "I heard that the holy belt was once worn by King Chinp'yŏng. It has been transmitted from generation to generation and is stored in the Southern repository." The king then performed purifying rites and perceived the belt. Eventually he offered it to T'aejo.

This year a wall was built for Sunju.

Wang Kyu and Hyŏng Sun were sent to Later Jin to offer congratulations for the emperor's accession.

T'aejo Twenty-first year [938]

Third year of the Tianfu era of Later Jin, first year of the Huitong era of Khitan

Spring, third month. A monk from India came. The king had the Sangha administration[147] prepare due ceremony and readied a dharma cart to welcome him.

Autumn, seventh month. The general of Pyŏkchin Prefecture, Yi Ch'ong'ŏn, died. Towards the end of Silla, many bandits plagued the region. Pyŏkchin was protected by Yi Ch'ŏng'ŏn, and the people depended on him for their safety. The king dispatched someone with a letter from the king, proposing to join forces to suppress the chaos. Yi Ch'ong'ŏn was very pleased, and sent his son Yŏng to lead troops in support of the king's campaign. The king approved this, and gave him the daughter of the *taegwang* Sado in marriage. He also confirmed Yi Ch'ŏng'ŏn as the

147 Literally, 'the two streets'. In Chinese Buddhism, the monk-registrars of the capital were divided along the two main sections of the Chinese capital, divided by the main thoroughfare; hence 'liangjie' 兩街 came to refer to the capital sangha administration.

general in charge of Pyŏkchin Prefecture, and showed him many favors. Yi Ch'ŏng'ŏn repaid this trust by drilling his troops and storing grain, so that the isolated forts [in his area] remained firmly in the hands of Silla and stood firm in a region where Paekche had to fight [so as to gain access to Silla]. He was thus a pillar of support in the southeast.

For the first time the era names of Later Jin were used.

The outer walls of the Western Capital were constructed.

Winter, twelfth month. The crown prince of T'amna, Mallo, came to court. He was granted the title of crown prince Star-leader (Sŏngju wangja 星主王子).[148]

This year walls were built for Yangam, Yonggang, and P'yŏngwŏn.

T'aejo Twenty-second year [939]

Fourth year of the Tianfu era of Later Jin, second year of the Huitong era of Khitan

Spring, third month. The *chwasŭng* Kongjik died. Kongjik was from Maegok in Yŏnsan. From his youth he was valiant, and served Kyŏn Hwŏn. In front of Kyŏn Hwŏn he hid his true feelings. His oldest son Chiktal, his second son Kŭmsu and his daughter were hostages of Kyŏn Hwŏn. Once Kongjik went to the court of Kyŏn Hwŏn and told Chiktal "Now I realize that this country is trapped in luxury and has no principles. Even though I am part of the inner circle here, I do not want to come back ever again. I heard that the Koryŏ ruler has an adequate civil bureaucracy to make the people at ease, and adequate military to prevent violence. Therefore he can take care of people from the four corners of the country. I want to pledge loyalty to him; what do you think?" Chiktal said "Since I have become a hostage here I have observed their customs. They merely rely on wealth and power, and enforce their affairs in a haughty and conceited manner. How could they manage the country like this! Now that you, father, want to turn to a wise ruler to protect our village, I think that this is a proper

148 Henceforth this would become the designated title for princes of T'amna (Cheju island).

decision. Together with my younger brother and sister, I will wait for an opportunity to join you. In case that fails, I will rely on your wisdom to ensure the continuation of your bloodline through your other son. In that case, I would die without regret."

Kongjik then decided to submit to Koryŏ together with his son Yongsŏ. Coming to the Koryŏ court, he told the king "In my humble village I heard about your transforming influence for a long time. Although I have no power to assist you, I would like to devote myself as a subject with utmost loyalty." The king was delighted and gave him the rank of *taesang*. He also granted him the emolument of Paeksŏng Prefecture[149] and horses from the royal stables as well as colored silk. His son Hamsŏ was made *chwayun*, and he gave the daughter of the *chŏngjo* Chunhaeng, a royal relative.

The king said, "you clearly discerned the difference between order and chaos, and seeing an opportunity to escape, you came to us. I find this truly worthy of praise, and have united our families in marriage, to show my generosity for the fact that you have devoted your mind and energy to protecting the border." Kongjik thanked him and then spoke the following words: "The Paekche prefecture of Ilmosan borders on my village, and now that I have shifted my allegiance, it is frequently raided and the people are not at ease. I would like to go and seize back the people of my village so that they are no longer robbed but can devote themselves to farming and sericulture. This will further strengthen their resolve to submit and be transformed." The king gave his permission.

Kyŏn Hwŏn was enraged and had Chiktal and his brother and sister brought before him, and had them seared off their thigh muscles. Chiktal died as a result. After Paekche had perished, Kŭmsŏ managed to return [to Maegok].

This year Later Jin sent the doctor of the academy Xie Pan to invest the king as Commander Unequalled in Honor (Rank 1B), Acting Grand Preceptor.

---

149 Now part of Ansŏng in Kyŏnggi Province.

Taean was fortified.

T'aejo Twenty-second year [940]

Fifth year of the Tianfu era of Later Jin, third year of the Huitong era of Khitan

Spring, third month. Kyŏngju was made into a Superior Area Command. All the names of prefectures etc. were changed.

Autumn, seventh month. Royal preceptor Ch'ungdam died. A stele was erected to his memory at Hŭngbŏp-sa in Wŏnju.[150] The king personally wrote the epigram.

Twelfth month. Kaet'ae-sa was completed. The king ordered that a dharma assembly of completion be held, and personally drafted the ritual text.[151]

This year for the first time the merit-reward land system was implemented.[152] From court ministers to military officials, regardless of their rank, depending on whether their personality or actions are good or bad, or their merit great or small, they are allotted in degrees [according to these criteria].

Sinhŭng-sa was repaired, and a merit subject hall was built in the temple; paintings of the merit subjects of the Three Han were painted on its walls. A Grand All-inclusive Assembly[153] was held for one day and one night, and this became an annual event.

The Later Jin returned our hostage, Wang Injŏk.

---

150 The stele's base and finial can still be found at the temple site, while the remaining fragments of the stele itself are in the National Museum of Korea. See Vermeersch, *Power of the Buddhas*, 249, 384.

151 Kaet'ae-sa, between Nonsan and Kyeryong, was founded in commemoration of T'aejo's victory over Later Paekche. The text has been preserved; see Vermeersch, *Power of the Buddhas*, 94–95.

152 *Yŏkpunjŏn* 役分田: generally regarded as a predecessor of the stipend land law system (*chŏnsikwa* 田柴科) implemented in 976.

153 Much'a taehoe 無遮大會

T'aejo Twenty-fourth year [941]

Sixth year of the Tianfu era of Later Jin, fourth year of the Huitong era of Khitan

Summer, fourth month. The *taegwang* Yu Kŭmp'il died. Yu Kŭmp'il hailed from P'yŏngju. As a general, he served T'aejo; whenever the king launched an attack and ordered him to go, he accepted, and never slept in his own home. Every time he returned victorious, the king welcomed and always showed him his affection. None of the other generals could compete with him. He was given the posthumous title Ch'ungjŏl, and he was enshrined next to T'aejo in the Royal Ancestor Shrine.

This year Koryŏ sent the *taesang* Wang Sinil to Later Jin to offer tribute.

T'aejo Twenty-fifth year [942]

Seventh year of the Tianfu era of Later Jin, fifth year of the Huitong era of Khitan

Winter, tenth month. The Khitan sent envoys, who brought with them fifty camels. The king, because the Khitan had previously broken a treaty of amity that they had made with Parhae, and destroyed Parhae soon afterwards, regarded them as extremely unprincipled. He thought they did not deserve to have an official relationship with their neighboring state Koryŏ, and broke off their exchange missions. Thirty members of the Khitan embassy were exiled to an island in the sea. The camels were tied to Manbu bridge, where they starved to death.

Yi Chehyŏn said: "King Ch'ungsŏn (r. 1308-1313) once asked me about this: 'During the time of our ancestor T'aejo, the Khitan sent us camels, which were tied up underneath a bridge; they were not given any fodder and died of starvation. Therefore the bridge became known as the camel bridge. Although the camel is not native to China, the country has always bred them. The emperor usually had several tens of camels. This was not an excess that did harm to the people; it would have sufficed to simply refuse them, why go as far as killing them through starvation?' To this I replied 'The founder of the dynasty, who has to pass on his legacy to his heirs—his foresight is remarkable and his consideration deep. This is something later generations cannot comprehend. Look at the example of Taizu, the founder of the Song dynasty, who reared pigs in the palace. Later Emperor Renzong removed them; however, later there was a sorcerer, but when they looked around they could not find anything to draw blood from [in order to break the sorcerer's spells]. Thus one knew that Taizu's foresight had even extended to such details. Yet this is also not a foregone conclusion. Who knows whether Taizu's intention of rearing pigs was not much greater than [preparing a cure for spells] by having something to draw blood from? The reason why our Taejo did this, was it that he wanted to thwart the barbarians' deceitful stratagems? Or was it that he wanted to prevent later generations' craving for [exotic] luxuries? The meaning of this is extremely subtle. Your highness should contemplate this deeply. Forceful action based on personal experience—this is not something a foolish subject can lightly advise on.'"

T'aejo, Twenty-sixth year [943]

Eighth year of the Tianfu era of Later Jin during the reign of Emperor Chu, sixth year of the Huitong era of Khitan

Summer, fourth month. The king went to the inner quarters and called for the *taegwang* Pak Surhŭi to personally give him his final instructions. He told him "I heard that when the great Shun was plowing in the mountains, he [was called and] in the end succeeded to Shao's throne. Emperor Gaozu arose from the thickets and marshes yet went on to establish the Han dynasty. I too emerged from a plain and simple background, and foolishly agreed to become king. Not fearing the heat of summer, and not avoiding the cold of winter, I burnished my body and labored my mind, and after ten and nine years managed to unite the Three Han. Undeservedly, I then sat on the throne for twenty-five years. Now my body is old, however, I fear for my progeny. If they are dissolute and if the ruling guidelines fall into decay then we should be greatly worried. Now I have composed some injunctions to pass on to later generations of kings, to browse in the morning and to investigate at night, they can serve as a precious mirror for eternity.[154]

The first injunction is: For our great dynasty we rely on the protective power of all the Buddhas. Therefore we have established Sŏn and Kyo monasteries, and sent out abbots to practice and manage their respective doctrines. If, in later generations, treacherous ministers control government and follow the monks' requests for an audience [to ask favors], the monasteries of the various doctrines will quarrel with one another for power. This has to be proscribed.

The second injunction is: All the temples have been established following Tosŏn's fathoming of the properties of the landscape. Tosŏn has said, "Except on places designated by me through divination, no constructions ought to be added, or else the virtue of the land will be damaged, and the dynasty will not reign eternally." We consider that if in later generations kings, princes, consorts, concubines, and court ministers designate their personal prayer temples or construct temples, there will be reason to worry! At the basis of Silla's collapse lies the competitive building of stūpas toward the end of the dynasty, making the land's virtue diminish. We should guard against this!

The third injunction is: Sons and grandsons of the legal wives of kings transmit the dynasty, and pass on the country to each other. Even though this has been a longstanding custom, yet there is the case of Danzhu 丹朱 who was unfit to succeed, so [his father] Yao passed on the throne to Shun; this was truly an act of public spirit. All those among the first sons who are not fit, should be replaced by the next son; if the next sons are all unfit, one should be chosen among the brothers of the king by the officials, and succeed to the king.

---

154 The fact that the injunctions were discovered in the house of Ch'oe Hang by the historian Ch'oe Chean has always aroused suspicion. See Koryŏsa 93.23a (Biography of Ch'oe Chean, appended to that of Ch'oe Sŭngno). For a good account of the problems surrounding the injunctions, see Remco Breuker., "Forging the Truth: Creative Deception and National Identity in Medieval Korea," *East Asian History* 35 (2008): 1–73. He argues that the injunctions in their current form were actually redacted during the reign of Hyŏnjong.

The fourth injunction is: Of old our country has esteemed Chinese customs, and followed China in terms of material culture, ritual, and music. Yet both the territory and the people are different in our Eastern Country, so there is no need for mindless copying. As for the Khitan, they are a country of wild animals, their customs are not the same and their language is also different. Be careful not to follow any of their clothing, organization, or measures!

The fifth injunction is: I have relied on the numinous protection of the mountains and rivers of the Three Han to achieve this great dynastic enterprise. The water virtue of the Western Capital P'yŏngyang is conducive, and [the city] is at the root of the earth veins of our country. We kings should go on a tour of inspection and reside there in the four middle months so that the total sojourn there amounts to more than 100 days per year.

The sixth injunction is: My greatest vow concerns the Yŏndŭng and P'algwan [festivals]. The purpose of Yŏndŭng is to serve the Buddha; the purpose of P'algwan is to serve the heavenly spirits, the dragon gods of the Five Peaks, the famous mountains, and great rivers. If in later generations there are treacherous ministers who propose to alter anything at all [to these festivals], they ought to be stopped. Also, from the beginning I made an oath that the days of the festivals should not coincide with days of mourning. When the ruler and his ministers celebrate together, one should still proceed with respect.

The seventh injunction is: It is very difficult for the ruler to obtain the hearts of his subjects. In order to do so, he must follow remonstrance and keep slandering at bay. Following remonstrance is the way to sagehood; slandering is like honey, but if it is not believed then it will stop of itself. If the people are given light corvée with due consideration of the season and are not taxed too much, and if the ruler understands how difficult is to wrest grains from the earth, then he will naturally obtain people's minds, and the country will prosper. The ancients said "Under the thick moss it will be easy to catch fish, with generous rewards good generals will emerge; birds will avoid the drawn bow, and under benevolent leadership people will be good." If rewards and punishments are right, then everything will fall in its place.

The eighth injunction is: South of the Cart pass,[155] beyond the river of Kongju,[156] the forms of mountains and other geographic features are conducive to rebellion, and the minds of people likewise. If people from prefectures and counties to its south would take part in court politics, or marry into the royal family or other powerful families and thereby obtain political power, this will either lead to confusion and throw the country in chaos, or, resentful of unification, they will attack the throne and instigate rebellion. Furthermore, as for their slaves belonging to official institutions or monasteries, or those performing various duties at fords or postal stations, some will throw their lot with the powerful to transfer their status or obtain exemptions, and some will attach themselves to the king or royal kin estates, and use crafty and deceitful words to manipulate power and sow chaos. There will be surely those among them who succeed in a calamitous rebellion. Even if they are commoners, they should not be given rank nor employment.

The ninth injunction is: the salaries of all the officials have been determined in accordance with the size of the country, and they can neither be increased nor decreased. Furthermore, according to the old statutes, salaries are set according to merit, and office is not given for private reasons. If those without merit or relatives and acquaintances receive a salary for free, then the people below will harbor resentment and start criticizing such policies. Those people will then not be able to enjoy the blessings of their salaries for long, so this kind of practice should be prohibited. Also, keep in mind that we have a strong and treacherous country as neighbor, so even in times of peace this peril should not be forgotten. Soldiers should therefore be protected and treated with consideration, and be exempt from corvée service. Every autumn their valor should be assessed, and those who stand out should be given rewards.

The tenth injunction is: Whether one is head of a family or state, one

155 Ch'a-hyŏn 車峴: name of a pass north of Kongju in South Ch'ungch'ŏng Province.

156 I.e. the Kŭmgang river flowing through Kongju.

should always be on one's guard, even when there is apparently nothing to worry about. Read widely in the histories and classics, and use those old examples as a warning or lesson for the present. The Duke of Zhou was a great sage, yet he used the chapter "Against Luxurious Ease" as a warning for King Cheng.[157] He had it put on the wall, so it could be contemplated every time [Cheng] entered or left the room.

All the injunctions end with the four characters "to be cherished with single mind." From then on it was passed on to succeeding kings as a treasure.

Fifth month. The king was indisposed.

Chŏngyu [20th] day. The chief councilors Yŏm Sang, Wang Kyu, Pak Sumun and others came to attend to the king. The king said "Emperor Wen of the Han left behind the following decree: 'Of all the myriad creatures in the under-Heaven who sprout forth or are born, there is none that doesn't also die. Dying is the principle of heaven and earth, and natural to all things. So why be deeply mournful?' The wise kings of old had such a firm mind [in their last moments]. I have been sick for twenty days already, and look at death as a return. So why worry? The words of Emperor Wen reflect my own intentions. As for all the affairs here and in the country that have not been settled, you gentlemen should settle them together with crown prince Wang Mu, and then report."

Pyŏng'o [29th] day. The king's illness grew worse, and he was moved to Sindŏk Hall. He ordered the academician Kim Ak to take down the draft of his last edict; when the words had been recorded, the king did not speak again. All those around him lost their voices because of their wailing. The king heard this and asked what the noise was. They answered, "Your highness is the father and mother of the people. Today you are about to discard your subjects, and therefore we are so pained that we cannot help ourselves." The king laughed and said, "the floating life has always been

157 This can be found in the *Book of Documents* (*Shujing*). The Duke of Zhou is the younger brother of King Wu, founder of the Zhou. King Cheng is the son of King Wu and second ruler of the Zhou dynasty.

like this." Shortly after having spoken these words, he died. The crown prince, members of the royal family and close ministers all beat the ground and wailed. All the officials lined up outside the gate of the Advisory Council. Wang Kyu came out of the gate to read the king's last edict, which said that all officials, both at the center and locally, should follow the crown prince in the assigning of duties and positions. Thereupon the crown prince took the throne, and led all the officials in lamenting [the deceased king].

Sixth month, *musin* [1st] day. The start of official mourning took place in the Sangjŏng Hall. Kim Ak read the king's posthumous edict.

Sayu [2nd] day. The king's coffin was placed in state on the western steps of the Sangjŏng Hall.

Kyŏng'o [23rd] day. The king was given the posthumous title of Sinsŏng Taewang, and the temple name T'aejo.

Imsin [25th] day. The king was buried in the Hyŏn-nŭng tomb. According to his bequeathed instructions, the system of mourning, burial, and burial mounds was to follow the precedent of the Emperors Wen of the Han and Wei, and was thus very simple and frugal. Queen Sinhye, of the Yu clan, was to be interred next to him. The queen was originally from Chŏngju, a daughter of the *samjung taegwang* Ch'ŏn'gung. Ch'ŏn'gung's family was very rich, and the people of his town called him their leader. Once, when T'aejo was still a general, he led his troops through Chŏngju, and rested his horse under an old willow tree. The queen then stood at a river near the road, and T'aejo saw that she looked virtuous. He asked which family she belonged to, and she answered "I am the daughter of the leader of this town." She invited him to take a rest and a meal, and T'aejo thus stayed at her house. Her family took very good care of his army, and later they slept together. But afterwards, T'aejo stopped seeing her. To preserve her chastity, she cut her hair and entered a nunnery. When T'aejo heard this, he summoned her and took her as his wife. It was she who urged him to take the throne by donning his armor, thus giving rise to the new dynasty.

Yi Chehyŏn commented with praise: "When I was serving King Ch'ungsŏn, the king once told me 'If our T'aejo had been born in China, his exploits and virtue would not have been less than those of Taizu of Song. Taizu originally served Shizong of the Later Zhou (950-960), who was a wise ruler. Shizong treated Taizu generously, and Taizu in turn did his utmost in serving his lord. When Emperor Gong came to power at a very young age, the empress dowager ruled in his stead. Through the pressure of his peers, he received the Zhou throne; this was something that he could do nothing about. When our T'aejo served Kungye, who was cruel and violent, he managed to secure two thirds of the territory; this was T'aejo's merit. But because the merit was so exceptional, Kungye harbored suspicions, so the situation was really precarious. But the people of the country had set their mind on him, and his generals pushed him to take the throne. Yet he firmly declined, and wanted to follow the integrity of the lord of Yanling.[158] But comforting the people and punishing the guilty [ruler], how could he escape this destiny! He loved life and hated killing, believed in just reward and punishing when necessary. He promoted sincere merit subjects and did not make random use of his power. In establishing the dynasty and transmitting the throne, he followed the same principles.

Now as for Song Taizu, while the ruler surnamed Li from Southern Tang (937-975) could lay on the couch snoring [because he was safe in the south], [in the case of the northern dynasties] the Later Jin (936-947) had offered the sixteen prefectures beyond the mountains as a tribute to the Khitan; yet he regarded these prefectures as his own, and after absorbing the Northern Han (951-979), he was ready to eternally expel them so as to settle the border of Qin and Han times.[159] After our T'aejo ascended the throne, Kim Pu had not yet become his guest and Kyŏn Hwŏn was not yet his prisoner, yet still he frequently went to the Western Capital to inspect the northern

158 Refers to a story about the fourth son of King Sumeng of Wu. Though wiser and more capable than his three older brothers, he chose not to upset the correct order of succession and retired; eventually he was enfeoffed as lord of Yanling.

159 This refers to the 16 prefectures of the Yan and Yun region (around modern Beijing) ceded by the Later Jin Emperor to the Liao in 938. Despite Taizu's ambition to recover them, he never managed to do so.

border. His intention was that the old territories of King Tongmyŏng were our family, so like an old rug it had to be rolled up and kept in possession.[160] How would he stop at controlling Kyerim and catching the Mallard?[161] From this perspective, although the scale is different, in terms of their ambition and virtue the two dynastic founders can be said to be similar yet belonging to different territories.'

King Ch'ungsŏn was intelligent and loved history. All the refined and learned gentlemen of the Middle Plains, such as Wang Gou, Yan Fu, Yao Sui, Yao Bi, Zhao Mengfu, and Yu Ji all came to visit him, and discussed with him for a long time."

The historian comments: "T'aejo ruled those below with magnanimity and was wise and discerning in using force. He treated people with sincerity so that those near and far all responded to his rule. The benevolence of his loving of life sprang from his Heaven-granted nature, and his concern for the people came from his utmost feelings. When Kyŏn Hwŏn and his son acted like barbarians he attacked and seized them. When Kim Pu and his ministers came to submit, he treated them with propriety. When the Khitan used their strength to invade and destroy another country he cut them off. Since Parhae's weakness had cost them their territory and they had nowhere to turn to, he comforted them. He traveled frequently to the Western Capital because it was the place of origin [of Koryŏ]. He personally inspected the northern border because it continued an ancient, uncivilized custom. Although his founding of the dynasty was not greatly concerned with Rites and Music, he set a model for the ages and was deeply humane and munificent, thus cultivating a country that lasted five centuries."

---

160 淸氈必席: I am not certain about the meaning of this expression.

161 I.e. the Amnok (Green mallard) River.

2. Hyejong, Chŏngjong, Kwangjong, Kyŏngjong, Sŏngjong, Mokchong

Hyejong, Righteous and Respected Great King

His given name was Mu 武, and his courtesy name Sŭnggŏn 承乾. He was the oldest son of T'aejo, and his mother was Queen Changhwa, née O. He was born in the *imsin* year, the second year of Qianhua of Later Liang [912]. His mother had dreamt of a dragon entering her bosom, and not long after T'aejo set up camp in Naju. He saw her and went to her, and she became pregnant. His strength and set of *ki* was vast, his wisdom and valor beyond the pale. He established his merit when joining T'aejo in his subjugation of Later Paekche. He was on the throne for two years, and lived to the age of thirty-four.

Hyejong First year [944]

First year of the Kaiyun era of Later Jin, seventh year of the Huitong era of Khitan

The king sent the vice-chancellor of the State Council, Han Hyŏn'gyu, and the vice-minister of the Ministry of Rites and Receptions, Kim Yŏm, to Later Jin to announce his succession and also to congratulate the emperor on vanquishing the Khitan.

Winter, twelfth month. The minister of the Hallim Academy and Manager of Affairs[1] Ch'oe Ŏnwi died. He was a Silla person, and was of generous and magnanimous disposition. From a young age he was good at letters, and when he was eighteen he traveled to Tang China where he passed the civil service examination. Only when he was forty-two did he return to his country, where he served as executive at the office of state affairs in Silla, and also scholar at the Academy of Fine Writing. When Silla submitted to Koryŏ, T'aejo made him tutor of the heir apparent, and he was also put in charge of writing and composition at court, so that all the boards and inscriptions of palace buildings were written and determined by him. At one time or another he also tutored all the nobles. He was seventy-seven when he died, and was given the posthumous title of "hero of letters" (Munyŏng 文英).

Hyejong Second year [945]

Second year of the Kaiyun era of Later Jin, eighth year of the Huitong era of Khitan

Later Jin sent the Chief Minister at the Court of Entertainments Fan Kuangzheng and the Frontrider for the Heir Apparent Zhang Jiying to invest the king as Area Commander-in-chief with Special Powers of Hyŏnt'o 玄菟, Pillar of State and Emissary of a Great Righteous Army, King of the Country of Koryŏ.

The daughter of the *taegwang* Wang Kyu was the sixteenth spouse of King T'aejo, and she gave birth to a son who was known as the Prince from the Kwangju palace. One day Wang Kyu accused the king's younger brothers Yo (later King Chŏngjong, r. 945-949) and So (later King Kwangjong, r. 949-975) of plotting against the throne. The king knew that it was not true, and

---

1 *P'yŏngjangsa* 平章事: according to Hucker (no. 4703), a designation for someone who, in addition to his regular appointment, also served concurrently as a state councilor. Formally this co-assignment was to the Secretariat-Chancellery, so that it can also be regarded as an appointment to that Department. Since the Three Departments (Samsŏng) were otherwise not yet operative in Koryŏ, this is actually the title he had received in Silla.

showed them even more affection than before. Then Auxiliary at the Bureau of Astronomy Ch'oe Chimong petitioned: "A comet has entered the Purple Subtlety star [of the Big Dipper], which means that the country is faced with bandits." The king understood this as a response to Wang Kyu's plot against his younger brothers, yet he did not punish him. Wang Kyu then gave the oldest princess in marriage to Wang So in order to strengthen his influence and power. Following her mother's surname the princess was called Hwangbo. Later all those who took a spouse with the same surname avoided their original name and used instead the surname of the wife's mother.

The historian comments: "When taking a spouse, choosing someone with a different surname is basic propriety. Even over 100 generations of marriage this should not happen. How could Hyejong marry his younger brother to a princess? This is how the customs were at the time. T'aejo was a ruler who stood out amongst his generation, modeling his laws on the ancients; yet although his mind was set on transforming customs, people's habits were so entrenched that customs could not be changed. From that time onward, it became a family rule, and it was not considered strange. Towards the middle period [of Koryŏ], marriage between cousins or close kin was forbidden, yet marriage between those of the same surname could not be forbidden. As the *Zuo zhuan* says, 'If man and wife are of the same surname, their descendants will not prosper.'[2] What goes for people of the same surname, applies even more to those who are closely related! Now we can see here that people took cousins as their spouse, and the more this is the case the fewer descendants are created. Though the dynasty lasted 500 years, in the end the branches of the royal clan numbered only a few dozen. Only then do we realize how profound the system of the former kings is. May this be a warning!"

---

2 This can be found in an entry for the 23rd year of Lord Xi [637 BC]. See Stephen Durrant, Wai-yee Li, and David Schaberg, *Zuo Tradition / Zuozhuan. Commentary on the "Spring and Autumn Annals"* (Seattle: University of Washington Press, 2016), vol. 1, 369.

Wang Kyu plotted to enthrone [his grandson] the prince of the Kwangju palace. At night when he spied that the king was fast asleep, he sent his retainer to penetrate the royal bedchamber. He was about to commit the treasonous offence [of killing the king], but the king became aware of him and struck him dead with one blow of the fist. He ordered his attendants to drag him away and never again raised any questions. One day the king was indisposed and stayed in the Sindŏk Hall. Ch'oe Chimong again memorialized that a dangerous change was afoot, and that the king would be advised to move. The king secretly went to Chunggwang Hall. At night Wang Kyu sent someone who bore a hole in the wall to enter, but the royal bedchamber was already empty. The king knew that it was Wang Kyu's work yet again did not punish him. Later, when Wang Kyu saw Ch'oe Chimong, he drew his sword and scolded him, saying "Surely the king's moving was your plan!" After Wang Kyu's plots against the king, the king became very nervous and always was surrounded by armored guards. His mood changed unpredictably from joyful to angry, and he promoted insignificant people. He gave rewards to military and civil officials without respecting any sense of proportion, so that everybody became exasperated and resentful.

Autumn, ninth month. The king was seriously ill but the ministers could not enter to see him, as sly minnows attended the king. On the *musin* [15th] day the king died in the Chunggwang Hall. He was given the posthumous title of Righteous and Respected Great King (Ŭigong taewang 義恭大王) and the temple name Hyejong. He was buried at Sun-nŭng, and the ministers made his younger brother Yo the next king.

Yi Chehyŏn commented in his eulogy: "Yufu requested to kill Lord Huan, because he wanted to obtain the position of Grand Councilor. Lord Yin did not honor this request, but neither did he punish [Yufu]. In the end, this led to the calamity of Weishi [where Lord Yin was killed].[3] In slandering the

---

3 This refers to events in the Spring and Autumn Period (771–476 BC) of Chinese history. See *Zuo Zhuan*, eleventh year of Lord Yin [712 BC]. Durrant, Li, and Schaberg, *Zuo Tradition*, vol. 1, 67.

king's two younger brothers, Wang Kyu had the same intention as Yufu. Hyejong did not deal with the crime, but to keep an eye on him let him stay close. The fact that he escaped a 'knife concealed in a sleeve' and a 'wall[-bursting] invader' can be called fortuitous. At the time, it was not long since T'aejo had passed on the throne. The fact that Wang Kyu displayed such lack of righteousness and yet managed to attract support can be compared to Cao [Fei's usurpation of the Later] Han or [Si]ma Yan's [usurpation] of the Wei. How could [Wang Kyu] not have been disposed of? How tragic! It is difficult indeed to keep the inferior people at bay. We should take this as a warning!"[4]

Kiyu [16th] day. Wang Kyu killed Pak Surhŭi. Pak Surhŭi was a brave person. When he was eighteen, he became a guardsman of Kungye. Later he served T'aejo, and proved his merit on the battle field many times. On his deathbed T'aejo tasked him with protecting Hyejong. When Hyejong lay ill in bed, he clashed with Wang Kyu. He commandeered more than a hundred troops under his personal authority [to challenge Wang Kyu], but the king suspected him of rebellious intentions and exiled him to Kapkot.[5] Wang Kyu doctored a royal decree and had him killed. Later he was given the posthumous name Ŏmŭi 嚴毅, and was posthumously made grand preceptor. His tablet was enshrined next to that of Hyejong at the royal ancestor shrine.

Wang Kyu was executed. When the king [i.e., Chŏngjong] first learned of Wang Kyu's treacherous plans, he secretly made preparations against a rebellion with the *taegwang* Wang Singnyŏm from the Western Capital. When Wang Kyu was about to start a rebellion, he led troops into the capital and encircled him. Wang Kyu did not dare to react. He was expelled to Kapkot, and then someone was sent there to execute him. More than 300 of his party were also executed.

---

4 For a more sober account of the possible reasons for Wang Kyu's attempt to take the throne, see H.W. Kang, "The First Succession Struggle of Koryŏ, in 943: A Reinterpretation," *The Journal of Asian Studies* 36, no. 3 (1977): 411–428.

5 Kapkot 甲串: place name on the northern part of Kanghwa island.

Chŏngjong, Literate and Luminous Great King

His given name was Yo 堯 and his courtesy name Ŭich'ŏn 義天. He was the second son of T'aejo. His mother was Queen Sinmyŏng, née Yu. He was born in the *kyemi* year, the sixth year of T'aejo's reign [923]. By nature he loved Buddhism, and was also deeply impressed by prognostication. He was on the throne for four years and lived to the age of twenty-seven

Chŏngjong First year [946]

Third year of the Kaiyun era of Later Jin, ninth year of the Huitong era of Khitan

Spring, first month. The king went to visit the Hyŏn-nŭng tomb [of King T'aejo]. On the eve of the offering, he heard a voice out of thin air saying "You, Yo, should know that preserving a compassionate heart for the poor people is the key task of a ruler of men."

This year Heaven produced the sound of drums, and the king granted a general pardon.

The king prepared the ritual implements and provisions to enshrine Buddhist relics. He personally walked as far as ten *li* to Kaeguk-sa where they were to be enshrined. He also donated 70,000 *sŏk* of grain to major temples to establish foundations for the *Sūtra of Buddha's Name* and foundations for broad learning so as to encourage the study of the dharma.

Chŏngjong Second year [947]

Twelfth year of the Tianfu era proclaimed by later Han emperor Gaozu, first year of the Tianlu era of Emperor Shizong of Liao

In spring, the king sent the *taegwang* Pak Sumun to fortify Tŏkch'ang Garrison and to construct the royal city in the Western Capital as well as walls for Ch'ŏrong, Tannŭng, Samch'ŏk and T'ongdŏk.

In autumn, the king sent the *taegwang* Pak Sugyŏng to fortify Tŏksŏng

Garrison.

The Bright Army Office (Kwanggun-sa 光軍司) was established. Originally, the son of Ch'oe Ŏnwi, Ch'oe Kwangyun 崔光胤, was sent as tribute scholar to Jin to study, but he was captured by the Khitan, and because of his talent they employed him and gave him office and titles. When he was serving as envoy in Kwisŏng,[6] he learned that the Khitan were planning to invade us, and sent a letter to report this. Thereupon the king ordered his officials to select 300,000 troops and called them the Bright Army.[7]

Chŏngjong Third year [948]

First year of the Qianyou era of Emperor Yin of Later Han, second year of the Tianlu era of Liao

Autumn, ninth month. Somugae and others from the Eastern Jurchen came to offer 700 horses as well as local products. The king went to the Ch'ŏndŏk Hall to receive them, but suddenly there was thunder and rain, and animals and people were struck by thunder. Also, the western corner of the hall was struck. The king was very scared, and close ministers escorted him to the Chunggwang Hall. Subsequently, the king was indisposed, and granted a pardon.

For the first time the era names of the Later Han were used.

Chŏngjong Fourth year [949]

Second year of the Qianyou era of Later Han, third year of the Tianlu era of Liao

Spring, first month. The *taegwang* Wang Singnyŏm died. Wang Singnyŏm

6 Kwisŏng 龜城: "Turtle city": in N. P'yŏngan Province, once part of Koguryŏ and then of Parhae; after the fall of Parhae it was occupied by Jurchen, so Ch'oe Kwangyun was probably on a mission to the Jurchen.

7 In honor of Ch'oe Kwangyun; the first character of his name, Kwang, means bright.

was a cousin of T'aejo. Because for a long time he had diligently and respectfully guarded the Western Capital and suppressed the revolt by Wang Kyu, he was bestowed the position of merit subject supporting the country, and granted the rank of *taesŭng*. He was also posthumously granted the title of Imposing Tranquility (Wijŏng 威靜) and the rank of grand preceptor. Later he was enshrined in the royal ancestor shrine.

Third month, *pyŏngjin* [13th] day. The king was seriously ill, and summoned his younger brother So; he passed on the throne to him, and moved to the Chesŏg-wŏn, where he died. He was given the posthumous title of Literate and Luminous Great King (Munmyŏng taewang 文明大王) and the temple name Chŏngjong. He was buried in the An-nŭng tomb. During his reign, because of his belief in prognostication he was planning to move the capital to the Western Capital. He raised a corvée labor force and ordered the chancellor, Kwŏn Chik, to construct a palace. The corvée labor continued without respite, and moreover households were moved from Kaegyŏng to fill up the new capital. The masses were full of resentment and criticism was mounting. When news broke of the monarch's death, those drafted for labor danced with joy.

Yi Chehyŏn commented in his eulogy: "Chŏngjong, despite the fact that he incorporated the dignity of a ruler, walked nearly ten *li* to a Buddhist temple to enshrine some relics, and moreover distributed 70,000 *sŏk* of rice in a mere day to all the monks. Yet with just one censure from Heaven, he lost courage and became ill. This illustrates the saying I have heard long ago, namely that a ruler seeking blessings does not receive any reward. But as his disease grew more and more grave, he still could pass on the dynastic mantle to his younger brother, and thus prevented people of Wang Kyu's ilk of taking advantage of a power vacuum; this deserves praise."

Autumn, eighth month. [The new king] ordered the *taegwang* Pak Sugyŏng and others to investigate those who had merit in labor at the founding of the dynasty, and bestow grain on them according to the amount of labor; this became a precedent for [bestowing] grain as reward.

[The new king] ordered the *wŏnbo* Sikhoe and the *wŏnyun* Sin'gang and others to determine the quota of annual tribute from all prefectures and counties.

Kwangjong, Great King of Great Accomplishment

His given name was So 昭 and his courtesy name Ilhwa 日華. He was a younger brother of Chŏngjong through the same mother. He was born in the *ŭlyu* year, the eighth year of T'aejo's reign [925]. He treated his subjects with courtesy, and was adept at listening and sharp in decision making. He felt compassion for the poor and weak and esteemed Confucian learning. From early in the morning till late at night he was diligent in his work, and established a peaceful government for everyone. Yet in his later years he believed in slander, and killed excessively. He also believed in Buddhism, and donated riches without restraint. He was on the throne for twenty-six years and lived to the age of fifty-one.

Kwangjong First year [950]

Third year of the Qianyou era of Later Han, fourth year of the Tianlu era of Liao

Spring, first month. A storm uprooted many trees. The king asked about the art of suppressing calamities, and the Bureau of Astronomy opined "Nothing is better than cultivating virtue." From then on the king frequently read the "Essentials on Government from the Zhenguan era."

Changch'ŏng Garrison was fortified.

In the autumn, Wihwa Garrison was fortified.

Kwangjong Second year [951]

First year of the Gwangshun era of Emperor Taizu of Later Zhou, first year of the Yingli era of Emperor Muzong of Liao

The king founded Tae Pong'ŭn-sa to the south of the city walls, and made it the memorial shrine for T'aejo. He also established Puril-sa in the eastern suburbs as the memorial shrine for his deceased mother, Lady Yu.

Winter, tenth month. The nine-story pagoda of Chunghŭng-sa in the Western Capital was destroyed in a fire.

Twelfth month. For the first time the Later Zhou era names were used.

Kwangjong Third year [952]

Second year of the Gwangshun era of Later Zhou, second year of the Yingli era of Liao

In spring, Ansak Garrison was fortified.

This year, the king sent the vice-chancellor of the State Council, Sŏ Pong, to Later Zhou to offer local goods as tribute.

Kwangjong Fourth year [953]

Third year of the Gwangshun era of Later Zhou, third year of the Yingli era of Liao

Later Zhou sent the Chief Minister of the Court of the Imperial Regalia, Wang Yan, and the Vice-Director of the Directorate for Palace Buildings, Lü Jibin, to invest the king as Lord Specially Advanced, Acting Grand Guardian, commissioned as Area Commander-in-chief with Special Powers of Hyŏnt'o, Emissary of a Great Righteous Army and Censor-in-chief, King of the Country of Koryŏ.

Winter, tenth month. The nine-story pagoda of Hwangnyong-sa in Kyŏngju burnt down.

Kwangjong Fifth year [954]

First year of the Xiande era of Emperor Shizong of Later Zhou, fourth year of the Yingli era of Liao

In spring, Sungsŏn-sa was built to pray for blessings for the deceased mother of the king.

Kwangjong Sixth year [955]

Second year of the Xiande era of Later Zhou, fifth year of the Yingli era of Liao

The king dispatched the *taesang* Wang Yung to Later Zhou to offer local products as tribute, and the vice-chancellor of the State Council Sunjil to congratulate [Emperor Shizong] on his accession.

Kwangjong Seventh year [956]

Third year of the Xiande era of Later Zhou, sixth year of the Yingli era of the Liao

Imjin County offered a white pheasant.

Later Zhou sent the Director of the Directorate for Palace Buildings Xue Wenyu to invest the king with the rank title Commander Unequalled in Honor (1B) and the office of Acting Grand Preceptor. All the officials were permitted to wear the Chinese style of hats and gowns. The former inspector for the military commissioner, the Case Reviewer for the Court of Judicial Review, Shuang Ji, came together with Xue Wenyu but had to stay behind because of illness. When he got better, he was called to the palace to meet the king, and he accorded well with the king's intentions. The king liked his talents, and requested that he be made an official. The officials then issued the necessary documents and went through the necessary procedures to appoint him. Before the end of the year, he was appointed to an office, which aroused great discontent at the time.

The king ordered a general assessment of all slaves in the counties, so as to differentiate between genuine and fake slaves. Countless slaves betrayed their masters, and as a result many despised the king: many sighed in discontent and were full of resentment. The queen pleaded with all her might, but the king did not relent.

Kwangjong Eighth year [957]

Fourth year of the Xiande era of Later Zhou, seventh year of the Yingli era of Liao

Spring, first month. The king watched an archery contest on the polo court.

Kwangjong Ninth year [958]

Fifth year of the Xiande era of Later Zhou, eighth year of the Yingli era of Liao

Summer, fifth month. The king appointed the Hallim academician Shuang Ji to serve as examination administrator. He tested candidates on the composition of poems, prose poems, and odes as well as a policy essay so as to select presented scholars. The king went to Wibong pavilion to display the roster of successful candidates. The top rank went to Ch'oe Sŏm and one other person, while in the classics section three candidates were chosen, and in the prognostication category two.[8] On the basis of Shuang Ji's proposal, this was the first civil service examination (*kwagŏ*) [ever held in Korea]. This marked the beginning of the flourishing of literary culture.

Black cranes gathered at the Hamdŏk Hall.

This year, the Later Zhou dispatched the assistant office chief at the Bureau of Waterways and Irrigation, Han Ŏn'gyŏng, and the Chief Steward

8 The main civil service examination was known as the composition test (*chesul-ŏp* 製述業), which gave those who passed the title of presented scholar (*chinsa* 進士), followed in terms of importance by the classics test (*myŏnggyŏng-ŏp* 明經業). Apart from these two tests giving access to the civil service, there were also various examinations for professionals, including prognostication (*pogŏp* 卜業) and medicine (*ŭiŏp* 醫業). See *Koryŏsa* 73, *sŏn'go* 1.

of the Sedan-Chair Service, Kim Ŏnyŏng, together with several thousand rolls of brocade, rice, cloth, and copper.[9]

Kwangjong Tenth year [959]

Sixth year of the Xiande era of Later Zhou, ninth year of the Yingli era of Liao

In spring, the king sent the *chwasŭng* Wang Kŭng and the *chwayun* Hwangbo Wigwang to Later Zhou to offer local products as tribute.

In autumn, envoys were sent to Later Zhou.

Later Zhou sent the Courageous Guard of the Left, General Dai Jiao.

In winter, envoys were sent to Later Zhou to offer copper and crystal as tribute.

The Censor and Prefect of Qingzhou, Shuang Zhe, came from Later Zhou. He was given the rank of *chwasŭng*. Shuang Zhe was the father of Shuang Ji. Having heard that his son had received the favor of the king, he came together with the returning envoy Wang Kŭng.

Kwangjong Eleventh year [960]

First year of the Jianlong era of Emperor Taizu of Song, tenth year of the Yingli era of Liao

Spring, third month. Ch'oe Kwangbŏm with six others passed the composition test, one passed the classics examination, and three the medical examination.[10]

---

9 Since the names are clearly Korean, perhaps these two officials had taken part in the Chinese civil service examination and were now sent back to Koryŏ.

10 This is the standard way of reporting the examination passers. While the text says "崔光範等七人", i.e. "Ch'oe Kwangbŏm and others, seven people," it is habitual to give only the name of the top ranking passer, and not the others. Since the number seven is inclusive of the top passer, I have here and elsewhere adapted the numbers to conform to English usage. Also note that the original texts says that it is the king who granted the pass certificates.

The official dress of the officials was determined. Those of the *wŏnyun* rank and above wore purple outer robes; those of the *chungdanggyŏng* rank and above wore red outer robes; those of the *tohanggyŏng* rank and above wore dark red outer robes; those of the *sojubak* rank and above wore green outer robes.[11]

Kaegyŏng was made the Imperial Metropolis (Hwangdo 皇都) and the Western Capital (P'yŏngyang) the Western Metropolis (Sŏdo 西都).

Sŭphol was fortified and promoted to Kaju Prefecture; Songsŏng was also fortified and promoted to T'akchu Prefecture.

The Arbiter of Agricultural Books and History Kwŏn Sin accused the *taesang* Chunhong, the *chwasŭng* Wang Tong and others of plotting sedition, and they were demoted. From then on slanderers and sycophants got their way, and ensnared the loyal and righteous. Slaves sued their masters, and sons accused their parents. The prisons were often overflowing so that temporary ones had to be built. Continuously those who were without guilt were sentenced to the death penalty. The king's jealousy and fear grew day by day, and many in the royal clan could not protect themselves. Even his first son Chu was not spared such suspicion, and the king did not let him come near. Everybody lived in fear, and nobody dared to utter a word to the other.

Kwangjong Twelfth year [961]

Second year of the Jianlong era of Emperor Taizu of Song, eleventh year of the Yingli era of Liao

Summer, fourth month. A big flood inundated the homes of many people, and the color of the water turned red.

This year a Directorate for the Repair of Palace Buildings was installed; the king moved to the residence of the *chŏnggwang* Wang Yuk.

Wang Kŏ and six others passed the composition test [of the civil service

---

11 Except for the *wŏnyun* rank, the other ones are here mentioned for the first and only time.

examination] and one the classics examination.

Kwangjong Thirteenth year [962]

First year of the Qiande era of Song, twelfth year of the Yingli era of Liao

In winter, the king dispatched Vice-chancellor of the State Council Yi Hŭngu to Song to present local products.

Kwangjong Fourteenth year [963]

First year of the Qiande era of Song, thirteenth year of the Yingli era of Liao

Summer, sixth month. The king returned to the palace, and issued the following proclamation: "For a long time I have lived outside of the palace, and have been unable to personally listen to the many memorials by officials, and therefore I am worried that many of my subjects have started to suspect that I have blocked them. Now that the repair of the palace has been completed, I have again a place to attend to politics. All you officials, I will respect the affairs of all of you, and as of old you should send forth your opinions on all matters, so that we will be as close as 'fish and water,' nobody should come in between the ruler and his ministers."

Autumn, seventh month. Kwibŏp-sa was constructed, and a Foundation to Save the Endangered was established.

Winter, twelfth months. For the first time the Song era names were put into effect.

Song sent the envoy of investiture Shi Zan and others to Koryŏ, but on their way their ship encountered a storm, and ninety people of the embassy drowned. Only Shi Zan escaped death, and the king consoled him with lavish concern.

Kwangjong Fifteenth year [964]

Second year of the Qiande era of Song, fourteenth year of the Yingli era of Liao

Spring, third month. Kim Ch'aek passed the composition test [of the civil service examination], one person passed the classics examination, and one the divination examination. The king went to the Ch'ŏndŏk Hall to give a banquet to all officials. He ordered Kim Ch'aek to take off his ordinary clothes and wear official robes and attend the banquet.

Autumn, eighth month. The Minister of Education Pak Sugyŏng died. He was endowed with great courage, authority, and wisdom, and served T'aejo as a *wŏnyun*. When Later Paekche invaded Silla numerous times, T'aejo ordered him to go there and strengthen Silla's defenses. He encountered Kyŏn Hwŏn on two occasions, but [at the second encounter] he pulled off an ingenious plan and defeated him. At the battle of Chomul Prefecture, T'aejo divided his army into three divisions, and made the *taesang* Chegung supreme general, the *wŏnyun* Wang Ch'ung middle general, and Pak Sugyŏng and Ŭnnyŏng lower general. When the battle started, the supreme and middle generals lost the advantage, only Pak Sugyŏng managed to gain the upper hand. T'aejo was greatly pleased, and promoted him to *wŏnbo*. But Pak Sugyŏng said, "Seeing that my older brother Pak Sumun is *wŏnyun*, but that I am placed above him, I would rather not make myself ashamed [by accepting a position higher than my older brother]." The king then made both of them *wŏnbo*. During the battle for Palsŏng, T'aejo had been completely surrounded, so he had to rely on Pak Sugyŏng's fighting skills to escape. During the *kyŏngja* year (940), when the merit-reward land system was implemented, he was especially granted 200 *kyŏl* of land. At the beginning of King Chŏngjong's reign, he was instrumental in helping to suppress a rebellion. At this time [i.e., during Kwangjong's reign], his sons Sŭngwi, Sŭnggyŏng, and Sŭngnye were slandered and thrown in jail. Thereupon he died of worry.

Kwangjong Sixteenth year [965]

Third year of the Qiande era of Song, fifteenth year of the Yingli era of Liao

Spring, second month. He granted his son Wang Chu the clothes of an adult [since he had reached the age of 20], and made him first heir, chief executive for all military affairs, and minister of the Advisory Council. [To mark the occasion] he held a banquet for all officials in the Changsaeng Hall.

The king dispatched the *taesŭng* and minister of the Department of Administration, Wang No, to Song to offer local products as tribute. The emperor gave him the office of junior vice-director of the Department of Ministries, and an effective fief of 300 households.

Autumn, seventh month. The minister of the Advisory Council, Sŏ P'il, died. Sŏ P'il hailed from Ich'ŏn, and he was very perspicacious. Originally he was promoted to the court for his clerical work [at the local level]. The king once conferred golden wine vessels on his councilors Wang Hammin, Hwangbo Kwanggyŏm, and Sŏ P'il. Only Sŏ P'il refused the gift, saying "I already undeservedly occupy the position of chief councilor, and receive the ruler's favor without merit; now receiving these golden recipients makes me even more apprehensive. Moreover, clear levels of distinction should be made in the use of clothing and vessels; luxury and frugality reflect corruption and good government respectively—If ministers use golden vessels, then what should the king use?"

The king replied, "You can take a treasure to be worthless, but I will take your words as a treasure worth cherishing." Later he went to see the king and said "I wish that your majesty would not reward those without merit, and that you do not forget those with merit." The king agreed, but the next day sent a close confidant to ask him about who those were with merit and those without merit. Sŏ P'il said, "As for those with merit, that is someone like the *wŏnbo* Sikhoe. As for those without merit, that is someone like the one facing me now. Please report to the throne my answer."

At the time, the king greatly esteemed Chinese who had settled in Koryŏ. He selected the houses of officials for them and gave them their daughters. One day Sŏ P'il told the king, "My house is rather big, so I would like to present it [as a residence for the resettled Chinese]." The king asked him about his motivations, and Sŏ P'il answered "Today on behalf of the resettled Chinese you choose positions to employ them, and you choose residences to house them. All those old families of standing have now lost their residences. I am foolish, but sincerely concerned for my heirs, I figure that if the house of a chief councilor is not big, then they may keep it. Now that I am still alive, please take my house. With the remainder of my emolument I will buy a small house, and have no regrets." At first the king was greatly angered, but then realized his intention and praised him; henceforth he no longer requisitioned the homes of officials.

In the palace stables a horse died, and the king wanted to punish its keeper. Sŏ P'il quoted the passage from the *Analects* where the master "did not ask about the horses"[12] to correct the ruler, and as a result the keeper of the horse escaped the punishment. Thus he never shunned straight and correct words [even if it put him in danger]. He was posthumously entitled Chŏngmin, and enshrined next to the king in the Ancestral Shrine.

Kwangjong Seventeenth year [966]

Fourth year of the Qiande era of Song, sixteenth year of the Yingli era of Liao

Ch'oe Kŏŏp and one other person passed the composition test [of the civil service examination].

Kwangjong Eighteenth year [967]

Fifth year of the Qiande era of Song, seventeenth year of the Yingli era of Liao

Nangnŭng Prefecture was fortified.

12 Confucius, *Analects* 10.11: "There was a fire in the stables. When the master returned from court, he asked if anyone was hurt. He did not ask about the horses."

Kwangjong Nineteenth year [968]

First year of the Kaibao era of Song, eighteenth year of the Yingli era of Liao

Summer, fifth month. Wihwa Garrison was fortified.

This year, the king built Honghwa, Yuam, and Samgwi temples. The king, believing slander, had killed many, so he harbored many doubts and fears; to get rid of his criminal karma he widely established vegetarian banquets. Those without a fixed abode pretended to become monks so as to fill their bellies. Those begging for food came from everywhere to get food; sometimes cakes, rice, beans, and firewood were donated along the roads of the capital and outside of it in uncountable numbers. Successive "stations to release creatures" were established, and the king went to nearby temples to read Buddhist scriptures. He forbade the slaughter of animals, so that the palace meat had to be procured in the market shops.

Kwangjong Twentieth year [969]

Second year of the Kaibao era of Song, first year of the Baoning era of Emperor Jingzong of Liao

Winter, eleventh month. The king's younger brother Wang Uk died.

Yŏngsak Garrison was fortified.

Kwangjong Twenty-first year [970]

Third year of the Kaibao era of Song, second year of the Baoning era of Liao

Ansak Garrison was fortified.

The king went to Kwibŏp-sa.

Kwangjong Twenty-second year [971]

Fourth year of the Kaibao era of Song, third year of the Baoning era of Liao

Winter, twelfth month, *imin* day. There was an earthquake.

Kwangjong Twenty-third year [972]

Fifth year of the Kaibao era of Song, fourth year of the Baoning era of Liao

Spring, second month. There was an earthquake.

Autumn, eighth month. An amnesty was declared.

This year Yang Yŏn and three others passed the composition test [of the civil service examination].

The king dispatched the Vice-chancellor of the Advisory Council, Sŏ Hŭi, to Song to present tribute. The emperor decreed that the king [of Koryŏ] should be granted a stipend village, and also bestowed him the title of merit subject to promote sincerity, smoothen edification, protecting integrity and guarding righteousness; Sŏ Hŭi was given the post of acting vice-minister of the Board of War; vice-minister at the Department of Administration and deputy envoy Ch'oe Ŏp was made acting chief minister of the Court of the National Granaries and assistant to the censor-in-chief; Vice-Chancellor of the State Council Kang Ye was made acting office manager for various directorates and lesser offices; Vice-Director of the State Council Yu Ŭn was made acting office chief in the Treasury Bureau.

Kwangjong Twenty-fourth year [973]

Sixth year of the Kaibao era of Song, fifth year of the Baoning era of Liao

Spring, third month. Paek Sayu and one other person passed the composition test [of the civil service examination].

This year, the garrisons of Changp'yŏng and Tanp'yŏng, as well as Koju, were fortified. The walls of Sindo were repaired.

Kwangjong Twenty-fifth year [974]

Seventh year of the Kaibao era of Song, sixth year of the Baoning era of Liao

Spring, third month. Han In'gyŏng and one other person passed the composition test [of the civil service examination].

In this year the lay believer Yŏn'ga from the Western Capital planned treason and was executed.

Kwangjong Twenty-sixth year [975]

Eighth year of the Kaibao era of Song, seventh year of the Baoning era of Liao

Summer, fifth month. The king felt indisposed, and died on the *kabo* [23rd] day of this month in the royal bedchamber. He was posthumously entitled Great King of Great Accomplishment (Taesŏng taewang 大成大王) and granted the temple name Kwangjong; he was buried at the Hŏn-nŭng tomb. When the heir apparent ascended the throne, he declared a general amnesty. Those sent into exile returned, those stuck in prison were released, those indicted by implication were forgiven, cases that were stuck were resolved, people were restored to their former position and rank, debts were cancelled, taxes reduced, temporary prisons demolished, and slanderous tracts burned. Everybody, both in the center and in the provinces, rejoiced greatly.

Yi Chehyŏn commented in his eulogy, "When Kwangjong employed Shuang Ji, can it really be called 'in establishing sagehood there are no limits?' Was Shuang Ji really a sage? Then why did he fail to bring the king to goodness, and fail to prevent him from believing slander and meting out excessive punishment? In so far that he established the examination system to select scholars, it cannot be denied that he had merit when going along with and making more accomplished Kwangjong's intention of using culture and refinement to reform customs. But because of his tendency towards resplendent and superficial writing, he left a bitter legacy for later generations."

Winter, tenth month. [King Kyŏngjong] made the *chŏngsŭng* Kim Pu minister of state and granted him a stipend village of 10,000 households.

[King Kyŏngjong] bestowed posthumous titles on six generations of his ancestors.

Kyŏngjong, Great King of Presenting Harmony.

His given name was Chu 伷, and his courtesy name Changmin 長民. He was the oldest son of King Kwangjong, and his mother was Queen Taemok, nee Hwangbo-ssi. He was born in the sixth year of Kwangjong (*ŭlmyo* year), on the *chŏngsa* day of the ninth month. He was gentle and conscientious of character, and did not like games and play. However, in his later years he grew tired of the myriad affairs of government, and started to indulge in entertainments on a daily basis. He was infatuated with music and women, and loved to play *go*. He kept the company of inferior people and kept worthy scholars at bay. As a result, government and morals greatly declined. He was on the throne for six years and died at the age of twenty-seven.

Kyŏngjong First year [976]

First year of the Taiping xingguo era of Song Emperor Taizong, eighth year of the Baoning era of Liao

Spring, second month. The king determined the grave size of civil and military officials.

Winter, eleventh month. Song sent the Vice-commander (in the heir apparent's guard?) of the junior fifth rank[13] Yu Tingchao and Aide at the Court of the National Granaries Xu Shaowen to invest the king as Grand Master for Splendid Happiness[14] and Acting Grand Mentor commissioned with extraordinary powers over all military affairs in Hyŏnt'o Prefecture, Great Obedient General and Commander-in-Chief of Hyŏnt'o Prefecture with a stipend village of three-thousand households.

The king sent an embassy to Song to congratulate [Emperor Taizong] on his accession.

Owls filled the sky during the day, flying and hooting.

The Executive Official Wang Sŏn was banished. Originally, the king had allowed the sons and grandsons of officials who had been slandered under Kwangjong to take revenge on their foes. Subsequently people took avail of this to kill each other, so that new grudges were declared. In such a situation, Wang Sŏn, on the pretext of taking revenge on his foe strangled the son of T'aejo, the Prince of the Ch'ŏn'an Palace. Thereupon the king demoted Wang Sŏn and forbade the wanton killing [on the pretext of] settling scores with enemies.

The king made Sunjil and Sinjil Left and Right Executive Official, which they both combined with the position of minister of the Royal Secretaries. The *wŏnbo* Suyŏ was appointed administrator of the Royal Kitchen, which was a position as attendant councilor to the king.

For the first time officials ranks and prestige title ranks were set, together with farm- and woodland ranks for each grade.[15] Regardless of whether the office rank was high or low, the amount of land was determined by the person's [administrative] rank.[16] Starting from the purple robes, eighteen

---

13 *Chwasaŏbusol* 左司禦副率: Not found in Hucker. The first three characters correspond to a rank title in Chosŏn (5B), while the last two appears to be a military-type rank.

14 A prestige title of rank 2B.

15 This is the famous *Chŏnsikwa* 田柴科 (stipend land) system; interpretations on how to interpret this system vary widely, but it is definitely the first step in building a centralized bureaucratic system.

16 The traditional Chinese bureaucracy was based on a system of nine ranks (which were further subdivided) on the one hand and numerous offices on the other. Offices were

ranks were made. The first rank was granted 110 *kyŏl* of farmland and an equal amount of woodland; lower grades were given consecutively lower amounts. For the civil officials, from the red robes upwards there were ten ranks, from the dark red[17] robes there were eight, and from the green robes ten. For the military officials, from the red robes upwards there were five ranks. For the specialist officials, from the red robes upwards there were ten ranks, from the dark red robes upwards eight, and from the green robes upwards ten. All were granted farm- and woodland according to their rank.

This year, Kim Haengsŏng was sent to Song where he enrolled in the National Academy and eventually passed the examination.

Kyŏngjong Second year [977]

Second year of the Taiping xingguo era of Song, ninth year of the Baoning era of Liao

Spring, third month. The king went to the Dragon Ship in the Eastern Pond to personally test the presented scholars, and Ko Ŭng and five others passed the composition test; he ordered them to immediately take off their ordinary clothes and wear their official robes.

The king granted the merit subjects as well as the castle lords of Hyang'ŭi and Kwisun merit land according to rank.

The king sent envoys to Song to present horses, armor, and weapons.

Kyŏngjong Third year [978]

Third year of the Taiping xingguo era of Song, tenth year of the Baoning era of Liao

Summer, fourth month. The *chŏngsŭng* Kim Pu died. He was posthumously

---

generally only granted to people of a certain rank, although there could be exceptions, so the rule seems to be to base reward on rank rather than office. However, the passage could also imply that the salary is determined by the person's capacity.

17 Here I read 緋 for 裶.

granted the title of Kyŏngsun[-wang].

Song sent the Companion to the Heir Apparent, Zhang Bo, on a mission of inquiry.

Kyŏngjong Fourth year [979]

Fourth year of the Taiping xingguo era of Song, first year of the Qianheng era of Liao

Spring, third month. Wŏn Chingyŏn and others passed the composition test of the civil service examination.

Summer, sixth month. Song dispatched the Audience Usher for Court Service Wang Zhuan to invest the king as Director of the Chancellery, and granted a stipend village of one thousand households.

This year, several tens of thousands of Parhae people came to submit.

Ch'ŏngsae Garrison was fortified.

Kyŏngjong Fifth year [980]

Fifth year of the Taiping xingguo era of Song, second year of the Qianheng era of Liao

Summer, fourth month. The interest rates for grains and cloth were determined. For grains, it was set at five pecks per fifteen pecks;[18] for cloth it was set at five feet per fifteen feet. This became a constant norm.

This year, Ch'oe Chimong was made *taegwang* and minister at the Advisory Council, Marquis of Tongnae Prefecture with a stipend village of one thousand households, and pillar of state. One day, Ch'oe Chimong had warned the king as follows: "A strange star has invaded Alpha Herculis; please, king, put the guards on alert against any eventuality." Not long after, Wang Sŭng plotted treason, and when the affair came to light he was executed. The king bestowed royal robes and a golden belt on Ch'oe

18 *Tu* 斗: usually pronounced *mal* in Korean, a unit of volume; see table of weights and measures.

Chimong.

Kyŏngjong Sixth year [981]

Sixth year of the Taiping xingguo era of Song, third year of the Qianheng era of Liao

Summer, sixth month. The king was indisposed.

Autumn, seventh month. The king's disease lingered on without signs of improvement. On the *kapchin* [9th] day he summoned his nephew, the Prince of Kaeryŏng, Wang Ch'i, and passed the throne to him. He also left the following instruction, the gist of which is as follows: "Continuing what was not yet finished by the four preceding kings, I received authority over the Three Han, and took charge of the protection of mountains and rivers, land and fields; I took care of the ancestral shrine and the altar for land and grain deities. Day after day without end, for seven years, I did not let my guard drop even once. Because of all this toil, I became seriously ill. Now I look forward to releasing my spirit of this heavy burden, and passing on the sage throne so as to relieve my worries. The rightful heir, the prince of Kaeryŏng, Wang Ch'i, is a sage amongst our family, someone whom I deeply cherish. He will surely be able to uphold the great enterprise of our forefathers, and protect the great institutions of the country. Lo! You lords and ministers, you should respectfully uphold my nephew [as the new king] and ensure the eternal peace of our great country. Whenever I read in the *Classic of Ritual* the passage 'a man should not die in the hands of women,'[19] I always sighed and kept it before my mind. Now that the day has come, all the consorts and concubines have already been sent away, so that if I cannot draw out my life any longer and the moment of death comes, I will have no regrets. As for the degree and length of wearing mourning, the system of the Han dynasty should be followed. Converting months into days, on the thirteenth day the minor anniversary [of death], and on the twenty-seventh

19 From the *Da Dai Liji*, chapter "Sang Da Ji," 1st paragraph. This means that at a man's moment of death, no women should be present.

day the major anniversary should be held. The size and design of my tomb and mound should be modest. As for those entrusted with protecting the garrisons in the Western Capital, Annam, Tŭngju, and other provinces, since they have charge of military affairs, their task is anything but light. They cannot lightly leave their posts to come to the palace [for the funeral and mourning], so they should remain at their posts, mourn for three days and then take off the mourning clothes. All other affairs I entrust to my successor." On the *pyŏng'o* [11th] day the king died in the main bedchamber. He was posthumously entitled Great King of Presenting Harmony (Hŏnhwa taewang 獻和大王) and given the temple name Kyŏngjong. He was buried at Yŏng-nŭng.

Yi Chehyŏn commented in his eulogy, "When Lord Tengwen asked Mencius about the well-field system, Mencius answered: '[...] Benevolent government must start with the drawing of boundaries. If the boundaries are not correctly drawn, the land will not be divided into equal squares, and the grain-salaries will be unequal. Therefore, violent rulers and corrupt ministers are invariably indolent in drawing boundaries. If the boundaries are correctly drawn, the distribution of lands and the regulation of salaries can be settled simply by sitting on your throne.'[20] Now the territory of the Three Han does not allow the meeting of carts or ships from all directions. There is no abundance of products, nor profit from trade. The people solely rely on what the land offers, and the majority of this land south of the Amnok River is mountainous. There is almost no land that is continuously fertile over the years. So, if we are indolent in the matter of drawing boundaries correctly, the damage will be infinitely larger than in China. T'aejo succeeded the decadence and chaos of Silla and the indulgence and violence of T'aebong, and had to rebuild everything from the ground up. There was not a day he could rest, so in the end [his land reforms] stopped at allocating portions of grain [from government offices]. After the first four kings, Kyŏngjong

20 See *Mencius* 3A.3, "Teng Wen gong." Only part of Mencius' answer is quoted by Yi Chehyŏn.

finally succeeded in creating the land rank system. Even though it had a rough quality, it corresponded to the intention of a hereditary salary[21] of the ancients. As for a tax of one ninth [of the harvest], a tax of one tenth [of goods produced], or how people should treat gentlemen or the ordinary person, there was no opportunity to debate this. Later generations frequently wanted to fix this, yet in the end only managed some window dressing. Since the fixing of boundaries was not considered an urgent matter from the beginning, if the source is muddied up how could the river downstream be clear? Alas! At that time there was none among the officials who put in enough effort to lecture the king on how Mencius strove to implement the ancient codes of law."

Eighth month. [The new king] went to Wibong pavilion and declared a general amnesty. There was a three year exemption of corvée labor, and taxes were reduced by half. Civil and military officials were promoted by one rank.

Winter, eleventh month. He posthumously titled his deceased father as Great King Proclaiming Felicity (Sŏn'gyŏng taewang 宣慶大王), with the temple name Taejong 戴宗. The tomb mound was called T'ae-nŭng, and subsequently the king went to pay his respects there.

Sŏngjong, Cultured and Virtuous Great King

His given name was Ch'i 治, and his courtesy name On'go 溫古. He was the second son of Wang Uk 王旭, the seventh son of T'aejo. His mother was Queen Sŏnhŭi, née Yu-ssi. He was born in the eleventh (*kyŏngsin*) year of King Kwangjong (960), on the *sinmyo* day of the twelfth month. He exuded a natural authority and was strict and upright; his talents were broad and encompassing. He established laws and institutions, esteemed and encouraged loyalty and righteousness, obtained [the counsel of] wise people

21 *Serok* 世祿: this would seem to contradict the meritocratic ideals of serving according to one's talent.

and aided the ordinary people; there was much to admire in his government. He was on the throne for sixteen years and lived to the age of thirty-eight.

Sŏngjong First year [982]

Seventh year of Daping xingguo of Song, fourth year of Qianheng of Liao

Spring, third month. The king changed the name of all offices. The Advisory Council became the Royal Secretariat-Chancellery (Naesa munha [song] 內史門下省), and the State Council became the Department of State Affairs (Ŏsa tosŏng 御事都省).

Summer, fourth month. The king ordered that all men older than ten years should wear caps.

Sixth month. The king decreed: "The ruler's virtue depends on his ministers. I have been freshly entrusted with a myriad different duties, and fear that there are deficiencies in my administration of them. All capital officials above the fifth rank should send me a letter discussing the merits and demerits of my policies."

The *chŏnggwang* and selection official, pillar of state Ch'oe Sŭngno, sent a letter, which in outline went as follows:[22] "...Humbly I think of the historian Wu Jing [670–749] of the Kaiyuan era [713–742], who compiled and presented a work entitled *Zhenguan zhengyao* (Essentials of Government of the Zhenguan era) to encourage Emperor Xuanzong (r. 713–756) to diligently practice government as Emperor Taizong (r. 626–649) had done. Because the essence of the situation is similar, despite the fact that it

---

22 Ch'oe Sŭngno's long-winded memorial can also be found in his biography (KRS 93.2b–22a). Apart from a few paragraphs, it is quoted here almost completely, including the lengthy evaluation of the first five reigns of Koryŏ and then twenty-two specific issues he wanted to raise. Originally, his memorial is said to have contained twenty-eight, but six have not been transmitted. For the translation, I am heavily indebted to the translation provided by Hugh Kang and Edward Shultz in Peter H. Lee ed., *A Sourcebook of Korean Civilization* (New York: Columbia University Press, 1993), Vol. 1, pp. 273–292. Note that this translation does not follow the original order of the memorial and is based on the version found in Ch'oe Sŭngno's biography.

is from a different country, the great policies of Taizong can be a model for us too.

Since King T'aejo founded the country, all that I have come to learn I still know by heart.[23] Now I have respectfully recorded the policies and transformative power of the past five reigns, noting their good and bad effects, both as a model and as a warning for you, king, to contemplate.

I respectfully venture that when our T'aejo, Divinely Sagacious Great King, came to the throne, the world was in chaos [but] his destiny was such that it occurs only once every thousand years. In the beginning, to quell the chaos and remove the wicked, Heaven produced the previous sovereign [Kungye], who assisted him [in his destiny]. Later, in accordance with a prophecy he received the mandate. People recognized his sagely virtue and turned to him. At that time, it so happened that Silla destroyed itself and that Koguryŏ saw the chance to reemerge. Without leaving his hometown [i.e., Kaesŏng], he constructed a palace. Calming the turbulent waves of the Liao and P'ae Rivers and acquiring the ancient lands of Chin-Han, within nineteen years he reunited the realm; no merit can be greater than this.

As for the Khitan, since they share a border with us, it is only natural that we established good relations with them from the beginning. They also sent envoys to request peaceful relations, yet we cut off interactions with them because, after having first established peaceful relations with Parhae, they suddenly became suspicious, and overnight attacked and destroyed them, breaking the old covenant. T'aejo regarded this as the utmost disregard for the Way, and therefore did not deign them worthy for diplomatic relations. The camels they offered he discarded and did not feed. His far-sighted policies and plans to prevent calamities before they arose were like this; they protected the country even before it was in danger.

After the Khitan troops had already destroyed Parhae, with the fall of Holhan fortress the crown prince of Parhae, Tae Kwanghyŏn, seeing that our country had emerged as a state that upheld righteousness, led the remaining

23 Ch'oe Sŭngno, born in 927, was presented to T'aejo as a precocious talent at the age of 12; T'aejo is said to have been so impressed that he gave him an appointment. He died in 989.

populace of several tens of thousands of households, marching day and night they hurried to get here. T'aejo took pity on them and treated him generously. He bestowed the [royal] surname on him as well as a name, and registered him in the royal genealogy. He was allowed to offer sacrifices to the royal ancestors of his country, and civil and military officials from the highest to the lowest were all granted titles of nobility. Thereby, through his swift actions to preserve a defunct state and continue its interrupted lineages he convinced, those far off to submit.

Now Kyŏn Hwŏn of Later Paekche had an evil nature and loved to foment chaos; he killed the ruler [of Silla] and oppressed its people. Without caring about sleep or food, T'aejo immediately raised an army to punish this crime. When the task was completed, [Silla] regained its authority. Thus, he did not forget the previous ruler [of Silla, who had been killed] and lent support in a crisis like this!

From the waning days of Silla to the beginning of our dynasty, the people living on the northwestern border frequently suffered from the Jurchen horsemen who came to plunder. T'aejo took personal responsibility for this as sovereign, and sent a good general to guard the border. Without even having to wield a short sword, [rather than attacking], the barbarian hordes came to submit. After this the dust settled down in the area beyond the border, and the border region itself was without worries. This is how, by knowing how to employ the right people, he mollified those afar and brought them closer.

Silla's king and ministers, feeling that their fortunes had been depleted and that their number was up, came to submit of themselves. Refusing three times to accept, he finally relented and allowed them to surrender. Of the more than 110 fortresses lying in the east between Myŏngju and Hŭngnye District, there was none he did not embrace with benevolence, so in due time they came to submit. This is how he knew how to yield in a proper way, and managed to make everyone without fail submit.

Only in pacifying Later Paekche in the south he had no option but to use the military, and on several occasions he raised a great army. However, beneath his banners and in front of his armored cavalry, some surrendered right in the face of battle, and some surrendered from afar. Even if the sword blades made contact, there was no intention of killing. Truly, the benevolent person has no enemies! By then Kyŏn Hwŏn had amassed cruel acts for several dozen years, but was eventually imprisoned following a coup by his son. Escaping, he ran to us, and requested troops to quell the rebellion. When T'aejo heard this, he received him with lavish courtesy. When Kyŏn Hwŏn died, T'aejo provided ample assistance for the funeral. Thus, his Way reached both the world of the dead and of the living, and his righteousness made no distinction for a person whether he was alive or dead.

When he came to pacify Later Paekche, when his chariot entered the cities, he took pity on the impoverished population and consoled them sincerely. He instructed his troops not to harm them even the slightest bit. Moreover, since north and south had been long divided, the new and old [systems] were still very different; yet from the first to the last he supported everyone as if they were one and the same [people], such was his magnanimity and all-embracing mind.

After achieving unification [in 936], he worked diligently at governing for eight more years. He served the great [i.e., China] with propriety and treated the neighboring countries with respect. In times of peace he was not lax; when meeting those of lower status he remained respectful. He valued the way and virtue, and cherished frugality. He did not attach great importance to the palace buildings; they were only built to more or less keep out rain and wind. He disliked clothing, and only dressed sufficiently to protect against heat or cold. He liked the wise and enjoyed goodness, discarded selfishness and followed others. His respectful and courteous mind stemmed from his Heaven-bestowed nature. Moreover, having been born and grown up among ordinary people, he had grown used to hardship and danger. He could always discern whether people's feelings were genuine or not. He could also always tell in advance if something would turn out to be good or bad. Therefore, rewards and punishments were always given at the right time, and right and wrong were always clearly distinguished. Thus in his knowledge of when to punish and when to reward, he completely embodied the way of emperors and kings.

Moreover, when he came to know someone, he never forgot about their talent, and always used those below to their full potential. He never had doubts when employing the wise, and did not hesitate to eliminate the evil. He esteemed Buddhism and cherished Confucianism. Having a ruler thus endowed with virtue was truly a blessing for the country. Ah, how fortunate!

But since it was the very beginning of the dynasty, the days since peace had been established were few indeed. The ancestral shrine and the altar for earth and grain gods did not yet shine in all their glory, while rites, music, and culture were still not completed. As for the ranks and statutes of officials and offices, as well as the rules and ceremonies for center and provinces—these had not yet been completed. His sudden death was a great misfortune for the people; Heaven's way is truly hard to fathom, how unfortunate!

King Hyejong was heir apparent for a long time, and often took care of administrative or military affairs. He followed propriety and respected his teachers, and was good at receiving guests and officials. Thus his good reputation spread throughout the court and beyond. Therefore when he succeeded to the throne, at first everybody was happy. Then somebody slandered his brother Chŏngjong, alleging that he harbored treasonous plans. When Hyejong heard this, he did not reply, and did not make any enquiries. He treated his brother with even more affection and consideration, and everything was as before. Therefore people admired his great tolerance. After a while however, he started to neglect virtuous government, and became overly concerned for his safety. He surrounded himself completely with armored guards who always followed him. He became too suspicious of others, and thus his embodiment of the kingship was greatly diminished. Moreover, he showed favoritism in rewarding military officers, and since favors were distributed unevenly, people in the capital and beyond grew resentful and disaffected, and people started showing signs of dissent. Then, the year after taking the throne, he fell ill, and spend long periods of time secluded in his bedchamber. As a result, court officials and wise people no longer could approach him, but inferior people from villages and hamlets were frequently with him in the inner quarters. When his illness became more severe, he grew angrier every day. During the three years of his reign, the people did not see any virtue [from the ruler], and it was only on the day of his death, that they were more or less released from this calamity. How truly painful this was!

While Chŏngjong was still waiting in the heir-apparent's residence, his reputation already spread. As Hyejong's illness lingered on for a long time, Wang Kyu and others secretly made their plans with an eye to taking over the royal house. Chŏngjong knew of this in advance, and together with loyal officers of the Western Capital he secretly made plans of his own in preparation [of the expected coup]. Thus when the rebellion was about to break out, soldiers arrived in great numbers, and therefore the treasonous plan could not succeed, and the evildoers were all executed. Even though this was due to the Heavenly Mandate, it still was planned by man, so how is it not admirable! From Chŏngjong's accession till now it has been thirty-eight years. The fact that in this period the royal line was not interrupted was thanks to Chŏngjong's efforts. After succeeding to his brother, he worked tirelessly day and night, giving his all in pursuit of truth and justice. Sometimes he would light the candle and receive court ministers [at night]; sometimes he would forego meals to listen to the myriad affairs of government and make decisions. Therefore, after he ascended the throne, everybody was pleased. However, because of his erroneous belief in prognostication, he decided to move the capital. Because he was by nature strong-willed and stubborn, he did not change his mind on this, and pushed through his plans with violence if needed. Corvée labor was raised and people were mobilized, giving rise to resentment and enmity. As a result, calamities arose at a speed that was quicker than a shadow or an echo. But before the capital could be moved west, the king departed his throne forever, how lamentable!

By instruction of Chŏngjong, Kwangjong received the mandate. He was even more courteous towards those below him, and in judging people he never lost impartiality in his evaluation. He was also never biased towards his relatives or those of high birth, and held the powerful in check. He never rejected those who were far removed or of base origin, and extended favors towards widows and orphans. For the first eight years of his reign, his government and instructions were transparent and fair, and there was no excess in either punishment or reward. But since Shuang Ji submitted himself to our country, he greatly esteemed literati, and extended excessive favors towards them. As a result those without talent were randomly selected for office, and suddenly transferred [to a better office] without regard for seniority. In less than a year they rose to the top posts of the bureaucracy. The king invited them day and night, as if he could not get enough of seeing them; this seemed to be a pleasure for him, but he neglected the affairs of state, instead banqueting and making merry without a break. Thus ordinary people from all over the country were all received with special courtesy, and young people without experience competed for offices while the old, virtuous elites gradually disappeared.

Although Chinese customs were cherished, the statutes and law codes of China were not adopted. Although Chinese scholars were treated with courtesy, the eminently talented of China were not employed. While the ordinary people's resources, which were the product of their sweat and blood, were wasted, the king merely gained empty praise from all quarters. As a result, the king never again regained his concern and diligence for state affairs nor met with important guests or officials. Therefore jealousy and envy reigned, and consultations between the king and his officials were increasingly strained. There was no one who dared to speak out and give a frank evaluation of current policy. Moreover, the king was increasingly infatuated with Buddhism, and frequently organized Buddhist events. Maigre feasts for monks were already frequent, and incense offering for special vows were also numerous. He prayed only to obtain blessings and longevity for himself, and exhausted limited resources and manpower to create limitless causality [for future rewards]. Taking lightly the most venerable office of the king, he liked to do small good deeds. In organizing banquets and plays, it was always done with utmost extravagance. The fact that everything appeared alright on the surface he regarded as the result of karmic power, so he did as he pleased, without thinking about correcting his behavior. The palace buildings thus much exceeded their due scale, and clothing and food were also excessively rich and decorated. Public works proceeded without regard for the season, and because their construction was so intricate, work continued without rest. Calculating roughly on the basis of these projects and events, what he spent in one year would have sufficed as T'aejo's budget for ten years. Moreover, in his later years he killed many innocent people.

I foolishly believe that if Kwangjong had always practiced frugal, upright, and diligent government as in his early years, his life span would surely have exceeded the age of fifty! What is even worse, however, is that during a period of sixteen years between the *kyŏngsin* [960] and the *ŭlhae* [975] years, the treacherous and heinous vied for advancement, and slander and calumny reigned. If the gentleman has no way to embrace and educate them, the small-minded will get their way. It even got to the point where children acted against their parents and slaves accused their masters. Those above and those below were divided against each other, and even officialdom was racked by divisions. Old ministers and experienced generals were killed one after the other, and even family and marital bonds were severed.

Moreover, while Hyejong managed to protect his brothers and Chŏngjong succeeded in protecting the country and their sense of justice was thus strong, yet both failed to protect the lives of their only sons. As for Kwangjong, in his later years he started harboring doubts and jealousy about his only son, and therefore even though he was still in the heir apparent's palace, Kyŏngjong could never be at ease; fortunately, however, he still could succeed to the throne. Alas! How is it possible that early on he was so good and managed to establish his reputation early on, yet later it came to this! This is deeply sorrowful.

Kyŏngjong was born deep inside the palace and was raised by palace women, so he had no experience of affairs outside the palace walls. But thanks to his inborn intelligence he managed to avoid regrettable incidents, and eventually succeeded to the throne. Once he had become king, he burned all the records of slander and calumny that had built up over the years, and released those who had languished innocently in jail for years. Thus resentment and anger were resolved, and both the court and ordinary people rejoiced. However, he was ignorant about the basics of politics, and had to rely on powerful families, which harmed the royal family. Thus the signs of imminent calamity were there from the beginning, and though he eventually realized his mistakes, there was no one he could turn to to resolve them. From this time on right and wrong were not separated, and rewards and punishments were not uniformly administered. Unable to mend this state of affairs, his initial diligence gave way to torpor, and eventually he turned to women and local music for pleasure and divertissement, and eventually turned to chess and go, which he could play all day without getting tired. He was surrounded only by eunuchs and courtiers, and as a result the words of wise gentlemen had no way of getting through to him, but the words of the small-minded people sometimes did get through. In the beginning he had a lofty reputation yet in the end lost his virtue; this is what is called "there is none who does not have a good beginning, yet few who manage to bring things to a good end." Loyal ministers and valiant scholars, who would not regret this state of affairs? This is something that your highness knows through personal observation.

Yet Kyŏngjong also did things for which he deserves praise. When he first became ill, before it turned serious he called your highness while lying in the inner chambers. Holding your hand he told you "I entrust you with the army and the country." This was a blessing not only for earth and grain gods, it was also fortunate for the people. Only Hyejong and Kyŏngjong have succeeded to the throne as heir apparent, so there were no expectations towards other people. When we arrive at a situation where there is no clear instruction regarding which of the cousins and brothers [are chosen], conflicts will necessarily arise. When Hyejong died of illness in the inner palace in his second year on the throne, he had a son called Prince Hŭnghwa. Besides the fact that he was still young, since there was no clear instruction [from Hyejong on his successor], the matter was settled by the king's younger brothers. Although Chŏngjong himself had been put forward by his ministers, to continue the great dynasty, right before he died he passed on the throne to [his brother] Kwangjong. Thus the ancestral shrine and the shrine to the earth [and grain] deities remained unperturbed. The instructions for posterity left behind by Chŏngjong and Kyŏngjong were truly wise!

I once observed that for the successive kings Hyejong, Chŏngjong and Kwangjong, when each came to the throne they faced an unsettled situation, so in the end half of the civil and military officials of the two capitals were killed or maimed [in succession struggles]. Moreover in the latter years of Kwangjong's reign the realm was in turmoil and slander flourished. Among those who were tried and punished, the majority was innocent. The merit subjects of successive kings as well as experienced generals could also not avoid executions and all perished. By the time Kyŏngjong ascended the throne, only about forty of the old ministers had survived. But during his reign too many were harmed; but since they were slanderers and young opportunists, they do not deserve our pity. Only the Princes of Ch'ŏnan and Chinju, since they were directly related to the august dynastic family, were not put on trial by Kwangjong, who showed his magnanimity.[24] Kyŏngjong too wanted to protect them, but powerful ministers criminally inflicted harm on them; this was really agonizingly sad.

I humbly venture that thanks to the virtue of previous kings, your majesty has encountered a time of revival. Thanks to the considerateness of the previous king, who resigned and handed you the throne, you could follow in the footsteps of the great sage kings' munificent project. There is not a single being who is not happy, and not a single man who has not obtained his position. Those in the capital and in the provinces are equally joyful, and men and spirits congratulate each other. This is what is called

24 These appear to be sons of T'aejo through his union with the Lady of the Ch'ŏnan-bu court 天安府院夫人 (surname Im, from Kyŏngju), and Lady Sukmok from Chinju 肅穆夫人 (surname unknown). See *Koryŏsa* 88.

"Heaven bestows, people give [to one another]." Your majesty, if you can follow the practices of T'aejo, it would be the same as Emperor Xuanzong pursuing the model of Taizong [of Tang]. Your majesty can also take lessons from the more recent events during the reigns of your four predecessors. Thus Hyejong had the merit of safeguarding the "flesh and bones" [of the dynasty], which can be called the principle of great friendship [towards his brothers]. Chŏngjong knew of the sprouts of rebellion in advance, he managed to quell the palace revolt, and make the ancestral shrine as well as the altar of the earth [and grain] gods tranquil again, transmitting them to the present; this can be called the wisdom of great planning. The government of Kwangjong's [first] eight years can be likened to that of the three dynasties [Xia, Shang, and Zhou]. Moreover, the court rituals were worth watching. This can be called "good and bad were evenly distributed." Kyŏngjong released several thousand innocent prisoners and burned all the slanderous documents that had accumulated over the years. This can be called the utmost magnanimity.

In outline, these are the achievements of the four king's administrations before you. Your majesty should retain from these the good policies and put them into effect, and observe what is not good and take that as a warning. Do not concern yourself with matters that are not urgent, and avoid expending your energy on projects that have no benefit. The ruler should be at ease above, and the people will then experience joy below. With a mind that starts from goodness, your ideas can be beautifully concluded. Take heed every day, and even when at rest don't let up. Even though you are worthy as a ruler, do not flatter yourself. Even if you are rich, talented, and powerful, don't be arrogant. If you act like this, blessings will come without seeking them and calamities will be averted without prayer. Then, as a sage ruler, how could you not enjoy 10,000 years on the throne? How could the dynasty not last a hundred generations?

Your subject has also recorded a list of twenty-eight policy proposals[25]

[25] *Simu* 時務: current affairs would probably be a better translation. As is explained at the end, six of the 28 have gone missing. Also, they are not numbered in the original; the

which are attached to this memorial. First: It has been forty-seven years since our country united the Three [Kingdoms], yet the soldiers cannot yet rest in peace, and grain provisions are still completely depleted [for the military]. The reason for this is that we border the barbarians to the northwest, and there are many places on the border that need to be defended against them. Your majesty, please keep this in mind carefully. T'aejo intended to make the Mahŏl Rapids the border of our country, but our suzerain determined that the stone wall along the banks of the Amnok River should be the border. I implore you to choose a buffer zone for the border, and to select local people who are good at archery and horseriding and entrust them with the defense. Also, select two or three among them as adjudant officers to lead them. Then, the capital army will be relieved of the burden of taking turns to guard the border, and we will greatly reduce the expenses for transporting provisions.

Second: I have furtively observed that your majesty sometimes personally pulverizes tea or grinds barley for merit[-producing] maigre feasts. Your subject is confused by this and deeply regrets the effort and labor of your august body. This kind of abuse started under Kwangjong who firmly believed in slander and evil accusations, and killed many innocent people. Deluded by Buddhist stories of retribution, he wanted to remove the evil karma he had produced, and confiscated offerings that had been made by the blood and sweat of the people. He held many Buddhist events: sometimes he held a Vairocana expiation rite; sometimes he offered a vegetarian banquet to monks on the polo court; sometimes he held a rite for all the spirits on land and water at Kwibŏp-sa.[26] Every time there was a Buddhist festival he would give food to begging monks or distribute cakes and fruit from the palace ritual site to beggars, or turn fish ponds such as those at New Pond, Cave Entrance or Mt. Mari into places to release living beings.

numbers have been added by the translator for clarity, but may or may not reflect the original sequence.

26 *Much'a suryuk hoe* 無遮水陸會: an "unimpeded water and land ritual;" an offering to pacify all unsettled spirits. Kwibŏp-sa had been established in the capital Kaesŏng by Kwangjong in 963 for the monk Kyunyŏ.

Four times a year he would send envoys to nearby temples to read Buddhist scriptures [on behalf of the creatures]. Also, since he forbade the taking of life, he did not allow the palace cooks to slaughter animals but had them buy the meat for offerings in the market. He also made officials high and low as well as ordinary people expiate sins by having them carry grain, beans, firewood, charcoal, and horsefodder, and giving it to a countless number of people on the streets of the capital and beyond. However, when he started to believe in slanderous accusations, he looked at people as if they were grass; those killed were so numerous the corpses piled up like a mountain. He frequently squeezed people to the bone to provide offerings to the Buddha. If the Buddha had a spirit, how could he accept these offerings! At that time, sons betrayed their fathers and slaves betrayed their masters. All those who had committed crimes dressed up as monks and went begging for food. They mingled with genuine monks and added to the vast numbers who went to maigre feasts. What possible benefit could there be in this? Furthermore, he let the monk Sŏnhoe manage the donations, and provided him with cakes and rice, which were wantonly used for other causes. This is not how one obtains a long life, and in the end Sŏnhoe's corpse was exposed by the side of the road and he became the object of ridicule at the time. Your majesty, please maintain the uprightness of the sovereign's body, and do not engage in acts without benefit.

Third: During the reign of T'aejo, the dynasty's royal guard troops were merely entrusted with the defense of the palace compound, so they were not that numerous. But by the time of Kwangjong, because of his belief in slander, he executed or censored many generals and ministers, and since he grew suspicious [of everyone around him], he simply selected strong looking guys from prefectures and counties and made them royal guards. People at the time thought this was excessive and without benefit. During the reign of King Kyŏngjong, the number of royal guards slightly decreased, but to this day it remains excessive. I humbly request your majesty to honor the principles of T'aejo's time, merely retain those that are truly strong and brave, and dismiss the rest. This will lessen the people's complaints and grievances, and allow the country to build up a reserve.

Fourth: Your majesty donates soysauce, wine, soybean paste, and soup to people passing along the roads. Your servant presumes that your majesty wants to emulate King Kwangjong and thereby eliminate bad karma. But the intention of securing good causality by indiscriminate donations is what is called "small favors do not spread everywhere." If you are clear and consistent in rewards and punishments, censor evil and encourage good, this suffices to obtain blessings. Insignificant matters such as these are not what a ruler of men occupies himself with, so please desist from doing so.

Fifth: Our T'aejo was sincere and attentive in serving the great, yet only once every few years he sent presents to China to maintain the appropriate diplomatic protocol. Nowadays, not only diplomatic missions, but also trade missions are both frequent and large in size. I'm afraid that China will find this demeaning. Also, because of the frequent traffic many ships are lost at sea and many lives lost. I request that henceforth diplomatic and trade missions are combined, and that the remaining irregular trade missions are completely forbidden.

Sixth: For the endowments in cash or grains of Buddhist temples, monks of each temple send out people to prefectures and counties to collect the due interest each year, causing great distress and hardship to the people. I request that this should all be forbidden; the money and grain [of the endowments] should be transferred to the manors of the temples. If the administrators of the temple have tenants, these should be taken away and attached to the temple manors; thereby the people's distress should be lessened somewhat.

Seventh: As for the king's management of the people, since he cannot go to each and every home and inspect it daily, therefore he dispatches magistrates to inspect whether the people are doing well or not. After our T'aejo unified the country, he wanted to establish a local bureaucracy,[27] but since it was still the formative phase of nation-building, and the task was complex, it was never achieved. Now I cannot help observing how local

---

27 *Oegwan* 外官: the system of officials serving outside the capital, from provincial governors and inspectors to local magistrates.

potentates avail themselves of the cloak of public office and oppress the people, who are at their wits' end. Please, your majesty, install a system of local bureaucracy. Even if they cannot be dispatched to all localities at once, you could still install one office for ten or more localities combined, and allocate two or three officials to each office to take charge of matters.

Eighth: Humbly I perceived how your majesty dispatched officials to welcome the monk Yŏch'ŏl, of the Sagul-san school,[28] into the palace. Ignorantly, your servant assumed that since Yŏch'ŏl, as someone who can produce blessings for people, is living on land that is owned by your majesty, and eats and drinks food and water that is also provided by your majesty, therefore he should as a matter of course be ready to pray for blessings for the dynasty every day; why go to the trouble of expecting him to produce blessings only after he has visited the palace? Formerly, there was a monk called Sŏnhoe who, to avoid corvee duties, became a monk and resided in the mountains. Kwangjong esteemed him greatly and extended courtesy to him, yet in the end he died a violent death and his corpse was exposed next to the road. If a monk's body can meet with such misfortune, then how could it procure blessings for others? I request that Yŏch'ŏl be returned to his mountain so as to avoid the kind of ridicule that Sŏnhoe incurred.

Ninth: In the time of Silla, the nobles, ministers, officials, and ordinary people wore clothing and shoes that were differentiated in color and quality according to rank. When the nobles, ministers, and officials went to court audiences, they wore their official robes and held [their official tablets]; when they retired, then they changed into comfortable clothing. Ordinary people were not allowed to wear patterned or colored clothing so as to distinguish base from noble, and who is worthy of respect and who not. Therefore, even though the official robes were not native products, they sufficed for the use of the officials. Since the time of T'aejo, in our dynasty people wear what they please regardless of whether they are noble or

28 One of the so-called Nine Mountain schools, Chan lineage schools established in the Late Silla period. The monk Yŏch'ŏl is otherwise unknown.

base. If an official had a high rank yet his family was poor, then he could not obtain official robes. If someone did not have an official position yet his family was rich, then he wore clothing of silk gauze and embroidered brocade. In our country, since products of good quality are scarce but coarse products numerous, all patterned and colored clothes are not locally made. However, since everyone wears them, I'm afraid that when we receive foreign envoys we embarrass ourselves because the officials do not wear the appropriate ritual clothes [while ordinary people do]. I beg your majesty to make all officials at court audiences follow Chinese and Silla custom and wear official robes and carry a tablet. When they address the throne, they should wear either small shoes with thick Korean socks, silk shoes, or leather shoes. Ordinary people should not wear patterned or colored fabrics or plaited silk, but only plain silk.

Tenth: Your subject has heard that monks when they travel to other prefectures or counties use the government hostels and postal stations for staying the night. They harass the official clerks at these places and curse them for their [lack of attention] in receiving them or for their slowness in bringing food or provisions. The clerks suspect they may be under royal orders and do not dare to talk back. There is no greater abuse than this! Henceforth monks should be forbidden from using government hostels or postal stations to eradicate this kind of abuse.

Eleventh: It is impossible not to follow the institutions of China, however the local customs of other countries all follow the local characteristics and are difficult to change completely. In instructing music, ritual, poetry, and writing, and the way ruler and minister, father and son should treat each other, it is fitting to follow the Chinese model to reform base customs. As for the rest, such as transport means, clothing, and other things, we can follow the local tradition to achieve balance between luxury and modesty. Not everything should be forcibly unified.

Twelfth: The residents of the various islands live amidst the sea because of the crimes committed by their forebears. I reckon that their lives are extremely difficult. Moreover the Court of Royal Entertainments[29] requisitions [tribute goods] from them at will throughout the year. Daily they become poorer and more destitute. I request that following the example of normal prefectures and counties, their tribute and corvée duties are equalized.

Thirteenth: In the spring our country organizes the Lantern Festival and in winter the P'algwanhoe. People are drafted far and wide, and their labor impositions are severe. Please reduce the number of people drafted so that we can save on manpower. Also, various effigies are manufactured; expenses are quite high, but once presented they are then destroyed; this is highly unconventional. Furthermore, effigies should only be used for inauspicious (i.e., funerary) rites. When Chinese envoys came here and saw them, they thought them inauspicious and covered their faces, quickly passing them by. Please let them no longer be used hereafter.

Fourteenth. According to the *Book of Changes*, "The sage moves the heart of people, and the under-Heaven achieves peace."[30] According to the *Analects*, "The one who governs without acting, he is none other than King Shun. What does this mean? He took on a respectful bearing and correctly faced south, and that was all."[31] That by which the sage moves Heaven and earth is his pure and unified virtue, and a mind that has no selfish desires. If your majesty maintains a humble mind, always preserves an attitude of respect and awe, and treats ministers and those below with courtesy, then who would not exert his mind and power to inform you of devious plots when serving as your officials, and have only the ambition to help when not serving? This is what is called "the ruler treats the subject with courtesy when employing him, and the subject is loyal when serving."[32] Please, your

---

29 Kwangnok-sa 光祿寺: as the translated title indicates, this office was in charge of royal banquets. While I follow Hucker's translation (no. 3348), I have replaced "Imperial" with "Royal." It does seem somewhat incongruous that this office would trouble people from far-off islands, since the foodstuffs they could contribute would likely be not very refined.

30 See *Yijing*, "Xian" (hexagram 31), Tuan Commentary. See the translation of this commentary by Richard Wilhelm, *I Ching or Book of Changes*, 541.

31 See *Analects* 15.5.

32 *Analects*, 3.19.

majesty, take heed of this at all times and keep trying to observe it better and better, do not indulge in arrogance, and keep a respectful demeanor when receiving those below you. Even if you have to deal with someone who committed a crime, settle the punishment according to law, and we may expect a dynasty where peace reigns.

Fifteenth. Apart from the palace slaves who performed duties in the palace, T'aejo sent the rest to the outskirts of the city to till the land and pay taxes. Apart from the horses in the royal stables that were not immediately needed for court activities, T'aejo sent the rest to stables outside the capital city to be fed; thus he could save expenses for the country. By the time of King Kwangjong however, since he held many Buddhist services, corvée labor duties became more burdensome by the day, and he drafted slaves from outside the palace to make up for the lack of manpower. When palace finances were insufficient for payments, he used up the rice of the storehouses. Nowadays there are many horses to raise in the palace stables and expenses are high, a burden borne by the people. If there is unrest at the border, army provisions will be insufficient. I entreat your majesty to follow the system of T'aejo's time to the letter, and determine the number of palace slaves and palace horses accordingly. The rest should all be allocated to other places.

Sixteenth. It is a common custom among the people to plant good [seeds] so as to achieve fame [in a future life]. Everybody builds temples according to their vows, their number is really high. Furthermore, there are many monks in the capital and in the provinces who compete to construct temples; they push the local leaders to draft people for the construction work, who make this a more urgent task than labor for the state. The people suffer greatly because of this. I entreat your majesty to forbid this strictly and completely, so as to remove this [unnecessary] toiling.

Seventeenth. According to the *Classic of Rites*, "The hall of the Son of Heaven [was ascended by a stairway] of nine steps, that of the prince by seven steps ..."[33] From old there have been such rules and regulations, yet

---

[33] *Li ji*, "Li qi" 9.

lately people do not honor the distinction of high and low. Even if they are of low status, if they have wealth and power, they all give priority to building [big] houses. Thus in all the prefectures, counties, postal stations and ferries, the mighty compete with each other in building big houses that surpass all regulations about size. They not only deplete the power of one family, by making ordinary people work [toward the construction of these houses], their excesses are enormous. Prostrate, I hope that you will order the officials of the Ministry of Rites to set measures for the size of houses of those of high and of low status. Let those in the capital and in the provinces observe those rules on size, and if among the houses already built there are some that exceed the limits, let them be destroyed to set an example.

Eighteenth. The copying of sutras and the sculpting of Buddhist images is done for the sole purpose of transmitting them for a long time. Why use precious materials to adorn them when doing so arouses the minds of thieves and robbers? The ancients used yellow paper for the scriptures and sandalwood for the rollers. For the statues they did not use gold or silver, copper or iron, only stone, clay, or wood. Thus there was no one who stole or destroyed them. During the Silla period, gold and silver were used for scriptures and statues, and they were excessively luxurious. In the end Silla collapsed, and merchants stole and destroyed Buddhist statues to convert them into items that could be sold for profit. These days those customs are still around, so I entreat you to strictly forbid them so that this wastefulness can be mended.

Nineteenth. In ancient times, after the virtue of the Jin dynasty had declined, [the eight great families with surnames] Luan, Xi, Xu, Yuan, Hu, Xu, Qing and Bai ended up as slaves. As for the descendants of merit subjects of our own state, even though they have received successive royal edicts promising promotion and emolument, they have yet to receive any official title. They are mixed up with official slaves and have to endure the taunts of newly risen officials, they have had much cause for grievances to emerge. Moreover, in the latter years of Kwangjong's reign, since many officials were killed or expelled, the descendants of great families could not succeed to their families' [position in society]. I request your majesty to honor the promises of successive decrees and give employment and salaries to the descendants of merit subjects. Furthermore, the [recipients of the] *kyŏngja* year (940) merit-reward land (*chŏnkwa* 田科) distribution, as well as those who entered the bureaucracy after the establishment of our dynasty should also be considered and given ranks and office so that grievances can be allayed and calamities averted.

Twentieth. Although worshiping and believing the Buddhadharma is certainly not bad, the way that rulers, officials, and ordinary people produce merit is not the same. In the case of ordinary people, they labor by using their own force, and spend by using their own wealth. Thus they do not harm others, and [using their wealth to produce merit] is acceptable. Rulers on the other hand labor by using the force of the people, and spend the people's wealth. For this reason, when Emperor Wu of Liang used the venerable body of the son of heaven to produce the good deeds of an ordinary person, people thought it unacceptable. Therefore, rulers should deeply consider why this is the case, and in all affairs weigh up the middle way so as not to harm ministers and people.

Your subject has learned that fortune and misfortune, aristocratic and base are all received at birth, and should therefore be accepted as they come. Moreover, those worshiping the Buddha's teachings are only planting causality for a future life, so there is scant benefit in seeing the rewards [since they lie in the future]. I'm afraid that this is not where the principles of governing the country reside. Moreover, the Three Teachings [of Confucianism, Buddhism, and Taoism] each have their own area of expertise, so they should not be confounded and seen as one and the same. Practicing Buddhism is the basis of cultivating one's body; practicing Confucianism is the source of governing the country. Cultivating one's body is for the benefit of one's future life; governing the country is a task for the present. The present is extremely close, while the future life is extremely far. Rejecting what is close to pursue what is far, isn't this a mistake? A ruler of men should single-mindedly avoid selfishness and dedicate himself to all beings. What use is it to make people toil against their will and waste the grain stored in the warehouses to pursue something that has absolutely no benefit? In the past, the father-in-law of Emperor Dezong (r. 780-805), Wang Jingxian, and his son-in-law, Gao Tian, cast a gilt bronze Buddha statue and offered it to the emperor so as to extend his life. Dezong however said "In my view, merit that is made on behalf of others, is not true merit" and he returned the statue. Thus, although their feelings [of affection toward the emperor] did not produce a result, the emperor was adamant that subjects and ordinary people should not engage in practices without benefit. In our dynasty, the Buddhist lecture meetings in every season, as well as the memorial feasts for deceased kings and queens are a long-standing tradition, they cannot be changed, but as for other [Buddhist events], anything that can be reduced should be reduced.[34]

Twenty-first. According to the *Analects*, "Offering to spirits that do not belong to you is flattery."[35] According to the *Zuo Commentary on the Spring and Autumn Annals*, "If a spirit does not belong to your family, it will not partake of the sacrificial food."[36] This is what one may call "licentious offerings do not produce blessings." Among the offerings at the Royal Ancestor Shrine and the Altar for the Earth and Grain Deities, there are many things that are still not according to the norm. Yet the offerings to mountain spirits and the rituals for stars and planets are profuse and excessive in scale. This is what one may call "In sacrificing one should not aim for frequency; if they are held too frequently, they become burdensome, and if they are burdensome they are not carried out respectfully." Even though your majesty cleanses your mind with utmost respect, and is not in the least indolent, if the sacrificial officials come to regard this as a routine affair they become resentful and lazy, and will not have any respect, will the spirits then enjoy the offerings?

---

34 Here a lengthy part on the correct time of performing rites has been left out. See Shultz and Kang's translation in *Sourcebook* I: 286-287.

35 *Analects* 2.24.

36 *Chunqiu Zuo zhuan*, 31st Year of Lord Xi. Durrant, Li, and Schaberg, *Zuo Tradition*, vol. 1, 441.

Formerly, whenever Emperor Wen of Han held a sacrifice, he made the officials carry it out with respect but did not allow them to pray [for blessings]. His judgment was beyond the pale, this can be called great virtue. If the spirits have no knowledge [of our affairs], how could they bestow blessings? But if they have knowledge, if the individual pursuit of one's own good is something that is difficult for the gentleman to accept, how much more so for spirits? The expenses for sacrificial offerings all come from the blood and sweat of the people, who give their labor and power. Your subject foolishly believes that the blessings obtained through the joy of letting people rest exceeds the blessings obtained through prayer. I wish that your majesty would do away with the superfluous prayer offerings, and would always maintain a self-respecting yet self-critical mind that can match Heaven, then calamities will disappear of themselves, and blessings will come naturally.

Twenty-second. The laws concerning commoners and base people in our country have long antecedents. When our T'aejo founded the dynasty, his subjects, apart from those who originally possessed slaves, did not possess slaves. Then they obtained them later as prisoners of wars during military campaigns, or purchased them. T'aejo originally wanted to free the prisoners of war and make them commoners, but considering that by doing so he might upset the merit subjects, he allowed them to do [with the slaves] as they pleased. For the next sixty years, there was no one who appealed against this. Only during Kwangjong's reign was there the first inspection of slaves to distinguish the real from the fake. There was no one under the merit subjects who did not suppress groans of resentment. However, no one dared to remonstrate. Even when Queen Taemok sincerely remonstrated, [her husband the king] did not listen. The base and slaves took heart from this and slighted the nobles. Those who vied to make accusations and plotted against their former owners were numerous beyond count. Kwangjong brought this disaster upon himself, but he could not make it stop. In the last years of his reign those who had been unjustly killed were numerous, and the loss of virtue was severe.

Formerly, Hou Jing encircled the palace of the Liang [Emperor Wu].[37] The family slave of the emperor's close minister Zhou Yi climbed over the walls and surrendered to Hou Jing. Hou Jing gave him the title of Unequaled in Honor. The slave rode a horse dressed in brocade robes and in front of the walls shouted "Zhou Yi served as an official for fifty years yet just got the title of Capital Commandant; I have barely started serving Hou Jing yet have reached the highest office already." Thereupon all the servants and slaves in the city fought to get out and submit to Hou Jing, and the palace subsequently fell. I implore your majesty to deeply reflect on the significance of this event, and that you will not allow the base to ridicule the noble; take a neutral position when dealing with divisions between slaves and masters. In general, those who hold high office will hardly ever act against the law since they know its principles. Those who hold insignificant offices, when they commit a wrong, their knowledge is sufficient to cover up the wrong. How could the good produce something that is base? It is true that in the palace and among the powerful ministers there are those who abuse their power and commit wrongdoings, at present the mirror of government does not reflect any selfish interests, so how could anyone transgress? Although King You and King Li of Zhou lost the way, the virtue of King Xuan and King Ping could not be concealed. Although Queen Lü of Han was not virtuous, this could not obscure the wisdom of Emperor Wen and Emperor Jing. All you should do is adjudicate the current affairs judiciously with an eye for detail so there will be no regrets. There is no need to go back and reopen past cases, which will merely lead to strife.

Ch'oe Sŭngno saw that the ruler had a strong will and talent, and therefore presented this memorial. The remaining six points were lost in the military conflict of the *kyŏngsul* year (1010).

Winter, tenth month. The king decreed as follows: "If among the people there are those who give out loans to collect interest, they are not allowed to

37 This refers to Hou Jing's siege of Jiankang, the capital of the Liang Dynasty (502–557) in 549. After capturing the city, he held Emperor Wu (r. 502–549) captive until the latter's death later the same year.

take more interest if it reaches the same amount as the money loaned."

Twelfth month. The king decreed as follows: "For the memorial day of the father or mother of an official, give one day and two nights off. For the memorial day beyond the mourning period of a grandfather or grandmother, if they have no living son, then follow the precedent of the memorial day for a father or mother."

This year, the Vice-chancellor Kim Uk was sent to Song to announce the succession.

The king's birthday was called the Ch'ŏnch'un [thousand springs] festival. The usage of naming celebrations [of the king's birthday] started with this.

Sŏngjong Second year [983]

Eighth year of the Daping xingguo era of Song, first year of the Tonghe era of Emperor Shengzong of Liao

Spring, first month. The king went to the Round Altar (Wŏngu 圜丘) to pray for a good harvest and enshrined T'aejo. The king personally performed the ceremony of the first plow, and made a sacrifice to the inventor of agriculture, Shennong, and enshrined the god of agriculture, Houji. This was the beginning of the harvest prayer and the first plowing.

The king feasted his ministers in the Ch'ŏndŏk Hall and bestowed gifts commensurate to rank.

The king made Ch'oe Sŭngno executive chief of the Chancellery.[38]

Second month. The king established the twelve departments,[39] and abolished the positions of *kŭmyu* and *chojang*. *Kŭmyu* and *chojang* are the titles of officials dispatched to localities outside the capital.

Third month. Song dispatched the Vice Minister for Imperial Entertainment Li Juyuan and the Vice Director of the Directorate for Palace

---

38 This is a problematic passage in so far that the Chancellery was established only later the same year, and the full administrative system was only implemented under Munjong.

39 Mok 牧: literally "shepherdship." Rather than neat territorial divisions, this should be seen as twelve important prefectures that had stewardship over nearby prefectures and counties.

Buildings to invest the king as Grand Master for Splendid Happiness (Rank 2B), Acting Grand Guardian, Commissioner with Special Powers over all military affairs in Hyŏnt'o Prefecture, Commander-in-chief of Hyŏnt'o Prefecture, and in addition Emissary of a Great Obedient Army, Supreme Pillar of State with a stipend village of 2,000 households. He was also enfeoffed as King of the Country of Koryŏ. The king received the investiture and issued an amnesty.

The king went to the Sangjŏng Hall and bestowed one horse each on military and civil officials above the rank of *wŏnyun*.[40]

Summer, fifth month. The *chwasŭng* Sŏ Hŭi was made minister of defense, and the *taesang* Chŏng Kyŏmyu minister of public works.[41]

Ch'oe Ŏnhaeng and four others passed the composition test of the civil service examination.

For the first time, [the Chinese system] of Three Departments, Six Boards, and Seven Directorates was instituted.[42]

Sixth month. The *kwangno-gyŏng*[43] Sŏl Sin'u was made minister of justice.

Autumn, seventh month. On the *imsul* [9th] day the Lady of the Myŏngbok Palace, née Hwangbo, died. The king had already mourned [his mother] Queen Sŏnŭi at a young age, and had grown up under her.[44] Therefore he deeply lamented her death and provided the best possible funeral ceremony. His grief deeply moved those around him. On the *kyeyu* [20th] day, he led the officials from the funeral hall where the body lay, and they wailed. On

40 Rank six, level ten; see table 2.

41 New terms are used for these offices (e.g. *ŏsa* 御事 for minister rather than *yŏng* 令), showing the administrative reforms Sŏngjong undertook at the beginning of his reign.

42 Samsŏng 三省–yukcho 六曹–ch'ilsa 七寺.

43 Originally not a rank, but an office, i.e. that of Chief Minister of the Court of Imperial Entertainments; it is here likely used as a rank title.

44 Queen Sŏnŭi was a daughter of T'aejo through his marriage with Queen Chŏngdŏk, who was a daughter of Yu Tŏg'yŏng from Chŏngju. The Lady of the Myŏngbok Palace, whom Sŏngjong renamed Queen Sinjŏng, was the daughter of the strongman of Hwangju, Hwangbo Chegong, and also a spouse of T'aejo. Her daughter was Queen Taemok, Kwangjong's spouse. Her son Anjong would become the father of King Hyŏnjong. See *Koryŏsa* 88 (biographies of queens), 91 (biographies of princesses) for their biographies.

this occasion he bestowed the posthumous title of Queen Dowager Sinjŏng Mother on her. The tomb was called Su-nŭng.

Ninth month. The *chwasŭng* Yi Chibaek was appointed Grand Master of Remonstrance.

Winter, tenth month. Six wine shops were established.

Eleventh month. On the *kapcha* [13th] day the sun reached its nadir, and the king went to the Wŏnhwa Hall to receive felicitations from his government. Later he gave a feast for all his ministers in the Sahyŏn Hall.

Twelfth month. The Ch'ŏnch'un 千春 Festival was renamed the Ch'ŏnch'u 千秋 [Thousand autumns] Festival, and the king gave a feast to his ministers.

The titles of all offices for local functionaries [*hyangni* 鄕吏] in all localities were changed.

The king ordered the selection of presented scholars. He personally took charge of the confirmation test, and selected three people including Kang Ŭnch'ŏn as presented scholar, and one scholar as master of classics. This marked the beginning of the confirmation test.[45] Kang Ŭnch'ŏn is none other than Kang Kamch'an.

Sŏngjong Third year [984]

First year of the Yongxi era of Song, second year of the Tonghe era of Liao

Spring, third month. On the *kyŏngsin* [10th] day a sacrifice for rain was held for the first time.

Yi Chong and two others passed the composition test of the civil service examination.

Summer, fifth month. Lightning struck the pillars of the gate to the Ministry of Punishments. All the officials [in that ministry], from minister to assistant office chiefs, were reprimanded and forced to resign.

---

45 *Poksi* 覆試. This was a test to confirm the quality of those selected in the civil service examination.

During this year the colors of the military officials dress were determined.

The king ordered the minister of punishment, Yi Kyŏmŭi, to build a fortress along the banks of the Amnok River which was to function as an access gate [to control border movement]. The Jurchen military rallied to stop this, took Yi Kyŏmŭi hostage, and retreated. The Koryŏ troops were scattered and the fortress could not be finished. Only one in three of the soldiers returned.

Han Suryŏng was sent to Song to offer local products.

Sŏngjong Fourth year [985]

Second year of the Yongxi era of Song, third year of the Tonghe era of Khitan

Summer, fifth month. Song sent the Chamberlain for Ceremonials Wang Zhu and the Director of the Palace Library Lü Wenzhong to invest the king as Acting Grand Mentor, and following precedent also as Commander-in-chief of Hyŏnt'o Commissioned with Extraordinary Powers over military affairs in Hyŏnt'o, cum Greatly Obedient Military Envoy and King of Koryŏ. He was granted a stipend village of one thousand households, and the same prestige and merit title as in the previous investiture. The king received the investiture and declared an amnesty.

Chin Yang and two others passed the composition test of the civil service examination.

Song was preparing to attack Khitan territory to recover the area of Yanzhou and Jizhou.[46] Since our territory was adjacent to that of the Khitan and as we had been invaded by them, they sent the Investigating Censor Han Guohua with an imperial edict which read as follows: "Ever since we inherited the throne and took charge of the realm, even plants and trees, insects and fishes, there was none that did not benefit; among the Chinese or the barbarians, there was none that did not lead

46 Names of prefectures in the region of modern Beijing, which had been ceded together with a number of others by the rulers of Later Jin to Liao in 938.

his underlings to follow us. Only these northern caitiffs have revolted against the sovereign plan. The territory of Youdou and Jizhou belongs to China, but because of the many troubles in the [Later] Jin and [Northern] Han periods, the barbarians took them away. Now the government of our dynasty reaches everyone within its territory, and writing and cart widths have been unified. How can we leave the people [of those prefectures] mired in uncivilized customs? Now I have instructed the various armies to go on an expedition to extirpate this malign influence. The crack troops have already cleared the way for our main army, and we are looking forward to the execution [of the enemy soldiers] and the celebration of our reunification. Now I know that the king of Koryŏ has long admired Chinese culture, and in daily life embraces wise government. You display loyalty and sincerity towards us, and rule your country with propriety and righteousness. However, being adjacent to those dog-like barbarians is like suffering from a poisonous scorpion. But now you have the chance to wash away all the anger that has accumulated over the years. If you ready your troops, and we take turns in coordinated attacks against them, the combined force of our neighboring countries will wipe out the enemy. The valor of our armies, marching to the same beat, will ensure our victory over those nearly defeated caitiffs; a good time like this does not come twice. If you agree to this plan, all the captured prisoners of war as well as cattle, treasures, and weapons will all be given to the generals and soldiers of your country as encouragement and reward."

The king prevaricated and did not send troops, so Han Guohua continued to pressure and cajole him. Only then did the king give his permission to send troops, to meet [the Chinese army] in the west. After [he secured this promise], Han Guohua returned.

What happened before all this is that the Khitan, to attack the Jurchen, passed through our territory. The Jurchen accused us of leading on the enemy and thus bringing on disaster on them. [When they] offered horses as tribute to the Song, they therefore craftily accused Koryŏ of colluding with the Khitan to boost their power and to help them in grabbing people [as slaves or hostages]. When Han Suryŏng traveled to Song [in 984], the emperor produced the accusations that the Jurchen had presented to him on a wooden tablet,[47] and told Han Suryŏng "Return to your country and tell [the king] to return those people." When the king heard this he was very worried and afraid, so when Han Guohua came he told him "The Jurchen are full of covetousness and deceit. The previous winter they twice sent a wooden tablet saying that the Khitan were about to reach their borders. We suspected that this information might be false, and did not immediately try to aid them. When the Khitan effectively came, they killed or captured a great many people. The remaining people fled to our country, and took refuge in the jurisdictions of Hoech'ang, Wihwa, and Kwanghwa within our borders. The Khitan troops who pursued them called out to our troops saying 'The Jurchen frequently raid our border cities; now we have taken revenge, we will reorganize our troops and return.' Thereupon, we provided provisions to the more than 2,000 Jurchen who had fled to us and sent them back to their home. Unexpectedly, they secretly sent troops to our country and killed or plundered our officials and people. They pursued the strong able-bodied men to sell them as slaves. Since they have for generations served China, we did not dare to retaliate. How could we expect that they could send slanderous accusations against us to confuse the emperor? Our country has always faithfully observed the imperial calendar, and pursued tribute relations faithfully, basking in the favor of the imperial court. How would we dare to harbor disloyal feelings and seek relations with other countries? Moreover, the Khitan dwell on the other side of the Liao Sea, and there are moreover two more rivers that separate us, so there is no way for us to go there. Furthermore, among the Jurchen who fled the troubles there are more than ten who received official positions in our country. Also, among the envoys who were called to the imperial court to present tribute, you can call them to court to sift through all the facts in this story and

---

47 Mokkye 木契: apparently the Jurchen and also the Khitan often used wood as a medium for official communications, perhaps because they lacked paper or because it was more appropriate for important communications to foreign powers.

establish the truth. Please relay what I said to the emperor." Han Guohua agreed to do this.

Winter, tenth month. It was forbidden to relinquish one's house to turn it into a temple.

This year, regulations for the five mourning grades and the commensurate number of holidays for officials were newly established. In the case of mourning clothes to be worn for three years, hundred days are granted. For mourning clothes to be worn for a year, thirty days are granted. For mourning clothes to be worn for nine months twenty days, and for those worn for five months fifteen days; finally for mourning clothes worn during a period of three months, seven days of holidays are granted.

Sŏngjong Fifth year [986]

Third year of the Yongxi era of Song, fourth year of the Tonghe era of Khitan

Spring, first month. The Khitan sent Kwŏllyŏl to propose a peace treaty.

Third month. Ch'oe Yŏngnin passed the composition test of the civil service examination.

For the first time, edicts (*cho* 詔) were called "royal instructions" (*kyo* 敎).

Summer, fifth month. A royal instruction said "For a country, the people are its foundations; for the people, food is like Heaven. If you want to embrace the mind of the ordinary people, you should simply refrain from interfering with their essential tasks during the three [main seasons for] agriculture. You, officials of the twelve departments and all prefectures and garrisons, from now till autumn you should stop making people perform various [corvée] tasks, and make them focus only on agriculture. I will send out officials to assess whether agricultural lands are fallow or cultivated, and whether local prefects are diligent or not [in enforcing this measure]. On the basis of this, rewards will be given or punishments meted out."

Autumn, seventh month. A royal instruction read "I heard that 'virtue consists of nothing but good government. Government lies in nurturing the people; for a country, the people are its foundations; for the people, food is like Heaven.' Thus our T'aejo constructed black granaries for the relief of the poor people, and this became a permanent institution. Now the population is gradually increasing and the provisions are no longer sufficient, so they should be increased by 10,000 *sŏk* of rice. Also, the name shall be changed to 'righteous granaries.' It is my wish that all prefectures have these righteous granaries. Local offices should inspect the population size of their locality and also itemize what is in their granaries, and report this to me."

A royal instruction said: "I am ashamed of my habitual lack of virtue, yet sincerely esteem Confucianism and wish to make the customs of the Lord of Zhou and Confucius flourish, in the hope of recreating the rule of Yao and Shun. Having established schools to nurture them and an examination system to select them, students have been sent from all the prefectures [to the capital]. My concern was that many may miss their hometown, so I have ordered that they should be able to either stay in the capital or return as they wish. [As for those who decided to return] please listen to my words, and do not neglect your study. To the 207 students who decided to return, please bestow 1,400 bolts of cloth, and to the fifty-three students who remain in the capital, bestow 106 caps and 265 *sŏk* of rice." Thereupon the king sent the Secretarial Receptionist Ko Yŏng'am to the Department of Guest Affairs to transmit this edict [throughout the country] together with wine and fruits.

A royal instruction said, "If there are people who hide and use runaway slaves, in accordance with the law statute that says 'one day [will be punished by] three feet of raw silk,' they will be penalized with thirty feet of cloth per day,[48] to be given to the original owner. However, even though the number of days is big, the total penalty should not exceed the original price of the slave."

Eighth month. For the first time, and throughout the twelve departments, those going to a locality to take up office were allowed to bring their spouse

48 Presumably because there was insufficient silk production in Korea, the penalty was transmuted to cloth.

and children.

Ninth month. A royal instruction warned officials of people in the departments not to clog up the prisons and courts, but to keep the granaries full for the relief of the poor. They should also encourage agriculture and sericulture, keep corvée labor light and taxes low, and settle affairs equitably.

This year, Ch'oe Han and Wang Im were sent to Song to matriculate in the academy.

Sŏngjong Sixth year [987]

Fourth year of the Yongxi era of Song, fifth year of the Tonghe era of Khitan

Spring, first month. A royal instruction read, "From the second month to the tenth month is the period when all the myriad things get born and grow, and thus it should be forbidden to set fire to the mountain areas. Those who disregard this ban shall be punished. Let this be a permanent rule."

Third month. The Minister of the Royal Secretariat Ch'oe Chimong died. Ch'oe Chimong hailed from Yŏng'am Prefecture in Namhae, and his name as a youth was Ch'oe Ch'ongjin. He had an optimistic nature and was upright and kind to others. Being intelligent and fond of learning, he was widely read in classics and histories, but was especially well versed in astronomy and prognostication. When he was eighteen T'aejo heard about his reputation and summoned him to analyze his dreams to look for auspicious signs. Ch'oe Chimong said "You shall definitely unify the Three Han." T'aejo was pleased and changed his name to "Chimong" (he who understands dreams). He granted him silk robes and an official position as royal assistant. Whenever T'aejo went on a military campaign, he always kept Ch'oe Chimong close by his side. When he ascended the throne, Ch'oe Chimong was always at the ready in the royal palace to give advice to the king. Hyejong gave him a position in the Bureau of Astronomy. When Chŏngjong executed Wang Kyu, in appreciation of his advice that a falling star augured an uprising, he bestowed on him slaves, a horse with a silver-encrusted saddle, and silver implements. Once he joined King Kwangjong on a trip to Kwibŏp-sa, but committed an offense after getting drunk and was banished to Oegŏl County.[49] There he stayed for eleven years until he was called back by Kyŏngjong, who made him Minister of the Advisory Council. When Sŏngjong ascended, he made him Executive Official of the Left, and Acting Minister of the Royal Secretariat, Supreme Pillar of State. He also bestowed the title of Merit Subject who Advanced Letters, Glorified the Transformation, and Established Principle. He also ennobled his parents. When he reached the age of seventy-eight, he thrice requested to retire, but each time it was refused. When he again sent a letter firmly requesting retirement, he was given exemption from court meetings, but had to personally attend to affairs in the Royal Secretariat (Naesabang) as before. Three years later he lay ill in bed, and the king sent physicians and medicine, and even went to personally enquire after his health. Every method that might cure him was tried, but he finally died at the age of eighty-one. When the king heard the news of his death, he was grief stricken, and ordered a condolence gift of 1,000 bolts of cloth, 300 *sŏk* of rice, 200 *sŏk* of barley, 200 horns of tea, and 20 *kŭn*[50] of incense. He also ordered officials to take care of the funeral. Ch'oe Chimong was posthumously invested as Grand Mentor of the Heir Apparent, and given the title Minhyu. Later he was further promoted to Grand Preceptor, and enshrined in the Royal Ancestor Hall of Kyŏngjong.

Summer, sixth month. Weapons from various prefectures were gathered and recast as farming implements.

Autumn, seventh month. A royal instruction read, "Slaves who have been manumitted are bound to become insolent towards their former masters as time passes. Currently, some have fought in sea battles instead of their masters, and some have spent three years in a grass hut beside the grave [of their master's kin]. Upon the master reporting this to the appropriate office, after confirming their merit and ascertaining that they are more than forty

---

49 Location unknown.

50 "Pound," on average 640 grams. See table of weights and measures.

years of age, they are given permission to shed their base status. However, if they are then found to have insulted their original masters, they have to return to base status and have to perform the labor assigned to them."

Eighth month. The king ordered Yi Mongyu to determine the forms of official documents that were passed on between the central bureaucracy and provincial bureaucracy, and between offices.

The king issued a royal instruction to the effect that Chŏng Uhyŏn had passed the composition test of the civil service examination, together with one person for the classics examination, one for the divination examination, two for the medicine examination, and two for the law examination. This was the first time that the roster was displayed and a royal instruction issued [to announce those who passed the examinations].

The king issued a royal instruction ordering that one doctor of classical learning and one doctor of medicine should be appointed in each of the twelve departments. This would ensure that the administrators of departments as well as those in charge of prefectures and counties would step up their efforts towards education and instruction. Furthermore, if there were those worth employing because of their talents in the classics, their filial love, or their medical expertise, in accordance with the old customs of the Han dynasty their deeds were to be recorded and they were to be recommended to the capital. This became a permanent rule.

Winter, tenth month. The P'algwanhoe in Kaesŏng as well as the one in P'yŏngyang were no longer held.

Eleventh month. Kyŏngju was changed to Eastern Capital resident governorship.

This year the five districts [of the capital Kaesŏng] were determined.

Sŏngjong Seventh year [988]

First year of the Duangong era of Song, sixth year of the Tonghe era of Khitan

Spring, second month. The Left Rectifier of Omissions Yi Yang sent the following memorial: "According to the *Monthly Ordinances* [of the *Book of Rites*], 'before the advent of spring an ox made of clay should be brought out to determine the timing of agriculture.' Please reintroduce such customs of old and make them a regular practice. According to the 'Ministers of the Court' chapter of the *Rites of Zhou*, 'In early spring decree that the queen should lead the people of the six courts, nurture the seed of early ripening and late ripening rice, and offer them to the king.' Now to pray for a good harvest your highness should hold the first plowing ceremony and the queen should definitely perform the ceremony of offering the seedlings. According to the *Monthly Ordinances*, after the emergence of vital energy in the first month of the year, no female animals should be used for sacrifices, and trees should not be cut. No young animals should be hunted or eggs taken, and people should not gather in large groups. Skeletons should be covered and corpses buried.' I request that these ordinances for the spring are promulgated so that all know what is forbidden at this time." The king followed his advice, and issued a royal instruction that was displayed in the capital and in the provinces.

Autumn, ninth month. Yi Wi and three others passed the composition test of the civil service examination, and two people passed the medical examination.

Winter, tenth month. Song sent the Executive of the Ministry of Rites Lü Duan and the Left Grand Master of Remonstrance Lü Youzhi to invest the king as acting Defender-in-chief, and grant him a stipend village of 1,000 households, with 500 households being effective. As before he was [recognized as] concurrent Greatly Obedient Military Envoy, Commander-in-chief of Hyŏnt'o Commissioned with Extraordinary Powers over military affairs in Hyŏnt'o, pillar of state and King of Koryŏ. The king's prestige titles and merit ranks were also as before. This year in the first month the Song emperor had personally conducted the first plowing, had issued a general amnesty, changed the reign title, and bestowed many favors on all official, both in the capital and in the provinces. Following this he sent Lü Duan and his retinue to invest the king and inform him through an edict of the amnesty. The king received the investiture, and pardoned all those who committed crimes lighter than that of murder. For those civil officials who had served for a long time, he changed [the color of] their robes. Those military officials who were advanced in years yet had no children, and had been on the military roster since the *kyemyo* year (943) he sent back to their home villages. To all civil and military officials he bestowed favors, and for those civil and military officials who regularly attended court audiences, he granted titles of nobility to their parents and spouses. He also reduced the debts of people and helped the destitute.

This year there was a locust plague. The king reduced the tax on assets; those fields which had been damaged 40 per cent were exempted from the land tax; those whose fields had been damaged 60 per cent were exempted from the land tax as well as the cloth tax; those whose fields had been damaged 70 per cent were exempted from the land tax, cloth tax, and corvée labor.

Ch'oe Sŭngno was made acting Director of the Chancellery.

For the first time the five shrines were established.

Sŏngjong Eighth year [989]

Second year of the Duangong era of Song, seventh year of the Tonghe era of Khitan

Spring, second month. A royal instruction read "I heard that those among the scholar-gentry at court and outside of it who fall ill cannot obtain a physician, and also do not have medicine. Thus, there are many who do not get better. From now on, for civil officials from rank 5 and above, and military officials from rank 4 upwards and above who fall ill, the office to which they belong should make a record and make arrangements for a physician and medicines so that they can be cured." All the officials sent a memorial of gratitude.

Third month. For the first time military commissioners for the Northeast region and the Northwest region were instituted. The director of the Chancellery, the royal secretary, and the director of the Department of

Ministries were appointed as officials in charge.[51] Furthermore there was one military commissioner and one chief military administrator,[52] both of the third rank. There were also two deputy chiefs, three administrative assistants, and four recorders. The officials in charge remained in the capital whereas the military commissioner went to a garrison [on the border]. The king personally handed him his military insignia, and gave him full authority over the border region.

Summer, fourth month. A royal instruction read "I greatly esteem academies and schools; sleeping or waking, I always worry about them. Recently, among the lists of names of people recommended from the provinces that I perused, only the Assistant Instructor at the National Academy Song Sŭngyŏn and the Doctor of Classics Chŏn Poin from Naju department in Namhae Province are teaching truly diligently. In this they fully accord with Confucius' intention of broad learning. In their tireless teaching, they correspond with my own mind of encouraging learning. They should be duly rewarded and promoted to show my special concern for excellence. Song Sŭngyŏn will be promoted beyond the ninth grade and will be made doctor at the National Academy, and also be granted one red official robe. Chŏn Poin shall be granted one official robe and fifty *sŏk* of grain. Henceforth, all those civil officials who have less than ten students, when their term of office ends and when they are to be transferred, their records should be presented to me so as to determine praise or censure. Of the classics doctors from the twelve departments, those who do not even have a single student who takes the civil service examination, when their term ends successfully they will still remain in the same office to censure their results [in not producing competent students]. Taking this into account when granting bureaucratic ranks shall become a permanent procedure."

---

51 Whether the term *pyŏngmasa* 兵馬使 (military commissioner) at this point refers only to an official, or to a full-fledged office, is a moot point. There is an entry for 1029 suggesting that it only became an office in that year, but already at this point it may have functioned virtually as a separate office. The three officials in charge represent the heads of the *samsŏng*, the three departments, that were formally established only under Munjong.

52 *Chibyŏngmasa* 知兵馬事.

Construction on the Ancestral Shrine (Taemyo 大廟) started. The king personally led his officials to carry building materials.

For the first time capital officials below the sixth grade were required to be tested four times before promotion; those from grade 5 upwards needed a royal decree. This became a permanent procedure.

Fifth month. The acting Director of the Chancellery Ch'oe Sŭngno died. Ch'oe Sŭngno hailed from Kyŏngju and was endowed with intelligence and wisdom. He loved learning and was good at composition. When he was twelve T'aejo summoned him to court and made him read the *Analects*. He praised him effusively and granted a salt basin. The next year the king ordered that he be affiliated with the Academy of Letters (Wŏnbong-sŏng 元鳳省) as a student, and bestowed a saddled horse as well as a regular food stipend of twenty *sŏk*. From this time forward he was entrusted with the composition of important letters. Ch'oe Sŭngno loyally served successive kings, and rose to the rank of executive chief of the Chancellery. He submitted a letter of resignation but it was not accepted. Shortly afterwards he was made director of the Chancellery, and invested as Lord of Ch'ŏngha, with a stipend village of 700 households. Repeatedly he begged to retire, but each time his requests were refused. Finally he died of illness at the age of sixty-three. The king was deeply saddened, and issued a royal instruction to praise his merit and virtue, and to bestow him posthumously with the office of Grand Preceptor. As a condolence gift the king granted 1,000 bolts of cloth, 300 *sŏk* of flour, 500 *sŏk* of non-glutinous rice, 100 ounces of frankincense, 200 cups of Noewŏn tea, and 10 pounds of leaf tea.

Autumn, eighth month. A royal instruction was issued to exhort and encourage students and students of medicine in all twelve departments and the various prefectures; they were also given wine and food.

Ninth month. On the *kabo* [16th] day a comet appeared, and an amnesty was declared. The king reproached himself, and proceeded with caring for the elderly and weak and bringing relief to the lonely and cold. He employed the old meritorious elite, and rewarded filial sons and chaste wives; he also waived or reduced people's debts.

Winter, twelfth month. A royal instruction read, "Formerly, during the months when the deaths of his parents were commemorated, Emperor Taizong of Tang forbade the slaughter of animals and ordered monks to burn incense, read scriptures and pray for no more than five days. All the more so for me, who grew up pitying my parents and becoming orphaned at a young age. Thus I have not had the chance to repay the ultimate grace they bestowed. Every time my thought turns to them, I want to honor their legacy so as to embrace them in me. From now on I allow for a five-day commemoration on the memorial days of T'aejo and of my father, and a three-day commemoration on the memorial day of my mother. During those periods incense should be offered, scriptures read, and prayers intoned. Also, in the months [in which the memorial days fall] no animals should be slaughtered and no meat eaten." Afterwards the king personally visited the memorial temples to offer incense on the memorial days of T'aejo and his parents. In later generations this became the regular custom.

Ch'oe Tŭkchung and seventeen others passed the composition test of the civil service examination, one passed the classics test, and one the divination test.

The Executive Han In'gyŏng and the Office Chief of the Ministry of War Wi Tŏg'yu were sent to Song. The Song emperor granted them the [prestige title of] Grand Master for Splendid Happiness [2B].

Sŏngjong Ninth year [990]

First year of the Chunhua era of Song, eighth year of the Tonghe era of Khitan

Summer, sixth month. Song dispatched the Chief Minister of the Court of Imperial Entertainments Zi Chengwu and the Junior Minister at the Court of Imperial Sacrifices Zhao Huacheng to invest the king as Merit Subject Promoting Sincerity and Smoothening the Transformation, granting him a stipend village of 1,000 household with 400 effective. The remaining [titles of investiture and ranks] were as before. The king received the investiture and declared an amnesty for crimes less serious than murder. From the civil and military officials down to craftsmen all received benefices according to rank. Originally our country's customs were deeply enthralled by ritual avoidance and yin-yang prognostication. Every time a foreign embassy came, a month and day had to be chosen to receive the imperial edict. After Zi Chengwu had been in the embassy hostel for over a month, he complained about this. The next day the king received the edict. From this time onwards only the day was chosen to receive it.[53]

Autumn, seventh month. The Right Rectifier of Omissions Kim Simŏn requested that Liu Xiang's "Explanation on the Six Types of Correct and the Six Types of Incorrect [Behavior of officials]"[54] together with the "Six Articles for Government" for regional inspectors of the Han Dynasty should be promulgated in the capital and provinces and posted on the walls of government offices as a warning and as encouragement. The king approved of this.

Ninth month. A royal instruction said: "Of all the basic [virtues] to govern a country, none exceeds filial piety. We dispatched officials to the six circuits to promulgate the instruction, which was aimed at finding filial sons, obedient grandsons, righteous husbands, and chaste wives. Now there was the commoner from Kurye County called Son Sunhŭng. His mother died of illness, so he made a portrait of her and offered to it. Once every three days he visited her grave and offered her food as if she were alive. Ch'adal and his two brothers from Chibul station in Unje County together cared for their mother. Because his wife was not diligent in looking after her mother in law, he divorced her. His two younger brothers also did not marry to devote themselves to care for her filially. When the mother of Pak Kwangnyŏm, from the Western Capital, died, he made a statue of her [his mother] from dead wood and offered to it with full rites. The commoner Nŭngsŏn from Nangsan Island in Namhae had a daughter called Hambu. When he died, she

---

53 Since before that both month and day had to be chosen, after the Chinese protested presumably an auspicious day within the current month was chosen.

54 Liu Xiang (ca. 77 BC – ca. 6 BC) was a Confucian scholar of the Western Han dynasty. This text can be found in the chapter on the "art of the minister" in his *Shuo yuan* 說苑.

turned his sleeping room into a funerary chamber, and for five months she presented him with food just as when he was alive. The daughter of Chŏng Kangjun, a commoner from Yŏng'il County, whose name was Cha'i, and the daughter Mr. Ch'oe from the capital, both became widows when still young, but did not remarry and filially served their parents-in-law. The Sub-colonel Cho Yŏng from Chŏlch'ung District buried his mother in the family garden, and offered to her in the morning and evening.

As for Hambu and the other seven sons and daughters, they should be granted insignia of virtue to be displayed at their dwelling, and they are exempted from corvée labor. In the case of taxable commoners (*paekchŏng* 白丁), they should be given public land as their personal household land. As for Ch'adal and his brothers, and Hambu and the other people, they are relieved from their [compulsory] residence in postal stations and islands, and may register themselves in a prefecture or county of their choice. Son Sunhŭng and four others should be made candidates for office so that their filial behavior can be made known. Now the Royal Recording Secretary Kim Simŏn and others should be dispatched to bestow 100 *sŏk* of grains to each, as well as two silver basins, and 68 bolts of colored silk and cloth. The sub-colonel Cho Yŏng is to be raised ten grades to Grand Master of Imperial Entertainments with Silver Seal and Blue Ribbon (3B), Acting General Censor, Left Military Marquis and Junior Colonel of the Wiik palace 衛翊府.[55] He should also be granted one official robe, 30 ounces of silver, and 20 bolts of silk.

Verily, the king is the leader of all people; and the multitude of people are the king's substance. If the people do good things, then that is the king's blessings; if they do evil things, that is also the king's worry. [Therefore] we manifest and make known filial behavior towards parents, and we should be intent on using this to ameliorate our customs. If an ignorant commoner deep in the remote mountains still is diligently thinking about filial piety, then how could the officials and scholars be indolent in honoring their

55 Translations of these titles are tentative; they appear to be too lavish in relation to the merit of Cho Yŏng; moreover, they mix civil and military titles.

forebears? If someone can be filial at home, he will perforce be a loyal minister for the country. All gentry and commoners alike should take heed of my words."

A royal instruction read: "Our T'aejo founded the Western Capital and dispatched members of the royal clan hither, and guarded it as the 'throat' of the kingdom. Every spring and summer, he travelled to the Western Capital to perform sacrifices. He wanted to protect the border region against barbarians and make the border defenses strong. Now I am ready to inspect the state of the terrain and assess the safety of the people; to assess whether the number of local officials is adequate, and whether local rituals should be reduced or augmented. As for the ritual guards, attendants, officials, royal luncheons, and musicians [who accompany the king there], these should all be reduced. The resident governor of the Western Capital and his staff, as well as the prefects of all the localities and the generals of the garrisons on the road there, should all remain in post [for the royal retinue]."

Winter, tenth month. The king went on a tour to the Western Capital. In all the localities that he passed through, he made all those who were imprisoned, except those who had committed one of the ten heinous acts or manslaughter, be released. He also granted elevation in rank to prefectures, counties, and postal stations commensurate with their status. To all officials of the Western Capital who were more than eighty years old, or who had mothers or wives that were eighty or more, he gave presents commensurate with their rank. Those among the ordinary people who were over eighty or who were seriously ill, he granted cloth and rice, again commensurate with their status. For those who were 100 or over, he made officials of the fourth rank of the Western Capital visit their family to enquire after their health. If there were soldiers among his retinue who had elderly parents, he allowed them to return earlier.

The king installed the Left and Right Military Garrison.

Twelfth month. The king made his nephew Wang Song Prince of Kaeryŏng.[56]

---

56 This is the later King Mokchong (r. 997-1009).

This year, the king issued a royal instruction to install a Scriptorium in the Western Capital. He made the students copy classics and history books, to store them in the Sciptorium. He ordered the censor to select officials for the Scriptorium and report their names to the throne.

The king sent the Executive of the Ministry of War Han Ŏn'gong to Song to thank the emperor for his kindness.

Sŏngjong Tenth year [991]

Second year of the Chunhua era of Song, ninth year of the Tonghe era of Khitan

Spring, second month. The king dispatched special envoys to enquire after people's health and other troubles throughout all the circuits.

Intercalary [second] month. For the first time the [Shrine for] the Deities of the Grain and Earth was established.

Ch'oe Hang and six others passed the composition test of the civil service examination and three passed the classics test.

Fourth month. Han Ŏn'gong returned from Song, and offered a copy of the complete collection of Buddhist scriptures. The king personally welcomed him into the palace, and declared a pardon through a royal instruction. Earlier, Han Ŏn'gong had been sent to Song to request the scriptures, and the emperor decreed that they should be granted. He also bestowed the titles of acting minister of war and censor-in-chief on him.

Autumn, seventh month. Because there was a drought, the king issued a royal instruction to take care of the elderly.

Winter, tenth month. The king traveled to the Western Capital. In every prefecture or county he passed through, if there was a father or elderly person who offered him beef or wine, he gave the wine to his soldiers and returned the beef. Among the households of commoners, if there were some who could not till the land because of illness he waived their land rent and taxes. For those whose disease was very severe he granted medicine. He also told the officials in charge that even though the purpose of the procession was to offer a sacrifice [in the Western Capital], it was also to inspect the provinces. All those of eighty or over were to be given special relief.

Han Ŏn'gong memorialized as follows: "The Security Council of the Song Dynasty corresponds exactly to the offices of those officials who are on permanent call in our court." Thereupon, for the first time the Security Council (Ch'umirwŏn 樞密院) was installed in Koryŏ.

The Jurchen from across the Amnok River were chased away and made to reside beyond Mt. Paektu.

The Hallim Academician Paek Sayu was sent to Song to give thanks for the bestowal of the Buddhist scriptures.

Sŏngjong Eleventh year [992]

Third year of the Chunhua era of Song, tenth year of the Tonghe era of Khitan

Spring, first month. A royal instruction read: "Without accumulating learning it is impossible to discover goodness; without employing the wise it is impossible to succeed. Therefore, within the capital I opened academies and institutes that foster Confucian skills, and in the provinces installed schools to encourage students to take a study course. I also encouraged the opening of comparative tests to deepen knowledge of the classics; yet I have as yet failed to discover a truly outstanding scholar. How can I be sure there is not someone who is obscuring wisdom and shielding talent? All those who have literary prowess or military skill should come to the palace to recommend themselves."

Summer, fifth month. A royal instruction commanded all capital officials of the fifth rank and above to recommend one person; his talents and virtue were to be described in a letter and presented to the throne together with the person's name.

Sixth month. Song dispatched the Chief Minister of the Court for Imperial Entertainments, Liu Shi, and the Vice Director of the Palace Library, Chen

Jing, to additionally invest the king as Acting Grand Preceptor with a stipend village of 1,000 households, 400 of which were effective; all other titles were as before. Earlier, when Paek Sayu went to Song, the clerk in charge of files, Chang Injŏn, had sent a memorial to the emperor about the situation [in Koryŏ], but Paek Sayu suspected that he had divulged state secrets. Thereupon Chang Injŏn did not dare to return [to Koryŏ]. Then the emperor ordered Chen Jing and the rest of the embassy to take him back, and sent a decree explaining that Chang Injŏn had not committed any crime. The king then sent a memorial, the gist of which is as follows: "This insignificant person only pursues my self-interest, how would I dare to mete out a punish that is excessive? Your highness from afar bestowed a munificent and graceful decree full of concern, so I already cleared Chang Injŏn of any wrongdoing."

Autumn, seventh month. Wang Uk 王郁 was exiled to Sasu County.[57] Wang Uk was the eighth son of T'aejo. His residence was located close to the private residence of Lady Hwangbo,[58] the spouse of Kyŏngjong. After Kyŏngjong passed away, she left the palace and moved here. Once she dreamt that she had climbed the Kok Pass and urinated, inundating the whole country, which was covered in a silver-like sea. When she asked a diviner about the dream, he explained that "you will give birth to a son who will become king and rule the whole country." The queen said, "I have recently been widowed, so how could I bear a son?" Later, however, she had an incestuous relation with Wang Uk. People did not dare to talk about this, since she was a daughter of Taejong.[59] One day when she was sleeping in the residence of Wang Uk, people in the house piled up firewood in the courtyard and set fire to it. The blaze alerted the king, who immediately came to see if everyone was alright; thus he found out what

57 Modern Sach'ŏn in South Kyŏngsang Province. Wang Uk later received the title Anjong.

58 She was later styled Queen Hŏnjŏng.

59 Taejong 戴宗, given name Wang Uk 王旭 (note the different spelling of this Wang Uk!). A son of T'aejo through his fourth wife, Queen Sinjŏng née Hwangbo. He married Queen Sŏnŭi, née Yu, a daughter through T'aejo with his sixth wife Queen Chŏngdŏk. Note also that this Wang Uk apparently passed on his mother's surname to his daughter.

had happened. Since Wang Uk had violated the norms of duty and honor, he was exiled. Queen Hwangbo had to return to her own residence, but when she reached the gate, the baby moved in her belly, so she grasped a branch of the willow tree in front of the gate, gave birth, and died. The king selected a foster mother to raise the child. When he became two, he summoned the foster mother with the child to see how he was doing; when they entered, the child looked at the king and called him "dad." When he was put in the king's lap, he fondled the lapels of his robes and again called him "dad." The king took pity on him, and said, the tears rolling from his eyes "the child misses his father." He was then sent to Sasu County to be with his father Wang Uk. The boy was none other than Wang Sun [the future King Hyŏnjong].

Ch'oe Han and Wang Im passed the examination for foreign guests in Song, were granted the office of assistant in the palace library, and returned home.

Ninth month. In Tŭngju, rice ears of seven inches and millet ears of one foot four inches appeared. The officials wanted to offer congratulations, but the king did not allow this.

Winter, eleventh month. The names of all greater prefectures, districts, prefectures, counties, passes, postal stations, rivers, and harbors[60] were changed.

Twelfth month. The Ancestral Shrine was finished. The king asked his ministers to discuss the relative order and position of the shrines for different kings, and also the protocol for the ancestral offerings, and report their conclusions to him.

A National Academy was established by royal instruction, and it was endowed with fields and estates.

The king personally sacrificed in the Ancestral Shrine.

---

60 州府郡縣關驛江浦

Sŏngjong Twelfth year [993]

Fourth year of the Chunhua era of Song, eleventh year of the Tonghe era of Khitan

Spring, second month. Ever-stable Granaries were established in the two capitals and the twelve departments.

Third month. A royal instruction read: "The son of heaven establishes an ancestral shrine with seven halls, and feudal lords ancestral shrines with five halls [to commemorate] the merits of ancestors and the virtue of the family. To the left are the Shao 昭 halls and to the right the Mu 穆 halls. Great filial piety moves the spirits, and utmost virtue affects heaven and earth. Now from last year we have finalized the Ancestral Shrine, so the place for sacrifices is complete and ready to be used for regular sacrifices in spring and autumn. The Shang dynasty had twelve lords over six generations, the Tang ten emperors in nine rooms. According to the *Jin shu*, 'Putting older and younger brothers next to each other [in the same room] is a departure from the Rites.' It is befitting that a spirit gets one room, but it is not right that a room should be limited in terms of spirits. That brothers are put in the same line [i.e. in one shrine chamber] is attested in ritual texts. This is all the more so for great King Hyejong; if we discuss him in terms of the same generation, then he cannot be separated off [into a separate chamber]. Together venerate the spirit tablets of Hyejong, Chŏngjong, Kwangjong, and Kyŏngjong in one shrine [chamber] which is part of the Great Shrine."

Summer, fifth month. The Jurchen on the northwestern border reported that the Khitan were readying an army to invade Koryŏ. The court deliberated that they were trying to deceive us, so no preparations were made.

Autumn, eighth month. Yi Yuhyŏn and nine others passed the composition test of the civil service examination, three passed the classics examination, and three the law examination.

The Jurchen again reported that the Khitan had arrived [at the border]. For the first time people realized the urgency of the situation, and military envoys were sent to all provinces to prepare troops.

Winter, tenth month. The Chancellor of the State Council Pak Yangyu was made supreme commander, the Vice-Chancellor of the Royal Secretariat Sŏ Hŭi was made middle commander, and Executive Chief of the Chancellery Ch'oe Ryang lower commander. Their army was placed in the northern border region to block the Khitan.

Intercalary [tenth] month]. The king went to the Western Capital and then proceeded to Anbuk District. There he heard that the Khitan general Xiao Sunning had attacked Pongsan Prefecture and captured our advance troop commander the Reviewing Policy Advisor Yun Sŏan and others. The king could thus not proceed further and returned. Sŏ Hŭi then led his troops with the aim of saving Pongsan. However Xiao Sunning made it known to him that his dynasty had already occupied the old territories of Koguryŏ, and that Koryŏ was thus infringing on its borders; hence this punitive expedition. He also sent a letter with the following contents: "Our great dynasty has already unified the four quarters; those who have not submitted will be annihilated, so please surrender quickly and don't tarry around here." When Sŏ Hŭi had read the letter, he returned and sent a letter to the king advising him to settle for peace. The king dispatched the Investigating Censor and Acting Deputy Director of Protocol Yi Mongjŏn to the Khitan camp to settle for peace. Xiao Sunning again sent a letter saying "800,000 troops have amassed here. If you do not come out to the river [presumably the Amnok] and submit, you will be annihilated. Both the king and his ministers should speedily submit before my army." Yi Mongjŏn reached his camp and enquired after the reason why the Khitan wanted to invade. Xiao Sunning said: "Your country does not care for the people's affairs, therefore we are entitled to effectuate Heaven's punishment on you. If you want to sue for peace, you should speedily come to submit."

Yi Mongjŏn returned. The king gathered all his ministers for deliberations. Some said that the king should return to his palace in the capital, and then at the head of his ministers and troops go there to surrender. Some said that he "should cut off all the territory north of the Western Capital and give it to them; a line should be drawn from Hwangju [in the west] to Chŏl Pass [in the east], which will be the border." The king was inclined to follow the latter opinion. He opened the granaries of the Western Capital, and after the people obtained their share, there still remained a lot, so as the king feared it would be used by the enemy, he ordered it to be thrown into the Taedong River. Sŏ Hŭi petitioned as follows: "If the food is sufficient, then the fortress can hold and the war can be won. In war, victory and defeat do not depend on strength or weakness, but on waiting for the right opportunity to make a move. How can you rashly order the rice to be thrown away! All the more so since food is the people's lifeblood. It would be better if it fell into enemy hands; vainly throwing it into the river is, I fear, not in accord with Heaven's intentions." The king agreed and ordered that the soldiers stop with throwing away the rice.

Sŏ Hŭi then added, "the several hundred *li* of territory between the eastern capital of the Khitan and our Anbuk District used to belong to the proto-Jurchen. Kwangjong took it and built fortresses such as Kaju and Songsŏng. Now the true goal for why the Khitan army came is nothing but to seize these two fortresses. Although they proclaim that they want to seize the ancient Koguryŏ territories, in fact they fear us. Now, seeing that their army is great in number and therefore handing over the territory north of the Western Capital cannot be called a plan. Isn't the territory north of Samgak-san also ancient Koguryŏ territory? Since man's desire is boundless, they will then keep asking for more, so should we then just keep giving? If we give up territory now, it will truly be a shame that lasts ten-thousand generations. Please your majesty, return to the capital and let us first fight them; after that it is still not too late to negotiate."

The former minister for taxation,[61] Yi Chibaek, petitioned as follows: "Since our divine ancestor [T'aejo] founded the nation until the present, there has not been a single loyal minister who wanted to rashly and without grounds give territory to an enemy; how tragic this would be! The ancients had a poem that goes as follows: 'A thousand leagues of rivers and mountains is nothing to a child; the officials of two reigns lamented

61 *Minkwan ŏsa* 民官御事.

Jiaozhou's actions.' Now, Jiaozhou was an important minister of Shu, who recommended a later ruler to offer territory to Wei.[62] Thus he was the laughing stock of a thousand generations. Rather than rashly cutting off territory and throwing it to the enemy, how about reviving the traditions of our first kings, namely the Eight Commandments celebration, Lantern Festival, and divine lad? Isn't this better than strange ways from a different country to protect the country and establish peace? If your highness agrees, then we should first inform the spirits [of our ancestors] and then either fight or sue for peace, that is up your highness." At the time, the king was much enthralled by Chinese culture, which made many citizens disgruntled. That is the reason Yi Chibaek mentioned this.

After Yi Mongjŏn had returned, since he did not report for a long time, Xiao Sunning attacked Anyung Garrison. But the senior colonel Taedosu and the junior colonel Kyŏngbang fought with him and carried the day. Xiao Sunning did not dare to advance again and sent someone to again urge Koryŏ to submit. The king sent as peace envoy the presenting official of the royal archives Chang Hyŏng to the Khitan camp. Xiao Sunning told him "You should send a high minister to talk in front of my army." Chang Hyŏng returned, and the king gathered all his ministers, asking "who can go the enemy camp and use his negotiating skills to remove the enemy army and establish merit that will last ten thousand generations?" There was no one among the ministers who replied. Only Sŏ Hŭi spoke: "Your subject is not bright, yet I do not dare not to follow your command." The king accompanied him to the river crossing, and holding his hands he comforted him and then sent him off. Sŏ Hŭi, carrying the state letter, entered the Khitan camp. He treated Xiao Sunning on equal terms, without flinching in the least. Xiao Sunning found this strange, and told Sŏ Hŭi: "Your country emerged in the territory of Silla; the territory of Koguryŏ belongs to us, but you have invaded it. Also, although our countries share a border, you cross the sea to serve Song. This is why our great country set out to punish

62 A story from the Three Kingdoms period in China; the 'later ruler' probably refers to a successor of Liu Bei, the founder of Shu Han, and mortal enemy of Cao Cao of Wei.

you. Now if you give up the territory [of Koguryŏ] and offer it to us, and establish tribute relations with us, everything will be OK."

Sŏ Hŭi replied "you are wrong. Our country is nothing but the former Koguryŏ. Therefore we have called it Koryŏ and made P'yŏngyang the capital. As far as borders are concerned, the eastern capital of your country is completely within our borders, so how can you talk about an infraction of your borders? Furthermore, both banks of the Amnok River are within our borders. Now the Jurchen have stolen themselves in between [our and your country] and are slyly but consistently deceiving everyone. All the roads [to Khitan territory] are completely blocked, even the sea routes they have infiltrated. The reason that we are unable to send tribute missions is none other than the Jurchen. If you could drive out the Jurchen and return our former lands so that we can build fortresses to protect the roads, how would we dare not to send tribute missions? General, if you transmit my words to your emperor, how could he not accept my words and feel pity?"

Since his words were brimming with righteous indignity, Xiao Sunning knew that he could not force Sŏ Hŭi [to bend to his will], so he transmitted his words to the Khitan emperor, who said "since Koryŏ is requesting peace, withdraw the troops." Sŏ Hŭi stayed in the Khitan camp for seven days and then returned. The king was extremely pleased, and went out to meet him at the river ferry. He also wanted to dispatch the chancellor, Pak Yangyu, as a goodwill ambassador to the Khitan emperor. Sŏ Hŭi again addressed the king: "Your subject has made a pact with the Khitan that only after they have pacified the Jurchen and we have recovered our territory will we send envoys to their court. Now we have barely recovered the territory within the river; if we request that embassies can only be sent after the territory beyond the river is occupied by us, there will then still be time to send envoys." The king replied, "since we have not sent tribute missions for a long time, I'm afraid that not sending one now will invite trouble." He then dispatched Pak Yangyu.

Sŏngjong Thirteenth year [994]

Fifth year of the Chunhua era of Song, twelfth year of the Tonghe era of Khitan

Spring, second month. Xiao Sunning sent the following letter: "Recently I received the following words from the emperor: 'However, not only have we established a trustworthy relation with that country for a long time, also our countries share a border. Even though the small serving the great is a firm rule or propriety, only if the beginnings are firm will the end be reached; only then will relations endure for a long time. If we do not prepare well, I fear that the envoys will find the road blocked. Following deliberations with that country, along the buffer roads fortifications should be built and walls moated.' In accordance with this decree, as you deem fit observe the Amnok well and among its western villages construct five fortresses. In order for the construction to start in the beginning of the third month, manpower should be brought to the construction sites. I humbly request the great king [of Koryŏ] to instruct your subjects to mark a course of 280 *li* from Anbuk District to the Amnok River and inspect where the terrain is favorable and determine the exact locations [for the fortresses]. Then order the construction of the fortresses to commence and raise the laborers so that they can start simultaneously on all the fortresses. Before that report on how many fortresses altogether are to be built. The most important thing is a road is opened through which carts and horses carrying tribute can freely pass. Forever upholding the imperial court [of Liao] is the surest way to establish peace and prosperity."

For the first time Khitan era names were used.

Third month. The king ordered his officials "those who are orphaned from a young age and have no one to support them should be given food by officials until the age of ten. When they reach the age of 10, they should be allowed to choose where they want to reside."

Summer, fourth month. The king personally offered sacrifices at the Ancestral Shrine. The spirit tablets of T'aejo, Hyejong, Chŏngjong, Kwangjong, Taejong, and Kyŏngjong were enshrined. An amnesty was declared and civil and military officials were promoted by one rank, and those in charge of rituals by two ranks. The people were treated to banquets for three days, while the orphans and those living alone were given relief. Old people and those who had been in office for a long time were given rewards; debts were remitted and those with overdue taxes were also acquitted.

The king dispatched the chancellor, Pak Yangyu, with a memorial to present to the Khitan; it announced the adoption of the correct [viz. Khitan] calendar, and requested the return of prisoners of war.

Sixth month. The king dispatched Wŏn Uk to Song to requests troops, so as to take revenge for the wars of the previous year. Song, however, told him that since the northern border had barely been pacified, they could not rashly take a decision [that would upset the peace]. They treated him with due protocol before sending him back. This marked the rupture in relations with the Song.

Autumn, eighth month. The king personally took the confirmation test for the presented scholars, passing eight people including Ch'oe Wŏnsin. Also, nine scholars who took the classics test were confirmed.

In this year, the Khitan dispatched the Chief Minister of the Court of Imperial Entertainment[63] Xiao Suguan and the Censor-in-chief Li Yuan with an edict to comfort and embrace Koryŏ.

The king ordered the Executive [of the Royal Secretariat-Chancellery?] Sŏ Hŭi to lead his troops to attack and expel Jurchen, and to build fortifications for the two garrisons of Changhŭng and Kwihwa, and for the prefectures Kwakchu and Kuju.

For the first time an official in charge of the Amnok river ferry was installed, and Yi Sŭnggŏn was the first to take charge; shortly after he was replaced by Ha Kongjin.

An envoy was sent to the Khitan to offer entertainment girls, but they were refused.

63 Following Hucker (no. 1666), I regard Chongluqing 崇祿卿 as Guangluqing 光祿卿, an alternative form because of a taboo on the "guang" character.

Sŏngjong Fourteenth year [995]

First year of the Zhidao era of Song, thirteenth year of the Tonghe era of Khitan

Spring, second month. A royal instruction read: "I am worried that those scholars who should devote themselves to letters, once they pass the examination are completely immersed in their tasks [as officials], and neglect their original vocation [i.e. the cultivation of literate culture]. For those who are not yet fifty and have not yet written any important missives for the throne, the Hallim Academy should set a topic, and every month they should present three poems and one rhyme-prose poem. For those officials serving outside the capital, they should write thirty poems and one rhyme-prose poem themselves [i.e. without a set topic] and at year-end present them attached to the [files] the accounting clerks[64] [brought to the capital]. The Hallim Academy should then grade them and report to me."

The king dispatched Yi Chujŏng to Khitan to present local products.

Summer, fourth month. The Executive [of the Royal Secretariat-Chancellery] Ch'oe Ryang died. He was originally from Kyŏngju, and was magnanimous by nature. He was good at composition and after passing the examination became Doctor of Cultivated Letters.[65] When the king had not yet been enthroned, he summoned Ch'oe as his master and friend. After becoming king, he appointed Ch'oe to office, and he did not let anyone down. Because of illness he took leave of his office. The king said to his ministers: "100 days after taking leave Ch'oe Ryang will give notice of his position as censor and selection official; I have already assented to this. Considering that Ch'oe has shown complete loyalty since I was still a crown prince to save me from my ignorance, when I think about his meritorious service, I would not dare forget it." Thereupon he restored him to office, and after several promotions he became Executive Chief of the Royal Secretariat-Chancellery and Editor of State History. Upon his demise, the king was greatly saddened, and gave him the posthumous title of grand

---

64 Kyeri 計吏: local clerks who had to compile accounts and present them to the capital.

65 Kongmun paksa 攻文博士: this title appears only in Ch'oe Ryang's biography.

preceptor to the heir apparent. As condolence gift he provided 300 *sŏk* of rice, 200 *sŏk* of barley, and 1,000 cups of Noewŏn tea, and he was buried with full honors. He was granted the posthumous title of Kwangbin, and afterwards received the posthumous office titles of defender-in-chief, grand guardian, and great assistant (*taegwang* 大匡). He was enshrined together with the king in the Ancestral Shrine.

Fifth month. A royal instruction was promulgated, changing the bureaucratic nomenclature.

Autumn, seventh month. Kaeju was changed to Kaesŏng District, and was given jurisdiction over six 'raw' counties and seven capital area counties.[66] Also, the ten provinces (*to* 道) were decided. Kwannae-do was given jurisdiction over 29 prefectures and 82 counties; Chungwŏn-do over 13 prefectures and 42 counties; Hanam-do over 11 prefectures and 34 counties; Kangnam-do over nine prefectures and 43 counties; Yŏngnam-do over 12 prefectures and 48 counties; Yŏngdong-do over nine prefectures and 35 counties; Sannam-do over ten prefectures and 37 counties; Haeyang-do over 14 prefectures and 62 counties; Sŏkpang-do over seven prefectures and 62 counties; P'aesŏ-do over 14 prefectures, four counties and seven garrisons.

The king held the confirmation test for presented scholars and five scholars including Yi Charim were passed, as well as three scholars for the classics test.

In this year the king ordered the Executive Sŏ Hŭi to lead troops and construct fortifications for Anŭi and Hŭnghwa fortresses.

The king sent Yi Chibaek to Khitan to offer local products.

The king sent ten boys to the Khitan to learn their language.

The king sent the Left Transmitter of Edicts (3A) Cho Chirin to Khitan to request marriage with the daughter of the prefect of the Eastern Capital [of Khitan], the commander of reserve horses Xiao Hengde;[67] [the emperor]

---

66 Chŏk-hyŏn 赤縣: not certain what this refers to; ibid. for Ki-hyŏn 畿縣

67 Fuma[douwei] 駙馬[都尉]: according to Hucker (no. 2083), among other things a title conferred on imperial in-laws; this would imply that Xiao Hengde had married a daughter of the Khitan emperor, hence the need to ask the emperor permission to marry the daughter of his son-in-law.

granted this request.

Sŏngjong Fifteenth year [996]

Second year of the Zhidao era of Song, fourteenth year of the Tonghe era of Khitan

Spring, third month. Khitan dispatched the Hallim Academician Zhang Gan and the Military Commissioner for the Loyal and Upright Army, Xiao Shuge, to invest the king as Area Commander Unequalled in Honor [prestige title, 1B], Director of the Department of Ministries, King of Koryŏ. When Zhang Gan and the others reached the western suburbs, an altar was constructed for the investiture ceremony; the king received the investiture with proper ritual and declared a general amnesty.

The king dispatched Han Ŏn'gyŏng to Khitan to present silk and other precious gifts.

Summer, fourth month. Iron coins were cast.

Autumn, seventh month. Wang Uk died in Sasu County. Wang Uk excelled in composition and was also proficient in geomancy. Before he died, he secretly left behind a bag of gold for his son Wang Sun,[68] with the instruction that after his death the gold should be given to a geomancer, who was to inter him in the Altar of the City Gods [precinct] in the Kwiryong ward of Sasu County. Also, he specified that he was to be buried face down. Wang Sun did as instructed, and during the burial asked that his father be buried face down. The geomancer then said "Why are you in such a hurry?"

The periods of leave for officials in mourning were determined. For the mourning after death three days were granted; for the first day and the 15th of the month [throughout the three-year mourning period] one day each was granted; for the sacrifice after two months and after a year, seven days each were granted; for the Tamje 禫祭 ritual held sixty days after the two-month ritual, five days were granted.

---

68 The later king Hyŏnjong (1009-1031). Wang Uk had been exiled to Sasu County because of the illicit relationship that produced Wang Sun (see above).

Winter, twelfth month, *chŏngsa* [21st] day. Kwak Wŏn and six others passed the composition test of the civil service examination, and six people passed the classics test.

This year Sŏ Hŭi made fortifications for Sŏnju and Maengju.

Sŏngjong Sixteenth year [997]

Third year of the Zhidao era of Song, fifteenth year of the Tonghe era of Khitan

Autumn, eighth month, *ŭlmi* [3rd] day. The king set out for the Eastern Capital, and gave a banquet to the assembled worthies; to all the officials and military grandees in attendance he bestowed presents according to rank, and all officials of the capital and the provinces were granted a promotion in their merit rank. He ordered officials to seek out and report to the throne people with remarkable talent and extraordinary ability who were living hidden among the hills and forests. Righteous husbands, faithful wives, filial sons, and obedient grandsons were granted honorary gates as well as presents, and the king also granted an amnesty. In the prefectures and counties where he passed through, he cut the taxes for the year in half.

Ninth month. The king subsequently traveled [further east] to Hŭngnye District, where he took residence in the Taehwa building and gave a banquet to the worthies. A big fish was caught in the sea. The king was indisposed. On the *kisa* [7th] day the king returned from the Eastern Capital.

Winter, tenth month, *muo* [27th] day. The king's illness gradually became worse, and he called his nephew the Kaeryŏng Prince Wang Song, and bequeathed him the throne. He then moved to the Ch'ŏnwang Temple in the palace. The Executive [of the Royal Secretariat-Chancellery] Wang Yung requested him to declare an amnesty, but the king replied, "death and life are determined by Heaven, so releasing those who are guilty to extend my life would be wrong. Moreover, what benefice would be left to bestow by my successor?" The king did not give permission [for an amnesty], and died. The same day Wang Song ascended the throne, and bestowed on his predecessor the title Civilized Brilliance (Munŭi 文懿), and the temple name Sŏngjong. He was buried in the Kang-nŭng.

Yi Chehyŏn commented in his eulogy: "King Sŏngjong established the Royal Ancestor Shrine and the Altar of the Earth and Grain Deities; he supported learning by fostering scholars and sought out the wise through the confirmation test; he encouraged magistrates to help the people when they were in need, and by rewarding the filial and chaste, he ameliorated the customs. Whenever he wrote an official missive the words and his intentions were sincere, and he took improving the customs to be his duty. As for the Khitan, they had set their eyes on devouring Koryŏ, and sent their army to invade. But Sŏngjong had already himself traveled to the Western Capital and sent out troops to pacify the north; this is exactly like Kou Zhun's stratagem for Shanyuan.[69] As for wishing to move the defense of the passes to Chŏl Pass [Chabiryŏng] and to throw the army provisions into the Taedong River, this was the advice of ignorant subjects, it was certainly not Sŏngjong's original plan. If only [the king] had contemplated Ch'oe Sŭngno's letter, and joyfully embraced it, he would have removed vain superficialities and firmly implemented matters of substance; by fostering a mind that favors antiquity he would have pursued principles that renovate the people; by implementing this without fail yet taking heed not to push it through too hastily, with his body and mind perfected, he would be able to extend this to other people; then one could envisage the state of Qi becoming like Lu, and Lu becoming the Way. [If so, then how] could Xiao Sunning contend that we neglect to care for the people and raise an army that has no legitimacy? How could Yi Chibaek advocate a policy of not reforming the customs so as to drive away the enemy? However, his settling the succession before turning old was a truly farsighted act for the country. His refusal to wantonly order a pardon

69 Kou Zhun (961-1023) advised Emperor Zhenzong to take a proactive stance against Khitan aggression, and occupy the city of Shanyuan to confront the invaders. However, by then it was actually too late already. See *Songshi* 281.9530 (See Nap-yin Lau, "Waging War for Peace? The Peace Accord between the Song and the Liao in 1005 AD,“ in *Warfare in Chinese History*, ed. Hans van de Ven (Brill: 2000), p. 210)

in his last moments, shows his clarity regarding matters of life and death. Isn't this what can be called 'one can truly act together with one who has the will'? Ah, how wise!"

Eleventh month. The king [i.e. Mokchong] sent the Commissioner for Audience Ceremonies Wang Tongyŏng to Khitan to announce the succession.

Twelfth month. The king went to Wibong Pavilion and promulgated an amnesty. Corvée labor was suspended for three years, and land tax for one year. He gave aid to the aged and rewards to the filial, forgave those implicated by proxy, and gave aid to the sick. He remitted the taxes of those in debt, and forfeited debts owed to the state. Civil and military officials were promoted by one rank, while the officials of rank 5 and higher were granted protected appointment privileges for their sons. The parents and spouses of officials who took part in court councils and those with an office corresponding to rank 7 or higher were given official titles. Those who had taken part in the presented scholar or classics examination ten times yet failed to pass, as well as calligraphers and geomancers with ten years of experience were all allowed to be granted office. All the spirits and deities of the country were granted merit titles, and as a result throughout the country a day of liberal drinking was granted. [Finally], he expressed respect for his mother, née Hwangbo, by bestowing the title of Queen Dowager Responding to Heaven, Opening Sagacity, Tranquil Virtue.

The Khitan dispatched the Great General of the Thousand Bull Division, Yelü Dilie, to congratulate the king on the Ch'ŏnch'u festival. [King Mokchong] received the edict and went to announce it to the coffin of King Sŏngjong.

Mokchong, Great King Proclaimer of Yielding

His given name was Song 誦, and his courtesy name Hyosin孝伸. He was the oldest son of King Kyŏngjong. His mother was Queen Hŏn'ae, née

Hwangbo. He was born on the *imsul* day of the fifth month of the fifth year of Kyŏngjong (980). King Sŏngjong raised him in the palace [after his father's death in 981], and when the time came for him to study, he ordered the Assistant in the Palace Library Kim Sŭngjo to assist him in his reading. His character was calm and self-possessed, with a strong sense of dignity. Thus at a young age he had the bearing of a ruler. But he was good at archery and horse riding, and loved alcohol and hunting, paying scant attention to the affairs of state. He indulged in those who flattered and fawned, and this led to ruin. He was on the throne for twelve years and lived to the age of thirty.

Mokchong First year [998]

First year of the Xianping era of Zhenzong of Song, sixteenth year of the Tonghe era of Khitan

Spring, first month. Chu In'gŏl and four others passed the composition test of the civil service examination, and seven people passed the classics examination. Earlier Sŏngjong had ordered the selection of presented scholars, but due to his illness this was not carried out, so this is why the ranks were granted this time.

Third month. All the village heads of all prefectures and counties who had reached the age of seventy were given the title of retired village head and were given half of their stipend land.

Kang Chujae and forty-nine others passed the composition test of the civil service examination, one passed by royal grace, twenty passed the classics test, twenty-three the law test, five the calligraphy test, and eleven the calculation test.

Summer, fourth month. The king went to the Ancestral Shrine to enshrine King Sŏngjong; an amnesty was declared.

The king's birthday was named as the Changnyŏng festival.

Because of the previous king's demise, the Khitan decreed that all the luxury goods offered should be returned.

Autumn, seventh month. The Grand Guardian and Minister of the Royal Secretariat Sŏ Hŭi died. He was the son of Sŏ P'il and he was known as a strict person. When he was eighteen he came first in the civil service examination. When King Sŏngjong traveled to the Western Capital he accompanied him, but when the king donned commoner's clothes to secretly visit Yŏngmyŏng-sa Sŏ Hŭi sent a memorial to remonstrate, so the king desisted, and sent him a saddled horse to reward him. During the war of the *kyesa* year [993], he carried a letter of state to Xiao Sunning's encampment. He asked the interpreters to ask Xiao about the proper ritual of greeting, and Xiao answered: "I am an important person from your suzerain country, so it behooves you to prostrate yourself in the courtyard." Sŏ Hŭi then said, "When a subject greets his sovereign, he does so from below. When great ministers from two countries greet each other, how could it be like this?" Thus it went back and forth two or three times, but Xiao did not yield. Sŏ Hŭi, enraged, returned to his quarters to lay down, and refused to get up. Xiao Sunning then finally allowed him to enter the hall to extend greetings. Sŏ Hŭi then rode his horse to the entrance of the encampment, and got off his horse to enter. They then greeted each other equally in the courtyard, and then mounted [to the reception hall] for full formal greetings. Sitting facing each other east-west, the discussions went back and forth, words and meanings were grave yet correct. Finally Xiao Sunning allowed the conclusion of peace, and after that wanted to hold a banquet to soothe the spirits. Sŏ Hŭi retorted "although our country has never lost propriety, our suzerain rallied an army and came from afar; therefore high and low were in a state of panic. Brandishing spears and swords, they have been gathering dew for a few days. How can we bear to have a banquet and make fun in such circumstances?" Xiao Sunning replied "When the great ministers of two countries meet, can't they have a joyful and amicable meeting?" After he kept firmly insisting, Sŏ Hŭi finally agreed to the banquet. After having a very joyful time he desisted and made ready to return. Xiao then presented him with ten camels, 100 horses, 1000 sheep, and all kinds of silk, 1,000 bolts altogether.

Sŏ Hŭi also accompanied the king on a trip to Haengju. King Sŏngjong went to Sŏ Hŭi's tent and wanted to enter, but Sŏ Hŭi said "A subject's tent is not a place where a ruler should stay." The king then told him to serve wine, but again Sŏ Hŭi objected, saying "A subject's wine is not something that can be offered to a sovereign." Sŏngjong then sat outside the tent and had royal wine served, which they drank together; the king then returned.

The Minister of the Foreign Relations Office, Chŏng Uhyŏn, sent a letter to the throne in which he discussed seven problems in current policies. They went against the king's will, so the king convened the state councilors, where he argued "Chŏng Uhyŏn dared to go beyond his duties to discuss topical affairs, how about punishing him?" All agreed with the king's decree, only Sŏ Hŭi said "among the ancients, there was no designated office for remonstrance, so how could there be the crime of exceeding the duties of one's office? Your subject has no talent, yet somehow sits on this state council. There are many things that we can discuss, but what Chŏng Uhyŏn has raised are all current problems, so it is I who should be punished [as a policy making official], while Chŏng should be rewarded." Sŏngjong was greatly enlightened by this, and made Chŏng investigating censor. He bestowed on Sŏ Hŭi a saddled horse, wine, and fruits.

When Sŏ Hŭi fell ill, Sŏngjong went to see him in person, and donated royal robes and horses to monasteries. Also he donated 1,000 sŏk of grain to Kaeguk-sa, all to pray for his life; there was nothing the king left undone. Yet Sŏ Hŭi died, reaching the age of fifty-seven. The king spent lavishly for his funeral and mourning, and granted him the posthumous title Ch'angwi. He was buried with full honors, and later co-enshrined with Sŏngjong in the Royal Ancestral Shrine.

The name of the Western Capital was changed to Hogyŏng.

Winter, eleventh month. The system for field and woodland ranks for civil and military officials, as well as for soldiers, was changed. [Henceforth] the first rank received 100 *kyŏl* of fields and 70 *kyŏl* of woodland, followed by gradually decreasing ranks, 18 in total. Those without rank were granted 17 *kyŏl.*

This year Kim Sŏngjŏk went to Song, where he passed the civil service examination.

Mokchong Second year [999]

Second year of the Xianping era of Song, seventeenth year of the Tonghe era of Khitan

Autumn, seventh month. The king constructed Chingwan-sa south of the capital as a memorial temple for the queen dowager.

Winter, tenth month. The king went to Hogyŏng [i.e., P'yŏngyang] to hold a maigre offering. He declared an amnesty and remitted the land tax [rent] for a year [for those living in the P'yŏngyang area], and cut it in half for all the counties and prefectures that he passed through [on his way to P'yŏngyang]. He enquired after the health of the elderly and bestowed presents on them. To soldiers of the two capitals and the garrison cities who were over eighty, those who had an official position received a higher rank, while those without a position were granted the title of Lieutenant Assisting the Military.[70] As for those officials and military who had accompanied the royal carriage, those of the eighth rank and below were granted presents commensurate with their rank. As for those students of medicine and prognostication in Hogyŏng, those who had been studying for twenty years but had already reached the age of fifty were given official titles. The widows of officials of rank 3 and above from Hogyŏng who had remained chaste were ennobled.

The Khitan sent the Right Attendant-in-ordinary Liu Ji to invest the king as Director of the Department of Ministries.

A person named Toyomido 道要彌刀 from the country of Japan and others, twenty households altogether, came to submit. The king settled them in Ich'ŏn where they became enrolled in the local household registers.

The king dispatched the Executive of the Board of Rites Chu Inso to

70 *Paeyung kyowi* 陪戎校尉.

Song China. The emperor especially summoned Chu Inso for an audience. Chu Inso declared to the emperor that his country people greatly admired Chinese customs, yet were suppressed and restricted by the Khitan. The emperor bestowed an edict and sent him back to his country.

Mokchong Third year [1000]

Third year of the Xianping era of Song, eighteenth year of the Tonghe era of Khitan

Winter, tenth month. The king established Sunggyo-sa as a memorial temple.

This year, fifteen people including Song Koeng passed the composition test of the civil service examination, and eight people passed the classics test

Tŏkchu was fortified.

Mokchong Fourth year [1001]

Fourth year of the Xianping era of Song, nineteenth year of the Tonghe era of Khitan

Winter, eleventh month. The king wanted to inspect local customs and traveled to Chungwŏn District.[71] He held a banquet for his high officials [in Chungwŏn] and declared an amnesty. Land rents of all the localities he passed through were remitted for a year, and the officials who traveled with him as well as the officials of the localities he had passed through were all promoted by one rank and granted gifts commensurate with rank. On the way back, when the king reached Changdan [County],[72] he told his Councilor Han Ŏn'gong: "This is your hometown (*pon'gwan*); considering your merits, I will promote it to Tanju [greater prefecture]."

This year a paddy field in Changyŏn County of Chungwŏn District

[71] Modern Ch'ungju.

[72] A locality with this name still exists on the northwestern side of P'aju. It is now cut through by the border between North and South Korea.

turned into a three-*kyŏl* large pond, the depth of which could not be fathomed.

P'yŏngno Garrison[73] was fortified.

Mokchong Fifth year [1002]

Fifth year of the Xianping era of Song, twentieth year of the Tonghe era of Khitan

Spring, third month. Pak Wŏnhwi and eight others passed the composition test of the civil service examination and nineteen people passed the classics test.

Summer, fourth month. The king held a sacrificial rite in the Ancestral Shrine and elevated the posthumous title of the deceased queen; he then declared an amnesty.

Fifth month. Military encampments for the Six Armies were established, and the soldiers serving there were exempted from corvée duty.

Sixth month. The mountain of T'amna [island] opened up four holes from which red liquid spouted for five days.[74] The liquid then turned into stone shaped like tiles.

Autumn, seventh month. A royal instruction read: "Recently I perused a memorial submitted by Chancellor Han Ŏn'gong, which stated 'now we have continued the practice of previous kings of using coinage and forbidding coarse hemp [for trading]. This has confounded local customs and has failed to produce benefits for the state; it has merely lead to an increase in people's resentment.' For commerce in tea, wine and similar shops, as before coinage should be used for trade. Apart from this, when the people trade among themselves, they are allowed to use local products [to barter]."

---

73 Believed to be located in Hŭich'ŏn-gun of North P'yŏng'an Province.

74 I.e. there was an eruption of Mt. Halla.

Mokchong Sixth year [1003]

Sixth year of the Xianping era of Song, twenty-first year of the Tonghe era of Khitan

Spring, first month. The king issued a royal instruction, ordering all doctors of letters and instructors of the three capitals and ten provinces to recommend their students, and to record the names of those who proved their worth. Local authorities are also requested to select the talented people within their jurisdiction, and to recommend them for the examinations every year; without fail this should become a regular practice.

Second month. A royal instruction read "Since last year there have been frequent abnormalities on the land and in the heavens, and we are also worried by the situation at the border. Now from the highest offices of state ministers above to the petty officials below, there is none who proffers straightforward and honest advice, all engage merely in flattery. How lamentable! If there were words [of advice] that went unheeded by me, this would be shameful; if in a dangerous situation no one would offer help, then who would be to blame? All the officials of rank 5 and above should write a letter to the king, containing words that are as curative as medicine and acupuncture, so that we can work together in supporting the affairs of state."

This year the fortifications of Tŏkchu, Kaju, Wihwa and Kwanghwa were repaired.

Queen Dowager Ch'ŏnch'u, whose surname was Hwangbo, forced prince Taeryang, Wang Sun [later King Hyŏnjong], to become a monk. What happened before is as follows. A person named Kim Ch'iyang from Tongju[75] was a relative of the queen on her mother's side. He was crafty and sly by nature, and once disguised himself as a monk and thus freely entered Queen Ch'ŏnch'u's palace, giving rise to many salacious rumors. When King Sŏngjong [heard about this] he had him beaten with the cane and sent into exile far away. After King Sŏngjong died, she called him back and granted him the office of secretarial receptionist at the Office for Audience Ceremonies. Within a few years she grew so fond of him that there was no

---

75 Tongju: ancient locality, located in modern Sŏhŭng, Hwanghae Province.

one to rival him [for her affections]. All the important offices were either given or taken away by him, so that the clique of his confidantes spread its tentacles across the country. He built a private mansion that numbered more than 300 bays; its terraces and pavilions, gardens and ponds were all extremely beautiful. Day and night he caroused there with the queen, without constraint or fear. In Tongju he established a shrine with the name plaque "Sŏngsuk-sa 星宿寺" (Temple of the constellations). Furthermore in the northwestern corner of the palace he established the Siwang-sa 十王寺 (temple of the Ten Kings of the netherworld). Its statues and paintings were weird and grotesque to the point that they are difficult to describe. Secretly they harbored disloyal intentions; to procure numinous protection, all vessels carried their intentions. Thus their bell inscription was as follows: "Since [we] were born in the Eastern Country, together we cultivated good seeds so that in later days when we reach the Western Realm, together we will achieve enlightenment." The king constantly wanted to banish him, but he was afraid of hurting his mother's feelings so did not dare to do so. Eventually the queen dowager gave birth to a son from her illicit relationship with Kim Ch'iyang. Together with Kim Ch'iyang she plotted to make him the next king. Thus they were jealous of Prince Taeryang and forced him to become a monk. At the time the prince was only twelve. Later he was residing at Sinhyŏl-sa on Samgak-san, and the queen on several occasions secretly dispatched someone to assassinate him. However an old monk at the temple dug a hole under one of the temple's rooms and hid him there. On top of it he placed a couch to protect the hiding place and thus avoided detection.

Mokchong Seventh year [1004]

First year of the Jingde era of Song, twenty-second year of the Tonghe era of Khitan

Spring, third month. The king reformed the law regarding the civil examinations. Previously the test had been taken in the spring months, but sometimes it took until autumn before the roster of successful candidates was released. Now for the first time it was decided that in the third month the [examination] venue would be opened [to admit examinees] and then shut off for ten days. On the first day, ten questions regarding the *Classic of Rites* were put up, the next day the candidates were tested on poetry and rhyme-prose. Skipping one day [for rest], on the [fourth day] candidates were tested on the policy essay. After the ranking had been decided and announced, the gates were opened. As for the various professional qualifications below the bright classics, the previous year in the eleventh month the tests were given, while the roster was released on the same day as the presented scholars. This became a regular practice.

Summer, fourth month. Hwang Churyang and fourteen others passed the composition test of the civil service examination, and four passed the classics examination.

Sixth month. The Director of the Chancellery Han Ŏn'gong died. He had a bright disposition and loved learning, yet when he took the civil service examination he failed to qualify. He received successive promotions and reached the position of director of the Chancellery. He received various honors and was the privileged recipient of a stipend village of 1000 households. He was also put in charge of editing the state history. Once, the king went to P'yŏngju, but when dusk fell it was extremely cold. The royal carriage was placed on the side of the road, and the king drank [with his ministers], and they did not continue their journey. Han then remonstrated with the king: "Your subject and the other ministers have drunk their full, but what about the military people?" The king praised him and bestowed a marten skin on him, ordered the royal carriage to depart and entered the temporary palace. Thus he always offered straight talk as the occasion necessitated. Now he had fallen ill, and the king bestowed medicine and physicians, and even a comfortable carriage to take him to hot springs for [medicinal] baths. He also ordered all localities [where he passed through] to provide for him. Also he bestowed three horses from the royal stable to defray expenses for prayers. In the end he did not recover and died. The king then bestowed lavish amounts of rice and cloth as condolence money, and posthumously appointed him Minister of the Royal Secretaries (Naesaryŏng 內史令), and bestowed the posthumous title of Chŏngsin 貞信. He was buried with full ceremonies, and was later co-enshrined with Mokchong.

Winter, eleventh month. The king traveled to Hogyŏng for a maigre offering, and declared an amnesty for crimes with a punishment lower than beating with the stick. The land tax for the people of the city was remitted by a year, and by half for prefectures and counties along the roads to the northern border. He also nourished the aged people [of Hogyŏng, i.e. P'yŏngyang] and increased the titles of gods of the surrounding mountains and counties.

Mokchong Eighth year [1005]

Second year of the Jingde era of Song, twenty-third year of the Tonghe era of Khitan

Spring, first month. The Eastern Jurchen raided Tŭngju and burned more than thirty settlements in its various prefectures and garrisons. The king sent a general to control them.

Third month. Local functionaries were purged and reduced so that only the twelve provincial army commands, four protectorates, and the protecting envoys, county prefects and garrison commanders of the eastern and northwestern military border districts remained. [The offices of] civil governor, drill sergeant, and regional inspector were all abolished.

Summer, fourth month. Ch'oe Ch'ung and six others passed the composition test of the civil service examination and three passed the classics test.

This year the Song literatus Zhou Zhu (K. Chu Chŏ) from Wenzhou came to submit. The king granted him the title of recorder at the Ministry for Protocol.

Mokchong Ninth year [1006]

Third year of the Jingde era of Song, twenty-fourth year of the Tonghe era of Khitan

Spring, second month. The king told his officials: "In recent years the autumn crops did not ripen [well], so ordinary people have difficulty feeding themselves. Those who have not paid the tribute tax (*kongbu* 貢賦) since the twenty-first year of the Tonghe era (1003), should be exempted. As for those who have run out of grain and have no seeds, the granaries should be opened and they should be provided with seeds."

Summer, fourth month. The king ordered all civil officials of rank six and above to select someone of talent and capable of leading the people; also, he added, if the person selected was worthy of reward, the selector would also be rewarded; however, if he deserved punishment the selector would likewise be punished.

Sixth month, *musul* [28th] day. Lightning struck the finial tile of the ridge of the Ch'ŏnsŏng Hall [of the palace]. The king was scared and worried, and blamed himself. He declared an amnesty, and increased the rewards for filial sons, obedient brothers, righteous husbands and chaste wives. He also raised the honorific titles of the deities of the country. For officials of the third rank and above he increased the merit rank. For those of rank four and below he raised their rank by one. For those officials of rank nine and above who had been officials for twenty years he changed the official clothing.[76] For those aged more than sixty, he elevated their office. He also reduced their cloth tax by half, and remitted the tax debts of those who had not paid before the *kapchin* year (1004).

This year a comet was observed.

Tŭngju, Kwisŏng and Yongjin Garrison were fortified.

Mokchong Tenth year [1007]

Fourth year of the Jingde era of Song, twenty-fifth year of the Tonghe era of Khitan

Spring, second month. The Khitan dispatched Yelü Yangui to invest the king to a higher level as merit subject Protecting Integrity, Upholding

76 Possible meaning: new official robes were provided.

the Country, Promoting Sincerity and Invested in Sagacity; Commander Unequalled in Honor, Acting Director of the Department of Ministries and Royal Secretary;[77] Supreme Pillar of State with a Stipend Village of 7,000 Households.

The nine-story pagoda of Chingwan-sa was constructed.

Summer, sixth month. Cha Wŏn and six others passed the composition test of the civil service examination, and thee passed the classics test.

Autumn, seventh month. The Censorate memorialized: "The person from Kyŏngju Yungdae feigns being a distant scion of Silla king Wŏnsŏng and has obtained recognition for 500 free people as slaves by giving presents to the palace person surnamed Kim and the Executive Han In'gyŏng, and the Executive of the Board of Personnel Kim Nak, thus making them his protectors. We have already investigated and obtained the facts, so please punish them." The king was enraged and banished Han In'gyŏng to Yangju and Kim Nak to an island in the sea. The person surnamed Kim was fined 100 pound of copper. The investigators were all praised.

Winter, tenth month. The king traveled to Hogyŏng to hold a maigre offering. He pardoned all those with a punishment of banishment or lower, and remitted the land tax [of P'yŏngyang residents] for a year. Taxes of the counties and prefectures he passed through were reduced by half. Honorary titles of the country's spirits were elevated.

Hŭnghwa Garrison, Ingnyŏng County and Ulchin County were fortified.

In this year there was an earthquake in P'yŏngyang.

T'amna reported the following: "An auspicious mountains arose from the sea." The king sent the Professor of the Taehak College Chŏn Kongji to inspect. The T'amna people told him that when the mountain first emerged, clouds and mist darkened the skies, and the earth shook with the sound of thunder. After seven days and nights the clouds and mist lifted [revealing for the first time the shape of the mountain]. It was more than 1,000 feet high, and more than 40 *li* in circumference. No grass or trees [grew on it] and

---

77 *Chŏngsa-ryŏng* 政事令: possibly a Liao term; according to Hucker from 950 to 1043 the Zhengsi sheng 政事省 functioned as the predecessor of the Secretariat (Zhongshu sheng).

its summit was covered by smoke. It looked as if it was made of sulphur.[78] People were afraid and did not dare approach it. Chŏn Kongji then went himself to just below the mountain, and made a drawing of its shape, which he presented to the king.

Mokchong Eleventh year [1008]

First year of the Dazhong xiangfu era of Song, twenty-sixth year of the Tonghe era of Khitan

Spring, third month. Son Wŏnsŏn and eight others passed the composition test of the civil service examination, and two candidates passed the classics examination.

Winter, tenth month. The king went to Hogyŏng.

T'ongju was fortified.

Mokchong Twelfth year [1009]

Second year of the Dazhong xiangfu era of Song, twenty-seventh year of the Tonghe era of Khitan

Spring, first month, *kyŏng'o* [14th] day. The king went to Sunggyo-sa.

Imsin day [16th]. The king went to the Sangjŏng Hall to watch the Lantern [Festival]. The oil from the Taebu storehouse[79] caught fire, and the fire spread to the Ch'ŏnch'u Hall. When the king saw the charred remains of the palace hall and the storage building, he sighed in grief and fell ill, and stopped listening to policy meetings.[80] The Royal and State Preceptor, the

---

78 There are various interpretations as to which volcano this might refer to, but it remains uncertain. Most volcanic formations on Cheju including Hallasan and Sŏsan Ilch'ulpong are much older than this account. The description and name (Sŏsan= Auspicious mountain) however fit the latter.

79 Taebu yugo 大府油庫: literally, the oil storehouse from the Palace Treasury.

80 Based on its name, the Ch'ŏnch'u Hall may have been connected to Queen Ch'ŏnch'u, Mokchong's mother, and hence the conflagration may have been interpreted as a Heavenly

Grand Physician Ki Chŏng'ŏp, the Grand Diviner Chin Hamjo, the Grand Scribe Pan Hŭiak, the State Councilor with the offices of Executive of the Ministry of Personnel and Assistant Executive in Political Affairs Yu Chin, the Executive of the Board of Personnel and Commissioner at the Royal Secretariat Ch'oe Hang, the Reviewing Policy Advisor and Deputy Commissioner at the Royal Secretariat Ch'ae Ch'ungsun and others took up residence at the Royal Academy of Letters.[81] The official in charge of the Royal Academy of Letters, the Executive at the Board of Construction Yi Chujŏng; the Transmitter of Edicts of the Right and Palace Censor Yi Chag'in; the officials favored by the king: manager of affairs at the Royal Academy of Letters, the First Office Chief Yu Ch'ungjŏng; the Presenting Official at the Court of Royal Audiences Yu Haenggan, and others, took up residence in the inner quarters. Also, the king's personal general Yu Pang and the senior colonels Yu Chong, T'ak Sajŏng, and Ha Kongjin took up positions at the nearby gate of the palace hall. The Vice Minister of the Board of Punishments Chin Chŏk also took up residence inside the inner quarters. The Executive of the Board of Taxation Ch'oe Sawi became Special Commissioner for the Taejŏng Gate. He ordered all palace gates closed, and enforced it very strictly. Only the Taejŏng Gate of the Changch'un Hall remained accessible. He also organized a Life-saving Assembly in the Changch'un and Kŏnhwa Halls.

Because Yu Haenggan was of beautiful appearance, the king loved him for his male physique. Every time he wanted to promulgate an edict, first he asked Yu Haenggan for his opinion, and only then released the edict. Because of this continuing affection and trust from the king, he grew arrogant and haughty, and treated the officials with contempt. Everybody was at his beck and call, so that even the ministers close to the king regarded him as a king. Likewise Yu Ch'ungjŏng was without skill or talent, but he

portent regarding her behavior. The Taebu Storage was renamed Changhŭng Storage in 1308.

81 Hallimwon [known as 學士院 in early Koryŏ], here identified as the "silver pavilion" (銀臺), which functioned as the office of transmission, receiving and processing important messages for and from the king.

was favored by the king. The king even assigned them the attendants of the royal drinking water storage; whenever they entered or left, these attendants followed them like a groom for a horse, it was exceedingly impudent.

Kapsul day [18th]. The Queen Dowager moved into the Changsaeng Hall. The king had been indisposed for several days and remained in the inner quarters, not wanting to see his officials. The state councilors were trembling with fear and requested permission to enter the inner chambers so as to enquire after the king's health. Yu Haenggan transmitted the following words from the king: "My body and energy are slowly improving, I will choose another day to see you." They requested again, but did not receive permission.

One day the king summoned state councilor Ch'ae Ch'ungsun into the royal bedchamber. The king dismissed those attending him and told him "My illness is slowly growing better, but I heard that on the outside there are people looking for an opportunity, do you know about this?" Ch'ae answered, "I tried to enquire about this but failed to get concrete information." The king then fetched a sealed letter from his pillow and handed it to him. It was a letter sent by Yu Ch'ungjŏng to the king, which read "The Junior Vice Director and State Finance Commissioner[82] Kim Ch'iyang is anxiously looking for an opportunity to commit what cannot be contemplated [i.e. treason], and is sending out people to hand over bribes so as to obtain their loyalty; he is still looking for internal support. I realized what he was up to and refused, and could not but alert you to this." The king then handed him another letter, this time from Prince Taeryang Wang Sun from Samgak-san. It read "A clique of crafty people have been sending people to threaten and persecute me; also, once they left some wine and food, but I suspected it may be poison so I didn't eat it but gave it to crows and sparrows; they died after eating it. Thus I am in a situation where they are out to harm me; please, your majesty, have mercy and save me." Having read this, Ch'ae Ch'ungsun said: "The situation is urgent! We should make plans as soon as possible." The king said "My illness is gradually getting

82 Here I read 三司使 for 三司事.

more and more serious, and it is matter of days before I enter the earth. Of T'aejo's grandsons, only Prince Taeryang is alive. You and Ch'oe Hang embrace loyalty and righteousness as a matter of course. You should do your utmost to assist so that the [altar of] earth and grain deities does not pass into the possession of another surname."

After Ch'ae Ch'ungsun left the inner quarters, he told Ch'oe Hang [what he had learned], and Ch'oe Hang said: "I have been worried for a long time. Now that the sovereign's mind is like this, it is a blessing for the earth and grain deities." Yu Ch'ungjŏng dispatched the Investigating Censor Ko Yŏnggi to tell Ch'ae and Ch'oe: "Now that his majesty is prostrate with illness, the clique of crafty officials is looking for an opportunity, so I fear that the [altar of] the earth and grain deities will pass to a different surname. If the sovereign's illness gradually worsens, we should make T'aejo's grandson the heir apparent." Ch'oe Hang and his colleague feigned surprise and said "Is T'aejo's grandson safe?" Ko Yŏnggi answered "Prince Taeryang is indeed alive, and is worthy of succeeding the throne." Ch'oe Hang and his colleague then answered "We already heard [that this is the case] a long time ago, so we should obey Heaven's command."

Yu Ch'ungjŏng again sent Ko Yŏnggi to tell them "I would like to go myself and discuss this with you, but there are servants and other people all around, so I am afraid this would arouse suspicion. I hope that you two gentlemen can come to meet me." Ch'oe Hang and Ch'ae Ch'ungsun discussed this and concluded "This is not a private affair, but something that concerns the royal dynasty so we should go and meet him." Thus they went to him and after the discussions had been concluded, Ch'ae Ch'ungsun reported to the king: "We should select one civil and one military official, who are to lead troops, including officers, and receive [Prince Taeryang]." Ch'ae Ch'ungsun then went back to consult with Ch'oe Hang and Ko Yŏnggi, and he proposed: "The Administrative Assistant of the Court Ceremonial Institute,[83] Hwangbo Yuŭi, is dedicated to the dynasty.

---

83 Sŏnwhi-wŏn 宣徽院: from Tang to Song this functioned as the Court of Palace Attendants, and was staffed by eunuchs; under the Liao and Jin however it functioned as the Court

Moreover, his father and grandfather established their merit for the country, so he is certain not to let this family tradition down and will exert himself." Then he was sent for, and he was reported to the throne. Then Ch'ae Ch'ungsun and the others again deliberated: "If there are many soldiers and officers to receive him, then the procession will be slow. I'm afraid that the clique of treacherous officials will move first with their treasonous plans. We should send only about ten-some people via a shortcut route to bring [the prince] back." The king agreed, and said: "you should dispatch them immediately, let there be no delay. I want to personally hand over the throne to him and entrust him with the army and the country. In case my illness gets better, just as Sŏngjong invested me, this precedent settled my role from an early moment, so nobody could take advantage of any hiatus. I have no sons and the succession has not been settled, giving cause for perturbation among my officials, this is my mistake. Nothing is more important than the dynastic project, so please, gentlemen, do your utmost." Having spoken, the king started crying, and Ch'ae Ch'ungsun also cried.

The king then ordered Ch'ae to make the draft of a letter to be delivered to Prince Taeryang, and personally started to grind the ink. Ch'ae immediately said "your subject will grind the ink himself, please do not exert your august body." The king said "I am so consumed with urgency that I do not feel the effort." The letter read as follows: "From antiquity the important matters of state have all been settled and assigned in advance, this has put people's mind at ease. Now I am struck down by illness, and treacherous people are looking for an opportunity [to replace me]. Because this insignificant person was previously inconsiderate, nothing has been settled or assigned, so the minds of officials are greatly perturbed. Therefore, since you are a direct descendant of T'aejo, set forth immediately. As long as I am still alive, I will personally entrust you with the dynasty and the altar. Then I will die without regrets. Should I continue to live, you will reside in the heir apparent's

Ceremonial Institute, "with broadened activities for supervising court activities" (Hucker, 2664). While there is no conclusive evidence as to which model was followed, given his lineage Hwangbo Yuŭi does not appear to have been a eunuch, so the latter option seems more likely.

palace, so that the minds of all will be at ease." The king then also ordered to add at the end: "The road is treacherous, and I fear that the traitors may have laid a trap to carry out an unexpected coup, so please take utmost care when you come here."

Now Yu Haenggan was not in favor of welcoming [Prince Taeryang] and establishing him as the successor. Considering that [the news of the decision] might leak out, Ch'ae Ch'ungsun deliberately left Yu Haenggan out of the loop. The letter was handed to Hwangbo Yuŭi, who, together with more than ten people including the Junior Colonel Mun Yŏn and others went to Sinhyŏl-sa to receive the prince. He also ordered the Military Administrator of the Kaesŏng Municipality, Kim Yŏn'gyŏng, to post 100 soldiers outside the city to receive him. Kim Ch'iyang knew about this but could not do anything about it. For several days he paced up and down, unable to act.

Previously, the king had come to realize that Yi Chujŏng had attached himself to the camp of Kim Ch'iyang, so he appointed him Vice-commissioner to the Chief Military Inspector for the Northwest, and he was dispatched that very day. Accordingly he summoned the Chief Military Inspector of the Northwest, Kang Cho, to join the unit [leaving with Yi Chujŏng]. Kang Cho received the order and went as far as Yongch'ŏn station in Tongju. There the Scribe at the Ministry of the Royal Secretaries Wi Chongjŏng, and the Chief Secretary of Anbuk Military Command Ch'oe Ch'ang, had once been demoted over a certain affair and felt deep resentment towards the court. They were always looking for ways of fomenting trouble. The two went to see Kang Cho and told him the following lie: "Our king's illness is severe and he is hovering between life and death. The queen dowager and Kim Ch'iyang are plotting to grab the Altar for the Grain and Earth Deities, but since you are away from the capital and in control of a sizeable army, they are afraid that you might not follow their plans, so they made this spurious command to summon you back. Please hurriedly return to the main road and raise a righteous army to protect the country and all its people. There is no time to lose." Kang Cho fully agreed with this assessment, and thought that the king had already expired and that the court was controlled by Kim Ch'iyang, so he returned to his main camp.

The queen dowager was afraid that Kang Cho would come, so she sent a trusted palace official to take control of Chŏl Pass and to block people from passing through. Kang Cho's father was worried by this and put a letter inside a bamboo stick. He made a slave shave his head to look like a monk, and instructed him to tell [people guarding the pass] that he was on his way to Myohyang-san. The "monk" urgently had to report to Kang Cho: "The king has already passed away, and evil forces are in control. Raise an army and return to pacify the country." The slave ran day and night, and when he reached Kang Cho's place he expired from exhaustion. However, Kang Cho found the letter hidden inside the stick and now believed even more that the king had died. Subsequently, together with his Vice-commissioner, the Executive at the Board of Personnel Yi Hyŏn'un,[84] he took charge of 5,000 armored troops. When he reached P'yŏngju he learned for the first time that the king had actually not yet died.

Kang Cho was dejected and sat with his head down for a long time. His generals then told him "This project has already been set in motion, we cannot stop it now." Kang Cho agreed, and made up his mind to depose the king. He did not know that the king had already decided to receive Prince Taeryang, and dispatched the Investigating Censor of the Branch Offices Kim Ŭng'in to lead troops and receive him.

Second month, *muja* day [2nd]. Kang Cho sent an address to the king: "Your majesty's illness is getting worse, but the most essential affair of the state has not yet been determined. Treacherous officials are looking for a chance [to foment rebellion], and you show undue favor to people like Yu Haenggan, who spread allegations and fawn on you. Awards and punishments are not determined according to clear criteria, leading to crisis and chaos. Now I want to determine who gets his due so as to realign people's minds, and remove the evil so as to allay people's anger. I have

---

84 Presumably Yi Chujŏng was supposed to replace him.

already determined that the Prince of Taeryang will be received in the palace. I am afraid that your majesty's feelings will be greatly shaken, so please take shelter in Yonghŭng-sa or Kwibŏp-sa. After I have removed the treacherous clique, please receive him in the palace."

The king replied "what you have reported I already know." On this day Hwangbo Yuŭi and Kim Ŭng'in together reached Sinhyŏl-sa. The monks thought that they might have been sent by the treasonous party, and kept the prince hidden. Hwangbo and Kim then together explained that they had come to receive and enthrone the prince. The prince then emerged, and Hwangbo and Kim escorted him back to the palace.

Kich'uk [3rd] day. The sun looked as if it had been veiled by a red curtain. Yi Hyŏn'un led his troops into the Yŏngch'u Gate and they made a great noise. The king was frightened, took hold of Yu Haenggan and sent him out to meet Kang Cho. T'ak Sajŏng and Ha Kongjin immediately ran over the Kang Cho's side. Kang Cho reached the Taech'o Gate and sat himself down on a "barbarian couch."[85] Ch'oe Hang emerged from the palace; Kang Cho got up and bowed respectfully. Ch'oe Hang said "Is there any kind of precedent for this?" Kang Cho did not respond.

Thereupon the soldiers stormed in. The king knew he could not get away, and together with the queen dowager they looked up to heaven and cried. Leading palace ladies, eunuchs, and Ch'ae Ch'ungsun and Yu Ch'ungjŏng, they went to Pŏbwang-sa. Kang Cho sat down in the Kŏndŏk Hall right below the royal throne, and his soldiers cried "Manse!" Kang Cho was startled and got up from the place near the throne. Kneeling, he said: "The person to succeed the throne has not yet arrived, so why are you making this kind of noise?" Suddenly Hwangbo Yuŭi and the others arrived with the prince. He was then immediately enthroned in the Yŏnch'ong Hall. Kang Cho deposed the king and made him "Country-renouncing Duke" [Yangguk kong 讓國公]. He made the secretarial receptionist at the Office for Audience Ceremonies Pu Am protect him. He also dispatched troops to kill Kim Ch'iyang and his son, as well as Yu Haenggan and others, seven people

85 Hosang 胡床: a kind of folding chair.

altogether. He banished the clique and the relatives of the queen dowager, more than thirty people, to sea islands. The king made Ch'oe Hang request a horse to Kang Cho, who sent one horse; they obtained one more from a local person. The king and the queen dowager rode the horses out of the Sŏn'in Gate. Upon reaching Kwibŏp-sa, he changed out of his royal robes and also changed his food, and then presented these [to the new king]. Kang Cho summoned them back together with Ch'oe Hang and others. The king told Ch'oe Hang, "Recently the conflagration at the palace storehouse and the tumultuous changes that took place, these are the result of my lack of virtue, so how could I resent [my dethronement]? All I wish for is to grow old in the countryside. Sir, please tell this to the new lord, and assist him well."

Thereupon he went towards Ch'ungju. Whenever the queen dowager wanted to eat, the [erstwhile] king offered the plates to her personally; whenever she rode her horse the king personally led it by the reins. When they reached Chŏksŏng County, Kang Cho dispatched the Chief Intendant of the Royal Pharmacy, Kim Kwangbo, to offer him poison. The king refused to drink it. Kim Kwangbo then told the king's personal guard, An P'ae, and his fellow guards, "Kang Cho told me 'you can order the personal guards to commit a great deed, and report it as suicide. If you refuse, I will give permission for you and your whole family [to be exterminated].'" At night An P'ae and the other guards murdered the king and reported that he had committed suicide. They fashioned a coffin from door panels, and made the hostel into a temporary funerary parlor. The queen dowager returned to Hwangju. A month later [the king] was cremated south of the county [of Chŏksŏng], his tumulus was named Kong-nŭng and his posthumous title was Sŏllyŏng 宣靈, his temple name Minjong 愍宗. There was none among ministers or ordinary people who did not feel pain and resentment. However, the new king did not know about this. It was only when the Khitan raised an army to chastise Koryŏ that the king found out that he had been killed. The king then changed his posthumous title to Sŏnyang 宣讓 and his temple name to Mokchong.

Yi Chehyŏn commented in his eulogy: "Qingfu's violation of ritual in the state of Lu; Lü Buwei's shifting of the blame onto Qin; Duke Hwan of Qi's killing of Aijiang; Emperor Qin Shihuang's quartering of Laoai—how can one recover from such humiliations that last a myriad generations! King Mokchong did not take heed and 'followed in the tracks of an overturned cart' from the beginning. Therefore mother and son both met with disaster, and the Altar of Earth and Grain nearly fell to ruin. How tragic! This was Sŏnyang's [Mokchong] misfortune. Or was it no misfortune?"

Kyŏng'in [4th] day. The king abolished the "Silver Terrace" (i.e. Royal Academy of Letters) and the Southern and Northern Courts of the Security Council.[86] Instead he established the Central Terrace Department (Chungdae-sŏng 中臺省),[87] which brought together the tasks of the previous three institutions. Kang Cho was made Commissioner of this institute, Yi Hyŏn'un Associate Commissioner, and Ch'ae Ch'ungsun Intendant. Yun Yŏ was made Junior Assistant Director of the Department of Ministries and concurrent Intendant [of the Central Terrace Department].

The king dispatched the Chief Minister of the Court of the National Granaries Wang Ilgyŏng to Khitan to announce the demise [of Mokchong] and the enthronement [of Hyŏnjong].

The Kyobang Palace was abolished and its 100 courtesans released. The Nangwŏn Pavilion was demolished and its precious birds and animals, all kinds of turtles and fish, were released into mountains and waterways.

Third month. The king's grandmother was posthumously ennobled as Queen Dowager Sinsŏng-wang.

Yu Yunbu was made Director of the Chancellery, and Yu Panghŏn Executive Chief of the Chancellery. Kang Cho was made Vice-minister of

86 Chungch'u nambug-wŏn 中樞南北院: It is possible that the Nambug-wŏn might be a separate institution, but more likely is that it should be read together with Chungch'u[-wŏn], the Security Council. What the "Southern and Northern Courts" refers to is not clear.

87 It was abolished again in the first month of 1011, after which the Security Council was reinstated. See next chapter. In the Chinese administrative system the "Central Pavilion" (Zhongtai) was another name for the Department of State Affairs (Shangshu-sheng). Hucker 1629.

the Board of Taxation and assistant executive in political affairs. Chin Chŏk was made Vice-minister of the Board of Punishment and assistant executive in political affairs. Yu Chin was made Vice-director of the Left and Wang Tongyŏng Vice-director of the Right at the Department of Ministries. Ch'oe Hang was made Senior Policy Advisor and Kim Sang'ŏn Junior Policy Advisor [at the Department of Royal Secretariat-Chancellery]. Ch'ae Ch'ungsun was made Executive at the Board of Personnel and concurrently Senior Policy Critic [at the Department of the Royal Secretariat-Chancellery].

Seventy-five military vessels were made and stationed at Chinmyŏnggu to protect against pirates from the northeast.

Summer, fourth month. The Acting Executive at the Board of Works Yi Yuhang was sent to Khitan to offer congratulations for the birthday of the queen dowager.

The deceased father of the king, Wang Uk, was posthumously ennobled as Hyomok taewang with the temple name Anjong. His deceased mother Lady Hwangbo was entitled as Queen Dowager Hyosuk-wang.

The king granted amnesty to all within the borders, gave sustenance to the old and sick, remitted outstanding taxes, and reduced corvée labor. He rewarded the merit subjects, gave presents to wise scholars, and employed the old meritorious elite. He removed female entertainers, secured military rations, and gave higher titles to various deities. He also raised the titles and emoluments of civil and military officials.

Fifth month. He made Lady Kim his queen; she was a daughter of King Sŏngjong.

He pardoned those with crimes punished by labor and lighter crimes, and increased the titles of civil and military officials by one grade. Those whose terms had been completed were given increased salary. Military of the capital armies were given cloth commensurate with their rank, and people from the southern provinces who had served in garrisons in the northeast were allowed to return to their fields and villages.

An Ch'angnyŏng and six others passed the composition test of the civil service examination, and two candidates passed the classics examination.

Sixth month. The northeastern region was plagued by locusts.

Autumn, seventh month. The king promulgated a royal instruction calling for advice; he ordered all civil officials who attended audiences (rank 5 and higher) to send a letter to the throne containing a frank assessment of policies.

The king went to the polo court, where he had gathered men and women over the age of eight and those gravely ill, 635 people in total. He bestowed wine and food, cloth and silk, tea and medicine, according to their station.

The Hallim Academician Ch'oe Hang was made Royal Tutor. A royal instruction read: "A king should treat the three elders as his father, and the five segments [of the day?] as his elder brothers, so as to rely on wisdom and have the assistance of virtue. When I was little I was in dire straits, and could not enjoy the benefit of instruction. Still I esteem the old models and would like to obtain people in that mold. The Hallim Academician Ch'oe Hang is perspicacious and talented, standing out among his peers. He should be given the title of literatus of the policy hall and made tutor to my humble person."

Eighth month. The Executive Chief of the Chancellery Yu Panghŏn died. Yu Panghŏn had a humane and considerate character. Even in unexpected situations he never lost his composure. He was strong in Confucian studies and never engaged in profitable activities. During the reign of Mokchong he became remonstrance official. When someone criticized him for not speaking out, he replied in a relaxed manner: "You may think that speaking out is [the only way to be] straightforward, but that is not how I see it."

Ninth month. There was an ongoing fog that continued into the winter.

Winter, tenth month. Wi Suyŏ was made Executive Chief of the Chancellery, and Chin Chŏk Executive Chief of the Ministry of the Royal Secretaries.[88]

Twelfth month. A royal instruction read: "Superfluously I came to inherit the project of my forefathers, so I do not dare to take it easy in any way.

88 Here still identified as the Naesa-sŏng 內史省.

Recently the autumn fog caused great damage, so I vacated the palace halls and reduced the number of dishes. For inviting such calamity, I reproached myself, and the mists duly lifted. I will further increase my respectfulness and awe, and strenuously exert myself in the affairs of government. However, all the affairs of the realm are difficult to handle by a single person. Since everyone looks up to the important ministers of state, I hope that they may offer some wise stratagems to remedy my deficiencies. The officials in charge of selection should scour the marshes and grasslands, so that there is no wise person left behind. The officials in charge of administering the law should adjudicate important crimes with the highest degree of compassion. Everybody should exert himself in the duty allocated to him. The prefects should support the widows and widowers, and the generals and officers should train, support and prepare the troops. Day and night we should remain vigilant and dedicated from beginning to end at our tasks."

The courtesy to be exchanged between civil and military officials when they meet on the road was determined.

3. Hyŏnjong

Hyŏnjong, Great King of Primordial Culture

His given name was Sun 詢 and his courtesy name Anse 安世. He was the son of Anjong, and his mother was Queen Hyosuk, née Hwangbo-ssi. He was born in the eleventh (*imjin*) year of Sŏngjong's reign (992), on the morning of the *imjin* day of the seventh month. He was intelligent and enlightened by humanity. He was a good student and a talented writer. When he first took the tonsure he resided at Sunggyo-sa. There a monk once dreamt that a great star fell into the courtyard of the temple and transformed into a dragon; the dragon again turned into a man, who was none other than the king. Because of this the community regarded him as extraordinary. Then he was transferred to Sinhyŏl-sa. Again, someone dreamt that they heard a cock crowing and the noise of sticks pounding laundry. They asked a soothsayer, who explained this dream through the local language: "a cock's crowing is called 'ko-gwi-wi,' and the sound of pounding 'ŏ-kŭn-dang.'[1] So these are omens that he will ascend the throne." He was on the throne for twenty-two

---

1 These appear to be onomatopoeic transcriptions: *kogwiwi* 高貴位 in Korean pronunciation sounds a bit like '꼬끼오', the sound of cock crowing. However, the characters literally mean "a high and precious seat," ie. the throne. 御近當 is likely also an onomatopoeic rendering of the sound of pounding, but it is not clear to me what the modern Korean equivalent might be. The characters could mean something like "the ruler is approaching what is his due."

years and lived to the age of forty.

Hyŏnjong First year [1010]

Third year of the Dazhong xiangfu era of Song, twenty-eighth year of the Tonghe era of Khitan

Spring, intercalary second month. The Lantern Festival was restored. It was the national custom to light lanterns for two nights around the full moon of the first month, from the royal palace and the capital to the villages and county seats. From the reign of Sŏngjong it had been abolished and was thus no longer held, but now its practice was reintroduced.

Summer, fourth month. The king personally held the sacrifice at the Ancestral Shrine.

Sŏ Sung and seven others passed the composition test of the civil service examination, and three people the classics examination. The Examination Administrator,[2] Son Mongju, petitioned that candidates were tested only on poetry and prose poems, but not on policy essays.

Fifth month. The king banished the First Office Chief of the Department of Ministries, Ha Kongjin, and the Defense Registrar of Hwaju Yu Chong, to distant islands. What had happened was this: Ha Kongjin had been in charge of the eastern and western border regions, but had abused his power to raise troops and invade villages of the Eastern Jurchen. However, he was defeated. Yu Chong had heard this and deeply resented the Jurchen. It so happened that ninety-five Jurchen came to the court. On their way they reached the Hwaju office, where Yu Chong had them killed. Therefore they were exiled. The Jurchen also told the Khitan what happened, and the Khitan leader told his ministers: "Kang Cho of Koryŏ killed his sovereign Wang Song and enthroned Wang Sun, this is insubordination. We should raise troops and punish him."

---

2 Chigonggŏ 知貢擧: office of someone in charge of the examination. See Kim Kaptong, *Koryŏ chŏn'gi chŏngch'isa* (Seoul: Ilchisa, 2005), 181, 208.

Autumn, seventh month. The Khitan sent the Reviewing Policy Advisor Liang Bing and the Supreme General Yelü Yun to enquire about what happened to the previous king.

Tŏkchu was fortified.

Eighth month. The king dispatched Vice-chancellor of the Ministry of the Royal Secretaries Chin Chŏk and the Junior Assistant Director at the Department of Ministries Yun Yŏ to the Khitan.

It was forbidden for monks and nuns to brew wine.

Ninth month. The king dispatched First Assistant Office Chief of the Department of Ministries Kim Yŏnbo to the Khitan to enquire after the emperor's health. The Second Assistant Office Chief of the Department of Ministries Wang Chwasŏm and the Aide to the Director for Palace Buildings Paek Ilsŭng were sent to the Eastern Capital of the Khitan to cultivate good relations.

Winter, tenth month, *pyŏng'o* day—first day of the month. The Vice Minister of the Ministry of Personnel, and Assistant Executive in Political Affairs Kang Cho was appointed commander of the field army. The Executive at the Ministry of Personnel Yi Hyŏn'un and the Executive at the Ministry of War Chang Yŏn'u were appointed his assistants. The Acting Vice-director of the Department of Ministries and Supreme General An Sogwang was appointed cavalry commander of the field army, assisted by Vice-censor-in-chief No Chŏng. The Director of Royal Workshops[3] Ch'oe Hyŏnmin was appointed Commander of the Left Army, and the Executive at the Ministry of Punishment Yi Pang as Commander or the Right Army. The Vice-minister at the Foreign Relations Office Pak Ch'ungsuk was appointed Commander of the Central Army. The Vice-minister of the Ministry of Punishments, Ch'oe Sawi, was made Overall Commander. Leading an

---

3 Sobugam 少府監: Directorate for Imperial Manufactories according to Hucker (5098); but for *shaofu* 少府 (Hucker 5097) he gives Chamberlain for the Palace Revenues. In Koryŏ it seems to have been in charge of storing and possibly providing goods needed in the palace, and also of providing technical skills. In early Koryŏ known as the Mulchang-sŏng 物藏省, changed to Poch'ŏn-sŏng 寶泉省 in 960 and shortly after to the name it carries here. Kam 監 here refers not to the office but to director. (*Han'guk kojŏn yong'ŏ sajŏn*)

army of 300,000 they marched to T'ongju to prepare against the Khitan [invasion].

Kyech'uk day [8th]. The Khitan sent the Reviewing Policy Advisor Gao Zheng, and the Reception Official at the Office for Audience Ceremonies Han Qi to announce that an army had been raised. The Assistant Executive in Political Affairs Yi Yegyun and the Second Office Chief at the Department of Ministries Wang Tongyŏng were sent to Khitan to request peace.

Eleventh month. The king dispatched the Royal Recording Secretary Kang Chujae to Khitan to congratulate the emperor on the winter solstice.

The Khitan sovereign sent the general Xiao Ning to announce that the emperor would personally take charge of the expedition.

The P'algwanhoe was restored. The king went to the Wibong Pavilion to watch the music performance. Originally, King Sŏngjong had abolished it because it was a miscellaneous, non-canonical performance, and moreover noisy and disturbing. On the day of the festival he merely went to Pŏbwang-sa to offer incense and then returned to the polo court to receive congratulations from the assembled civil and military officials. It had already been abolished for nearly thirty years when the Assistant Executive in Letters Ch'oe Hang requested its reinstatement.

Sinmyo day [16th] The Khitan sovereign himself led an army of 400,000 cavalry and infantry, which he called the "Righteous Army of Celestial Soldiers" across the Amnok River, and encircled Hŭnghwa Garrison. The Military Inspector, the Office Chief at the Ministry of Punishment Yang Kyu; the Garrison Commissioner, the Office Chief at the Ministry of Taxation Chŏng Sŏng; the Assistant Commissioner, the Recorder at the Directorate for Palace Buildings Yi Suhwa; the Adminstrative Assistant, the Director of the Office for Sacrificial Grain and Animals Chang Ho were united in holding the fortress firm and secure.

Imjin day [17th]. Ch'oe Sawi and the other officials in charge divided up the army into three divisions and left Kwiju toward the north in the direction of Yukton, T'angjŏng, and Sŏsŏng. They clashed with the Khitan but were defeated on all fronts.

The Khitan ruler rounded up some boys and girls who had been gathering grain outside T'ongju, gave them brocade clothing and a letter wrapped around an arrow. Together with more than 300 troops he sent them to Hŭnghwa Garrison to urge them to submit. The letter around the arrow read as follows: "The previous king Wang Song has served us well for a long time. Now the treasonous official Kang Cho has killed his sovereign and put a young boy on the throne. Therefore I am personally leading these crack troops to the border of your country. You should capture Kang Cho and bring him to my carriage, and then I will immediately retreat. If not, I will immediately proceed to Kaeju [Kaesŏng] and kill your wives and children."

On the *kyesa* day [18th] again an edict was wrapped around an arrow and stuck into the garrison gate. The edict read, "This is an order to the castle lord of Hŭnghwa Garrison, its soldiers, and its ordinary folks. We have assisted and protected the previous king Wang Song in the continuation of his ancestors' submission to us as vassals. While guarding the border lands he was suddenly assassinated by treacherous and evil people. I am ready to punish them with these elite soldiers. As for the others, if you submit in awe then you will be pardoned. You of all people, who received the grace and support of the previous king, should know from history the fate of those who rebel and of those who submit. Return to my embrace without hesitating and you will not regret."

The same day Yi Suhwa and the others composed a memorial in reply: "Those who take heaven as their hat and earth as their shoes, should know how to remove the treacherous and evil. Those who support their fathers and serve their rulers should be steadfast in loyalty and righteousness. If you go against these principles, then you should meet with disaster. Prostrating ourselves, we implore you to bow down to the level of the people and honor their feelings, and proceed with your grand designs on that basis. In order to set forth Heaven's design, why first pursue a small bird like the sparrow? If you get battle ready and take the lead, you will be able to vanquish even the fiercest enemy."

On the *kabo* day [19th], the Khitan ruler presented the garrison generals with brocade clothing, silver utensils, and other presents according to rank, and issued another decree: "I have examined the memorial you presented and taken note of the contents. We have taken on the mantle of the five previous sage rulers[4] to rule the 10,000 countries. If any [of my vassals] show loyalty and benevolence they should be rewarded; if any are rebellious and evil, then they shall be punished. Since Kang Cho killed his former king and installed that young pretender, he has been flaunting his crafty power and arrogating authority. Therefore I have personally set out to punish him and mete out the correct punishment, and am ready at the head of my full army at your doorstep. Earlier I especially promulgated an edict to show my willingness to embrace you. Perusing the reply you sent me, I perceive no intention to submit. What you have stated does not come from sincerity. The words are refined, but that is merely an empty display of respect. Moreover, as you have all been officials for a long time, you should know about rebellion and compliance. How can you lend support to the plans of the rebellious party, and not even consider redressing the wrong that befell your previous king? It is only when you look back on what brought peace and what delivered disaster that you can anticipate disaster or blessing."

Ŭlmi day [20th]. Yi Suwha again sent a reply. "Your servant and the others received your edicts lately, and promptly stated our true feelings. We merely hope that you will be moved to tears by the [true] crime, and ardently hope for the benevolence of releasing the snare [i.e. the siege of the garrison]. Enduring frost and snow, we will redouble our efforts to keep the people safe. Till our bones turn to ashes and our bodies to dust, we will always uphold the thousand-year sage rule."

When the Khitan ruler saw the letter he realized they would not submit.

Chŏngyu day [22nd]. The Khitan emperor broke the siege and dispatched another edict: "Make sure that you comfort the people and look after them. 200,000 of my troops will be stationed at Murodae north of Inju. With the remaining 200,000 troops I will move to T'ongju." The Khitan ruler then

---

4 Shengzong (r. 982–1031) was the sixth emperor of the Liao Dynasty.

moved to the foot of Mt. Tongsan.[5]

Kihae day [24th]. Kang Cho led his troops out of T'ongju. South of the city he divided the army into three, each separated by rivers. He set up one camp west of the city where the three rivers converged; this is where Kang Cho himself stayed. One camp was set up on a mountain near the city, and one was set up close to the city walls. Kang Cho had sword carts[6] set up in a battle line, so whenever the Khitan attacked the sword carts faced them in a single line, and there was none who did not fall down. The Khitan had to retreat several times. Kang Cho then started to make light of the enemy, and he played *go* with others. The Khitan advance troops under Yelü Pennu, together with the general[7] Yelü Dilu then attacked and destroyed the camp at the point where the three rivers meet. The garrison commander came to announce that the Khitan troops had arrived, but Kang Cho did not believe him, and said "If there is too little food in the mouth then it is not easy to get the taste; if there are more arriving then alert me again." Hurriedly the commander said "There are already many Khitan entering!" Kang Cho was startled and got up quickly saying "is this true?" Then it was as if suddenly he sensed King Mokchong standing behind him, cursing him, "You bastard! Don't think you can escape Heaven's punishment!"

Kang Cho then removed his helmet and knelt down, saying "I am guilty of a mortal crime! I am guilty!" But he hadn't finished speaking or the Khitan troops had already arrived and tied him up. Yi Hyŏn'un, the Assistant Office Chief in the Criminal Administration Bureau No Chŏn, the Investigating Censors No Ŭi, Yang Kyŏng, and Yi Sŏngjwa were all captured, while No Chŏng, the Aide at the Court for Royal Entertainment Sŏ Sung, and the Recorder No Che were all killed. The Khitan rolled Kang Cho into a carpet and carried him away. Our troops were in complete disarray and they successfully pursued them for several tens of *li*. In the end they chopped

---

5 Tongsan 銅山: not certain what locality this refers to, or whether this might refer to a ruse in that the Khitan did not go to the place they said they were going to.

6 Kŏm'gŏ 劍車: probably a two-wheeled cart with a protective shield on which swords or spears were mounted, and behind which the soldiers could hide whilst the enemy attacked.

7 Xiangwen 詳穩: a Khitan term for general. See Hucker 2367.

off 30,000 heads, while the provisions, armor, and weapons that had been thrown away was beyond count.

The Khitan ruler then removed Kang Cho's shackles and asked him "Will you be my subject?" Kang Cho replied, "I am a Koryŏ person, how can I additionally become your subject?" The emperor asked again but the answer was as before. He then pierced his flesh and asked again, but the answer was the same. The emperor then asked Yi Hyŏn'un and he replied "My two eyes have already witnessed a new sun and moon, with my whole mind, how could I miss the old mountains and rivers?" Kang Cho was angry and kicked out at him, saying "You are a Koryŏ person, how could you talk like this?"

By that time the Khitan cavalry had already advanced far. But ahead, the Left and Right Cavalry Generals Kim Hun, Kim Kyebu, Yi Wŏn, and Sin Yŏnghan had hidden their troops in an ambush at Wanhang Pass. Brandishing short weapons they suddenly emerged and defeated the enemy, forcing the Khitan to retreat somewhat.

The Khitan then forged a letter by Kang Cho and sent it to Hŭnghwa Garrison, urging them to surrender. Yang Kyu said "I came here on the orders of the king, not on those of Kang Cho. We will not surrender." Again the Khitan made No Chŏn and the Commissioner for Audience Ceremonies Ma Su take an urgent appeal to T'ongju, telling it to surrender. Everybody inside the fortress was trembling with fear. Senior Colonels Ch'oe Chil and Hong Suk flicked their sleeves [in anger] and got up, taking with them No Chŏn and Ma Su. Together with Defense Commissioner Yi Wŏn'gu, Vice-commissioner Ch'oe T'ak, Supreme General Ch'ae On'gyŏm, and Administrative Assistant Si Kŏun they closed the gates firmly and protected them; thus they were all of one mind.

Twelfth month, *kyŏngsul* day [6th day]. The Khitan troops entered Kwakchu. The Defense Commissioner, the Assistant Office Chief at the Ministry of Taxation Cho Sŏngyu had fled in the night. The Junior Policy Monitor Sŭng Iin and the supreme generals Tae Hoedŏk and Sin Yŏnghan, the Office Chief of the Ministry of Works Yi Yongji, and the Office Chief of the Ministry of Ritual Kan Yŏng'ŏn all died. The city thus vanquished, the Khitan left 6,000 troops to guard it.

Imja day [8th day]. The Khitan troops reached the Ch'ŏngsu River. The Regional Military Commander for Anbuk, the Executive at the Ministry of Works Pak Sŏm, had abandoned the fortress and fled, and all the local people had dispersed.

When the king first heard that the Khitan troops had arrived, he dispatched Senior Colonel Chi Ch'aemun to station troops in Hwaju to guard the northeast. As soon as news broke of Kang Cho's defeat, Chi Ch'aemun was ordered to move his troops so as to relieve the Western Capital. Chi Ch'aemun immediately set out together with the Military Logistics Commissioner the Attendant Censor Ch'oe Ch'ang and occupied Kangdŏk Garrison.

Kyech'uk day [9th day]. The Khitan army reached the Western Capital and set fire to the pagoda of Chunghŭng-sa.

Kab'in day [10th day]. Sukchu fell. On this day, No Ŭi acted as local guide and together with the Khitan person Liu Jing carried an appeal to the Western Capital urging it to surrender. The Vice-magistrate Wŏn Chongsŏk and his staff, Ch'oe Wi, Han Chil, Yang T'aek, and Mun An had already drafted a letter of submission. When Chi Ch'aemun heard this, he took his troops and reached the Western Capital, but the gates were closed. Ch'oe Ch'ang called the Branch Office Censor Cho Chagi and told him: "We came here on the king's orders in a forced march, yet you don't let us in, what does this mean?" Cho Chagi informed him that No Ŭi and Liu Jing had come with the instruction to submit, and then opened the gate. Chi Ch'aemun entered and made camp in the southern corridor of the old palace. Ch'oe Ch'ang remonstrated with Wŏn Chongsŏk, and told him to detain No Ŭi and Liu Jing and to firmly maintain the city, but Wŏn Chongsŏk did not listen. Ch'oe Ch'ang and Chi Ch'aemun then secretly made the plan to send soldiers north of the city and wait for the moment No Ŭi and the others would return [to the Khitan camp], ambush and kill them and burn the letter of submission. Since there were clearly those planning sedition within the city, Chi Ch'aemun left the city and set up camp to the south of the city. The only one who followed him was the Supreme General Chŏng Ch'ungjŏl. Suddenly the Chief Military Inspector from the Northeast region T'ak Sajŏng arrived with his army, and they joined forces and entered the city again.

The king, since the three armies had been defeated and all the counties and prefectures had fallen, sent a petition to request a court meeting. The Khitan ruler granted the request. He then ordered his soldiers not to plunder, and made Ma Baoyou magistrate of Kaesŏng and Wang Ba his assistant. He also sent Yilin at the head of 1,000 cavalry to protect Ma Baoyou.[8]

Ŭlmyo day [11th]. The Khitan ruler again sent Han Qi at the head of 200 elite cavalry to the North Gate of the Western Capital fortress. He called out: "The emperor yesterday dispatched Liu Jing and No Ŭi with an edict to instruct you; how is it possible that till now there has been no news? If you do not defy the order, please send out the magistrate and his staff to listen to my instructions." T'ak Sajŏng had heard what Han Qi was saying, and made plans with Chi Ch'aemun to let his subordinate Chŏng In and others make a lightning cavalry attack. Han Qi and more than 100 others were killed, and the rest were captured; none managed to return. T'ak Sajŏng made Chi Ch'aemun the vanguard for an attack on Yilin. In the battle Yilin and Ma Baoyou were defeated and fled. Only now were the minds of the people in the city slightly at ease.

T'ak Sajŏng returned to the city, while Chi Ch'aemun and Yi Wŏn camped at Chahye-sa. The Khitan ruler again sent Yilin to attack. A guard patrol reported that the enemy troops were camping at Anjŏng station and were of great strength. Chi Ch'aemun immediately rode off to inform T'ak Sajŏng.

Pyŏngjin day [12th]. Together with T'ak Sajŏng and the monk Pŏb'ŏn they led 9,000 troops to confront the enemy south of Imwŏn station. They cut

---

8 This passage is confusing; it suggests that the king asked for a temporary reprieve to call back all his ministers for a court meeting, yet since many fortresses were still holding out many officials would not be able to make it. Also, since Hyŏnjong was still in Kaesŏng (he would flee the capital on the 28th of that month), the fact that the Khitan sent their own magistrate suggests that they were virtually certain of victory.

off more than 3,000 enemy heads but Pŏb'ŏn was killed. The next day Chi Ch'aemun again went to battle with the Khitan and defeated and drove them away. Thereupon the soldiers and officials in the city climbed the walls to see what was happening, and finally left the city to pursue the enemy to the Horse Rapids.[9] But the Khitan troops turned around and defeated them. The Khitan then encircled the city. The Khitan ruler then stayed in a Buddhist temple west of the city. T'ak Sajŏng was afraid, and tricked his general Tae Tosu by telling him "If you go out through the east gate and I through the west gate and attack them from the front and the back, victory will be assured." Then with his subordinates and soldiers he sneaked out at night. When Tae Tosu left through the east gate he first realized he had been tricked; he also realized that his force was no match for the enemy, so he led his army to submit to the Khitan. With the generals dispersed or destroyed, the city was gripped with terror.

Sami day [15th]. The Recording Officer to the General Commander, Cho Wŏn, together with the Garrison Commander of Aesu Kang Minch'ŏm and the Junior Colonels Hong Ye and Pang Hyu, at a loss as to what should be done went to pray at the spirit shrine. They obtained a positive omen from the divination, and all of them put forward Cho Wŏn as commander. They gathered the dispersed troops, closed the gates, and guarded them firmly.

Kyŏngsin day [16th]. Yang Kyu left Hŭnghwa Garrison with more than 700 soldiers. When he reached T'ongju he gathered a further 1,000 soldiers. On the *sinyu* day [17th] he entered Kwakchu and fought the Khitan troops that had been stationed there, killing them all. He gathered up the remaining 7,000 men and women and transported them to T'ongju. That day the Khitan ruler attacked the Western Capital but failed to take it. He then broke the siege and moved east.

Kyehae day [19th]. A twisting wind suddenly arose at the spirit shrine in the Western Capital, and the Khitan soldiers and their horses all fell down.

The king recalled Ha Kongjin and Yu Chong and reinstated their titles.

Sinmi day [27th]. Chi Ch'aemun hurriedly returned to the capital.

---

9 Mat'an 馬灘: located near the Taedong River around P'yŏngyang..

On *imsin* [28th] day he reported the situation of the Western Capital and the defeat of the troops there. The assembled officials discussed whether or not they should surrender. Kang Kamch'an alone opined "The blame for the present situation rests with Kang Cho, so we should not be overly worried. However, we cannot overcome the numerical advantage of the enemy and should first evade their vanguard; later we can slowly regroup and get even with them." Then he advised the king to flee south. Chi Ch'aemun then requested "your servant is without talent and weak, yet I wish to be at your side to exert myself like a dog or a horse for your protection." The king said "Yesterday Yi Wŏn and Ch'oe Ch'ang hurriedly returned, and requested to follow and protect me, yet today there is no trace of them. Is this the actual extent of the righteousness of a minister? Now you sir have already exerted yourself in the field, yet still you wish to protect me, I am deeply appreciative of your loyalty." The king then offered him food and drinks, as well as a silver incrusted saddle and reins. That night the king and his queens, together with the Executive at the Ministry of Personnel Ch'ae Ch'ungsun and fifty personal guards left the capital.

Kyeyu day [29th]. When the royal group reached Tanjo station in Chŏksŏng County, a soldier named Kyŏnyŏng together with the station attendants brandished bow and arrows and were about to attack the royal retinue. Chi Ch'aemun shot at them from horseback and the bandits ran away. [Somewhat later] they suddenly emerged again from the southwest mountain and blocked the road. Chi Ch'aemun again shot at them and drove them away. Towards dusk the king reached Ch'anghwa County.[10] There was a local functionary who addressed him: "King, do you know my name and my face?" The king pretended not to hear him, and the functionary grew angry, and began to create a disturbance, making people shout "Ha Kongjin is coming with soldiers!" Chi Ch'aemun asked "For what reason is he coming?" The functionary said "He wants to catch Ch'ae Ch'ungsun and

10 Ch'anghwa-hyŏn 昌化縣: corresponds to modern Yangju, north of Seoul in Kyŏnggi Province.

Kim Ŭng'in."[11]

Kim Ŭng'in, the Executive Yi Chŏngch'ung, and the Junior Colonel Kukkŭn all fled. At night the bandits came again. All the attending officials, eunuchs, and palace ladies fled and hid themselves, only the two royal consorts Hyŏndŏk and Taemyŏng and their two ladies in waiting, and the Recipients of Edicts Yanghyŏp and Ch'ungp'il remained to wait on the king. Chi Ch'aemun was running in and out to gauge the situation and be ready to respond, so the bandits did not dare to approach. When dawn broke, Chi Ch'aemun requested that the two consorts first leave through the north gate; personally taking hold of the bit of the king's horse [so that it wouldn't neigh], between them they went to Tobong-sa.[12] The bandits did not notice. Ch'ae Ch'ungsun then also joined them. Chi Ch'aemun proposed the following "Last night the bandits were suspecting that Ha Kongjin [had arrived], so I request to go looking for him." The king was afraid that he would disappear and did not give permission. Chi Ch'aemun then said "If I your servant betrays his ruler by breaking his word or through his actions, Heaven will surely strike him down." The king then gave him permission, and he immediately went to Ch'anghwa County.

On the road he met Kukkŭn, who told him that even his clothes had been taken by the bandits. Chi Ch'aemun told him "You have not acted like a loyal servant, so you should count yourself lucky to be still alive." Just at that time Ha Kongjin and Yu Chong were on their way to the king's traveling court, and Chi Ch'aemun happened to meet them on the road; he told them everything that had happened with the bandits and after questioning them concluded that it had not been Ha Kongjin who was behind the disturbance. Ha Kongjin had met on the road the Executive Assistant of the Middle Army Ko Yŏnggi; after the defeat of his army he was on his way south, so they decided to travel together. At the time Ha Kongjin had about twenty soldiers under his command. Chi Ch'aemun then used the soldiers to surround the

---

11 While the antagonism of local people toward the king and his entourage is obvious, a lot of the details do not make immediate sense,

12 Likely located in the eponymous Tobong-san, where there is still a temple bearing that name. Located in Uijŏngbu, northeast of Seoul.

Ch'anghwa County [office] and ferreted out the bandits' lair. He managed to retrieve fifteen stolen horses and ten saddles.

Chi Ch'aemun then told Ha Kongjin and the others "If we return now together with you gentlemen, the king will surely get a shock. Please follow a little behind me, I will go by myself." When Ch'ungp'il saw him coming back at the temple gate, he hurried back inside to tell the king that Chi Ch'aemun had returned. Overjoyed, the king went out of the gate to welcome him, Chi Ch'aemun then told the king "I managed to retrieve what the bandits took; in fact, it was not Ha Kongjin who was responsible for this. As a matter of fact, I have come together with Ha." The king then welcomed Ha Kongjin and Yu Chong and comforted them.

Kapsul day [30th]. The king went to Yangju. Ha Kongjin reported, "The Khitan originally gave as a reason for the invasion that they wanted to punish the criminal; they have now caught Kang Cho. If we now sent an envoy to request peace, they will definitely turn their troops around." The king made a divination and obtained a good omen. He then dispatched Ha Kongjin and Ko Yŏnggi with a missive to be delivered to the Khitan camp. When they reached Ch'anghwa County, they handed the missive over to the Junior Colonel Chang Min and the Sub-colonel Chŏng Yŏl, instructing them to first go the [Khitan] army and tell them "Our king firmly wishes to come in person to the emperor's quarters, but is afraid of the military might. Also, because of internal chaos he has fled to Kangnam.[13] Thus he dispatched his trusted servants Ha Kongjin and others to report on the situation, but since Ha Kongjin and the others are also afraid, they did not dare to come here. Please gather your troops quickly [and return]." But before Chang Min and Chŏng Yŏl could reach their destination, the Khitan vanguard had already arrived at Ch'anghwa. Ha Kongjin and the others transmitted the above message to the Khitan soldiers, who asked where the king now was. Ha answered, "He is now heading toward Kangnam, but I don't know his whereabouts." Again they asked whether he was near or far, and Ha

13 Kangnam 江南: one of the ten provinces (*to*) organized by Sŏngjong in 995. It corresponds to the area south of the Kŭm River, with Naju as the main center.

answered, "Kangnam is too far, I don't know how many 10,000 of *li*." The pursuing troops then turned back.

Hyŏnjong Second year [1011]

Fourth year of the Dazhong xiangfu era of Song, twenty-ninth year of the Tonghe era of Khitan

Spring, first month, *ŭlhae* day, first day of the month. The Khitan ruler entered the capital walls, and burnt the Ancestral Shrine, the palace, as well as people's houses. Everything was laid to waste. That day the king reached Kwangju,[14] but lost track of his two queens and ordered Chi Ch'aemun to find them. When he reached Yot'an station he found them and returned them to the king. Delighted, the king decided to stay for three days [in Kwangju].

Chŏngch'uk [3rd] day. Ha Kongjin and Ko Yŏnggi reached the Khitan camp, and made the request for the army to return. The Khitan ruler allowed this, but detained Ha Kongjin and the others. When the officials accompanying the king heard that Ha Kongjin had been taken, they all panicked and ran away. Only the Executive Ch'ungsuk, Chang Yŏn'u, Ch'ae Ch'ungsun, Chu Chŏ, Yu Chong and Kim Ŭng'in stayed behind.

Muin [4th] day. The king set out from Kwangju and reached Pinoe Station. Chi Ch'aemun told him "[Most of the] attending military and civil officials have dispersed to the four directions on the pretext of looking for spouses and children. At night when it is dark, I am afraid there will be treacherous bandits who will come to steal. I request that special insignia are distributed to be inserted on the hats of civil and military officials so that they can be distinguished [from bandits]." The king followed his advice.

Kimyo [5th] day. Yu Chong advised the king: "My registered hometown (*chŏkhyang* 籍鄕) is not far from Yangsŏng, I request that we pass through there." The king was pleased and they went there. At night, Yu Chong and

14 Kwangju 廣州: in Kyŏnggi Province, south of the confluence of Namhan and Pukhan rivers. Not to be confused with the modern city of Kwangju 光州 in South Chŏlla.

Kim Ŭng'in forged a royal decree that the royal saddles should be thrown away, and gave them to the county people. The next day, all the county functionaries had disappeared. Yu Chong and Kim Ŭng'in then requested to send the two queens each to their hometowns, and send their guard troops to the eastern border to prepare for an emergency. The king consulted about this with Chi Ch'aemun, who said, wailing loudly "It is precisely because ruler and ruled have lost the way that we are struggling with misfortune and find ourselves on the run like this. Now more than ever we should act with humaneness and righteousness to recover people's minds. Discarding the queens so as to obtain life, how is this something that could be endured [by a humane person]?" The king replied, "The general's words are correct."

Next, as they were passing through Sasan County, Chi Ch'aemun saw a flock of wild geese that had descended on a field. To cheer up the king, he galloped towards the geese, who took flight. Turning his body, he looked upwards and released an arrow; hitting its target, a goose fell down. The king was very happy; Chi Ch'aemun got off his horse, gathered the goose and brought it to the king, saying "With a subject such as yours truly, why be afraid of some bandits?" The king laughed heartily, and praised him. When they neared Ch'ŏnan District, Yu Chong and Kim Ŭng'in made the following request: "We would like to go ahead to Sŏkp'a station and prepare the food to welcome you." They then ran away.

Sinsa [7th] day. They reached Kongju. The Military Governor for Kongju, Kim Ŭnbu, welcomed the king with proper ritual at the outskirts of the city, saying "What brought your highness to this extreme situation where you have to climb mountains and traverse rivers, enduring frost and snow?" He offered clothes, belts, and local products. The king was pleased with this gift and changed his clothing, and distributed the products among his retinue. At dusk they reached P'asan station. All the functionaries had fled, and there was no food left in the royal kitchen. Fortunately the food that Kim Ŭnbu had offered arrived just at that moment, and was divided for the evening and morning meals.

The king said to Chi Ch'aemun, "Queen Hyŏndŏk is pregnant, so it is not convenient for her to travel far. Her hometown (*pon'gwan*) Sŏnju is not far from here, so we can send her there." Chi Ch'aemun firmly held on to his earlier advice [not to send the queens away], but the king said "In this situation there is no other option." Then she was sent [to her hometown].

When they were staying at Yŏyang County, the officers and soldiers were restless and wanted to leave. Chi Ch'aemun then proposed "When your sagacious ancestor unified the country, he rewarded everyone with merit, no matter how small it was. How the more so now that we have encountered so many dangerous and difficult situations? To obtain their minds we should first reward them abundantly." The king followed his advice, and granted the rank of *chungyun*[15] to sixteen people including Hyŏn Anji.

Im'o [8th] day. They reached Samnye station. The Military Governor for Chŏnju, Cho Yonggyŏm, came to meet the royal retinue wearing ordinary clothing. Pak Sŏm advised: "Chŏnju is in the old territory of Paekche, which our sage ancestor [T'aejo] hated. Please your highness, do not go [to Chŏnju]." The king agreed and they went straight to Changgok station and stayed there. That evening Cho Yonggyŏm planned to put the king in his place through a display of strength. He gave the Transport Commissioner Yi Chae, the Chief Military Inspector Ch'oe Chŭp, and the Deputy Director of the Palace Administration Yu Sŭnggŏn a white flag to put on their caps, and banging drums and making a racket they approached [the station]. Chi Ch'aemun ordered that the gate be firmly shut and the bandits did not dare to enter. The king and his queens remained on their horses in the official residence of the station. Chi Ch'aemun climbed on the roof and asked: "What do you want to obtain by coming here and acting like that? Has Yu Sŭnggŏn come or not?" One of the rogues[16] answered "He has come." Chi asked again "Who are you?" The other asked "And who are you?" Chi Ch'aemun did not answer the question directly so one of the rogues said "You are general Chi!" Recognizing his voice, Chi Ch'aemun said "And you are

---

15 This is the lowest of 18 ranks for local functionaries (*hyangp'um* 鄕品), so it appears to be a rather stingy reward.

16 The text uses the word "bandit" (*chŏk* 賊) throughout, but it seems that in most cases it is used to designate "rogues" or "unsavory elements" rather than simply thieves.

the King's Attending General Ma Hanjo!" Then he used a royal summons to call Yu Sŭnggŏn before the king. But Yu Sŭnggŏn said "If you do not come outside, I do not dare to go inside." Chi Ch'aemun then went outside and called Yu Sŭnggŏn, and then led him before the king. Bursting into tears, Yu Sŭnggŏn told the king "What happened today is Cho Yonggyŏm's doing, I have no knowledge [of his intentions]. Please give me a summons to call Cho Yonggyŏm to your highness." The king gave his permission and Yu Sŭnggŏn then absconded. The king ordered Yanghyŏp to summon Cho Yonggyŏm and Yi Chae to come immediately. The officers wanted to kill them, but Chi Ch'aemun shouted them down. He ordered two people to take the horse of Princess Taemyŏng and sent them back to Chŏnju.

Ŭlyu [11th] day. The Khitan army retreated [from Kaesŏng].

Chŏnghae [13th] day. The king crossed No Pass and entered Naju.

Kyŏng'in [16th] day. At night, a scout erroneously reported that the Khitan army was approaching. The king panicked and ran outside. Chi Ch'aemun told him, "If the royal retinue moves at night the people will be startled and there will be commotion. Please go back to the temporary palace. I will first inspect what is going on, and after that there will still be sufficient time to move." When Chi Ch'aemun went out to see what was happening, the Secretarial Receptionist Song Kyun'ŏn and the Sub-colonel Chŏng Yŏl had arrived with a letter from the commanding general of the Khitan vanguard, the imperial son-in-law,[17] and a report by Ha Kongjin. Chi Ch'aemun took them into the temporary palace, and when the king read the report by Ha Kongjin, he realized that the Khitan army had already retreated. Overjoyed, be made Song Kyun'ŏn Recording Officer of the Privy Council and Chŏng Yŏl Junior Colonel of the king's guard armies. The letter of the emperor's son-in-law could not be deciphered, since it was written in the Khitan language and there was nobody who could read it.

Sinmyo [17th] day. The Sub-colonel of Kuju, Kim Sukhŭng, together with the Senior Colonel Poryang attacked the Khitan and killed more than

17 *Fuma* 駙馬: probably short for *fuma douwei* 駙馬都尉, "commandant-escort", a title usually conferred on imperial in-laws. (Hucker 2083)

10,000.

Imjin [18th] day. Yang Kyu ambushed Khitan troops at Murodae and killed more than 2,000. He also recovered more than 3,000 men and women who had been taken hostage.

Kyesa [19th]. Yang Kyu again fought the Khitan at Isu and pursued them to Sŏk Pass, killing more than 2,500 and freeing more than 1,000 hostages.

Ŭlmi [21st] day. The king started his return journey and stayed at Pongnyong County.

Pyŏngsin [22nd] day. Yang Kyu again battled the Khitan at Yŏrich'am and killed more than a thousand. He also recovered more than 1,000 hostages. That day there were three battles and each ended in victory.

Kyŏngja [26th] day. The king stayed in Chŏnju for seven days.

Im'in [28th] day. Yang Kyu again attacked the Khitan, this time the vanguard, at Aejŏn, and killed more than a thousand. Suddenly the Khitan main army under the emperor was upon them. Yang Kyu and Kim Sukhŭng fought them with all their might throughout the day, but his troops were depleted and they ran out of arrows, so they all died on the battlefield that day. Leading stray armies, for almost a month he battled the Khitan seven times, killing a great number of enemy soldiers and freeing more than 30,000 hostages. The number of camels, horses, and military equipment that he obtained was beyond count. Because of the frequent attacks by Koryŏ generals and because of the heavy rains, the Khitan horses and camels were exhausted and the troops lost their armor and arms.

Kyemyo [29th] day. The Khitan army crossed the Amnok River, but because the garrison commissioner Chŏng Sŏng attacked them from the rear after about half had crossed, many Khitan soldiers drowned. All the cities that had surrendered were recovered.

The Central Terrace Department was abolished and the Security Council was reinstated.[18]

Ch'ae Ch'ungsun was appointed Director of the Palace Library, Pak Sŏm Vice-minister at the Court of Royal Entertainments, and Chu Chŏ Executive

---

18 See Chapter 2, 4th day of second month of 1009.

at the Ministry of Rites and Auxiliary Academician at the Security Council.[19] Pak Sŏm had fled from Anbuk to the capital and helped his family move from there to his native Muan County. On the road he happened to meet the royal cortege and followed the king to Naju, but eventually resigned and returned [to his home county]. When he heard that the Khitan had retreated, he resumed his duty for the king. When the royal decree [of his appointment] came, there was a lot of discussion and derision.

Second month, *chŏngmi* [3rd] day. The king left Chŏnju and on the *musin* day [4th] reached Kongju where he stayed for six days. The Military Governor of Kongju, Kim Ŭnbu, made his oldest daughter prepare new clothes for the king, and as a result he took her in marriage. She became known as Queen Wŏnsŏng.

Yang Kyu was posthumously granted the office of Vice-minister of the Ministry of Works, and Kim Sukhŭng was posthumously made general.

The king granted the Senior Colonel Chi Ch'aemun 30 *kyŏl* of land. A royal instruction read: "As I had to flee from the marauders, I encountered countless setbacks on the road, yet the only one of my accompanying officials who did not flee was Chi Ch'aemun. Enduring wind and frost, traversing mountains and crossing rivers, he never ever held back from his exertions on horseback, and remained steadfast and loyal like pines or bamboo. Thinking about all his extraordinary exploits, how could I begrudge him this rare grace?"

Chŏngsa [13th] day. The king stayed in Ch'ŏngju. The Investigating Censor An Hongjŏm submitted the following memorial: "When the Khitan troops approached Changdan, a fierce snowstorm made it look as if the Spirit Shrine of Kam Peak was full of soldiers and horses carrying flags. The Khitan were spooked by this and did not dare approach. In ancient times when Fu Qin [Former Qin, 352–410] attacked Jin, in the distance it appeared as if the shrubs and trees of Bagong Mountain transformed into

---

19 中樞院直學士: this was an official of the senior third rank in Koryŏ; in the Chinese system however an Academician would have worked at the Hall of Worthies or similar academic institutions.

Jin soldiers. Scared, they retreated. The assistance rendered by spirits, how would it be different now from the past? I request that the relevant bureau repairs and recompenses the shrine." The king followed this advice.

A Lantern Assembly [festival] was held in the temporary palace. Subsequently it was regularly held on the full moon of the second month.

Kyŏngsin [16th] day. The king left Ch'ŏngju, and on the *chŏngmyo* [23rd] day returned to the capital. He entered the Such'ang Palace.

The Ministry of Punishment requested "Yu Ŏn'gyŏng received the country's favorable treatment for generations, but rather than repaying this privilege, he led others in submitting to the enemy. We request that his wife and children be banished." The king followed this request.

Third month. The king appointed Yu Chin as Executive Chief of the Royal Secretariat, and Cho Chirin and Ch'oe Sawi as Assistant Executives in Political Affairs.

Summer, fourth month. The king appointed T'ak Sajŏng as junior policy critic.

The king prayed for rain at the Ancestral Shrine. He also moved the markets and forbade the slaughter of animals. The use of parasols and fans was forbidden, and cases of those thrown in jail were reinvestigated [to clear the innocent]; the destitute were given relief aid.

The king ordered his officials to give grain to the wife of Yang Kyu, [daughter of] the lord of Ŭnyul Prefecture, Lady Hong, and to her son Yang Taech'un the title of Editor-collator. The king personally wrote the letter of instruction: "Your husband was very talented and resourceful, and he also understood the principle of governing. He put steadfastness into practice and always manifested sincerity, he was peerless in his loyalty. Recently at the northern border he pursued and captured the invading bandits, and kept cities and garrisons safe. Scoring successive victories, in the end he was felled and died. Always remembering his merit, every year I will grant you 100 *sŏm* of rice for the rest of your life."

No Chŏng was posthumously appointed Vice-minister at the Foreign Relations Office.

Since the Supreme Generals Ch'ae On'gyŏm and Sin Yŏnghan, the Senior Colonel Wŏn Tae, the Sub-colonels Ch'oe Wŏn, Sŭbyu, and Sŭng Iin, and the Aide to the Grand Astrologer Yu Int'aek had all died in battle, to condole their families they were given rice and cloth according to rank.

The king ordered officials to gather and bury the remains of all those who had fallen in battles across the country, and make offerings to them.

The king instructed the state councilors as follows: "According to the *Analects*, 'What use [to a blind man] is the assistant who does not steady him when he totters or supports him when he falls?'[20] According to the *Book of Documents*, 'Wood by the use of the line is made straight, and the sovereign who follows reproof is made sage.'[21] Those of you, my ministers, who have obtained righteousness, would not you devote all your mind to assisting [the king]? Since I impertinently took on the royal robes, I have encountered many hardships and danger. Day and night I struggled with overcoming fear and shame, and sought to overcome my faults. Gentlemen, please force yourself to assist me without rest, and there will be no instructions to follow from me [i.e. because the officials will anticipate the orders]."

The king prayed for rain at Song Peak, and it rained heavily.

The king sent the Office Chief of the Ministry of Works Wang Ch'ŏm to Khitan to thank them for withdrawing their troops.

The Yŏngbin and Hoesŏn Hostels were built to receive foreign envoys.

Fifth month. The leader of the Jurchen from the northeast Sŏŭltu came with seventy of his retainers to offer local products. Each was granted clothes and silver plates.

Honorary titles were granted to the spirits of P'yŏngyang: Mongmi, Kyoyŏn, To Chiam, and King Tongmyŏng.

The Executive Chief of the Chancellery Wi Suyŏ requested to retire on account of his age, but the king refused this, and granted him a table and cane.

---

20 *Analects* 16.1, "The Ji Clan." DC Lau, *Confucius—The Analects*, 138.

21 "Charge to Yue Yi" 4, *Shang shu*. Translation by James Legge, retrieved from ctext.org.

Autumn, seventh month. Ch'oe Sawi was made commander of the northwest field army, and Chang Yŏn'u and Ch'ae Ch'ungsun were appointed Security Councilors.

The Ministry of Punishment petitioned: "The Office Chief Paek Haengnin stayed behind in the capital when the king's retinue left for the south. He called himself vice censor-in-chief and together with Yi Illye and Kŏjŏng mustered servants and slaves to form an army, but in the face of the enemy they did not fight but simply dispersed. Please remove his name [from the roster of officials]." The king followed this.

An instruction by the king said "Last year when the Khitan encircled the Western Capital, the monk Pŏb'ŏn showed righteousness and sacrificed himself valiantly for the country. He should posthumously be given the [monastic rank of] prior (*sujwa* 首座)."

Eighth month. The Ministry of Punishment petitioned: "When the king went to the south, Cho Yonggyŏm, Yu Sŭnggŏn, Yi Chae, Ch'oe Chŭp, Ch'oe Sŏng'ŭi, and Im T'ak, made a commotion that frightened everyone in the temporary palace. We request that their names be removed [from the roster of officials] and that they be banished." The king followed this.

Mun Inwi was made Vice Director of the Department of Ministries, and Chang Yŏn'u supervisor temporarily taking charge of the Censorate.

[The court] debated [what should happen to] the party of Kang Cho loyalists. [It was decided to] exile T'ak Sajŏng, Pak Sŭng, Ch'oe Ch'ang, Wi Chongjŏng, and Kang Ŭn to islands.

A royal instruction read "We posthumously appoint Kim Sukhŭng as general. By himself he guarded the border cities, and valiantly he engaged the enemy. His merit was that of "the strength to cut [through the enemy as if they were] bamboo." In the end he lost his life through an enemy arrow. When remembering such valor of the past, it is fitting to show concern and give rewards. Annually give his mother Lady Yi 50 *sŏk* of grains for the rest of her life."

The king dispatched the Executive at the Ministry of Taxation Ch'oe Wŏnsin to Khitan.

The king went to the gate of the Kwan'in Hall and bestowed food on the elderly and infirm, the orphans and those who were gravely ill, all according to rank.

The king appointed the Assistant Executive in Political Affairs Ch'oe Sawi as resident governor of the Western Capital.

Song'ak's walls were enlarged and repaired.

A wall was constructed for the imperial enclosure of the Western Capital.

More than a hundred ships of the Eastern Jurchen attacked Kyŏngju.

Ch'ŏngha, Hŭnghae, Yŏng'il, Ulchu, and Changgi were fortified.

Ninth month. The Assistant Executive in Political Affairs Cho Chirin died. As an official, he essentially liked to imbibe wine, and day and night he made merry. King Mokchong appointed him as Executive at the Ministry of Personnel and official in charge of the Silver Terrace. But after that he formed factions and used revenue for his own ends, and was widely derided.

T'amna requested to follow the prefecture (*chugun*) system, and asked to be granted the official sealed letter [approving this system]. The king allowed this.

Winter, tenth month. The king appointed Yu Pang Assistant Executive in Political Affairs and Resident Governor of the Western Capital. Concurrently he was made Commander of the Northwestern field army.

The king dispatched the Office Chief of the Slave Agency, Kim Sung'ŭi, to Khitan with felicitations for the winter solstice.

The palace was repaired.

Eleventh month. The king dispatched the Executive at the Ministry of Punishment Kim Ŭnbu to Khitan with felicitations for the emperor's birthday.

Twelfth month. The king appointed Mun Inwi as Assistant Executive in Political Affairs.

A royal instruction read: "The wise kings of the past regarded the people as their own children. Now that we occupy the position of shepherd of the people, how would I dare not exert myself completely [to this end]? Now we are facing a year of famine, and the weather is exceedingly cold, so I fear that the widowers, widows, and orphans cannot avoid starvation or freezing to death. Order all local offices to give them clothes and food so that they do not lose their wherewithal."

This year the Executive at the Ministry of Rights Chu Ki petitioned to use the system of covering up names for the examination of presented scholars.

The Khitan killed Ha Kongjin. When he was detained by the Khitan, inwardly he planned to return to his country, but outwardly he showed loyalty and diligence. The Khitan ruler treated him with increased affection. Then Ha Kongjin and Ko Yŏnggi hatched a secret plan, and they petitioned the emperor: "Since our country is now already defeated, your servant would like to lead troops on an inspection tour and come back." The Khitan ruler gave his permission. Then they heard that the [Koryŏ] king had returned [to his capital], and the Khitan made Ko Yŏnggi stay in the central capital and Ha Konggjin in Yanjing. They were both given the daughters of good families in marriage. Ha Kongjin bought many good horses and placed them on a road leading east, as part of a plan to return [to Koryŏ]. Someone reported his plan, and the Khitan ruler interrogated him under torture. Ha Kongjin then revealed everything truthfully. Moreover he said "Your servant doesn't dare to have divided loyalties towards my home country. I deserve to die ten thousand deaths, it is better than being alive but serving the suzerain dynasty." The Khitan ruler admired his integrity and forgave him, but afterwards tried to convince him to change his allegiance and become loyal [to the Khitan]. Ha Kongjin refused to change his mind, however, and became even more intransigent. Thus in the end he met with disaster.

Hyŏnjong Third year [1012]

Fifth year of the Dazhong xiangfu era of Song, first year of the Kaitai era of Khitan

Spring, first month. A royal instruction read: "Recently it appears that the dress of monks is becoming gradually more luxurious, so that it is no different from ordinary people. Order the relevant authority to determine a dress code [for monks]."

The resident governorship of the Eastern Capital was abolished, and instead a Kyŏngju defense councilor was installed. Furthermore, the military governors for the twelve prefectures were abolished, and instead five regional military commissioners and seventy-five provincial commissioners of inspection were established.

Kung'olsan was fortified.

Second month. A royal instruction read: "As for the prefectures and garrisons of the northwest, since they suffered from the military invasions, the people lack material and food. Now the time of spring planting is near, but there is nothing to cultivate or plant. Order the officials of each province to provide food and seeds, so that the people do not lose their livelihood."

The Jurchen chief Masijŏ at the head of sons and brothers of thirty-family villages came to offer local products and horses.

A royal instruction read: "According to the *Analects*, 'If the ordinary people do not have enough, with whom else could the prince have plenty?'[22] Nowadays, because of the fighting, the people had no chance to do farming, and the roads are full of starving people. When I think about the plight of the people, as their father-like ruler, how could I alone be at ease? Order the kitchen servants to reduce the amount of food."

The king appointed Wi Suyŏ as Director of the Chancellery, Yu Chin as Executive Chief of the Chancellery, Ch'oe Sawi as Executive Chief of the Royal Secretariat, Ch'oe Hang as Vice-minister of the Ministry of Personnel and Assistant Executive in Political Affairs, Pak Ch'ungsuk as Vice-director of the Department of Ministries, and Ch'ae Ch'ungsun as Vice-minister of the Ministry of Rites.

Third month, *kyŏng'o* [3rd] day. There was an earthquake in Kyŏngju.

Seven people including Wang Fu, a person from Song, came to submit.

The heir-apparent overseer[23] [Wang] Chŏng died. He was a commoner

---

22 *Analects* 12.9, "Yan Yuan."

23 *T'aeja ch'ŏmsa* 太子詹事: According to Hucker (79), the *zhanshi* 詹事 is the supervisor of the household of the heir apparent, yet here it appears to be part of the title of a prince.

grandson of T'aejo. His father, the prince of Tongyang, was crafty and violent, and associating with a group of unworthies, he secretly harbored designs [on the throne]. Kwangjong made him take his own life, but Chŏng and his older brother the Vice-director of the Department of Ministries [Wang] Rim were spared on account of their youth. They escaped and hid among ordinary people, begging for a living. When Kang Cho grasped power he proposed to revive the Royal Clan, and gave Chŏng and his older brother titles of nobility. He also gave them slaves and an estate, and had their names entered into the Royal Genealogy for the first time. After he died he was granted the title On'gyŏl, while his father the Tongyang prince was given the title of Heir Apparent Hyoŭn.

A Royal Instruction read: "Among the eight [objects] of government of the *Great Plan*, food comes first.[24] This is verily the way to make a country prosperous and its army strong. Recently, people have become accustomed to fickleness and indulgence, ignoring the essentials they pursue the superfluous. They do not know how cultivate the land anymore. Make a selection of the craftsman of the silk weaving and various textile quarters, and send the rest to engage in agriculture."

Kim Ŭnbu returned [from Khitan] and reached Naewŏn-sŏng. The Khitan then instructed the Jurchen to seize him and bring him back [to the Khitan].

Summer, fourth month. It was forbidden to trade silk fans.

Director of the Chancellery Wi Suyŏ died. He was upright and sincere, and always upheld the law. During the reign of King Kwangjong he had been in charge of the royal diet, and for a long time he was not transferred to another position. Since he was the oldest of his court ministers, the king made much use of him.

The Khitan summoned the king to come in person to their court.

Fifth month. The Eastern Jurchen raided the counties of Ch'ŏngha, Yŏng'il, and Changgi. The king dispatched [the officials of] the Local Navy Command[25] Mun In, Kang Minch'ŏm, Yi Int'ak, and Cho Chagi to take

24 The *Great Plan* (Hongfan 洪範) is a chapter of the *Book of Documents*.

25 Tobusŏ 都部署: an office apparently installed by Hyŏnjong to take charge of administration

charge of the military in these districts and to attack and push them back.

The Court's Palace on the Road in Kyŏngju was demolished and the material used to repair the pagoda of Hwangnyong-sa.

The king personally went to Wŏn-nŭng, the tomb of Queen Hyosuk [his mother].

A royal instruction read: "Last year the Western Capital was plagued by drought and floods, and now the price of grain has soared. The people are in dire straits and lack everything. From the time I get up to the time I go to bed I keep worrying about this predicament. Order the local administration to open the granaries and provide relief food."

Sixth month. In Yongjin Garrison, [the houses of] 340 households burned down.

Because the temporary palace was low and cramped, the king ordered that consultations with the policy-making officials would take place once every five days.

The Song Chinese Ye Jutian, Lin De and Wang Hao came to submit.

The ritual officials requested that both at the capital and in the rest of the country celebrations be held for the king's birthday. A royal instruction read: "This insignificant person became orphaned at young age, and was forever prevented from nurturing [my parents]. Every time that the day comes when my mother went into labor, my mourning becomes deeper. How could I have a celebration when I can barely contain my grief? All celebrations in the capitals and the districts should be forbidden altogether. Only hold a Buddhist Rite for Long Life,[26] and make it a regular event."

The Investigating Censor Yi Int'ak was relieved of his duties. Yi Int'ak was in conflict with the Field Commander of the Northeast, Kang Kamch'an. Disputes and accusations did not cease, hence the king relieved him of his office.

Because of the drought, the king ordered his officials to revise the sentences of those imprisoned who had grievances, and release those with

---

and military affairs in border districts, especially on the sea.

26 *Ch'uksu toryang* 祝壽道場.

light sentences. Prayers were also offered at the shrines for spirits of the mountains and rivers.

The king dispatched the Executive at the Ministry of Punishment Chŏng Kongji to Khitan with greetings for the summer season, and also to report that the king could not travel himself due to illness. The Khitan ruler was enraged and issued a command that the six fortresses of Hŭnghwa, T'ongju, Yongju, Chŏlchu, Kwakchu, and Kuju were to be seized.

Autumn, seventh month. A royal instruction read: "When I was young and residing in Sasu, Ŏnhyo and Hyojil assisted us very diligently from the beginning. They should be granted good fields as reward for their assistance."

Eighth month, *pyŏngsin*, first day of the month. There was a solar eclipse.

The Japanese Panda 潘多 and others, thirty-five people in all, came to submit.

T'amna presented two big ships.

Kyŏngju was fortified.

Ninth month. The Head Military Attendant[27] Mun Yuryŏng was dispatched to the Naewŏn-sŏng of Khitan.

Winter, tenth month. Lu Shining, from the Chu area of Song, and others came to offer local products.

Intercalary [tenth] month. The Jurchen Moilla and Sŏŭltu, leading thirty households of their tribe came to Hwaju to request an alliance. The king granted this request.

The king dispatched the Vice-Minister of the Ministry of Works Chang Yŏng and the Executive of the Ministry of Rites Yu Chingp'il to Khitan.

Minjong was reburied to the east of the [capital] city, and his tomb was named Ŭi-nŭng. His posthumous title was changed to Sŏnyang [proclaimer of yielding] and his temple name to Mokchong. Originally, after Mokchong had been killed, the title and temple name that had been offered were determined by Kang Cho, so now they were finally corrected.

27 *Sŏdu kongbonggwan* 西頭供奉官: official of rank 7B at the Bureau of Royal Stewards (Aekchŏng-guk 掖庭局).

Kim Ŭnbu returned from Khitan.

The Khitan envoy, the Defender-in-chief Han Bin, arrived.

Twelfth month, *chŏngch'uk* [14th] day. An earthquake struck Kyŏngju.

A royal instruction read: "Formerly, in the Jin dynasty, when the great palace hall burnt to the ground, Du Yu and Xie Kun advised the throne to repair the "In praise of virtue" gate and temporarily enshrine the spirit tablets there to hold the offerings. Now because the virtue of this insignificant person is deficient, the ancestral shrine has been destroyed. Though my grief and sadness are profound, there has not been any opportunity yet to rebuild the shrine. Now I want to first make the wooden spirit tablets and place them in the Purification Compound.[28] Order the ritual officials to work out the details and report their conclusions to me."

The Khitan envoy, the Commissioner of the Office of Presentations Li Tingsi, arrived.

Statues were made for the Mongmyok Shrine in the Western Capital.

Changju and Kŭmyang were fortified.

Hyŏnjong Fourth year [1013]

Sixth year of the Dazhong xiangfu era of Song, second year of the Kaitai era of Khitan

Spring, first month. The king dispatched the Deputy Director of Protocol Chang Kye to Khitan.

Dai Yi, a person from the Min region in China, came to submit. The king conferred on him the prestige title of Gentleman-Confucian, and the post of Palace Stationer. He also granted him clothes, goods, and an estate.

Second month, *imo* [20th] day. There was an earthquake in Kyŏngju.

A royal instruction read: "Despite this unworthy body of mine, somehow I became the leader of the country. Because of my accumulated errors and transgressions these natural disasters come one after the other. Isn't there an

---

28 *Chaebang* 齋坊: an auxiliary complex to the ancestral shrine (or a tomb), where the buildings are located where the ritual officiant prepares himself for the offerings.

old saying that 'disasters do not happen randomly'? This makes me fearful and worried, and I do not dare to relax. Order the officials to find a way to make these disasters stop, and report them back to me."

The king dispatched the Commissioner of the Security Council Ch'ae Ch'ungsun to Khitan.

Third month. It was forbidden to cut pine trees and cypresses.

On the *sinch'uk* [10th] day there was an earthquake in Kŭmju.

The Khitan envoy, Left Palace Guard General Yelü Xingping, came to claim Hŭnghwa and five other fortresses.

Summer, fourth month. The king appointed the Assistant Executive in Political Affairs Chang Hyŏng as Resident Governor of the Western Capital.

Fifth month. The Khitan came to announce that they had changed their era name to Kaitai.

The Jurchen were leading Khitan troops so that they could cross the Amnok River, but Supreme General Kim Sŭngwi attacked them and drove them back.

The king betrothed the daughter of Crown Prince Kyŏngjang. Prince Kyŏngjang was the third son of Taejong.[29]

The king dispatched the Acting[30] Aide at the Department of Ministries, Kim Chakpin, to Khitan to offer congratulations on the change of era name.

Autumn, seventh month. The Khitan envoy, Left Palace Guard General Yelü Xingping, again came to demand the six fortresses.

Eighth month. The king went to Ŭi-nŭng tomb[31] and declared an amnesty.

Ninth month. Im Yugan and seven others passed the composition test of the civil service examination, and one person passed the classics examination.

A royal instruction read: "The Supreme General Upholding the Country Song Nŭng and the Cavalry General-in-chief Yu Son served our T'aejo and achieved merit in battle for him; this is already a century ago; both should

29 As seen in chapter 2, Taejong was a son of King T'aejo through his fourth wife. He was also the maternal grandfather of Hyŏnjong; thus he was marrying his cousin.

30 *Ch'a* 借: acting: this means that the recipient of this office did not have the required rank, so this was effectively a temporary appointment. In this case the office was of rank 3B.

31 The tomb of Mokchong and his queen. See *Han'guk minjok munhwa taebaekkwasajŏn*.

be granted [posthumously] the rank of Taegwang."

The Vice-Minister of the Ministry of Personnel and Assistant Executive in Political Affairs Ch'oe Hang was made Chief Compiler of the Dynastic History; the Vice-Minister at the Ministry of Rites Kim Simŏn was made State Historiographer; the Executive at the Ministry of Rites Chu Chŏ, the Drafting Advisor at the Department of the Royal Secretaries Yun Chinggo, the Attendant Censor Hwang Churyang, and the Junior Policy Monitor Ch'oe Ch'ung were all made State Historiographer.[32]

Winter, twelfth month, *muo* day, first day of the month. There was a solar eclipse.

Hyŏnjong Fifth year [1014]

Seventh year of the Dazhong xiangfu era of Song, third year of the Kaitai era of Khitan

Spring, first month, *im'o* (25th) day. A shooting star was seen in the Auriga Constellation.[33]

The palace was finished.

Second month, *kyŏngsin* (4th) day. A shooting start entered the Perseus constellation.

The Jurchen envoy Mandu of the Ch'ŏlli Country chief Nasa came to offer horses and marten and flying squirrel skins.

The king instructed that those over the age of seventy but without office should be given the rank of *chŏngwi*.[34]

Summer, fourth month. People were forbidden from wearing daggers.

The king personally conducted the offerings in the Purification Compound and conferred posthumous titles. At the time the Ancestral Shrine was not

---

32 I.e. they were put in charge of compiling the *sillok*, presumably of Mokchong's reign, but perhaps also for the earlier reigns, as these had been lost in the Khitan raid of the capital.

33 *Ogo* 五車: Auriga or the Wagoner is a constellation between the Great Bear and Orion.

34 *Chŏngwi* 正位: in the T'aebong and early Koryŏ system this would correspond to the 13th of 16 ranks. In the system of local officials' ranks (*hyangp'um*), it would correspond to rank 7B.

yet completed, so every time a memorial day rite had to be performed an official was dispatched to the deceased's tomb. Now that the Purification Compound had been repaired so that spirit tablets could be temporarily enshrined there, Mokchong was the first to be enshrined. An amnesty was declared for those with punishments of banishment or below.

Yu Chin was appointed Acting Grand Preceptor and Probationary Director of the Chancellery; Ch'oe Sawi Executive Chief of the Chancellery; and Kim Simŏn Executive Chief of the Department of Royal Secretaries.

U Hyŏnbu and ten others passed the composition test of the civil service examination.

Fifth month. Deputy Commissioner at the Security Council Chŏn Kongji died. He excelled at composing diplomatic correspondence and had been in office successively for more than twenty years. He was praised by the king for his diligence and exemplary work.

Sixth month. A Royal Instruction read: "Regarding the soldiers on defensive duties, for those that die on the road, officials should provide necessities for the funeral; the coffin with the bones should be delivered via the postal stations to his family. As for those who die on duty but whose names or place of origin are not recorded, the local administration should give them a temporary burial and record their age and appearance; let there be no questions or obfuscation on this."

The Finance Commission petitioned: "The price of goods has soared recently; one bolt of ordinary cloth now costs eight *tu* of rice. Even if there is a bumper harvest that drives down the price of grain, how is this possible? Please set the price according to the weight." This was followed.

The king promoted Chin Chŏk and Yi Yegyun to Executive Chief of the Chancellery, Wang Tongyŏng to Executive Chief of the Department of Secretaries, Yun Yŏ to Vice-minister at the Court of Royal Entertainments, and Wang Chwasŏm to Vice-Director of the Directorate for Palace Buildings. This was due the fact that they had all been sent as official emissaries to Khitan but had been detained and had not returned.

Autumn, seventh month. The Commissioner of the Security Council

Kang Kamch'an requested that the Altar for the Earth and Grain Deities be repaired, and that the Ministry of Rites debate and decide on the procedures and rites. The king followed this.

Eighth month. The king dispatched the Drafting Advisor at the Department of the Royal Secretaries Yun Chinggo to Song to offer saddle-cloths with dragons and phoenixes stitched in gold-thread fabric, and saddle cloths with embroidered dragons and phoenixes, two pairs each; he also gifted twenty-two good horses. He was to request allegiance to Song just as in former times. The Song emperor decreed that Dengzhou[35] should install a hostel for them on the sea where the Korean embassy would stay.

The Executive Chief of the Department of Royal Secretaries Kim Simŏn was made prefect of the Western Capital.

Ninth month. The Khitan sent their General Li Songmu to again demand the six fortresses.

Winter, tenth month. The Khitan dispatched their Dynastic Elder[36] General Xiao Dilie to invade T'ongju and Hŭnghwa fortresses. General Chŏng Sinyong and Sub-colonel Chu Yŏn fought and defeated them, killing more than 700. Those that drowned in the [Amnok] river were numerous.

Eleventh month, *kyemi* day, first day of the month. Supreme Generals Kim Hun and Ch'oe Chil at the head of several divisions caused a disturbance; the Commissioner at the Security Council Chang Yŏn'u and the caretaker [at the Security Council] Hwangbo Yuŭi were banished.

From the deployment of troops in the *kyŏngsul* year (1010) onwards, the total number of soldiers had increased. Because of this, the salaries for officials were insufficient. Hwangbo Yuŭi and others then proposed to take the perpetuity land[37] of the Capital Garrison to supplement the salaries, but the military officials thought that this was unfair. Furthermore, Ch'oe Chil was aggrieved that despite receiving successive military offices for merit at the border, he did not receive any civil offices. Thereupon Kim Hun

35 Port city on the northern shore of the Shandong peninsula, now part of Penglai city.

36 *Guojiu* 國舅: usually refers to a maternal uncle of the emperor.

37 *Yŏng'ŏpchŏn* 永業田.

and Ch'oe Chil, together with Pak Sŏng, Yi Hyŏp, Yi Sang, Yi Sŏm, Sŏk Panghyŏn, Ch'oe Kajŏng, Kong Mun, Im Maeng, and others, stirred up the anger of the multitude because of the grabbing of land, and convinced the soldiers of several divisions to follow them. Beating the drum and making a lot of noise they burst into the palace, and tied up Chang Yŏn'u and Hwangbo Yuŭi, beating them to within an inch of their lives. They then went to the main hall of the palace, and appealed directly to the king: "Hwangbo Yuŭi and his ilk have taken away our land and use it for themselves, effectively seeking their own profit, not the profit of the public. If you cut off the feet and fit them into shoes, what use will they be for the four limbs? All the soldiers are dejected and can no longer repress their feelings of anger and resentment. Please remove these parasites from the land and appease our feelings." The king was cautious not to go against their feelings, and for the time being followed their request. Then he had the two stripped of their office and sent into exile.

Ŭlyu (3rd) day. Kim Hun and the others requested that military officials of the *sangch'am* rank[38] and above would be given concurrent civil posts. He also requested to abolish the Censorate and replace it with the Golden Bird Terrace,[39] and to abolish the Finance Commission and replace it with the Capital Registrar Commission.[40]

A rumor was spread to the effect that monks from the temples on the north mountain had raised an army and were approaching the capital. There was great consternation and everyone was on their guard.

Twelfth month. The king declared an amnesty, but Hwangbo Yuŭi and Chang Yŏn'u were excluded. The king also reduced taxes by half, and granted emoluments to the descendants of T'aejo's merit subjects. He also bestowed favors on central and local officials according to rank.

---

38 *Sangch'am* 常參: those ranks that could take part in the daily court meetings. Usually rank 5 and above.

39 Kŭmodae 金吾臺: Probably named after the Golden Bird Division 金吾衛, one of the "six divisions" in the Koryŏ military system.

40 Tojŏngsŏ 都正署: for these two offices I have used explanatory rather than functional translations to differentiate from the original offices (Ŏsadae 御史臺 and Samsa 三司 respectively). They were both abolished the following year.

Hyŏnjong Sixth year [1015]

Eighth year of the Dazhong xiangfu era of Song, fourth year of the Kaitai era of Khitan

Spring, first month. The Khitan constructed a bridge over the Amnok River, and built protective walls to the west and east of the bridge. A general was sent to attack and destroy it, but he failed.

Kyemyo (22nd) day. The Khitan army encircled Hŭnghwa Garrison, but the Generals Ko Chŏg'yŏ and Cho Ik managed to repel them. On the *kapchin* (23rd) day they again invaded T'ongju.

Third month. The king went to the Western Capital.

He held a banquet for the assorted officials in the Changnak Palace, and had Kim Hun, Ch'oe Chil, Yi Hyŏp, Ch'oe Kajŏng, Sŏk Panghyŏn, Yi Sŏm, Kim Chŏngyŏl, Hyo Am, Im Maeng, Ch'oe Ku and others, nineteen people altogether, executed.

At the time, since the military officials had managed to obtain civil posts, government was now being conducted through too many gates, and the court was in chaos. The former defense commissioner of Hwaju, Yi Charim, secretly told the caretaker [of the Security Council] Kim Maeng: "Why doesn't the king put into effect a 'journey to Yunmeng' just like Emperor Gaozu of Former Han?"[41] Kim Maeng understood what he meant, and secretly petitioned the king to appoint him. Since Yi Charim had previously worked as a chief secretary[42] in the Western Capital, he had already obtained the minds of the people. Then he was appointed administrative assistant to the resident governor[43] of the Western Capital, and was ordered to travel ahead and make preparations. Then Kim Hun and the others were made drunk, and soldiers came in to kill them. Ch'oe Ku was a Confucian scholar, but he was also an office chief at the Ministry of War, in charge of guarding

---

41 This refers to a story about the first emperor of the Han Dynasty, Liu Bang, later given the temple name Gaozu (r. 202–195 BC). To eliminate a rival, rather than attacking him directly, he traveled to a place called Yunmeng and had him killed while he was away. Ban Gu, *Han shu*, biographies.

42 *Changsŏgi* 掌書記: Chief secretary. According to Hucker (no. 189), served on the staff of Surveillence Commissioners or prefectures.

43 *Yusu p'angwan* 留守判官.

the king; his character was coarse and vulgar, and he associated with Ch'oe Chil and his ilk. Therefore he was also killed.

The Khitan invaded Yongju.

The Jurchen attacked Kudup'o Garrison with 20 ships. The Local Navy Command of Myŏng-do[44] repelled them.

Summer, fourth month. The Khitan envoy General Yelü Xingping came, again demanding the six fortresses; he was detained and not allowed to return.

The king returned from the Western Capital.

Fifth month. Kim Ŭnbu was put in charge of the Security Council.

Sixth month, *kiyu* day, first day of the month. There was a solar eclipse.

Intercalary sixth month. Sasu County was upgraded to Saju.

Ouyang Cheng, a person from Quanzhou in Song, came to submit. He was made junior policy monitor.

Autumn, seventh month. The Golden Bird Terrace was abolished and replaced with the Censorate. All the institutions that had been requested by the military officials were abolished.

The Capital Military Command[45] petitioned: "Generals Chŏng Sinyong and Im Yŏngsa, together with 12,500 soldiers all have earned merit through their service at the border. Please raise their ranks as a reward." This was followed.

Eighth month. Minister of the Department of Royal Secretaries Yu Yunbu died.

Ninth month, *kab'in* [7th] day. The Khitan envoy, the Palace Gate General Li Songmu came to demand the six fortresses.

Kimi [12th] day. The Khitan came and attacked T'ongju and Hŭnghwa Garrisons. The Supreme General Chŏng Sinyong, Sub-colonel Chu Yŏn, Executive Captain Im Ŏk, Lieutenant Yang Ch'un, Aide to the Royal Physician Son Kan, and Aide to the Grand Astrologer Kang Sŭngyŏng,

---

44 Myŏngdo Tobusŏ 溟道 都部署: Myŏngdo likely refers to Kangnŭng (Myŏngju), while Tobusŏ is the name of a local navy command.

45 Tobyŏngmasa 都兵馬使

leading the troops attacked the Khitan from the rear, and killed 700 of them. However, Chŏng Sinyong and the five others were all killed in battle.

Chŏngmyo [20th] day. The Khitan attacked Yŏngju Fortress but could not subjugate it and retreated. Supreme General Ko Chŏg'yŏ and Generals So Ch'onghyŏn and Ko Yŏnjik, Executive Captain Kim Ki, Sub-colonel Kwang Ch'am and others went in pursuit but were killed. The Khitan soldiers took the Administrative Assistant to the Military Commander Wang Chwa and the Recorder No Hyŏnjwa captive and left.

Winter, eleventh month. The Vice-minister at the Ministry of Taxation Chang Yŏn'u died. Towards the end of Silla, his father Chang Yu, to avoid the chaos had traveled to Wu-Yue where he studied Chinese. Upon his return, King Kwangjong repeatedly appointed him to the Foreign Relations Office,[46] and whenever envoys came from China, he was in charge of receiving and looking after them. Chang Yŏn'u excelled in administrative work and had an illustrious career; he was praised by the king for his ability.

This year the Khitan seized the garrisons of Sŏnhwa and Chŏngwŏn and fortified them.

[During this year] the king dispatched the Executive at the Ministry of Taxation[47] Kwak Wŏn to Song to present tribute.[48] He also reported that the Khitan had been invading [Koryŏ] for the past several years.

Hyŏnjong Seventh year [1016]

Ninth year of the Dazhong xiangfu era of Song, fifth year of the Kaitai era of Khitan

Spring, first month, *kyŏngsul* [5th] day. The Khitan Yelü Shiliang and Xiao

46 Kaek-sŏng 客省: originally the Yebin-sŏng 禮賓省, but changed to this name in the 14th year of Sŏngjong's reign (995). *Koryŏsa* 76, 百官一, 禮賓寺.

47 *Mingwan sirang* 民官侍郎: Mingwan is another designation for the Ministy of Taxation.

48 Kwak Wŏn's mission is also attested in the *Songshi*, where his description of Koryŏ customs is quoted. See Sem Vermeersch, *A Chinese Traveler in Medieval Korea: Xu Jing's* Illustrated Account of the Xuanhe Embassy to Koryŏ (Honolulu: University of Hawai'i Press, 2016), 41. Of course, since the tribute relation with Song had been broken off, technically he could not present tribute, but that is the term used (*kongbangmul* 貢方物).

Juelie attacked Kwakchu. Our troops fought with them, and several tens of thousands died. They put military supplies in carts and returned.

Kab'in [9th] day. A Khitan delegation of ten people arrived at the Amnok River but they were not received.

The king posthumously made Chŏng Sinyong Junior Vice-director at the Department of Ministries, and Supreme Pillar of State; Chu Yŏn General; Im Ŏk Senior Colonel; Yang Ch'un Junior Colonel; Son Kan Chief Steward at the Palace Medical Service; and Kang Sŭngyŏng Grand Astrologer. He also ordered to appoint Chŏng Sinyong's son Kyunbaek as Junior Colonel and Chief Steward of the Livery Service.

The Ministry of War requested that Junior Colonels Chin Myŏng, Yu Ko, Ka Kanghyo and others, seventy-four in total, be posthumously raised by one rank as reward for their merit at the border. The king followed this advice.

A royal instruction read: "Because the harvest in the counties and prefectures of Kangnam was bad, many people are starving. Let the local officials provide grain and seed and make them encourage the people to engage in agriculture."

Due to the service rendered by the deceased General Ko Yŏnjŏk at his death, the king presented as funeral expense to his family fifty *sŏk* of rice, thirty *sŏk* of barley, and 100 bolts of cloth.

Taxes and local tribute for P'oju and other localities, nineteen altogether, were remitted for the year.

T'aejo's coffin was restored to the Hyŏn-nŭng timb. During the chaos of the *kyŏngsul* year [1010] it had been moved to Hyangnim-sa in Pua-san, but now it was finally restored to its original burial place.

Kwak Wŏn returned from Song. When he was in Song China, it so happened that the Jurchen also [were there to] complain that the Khitan had been pestering them for several years, preventing them from coming to the Song court. Due to his covenant with the Khitan, it was difficult for the Song emperor to reply, so the Scholar Qian Weiyan wrote a draft edict that went as follows: "The purpose of our rule is to direct and shepherd, and my mind is set on bringing peace to the people. Even though our territories are divided because what differentiates us, still I pursue everything with utmost sincerity, not letting anything come in between. When I think of your country, my heart is filled with sadness. But while wishing to take care of you, our border with the neighboring state [of Liao] has been longstanding, and we have well observed the covenant. What I look forward to is to live in peace and make the life of the people agreeable." When the emperor read this he was happy and said "Put this way, even if the Khitan see it there will be no harm done." Then he instructed Kwak Wŏn to visit the Kaibao temple. Secretly he told the escort commissioner, the Assistant Office Chief Zhang Shide, to gradually appraise Kwak of the situation. Together with Kwak Wŏn, Zhang Shide climbed the pagoda [of Kaibao temple], and softly told him "Now all the high and prominent buildings of the capital are all military garrisons. The emperor is ruling over a unified empire, and is moreover preparing the soldiers; every day he makes them train for battle so as to be ready for what happens at the northern border. If our emperor has prepared like this, how much more should this be the case for your country, where you face off with them across the border? Staying on good terms and giving the people rest is the best long-term planning you can make."

Second month. The Ministry of War requested that the Senior Colonels Ch'oe Koeng and Yi Kang and others, 159 people altogether, because of their merit in battle be given a rank higher by one grade. The king followed this request.

The Khitans Wangmei and Yanxiang and others, seven people altogether, fled to Koryŏ.

The family of Kim Hun and other [military who had caused a riot], including parents, spouses, brothers and sisters, grandfathers and grandchildren, and aunts and uncles, despite their guilt by association, were released. As for his sons and their halfbrothers, they were sent back to their hometown, but were excluded from habitual pardons.

On the *sinch'uk* [26th] day, Venus traversed the skies.

The Ministry of War requested that General Hwang Homaeng and others, thirty-nine people in total, because they had established merit in battle, be promoted by one rank. The king followed this.

The Khitan Caoen, Gaohu, and others, six people altogether, came to submit.

Summer, fifth month, *ŭlsa* [2nd] day. A son, Wang Hŭm,[49] was born to the king.

The Ministry of Punishment requested that in case an official or local administrator would enrich himself during an inspection, regardless of whether he had appropriated much or just a little, that he would be removed from office and exiled to his place of origin (*pon'gwan*). The king followed this.

The Khitan Ma'er Baoliang, Wang Bao, and others, thirteen households altogether, came to submit.

The soldiers Kyulsŏn and Yŏngmong from Kuju were planning a revolt, so they were executed.

The Khitan Yaodou, Zhifu, and others, six people altogether, came to submit.

Sixth month. The Khitan Zhang Lie, Gongxian, Shendou, You'er, Wang Chong and others, 30 households altogether, came to submit.

Autumn, seventh month. The Capital Military Command requested that the General Ko Chŏg'yŏ, the Senior Colonel Sŏ Kŭng, the Junior Colonel Suam and others, 3,108 people in total, because of their service at the [battle of] T'ongju, where they had captured or killed numerous [enemy soldiers], regardless of whether they were alive or dead, be promoted by one rank. The king followed this.

Kim Hyŏn and eight others passed the composition test of the civil service examination, and five passed the classics examination.

Yi Chuhŏn was appointed Junior Vice-director of the Department of Ministries.

The Khitan Youdao, Gaozong, and others, nine people altogether, came to submit.

---

49 He would later become King Tŏkchong (r. 1031-34).

A royal instruction read: "Recently, we heard that while the autumn harvest is nearly there, hordes of locusts are causing damage. Could this not be caused by the disarray in administration of punishment? Make sure that the prisoners in the capital and in the provinces being tried for crimes punishable with labor or banishment or lower, are released on bail, and that their cases are swiftly adjudicated."

Eighth month. The Khitan Zhujian, Congdao, and others, eight people altogether, came to submit.

Ninth month. Because of locusts and drought in the counties of Namgye,[50] the king avoided the main palace hall and reduced the amount of sidedishes; also drinking wine and performing music was forbidden in all the palaces.

The Khitan Luoken and others, five people altogether, came to submit.

Yi Chuhŏn was appointed resident governor of the Western Capital.

The Finance Commission requested that, to relieve the hunger in the localities of Kangnam, grains be transported from granaries within the pass; the king followed this.

The Khitan Fengda, Gaoli, and others, nineteen people altogether, came to submit.

Winter, tenth month. The king instructed that since robbers were numerous in the southern border region, all counties and prefectures should be strict in pursuing and apprehending them.

Eleventh month. The king bestowed twenty *kyŏl* of good farmland on the family of Chŏng Sinyong,

Ch'oe Hang was appointed Executive Chief of the Ministry of the Royal Secretaries, and Yu Pang Vice-Minister at the Ministry of Punishment and Assistant Executive in Political Affairs.

The king prayed for snow at the various lookouts.

The Khitan Kuangyier and others, ten people altogether, came to submit.

---

50 Namgye 南界: apparently refers to the area of Ch'ŏngha-myŏn in Yŏng'il-gun, S. Kyŏngsang Province. "Kye" is also a term used for the border circuits, but although there is a northern and eastern Kye, as far as known there was no southern Kye.

Twelfth month. The Vice-minister of the Ministry of Personnel, Kang Kamch'an, petitioned: I have twelve *kyŏl* of land in Kaeryŏng County; please let me donate it to military families. The king approved.

The Khitan Sefuda and others, six people altogether, came to submit.

This year the Song era names were restored.

Hyŏnjong Eighth year [1017]

First year of the Tianxi era of Song, sixth year of the Kaitai era of Khitan

Spring, first month. The Assistant Executive in Political Affairs Chang Hyŏng requested permission to retire; this was granted.

The king ordered all officials and local administrators to apprehend those that intentionally set fire to people's houses to seize their belongings.

It was again forbidden for people to donate their houses to make it into a temple, or for spouses or daughters to become nuns.

Third month. Chŏng Paegŏl and seven others passed the composition test of the civil service examination.

Summer, fourth month. The king dispatched the Executive Chief of the Chancellery Ch'oe Hang and the Vice-commissioner of the Security Council Yun Chinggo to Saju to bring back the coffin of Anjong. The king received [the coffin of his father] at the eastern suburbs, and he was reburied in the Kŏn-nŭng tomb.

Fifth month. Yi Kong was put in charge of the Security Council.

The Commissioner of the Security Council, Kim Ŭnbu, died. Kim Ŭnbu was diligent and upright by nature. The three queens [of Hyŏnjong], Wŏnsŏng, Wŏnhye, and Wŏnp'yŏng, were all his daughters. Posthumously he was granted the position of Director of the Chancellery.

Sixth month. There were plant-destroying insects.

Autumn, seventh month. The Khitan Guangzheng and others, seven households altogether, came to submit.

The Ministry of War requested that the *chŏngbo* Yi Yongbong, the *chŏngjo*

Im Sulgwang and others, thirty people altogether, be granted a promotion of one rank in the local administrative hierarchy for their merit at the border. The king followed this.

Lin Renfu and others from Quanzhou in Song, forty people altogether, came to offer local products.

Relief was provided for the poor people of the capital.

The Jurchen Malgal Moksa, leading [the people] of his community, came to court. He was granted a title and also given clothes and presents.

The Khitan Maiseduoyi, Zheng Xin, and others, forty people in total, came to submit.

The king dispatched the Executive at the Ministry of Punishment Sŏ Nul to Song to present local products.

Junior Vice-director of the Department of Ministries An Sogwang died. He came from a family of military officials, and he was strongly built and handsome, with an air of authority. He loved hawks and horses. When Mokchong came to the throne, in reward for his assistance he was put in charge of the royal guards. He received extraordinary favors and attention.

Eighth month. The Khitan Guoxuyi and others, three households altogether, came to submit.

The king went to Kŏn-nŭng, [the tomb of his father].

The Eastern Jurched Kaedabul and others, four people altogether, came to submit. They requested the chance to establish merit at the border, and received permission. The king also bestowed presents on them.

The Western Jurched Kaesin seized the monk Daozun from the Eastern Capital of Khitan and came [to present him at court].

The Khitan Xiao Hezhuo surrounded Hŭnghwa Garrison and attacked it for nine days, but could not take it. Then the generals Kyŏnil, Hong Kwang, and Ko Ŭi charged out to fight, and defeated them. They killed or caught many [enemy soldiers].

The Black Water Malgal Aribul and others, six people in total, came to submit. They were resettled in various counties of Kangnam.

Ninth month. The Khitan Qunqi and Kunji, the Jurched Kojŏ and others, ten households altogether, came to submit.

The Khitan Wudou and others, eight people altogether, came to submit.

The king went to the Sŏnjŏng Hall to inspect the troops.

There was drought and locusts. The king shunned the main hall and reduced the consumption of sidedishes.

Winter, eleventh month, *kihae* [5th] day. Venus passed through the sky.

Twelfth month. Ch'ae Ch'ungsun was appointed Commissioner to the Security Council.

The king visited the Hyŏn-nŭng tomb [of T'aejo] and declared an amnesty.

The king instructed: Make all the relevant local authorities repair and manage the royal tombs and graves of Koguryŏ, Silla, and Paekche. It should be forbidden to gather firewood from these places, and those who pass by should dismount.

Hyŏnjong Ninth year [1018]

Second year of the Tianxi era of Song, seventh year of the Kaitai era of Khitan

Spring, first month. The king dispatched a commissioner to the Western Capital to make sacrifices at the Portrait Hall of T'aejo, because the portrait had been redone.

The Western Jurched Mialtal and others, seven people altogether came to offer armor, helmets, and horses.

Kolsu, a person from Chŏng'an Country, fled to us.

The state councilors, leading all the other officials, came to present a petition urging the king to return to the main palace hall, and resume the eating of his habitual dishes, but the king refused.

The Eastern Jurched Sŏyulbul and the Western Jurched Aju, and others, more than forty people altogether, came to offer horses, armor, helmets, flags and pennants, sable skins, and flying squirrel skins.

Because of the recent fighting, the people of Hŭnghwa Garrison were destitute, and suffering from cold and hunger. They were provided with cotton cloth, salt, and soybean sauce.

The ministers frequently requested the king to resume dishes as usual, and the king consented.

Second month. The king bestowed tea and cloth according to rank to lieutenants and mariners and lower ranks of the Navy and Arbalest forces.

The royal commissioner of pacification post for all the provinces was abolished. In their stead were installed four protectorates (*toho* 都護), eight departments (*mok* 牧), fifty-six administrators of major and lesser prefectures (*chijugunsa* 知州郡事), twenty-eight garrison commanders (*chinjang* 鎭將), and twenty county magistrates (*hyŏllyŏng* 縣令).

The Western Jurchen Nŭnggŏ and Kŏi, and others, came to present animal skins, iron armor, and horses.

The king went to Sŏnhwa Gate to inspect the archery display.

A royal instruction read: "According to the *Book of Rites*, in the last month of spring, the prisons should be inspected and fetters and handcuffs removed.[51] The law courts of the capital and the provinces should observe the 'Monthly Ordinances' [of the *Book of Rites*], so as to induce the Yang force and harmony. Make this a permanent rule."

The Eastern Jurched Noŏ, leading his community, came to offer horses and sable skins. The king bestowed clothes and presents on him.

The Capital Military Command requested to lend official oxen to the people of Hŭnghwa, who had endured many attacks and chaos and were without any cattle, so that they could till the land. The king followed this.

The Lieutenant Pak Myŏnggŭm of Yongju requested that the rank and office he had received for meritorious service at the border be transferred to his father. The request was granted.

Honorary titles were given to the spirits of all the country's rivers and mountains.

The Western Jurchen Mamun, Maaldal, and others came to present horses.

---

51 Actually this instruction can be found under the second month of spring rather than the third month; see the Yueling 月令 chapter of the *Li Ji* 禮記.

The king granted them produce and presents.

The Khitan Zhang Zheng and others, four people altogether, came to submit.

Third month. The Khitan Song Kuangxi, Yigai, and others, more than ten people altogether, came to submit.

The king ordered officials to gather and bury the remains of those who had died of hunger at the city outskirts and in the region around the capital.

The Eastern Jurched Arigo and the Western Jurched Nŭnggŏ and others, more than 100 people altogether, came to offer tribute and were granted ranks; they were also given silk.

Summer, fourth month, *mujin* [5th] day. Queen Kim died, and received the posthumous title Wŏnjŏng. She was buried in the Hwa-nŭng tomb.

Kyŏng'o [7th] day. A yellow mist covered the capital area for four consecutive days and many suffered from miasma. The king sent out physicians all around to cure them.

The Eastern Jurched Kut'ara and the Western Jurched Kŏil and others, more than twenty people altogether, came to present horses, weapons, and regalia; the king granted clothes and presents. The Western Jurched Moksa, Mokkae and others, 200 households altogether, came to submit.

Intercalary [fourth] month. The Director of the Chancellery, Yu Chin, and others presented the following petition: "The people are suffering from epidemics and the forces of Yin and Yang are all mixed up. This is all caused by the fact that the administration of punishments does not follow the right time. According to the 'Monthly Ordinances' [of the *Book of Rites*], in the third month prisons should be inspected and fetters and handcuffs removed, there ought to be no wanton beatings and litigations should be stopped. In the fourth month, those who have committed grave crimes should be sentenced leniently, and those with minor crimes should be released. In the seventh month, the prisons should be repaired and equipped with fetters and handcuffs, light crimes should be punished and small crimes adjudicated. Furthermore, according to the 'Ordinances for Prison Officers,'[52] from the

52 Okkwal-lyŏng 獄官令: probably from the Tang legal code.

beginning of spring to the autumnal equinox, no death sentence should be pronounced, but in case of heinous crimes and treason this law does not apply. Although this should be known, we fear that the law officials are not yet completely conversant with these guidelines, so please make sure that all officials in the country henceforth comply with them." The king followed this.

The Eastern Jurched chief Arodae and others came to present horses and sable fur. The king bestowed clothes and presents on them.

Wang Suzi, from the Jiangnan area of Song, and others, twenty-four people altogether, came to offer local products.

The pagoda of Kaeguk-sa was repaired and at this occasion more than 3,200 people were ordained as monks.

Fifth month. The Khitan Shifu came to submit.

100,000 monks were given food.

The Eastern Jurchen Una, T'ŭgo, Ibul, and others, more than thirty people altogether, came to offer horses and weapons; the king bestowed official ranks and gave clothes and presents.

Kang Kamch'an was made Resident Governor of the Western Capital and Executive Chief of the Ministry of the Royal Secretaries. The king personally drafted the letter of appointment, and later told him: "During the *kyŏngsul* year [1010] the Caitiff spears and halberds, numerous like dust, penetrated deep into the country, reaching the shores of the Han River. If it had not been for your strategy, the whole country would have worn their clothes with the lapels on the left."[53] People at the time considered [these words] a great honor.

The *chwayun* Kang Yunbong and others, nineteen people altogether, were promoted by one rank for their merit in battle.

There were plant-destroying insects in the northwestern border region.

The king instructed that all soldiers and officers from the various

---

53 *Chwaim* 左衽: stock expression for "barbarians," who were said to fasten their coats under the left arm, i.e. by putting the right side of the robe or coat over the left; the standard way was to fasten it under the right arm.

prefectures and garrisons who had established merit during the Khitan invasion of the *ŭlmyo* year [1015], be given a higher office rank; for those who had died sufficient condolence money should be given.

Hwang Chŏng and eight others passed the composition test of the civil service examination, and ten people passed the classics examination.

The Western Jurchen T'aŏk, Silbul, and others, ten people altogether, came to present horses, armor, and helmets; they were given higher offices and presents.

Sixth month. Ch'ae Ch'ungsun was appointed Vice-minister of the Ministry of Personnel and Assistant Executive in Political Affairs.

The Jurchen from the northwest Kaŭlbul and others, thirty people altogether, came to present horses and military equipment.

Hyŏnhwa-sa was established to pray for blessings for the deceased parents of the king.

On the *kyŏngsul* [19th] day, a shooting star emerged from the Big Dipper; it was more than forty feet long.

The Eastern Jurchen Nigori and the Western Jurchen Chemo came to court.

The Ministry of War requested that General Yang Ak and Senior Colonel Ham Chin and others, 449 people altogether, had established merit at the border and should be promoted by one rank. The king followed this.

Autumn, seventh month, *chŏngch'uk* [17th] day. Prince Wang Hyŏng was born.[54]

The Eastern Jurchen Oduju and others, more than thirty people altogether, came to present horses and military equipment. They were given clothes and presents.

Eighth month. The king instructed that the parents, spouses, and children of the officers and soldiers who had died on the northern border since the *ŭlmyo* year [1015] be given presents commensurate with rank.

Ninth month. The king went to the Sŏnhwa Gate and gathered the Three

---

54 The later King Chŏngjong (r. 1034–1046).

Divisions,[55] the Royal Soaring Eagle Army, the descendants of merit subjects, and those civil officials below rank six with military skills, and had them tested and graded.

The Executive Chief of the Ministry of the Royal Secretaries, Kim Simŏn, died. Originally he studied with the Policy Advisor Ch'oe Sŏm. Once while sitting [at his desk] he dozed off and dreamt that fire came out of Kim Simŏn's crane and shot up to heaven. He thought him an extraordinary person, and gave his daughter in marriage. After he passed the examination, he served in all of the Three Departments. When he was appointed to far-off provincial posts, he devoted himself to agriculture and to the local people. Therefore he gained a high reputation.

The Eastern Jurchen Niubul came to court, and was granted a higher local office.

Yun Chinggo was put in charge of the Security Council.

There was a general pardon.

Winter, tenth month. The Junior Vice-director of the Department of Ministries, Kim Nohyŏn, died. Kim Nohyŏn garnered praise for his diligence and talent. Whenever there was a construction project he was made overseer.

The king granted the Jurchen Moksa from Kuju and others, thirty-four people in total, more than 500 bolts of various types of silk and cloth, as a reward for catching bandits.

Executive Chief of the Ministry of the Royal Secretaries Kang Kamch'an was made Supreme Commander of the north-east field army.[56]

Chiefs of the Eastern and Western Jurchen Yŏmjigŏ, Ina, Sŏ Ŭlla and others, fifty people altogether, came to present horses, armor, helmets, and military equipment. The king granted them clothes and presents.

The king dispatched Junior Minister at the Foreign Relations Office Wŏn Yŏng to Khitan to request peace.

---

55 Samwi 三衛: not certain what this refers to; in Koryŏ there were two armies and six divisions (Igun yugwi 二軍六衛).

56 *Haengyŏng tot'ong-sa* 行營都統使.

The state councilors, on account of the fact that the falling star had already disappeared, urged the king to return to the main palace hall and resume the eating of side dishes. The king followed this.

Chŏn Poin was appointed vice-director of the Department of Ministries.

Usan country,[57] because it had been marauded by the Northeastern Jurchen, had abandoned agriculture, so the king granted them agricultural instruments.

Twelfth month. The Northeastern Jurchen Achao, Ŭlbul, and others, fourteen people altogether, came to present horses and military equipment.

The Khitan Wang Sui came to submit.

Musul [10th] day. The Khitan imperial son-in-law and commander, Xiao Sunning, set out with an invading army said to number 100,000. The king appointed the Executive Chief of the Ministry of the Royal Secretaries, Kang Kamch'an, as supreme commander, with Supreme General Kang Minch'ŏm as his assistant commander. At the head of 208,300 troops, they camped at Yŏngju, and went to Hŭnghwa Garrison to select 12,000 cavalry troops. They set them up for an ambush in a mountain valley, and with ropes bound together cowhides, with which they blocked a stream to the east of the fortress, and waited. When the bandits arrived, they released the blockage and launched an attack by the cavalry that had waited in ambush. The Khitan were greatly defeated, and Xiao Sunning led his troops straight towards the capital. Kang Minch'ŏm pursued them, and inflicted a heavy defeat on them at Raegu-san in Chaju. The Executive Cho Wŏn also attacked them at Horse Rapids, and killed more than 10,000 of the enemy.

The coffin of T'aejo was moved and brought to safety in Hyangnim-sa on Pua-san.

Kab'in [26th] day. The capital was put on high alert.

Those with sentences of banishment or lower were pardoned, and unpaid land rents older than two years were remitted.

On the *chŏngsa* [29th] day, a shooting star appeared in the Heavenly

---

57 Usan-guk 于山國: Ullŭng-do island.

Market Enclosure.[58]

Hyŏnjong Tenth year [1019]

Third year of the Tianfu era of Song, eighth year of the Kaitai era of Khitan

Spring, first month, *kyŏngin* [2nd] day. Kang Kamch'an, because the Khitan troops were pressing on the capital, sent the Administrative Assistant to the Military Commander, Kim Chonghyŏn, at the head of 10,000 troops to hurry ahead and protect the capital. The military commander for the northeast also sent 3,300 soldiers to the capital to assist.

Sinyu [3rd] day. Xiao Sunning reached Sin'ŭn County, which is about 100 *li* from the capital. The king ordered to bring all the families living outside the walls inside the city, clearing the fields to await [the enemy]. Xiao Sunning sent Yelü Haode with a letter. When they reached the T'ongdŏk Gate, he announced that the Khitan army was withdrawing. Secretly, 300 reconnaissance troops were sent to Kŭmgyo station. Hundred of our troops were then dispatched, and under cover of the night they killed them [i.e. Yelü Haode and his troops].

The Eastern Jurchen chief Una and others came to court.

Sinsa [23rd] day. The retreating Khitan army reached Yŏnju and Wiju. Kang Kamch'an and others ambushed them and killed more than 500.

Second month, *kich'uk* [1st] day. When the Khitan troops passed Kwiju, Kang Kamch'an and others attacked them on the eastern city outskirts. Both sides were evenly matched, and the battle remained undecided. Then, when Kim Chonghyŏn arrived with his troops, suddenly a wind started blowing from the south, together with rain. The flags fluttered north, and our troops took avail of the force of the wind to run at the enemy with doubled valor. The Khitan army fled north, with our troops pursuing and attacking them. From Sŏkch'ŏn to Pan-yŏng pass, the corpses covered the fields. The

---

58 *Ch'ŏnsiwŏn* 天市垣: One of the San Yuan or Three Enclosures, a traditional Chinese enclosure.

number of prisoners, horses, camels, armor and military equipment taken that day is beyond counting. Those who returned alive numbered only a few thousand. Never before had the Khitan army suffered a defeat such as this one. When the Khitan emperor received this news, he erupted in anger, and dispatched an envoy to blame Xiao Sunning: "This came about because you underestimated the enemy and penetrated too deeply into their territory. How would you dare face me again? I will tear the flesh from your face and then kill you."

Junior Vice-director of the Department of Ministries Chŏn Poin died. He was rash and short-tempered of character; as someone who had passed the classics examination, he was appointed to various academic positions. People at the time called him a true scholar.

On the *kab'o* [6th] day, the three armies returned victorious and offered the goods they had obtained from the enemy to the king. The king personally received them at Yŏngp'a station. Colored tents were set up and music and a banquet were prepared for the officers. The king personally put an eight-branched golden flower [ornament] on Kang Kamch'an's head. Holding a golden goblet in his left hand and Kang's hand in the other, he again and again comforted him and sighed [in admiration and relief]. Kang bowed in thanks, and professed that he did not deserve this. Then the name of the station was changed from Yŏngp'a 迎波 to Hŭngŭi 興義 [flourishing righteousness], and the station officials were given caps and belts like those of local administrators in counties and prefectures.

The king gave a banquet to all the officers in the Myŏngbok Hall and also expressed his recognition for the work of the three armies.

Third month, *muo*, first day of the month. There was an eclipse of the sun.

The Vice-director of the Department of Ministries, Mun Inwi, died. Mun Inwi was always straight and to the point, and did not like artifice. During the reign of King Mokchong, he was appointed to the palace of Queen Ch'ŏnch'u. When Kim Ch'iyang was killed, many officials of that palace were killed by implication. Only Mun Inwi escaped, thanks to the protection of Kang Cho.

Yu Paekpu, of the T'ongju Local Navy Command, and others, 173 people altogether, had died in battle against the enemy; the king posthumously granted them offices, and bestowed rice and barley on their families according to rank.

Aroda, envoy to the chief of Ch'ŏlli Country, Nasa, came to present horses.

The Ministry of Rites requested that it be forbidden for guards to wear metal armor fabricated in spring. The king followed this.

Summer, fourth month. Because the people of Suan, Sangsan, Hyŏpkye, Sinŭn, and other counties were suffering because of the Khitan soldiers, officials gave them grain and seeds.

Kang Kamch'an sent a memorial requesting retirement, but it was not granted; instead the king gave him a seating cushion and walking cane.

Chang Winam and others of the Local Navy Command at the Myŏngdo navy garrison apprehended eight pirate vessels. The king dispatched the station provisioner[59] Chŏng Charyang to Japan to return the 259 pirates that had been captured.

Fifth month. The land tax and taxes of Changsan, Haean, and other counties was remitted.

The Vice-director of the Court of Letters and Documents[60] of the Eastern Capital of Khitan, Lord Wuchang, came to court.

An envoy was sent to Ch'ŏlli Country to respond to their offering of tribute.

Sixth month. The Eastern Jurchen chief Nasabul and others came to court, leading a throng of people.

The Hallim Academician Kwak Wŏn requested that the policy essay be eliminated from the presented scholars examination, and replaced by a commentary, the topic of which should come from the *Book of Rites*. The king approved.

---

59 *Kongyŏngnyŏng* 供驛令: I have simply made an educated guess of the function of this office; it might well be something very different.

60 Munjŏg-wŏn 文籍院: it is not certain what kind of institution this is.

Yŏngp'yŏng Garrison was fortified.

Autumn, seventh month. I Ŭngbo and Yi Wŏn were made respectively Senior and Junior Vice-director of the Department of Ministries.

Chen Wenfan from Quanzhou in Song together with 100 other people came to offer local products.

The chief of the Western Jurchen Arabul, leading his people, came to present horses.

Yu Xuan from Fuzhou in Song together with more than 100 others came to present incense and medicine.

The Capital Military Command requested that those who had established merit in suppressing the Khitan forces, 9742 people altogether, each be given a promotion in rank and in office. The king approved.

Those households from Usan country who had previously fled here to escape the Jurchen raids were all sent back to their country.

A ceremony to glorify the parents of those who had newly passed the examinations was determined.

Eighth month. The king dispatched the vice-ministers at the Department of Rites Ch'oe Wŏnsin and Yi Suhwa to Song to offer congratulations for the new year.

The Commissioner of the Eastern Capital of Khitan, Vice-minister of Works Gao Yingshou, arrived.

The king dispatched the Assistant Office Chief at the Office of Merit Evaluation Yi Int'ak to the Eastern Capital of Khitan.

Director of the Chancellery Yu Chin died. Yu Chin hailed from Taewŏn County in Ch'ungju. All the queens surnamed Yu also belonged to the same lineage, so people regarded him as part of the royal in-law family. He was a man of integrity, and handsome in appearance. From the time of King Kwangjong he had filled positions close to the king, but had never served in provincial posts. Although he had never remonstrated the king, he still gained the trust of the high officials.

The Eastern Jurchen Moilla, leading his people, came to court. He was promoted in rank and in office.

Ninth month, *kab'in* day, first day of the month. The grand astrologer reported that there would be a sun eclipse, but because of the clouds it could not be observed.

Yang Kyu and Kim Sukhŭng were [posthumously] bestowed merit subject certificates.

Winter, eleventh month. Kang Kamch'an was made Acting Defender-in-chief, Executive Chief of the Chancellery together with Executive Chief of the Ministry of Royal Secretaries. He was also made Dynasty-founding Baron of Ch'ŏnsu County, with a stipend village of 300 households.

Households were moved from Kangnam circuit to repopulate the counties of Sangsan, Ich'ŏn, Suan, Sinŭn, Hyŏpkye, and Ubong.

T'aejo's coffin was reinterred at his Hyŏn-nŭng tomb.

Twelfth month, *kyemi* day, first day of the month. A son was born to the king; his name was Wang Sŏ.[61]

The chief of the Eastern Black Water [Malgal], Ch'udolla, came to offer horses and military equipment.

Ch'oe Sawi was made Merit Subject of Promoting Loyalty, Assisting Principle, and Equalizing Virtue, and was made Dynasty-founding Baron of Ch'ŏngha County, with a stipend village of 300 households. Kang Kamch'an was made Merit Subject for Promoting Loyalty, Assisting in Planning and Pacification of the Country. Yu Pang was made Merit Subject for Promoting Sincerity, Assisting Principle, and Supporting the Country, and was made Dynasty-founding Baron of Ch'ŏnsŭng County with a stipend village of 300 households. Ch'ae Ch'ungsun was made Merit Subject for Promoting Loyalty, Exhausting Fidelity, and Protecting the Dynasty, and was made Dynasty-founding Baron of Cheyang County with a stipend village of 300 households. Kang Minch'ŏm was made Merit Subject for Promoting Sincerity, Establishing Principle, and Venerating [the Dynasty].

The king visited the Hyŏn-nŭng tomb.

Sinhae [29th] day. A falling star appeared.

---

61 Later King Munjong (r. 1046–1083). His given name was later changed to Hwi.

Hyŏnjong Eleventh year [1020]

Fourth year of the Tianxi era of Song, ninth year of the Kaitai era of Khitan

Spring, first month. Chin Hamjo was appointed junior vice-director of the Department of Ministries.

The Black Water Malgal Alsigyŏng, Kojimun, and others, twenty-four people in total, came to offer local products.

Ch'oe Hang was granted the title of Merit Subject of Promoting Loyalty, Exhausting Fidelity, and Protecting the Dynasty.

The Western Jurchen chief Koduhwa came to offer local products.

Second month. Since the soldiers Hyŏg'yŏn and Yi Chŭng from Suan County, and Siŭmdal from Kuju, had died in battle, their families were lavishly rewarded.

The Eastern Jurchen Kŏmbulla and others, seven people altogether, came to present horses.

Because the Executive Chiefs of the Chancellery Chin Chŏk and Yi Yegyun, the Vice-chancellor of the Ministry of Royal Secretaries Wang Tongyŏng, Director of the Office of Water Control[62] Yun Yŏ, Vice-director of the Directorate for Construction and Maintenance Wang Chwasŏm, Assistant Executive at the Directorate of Royal Workshops Kim Tŏkhwa, Registrar at the Directorate for Construction and Maintenance Kim Chingho, and Director of the Palace Infirmary Kim Tŭkkoeng had been detained by the Khitan, their spouses were granted grain according to rank. The wife of Wang Chwasŏm was made Lady of Kaesŏng Prefecture, and her son Wang Ibo was appointed master scribe at the Ministry of Rites.

Huai Zhi from Quanzhou in Song and others came to present local products.

The king sent Yi Chag'in to the Khitan with a memorial requesting to be called a vassal again and to be allowed to offer tribute. Yelü Xingping and others, who had been detained, were also sent back.

---

62 Sajae-gyŏng 司宰卿: following Shultz' translation. Hucker surmises that the Sizai-si 司宰寺, meaning "court in charge of slaughtering" referred to the Court of Imperial Entertainments (Guanglu-si). Hucker 5785.

Third month. The Khitan envoy, the Acting Minister of Education Han Shaoyong, arrived.

The Jurchen General "Seeking Refuge in Virtue" Pulla came to court with his people.

The General P'aeng Hongp'ae and others, ten people altogether, because of their merit at the border, were promoted by one rank.

Ch'ae Ch'ungsun requested: "Those soldiers with parents older than eighty ought to be relieved of their duty to care for their parents; those civil and military officials caring for parents older than seventy and who do not have brothers, ought not to be appointed to offices outside the capital. Those whose parents are sick should be given 200 days leave to look after them." The king approved.

The king granted 300 *sŏk* of grain to the family of Chŏng Sinyong.

Summer, fourth month. The king invested his son Wang Hŭm as Commander Unequalled in Honor, Acting Grand Preceptor, Acting Ministry of Education, Minister of the Royal Secretaries, Supreme Pillar of State, Merit Subject Venerating Humanity Spreading Filiality and Aiding Circulation, and Prince of Yŏn'gyŏng.

The king held a banquet in Myŏngbok Hall for all military and civil officials who take part in the court audience [i.e. those of rank 5 and higher], and gave them presents according to rank.

The king dispatched the Vice-minister of the Ministry of Rites Yang Chŏk and Executive of the Ministry of Punishment Han Kŏhwa to Khitan to announce the investiture of the heir apparent. State councilor Yu Pang remonstrated, trying to stop this. The king did not accept his protests.

The Eastern Jurchen chief Tallo came at the head of his people to offer 300 *sŏk* of rice.

The officials petitioned: "earlier it was decreed that those over the age of eighty or those who were seriously ill would obtain the service of one able bodied working-age person, those over the age of ninety would get two, and those aged 100 would get five. However those defending the borders were not included. Please allow those defending the border the same exemption of service so that they can care for their parents."

Yi Wŏnhyŏn and nine others passed the composition test of the civil service examination, and three passed the classics examination.

The Black Water Malgal Oduna and others, more than seventy people altogether, came to offer local products.

Ch'oe Wŏnsin and Yi Suhwa were exiled because they had demeaned their role as ambassadors.

Sixth month. There were locusts in the northwestern region.

The king dispatched the Acting Vice-director of the Office of Water Control No Chipchung to the Eastern Capital of Khitan.

The chief of Pullae Country, Sagamun, sent the Jurchen Nouldal to offer local products.

Executive of the Chancellery Kang Kamch'an requested to retire. The king granted his request, and additionally gave him the title of Acting Grand Mentor, Dynasty-founding Vicsount of Ch'ŏnsu County with a stipend village of 500 households.

Autumn, seventh month. Because of the long-lasting drought prisoners were released.

Eighth month. One-thousand two-hundred and forty *kyŏl* of military land from Ansŏ circuit was gifted to Hyŏnhwa-sa. The two Departments [i.e. the Department of Ministries and the Department of Royal Secretary-Chancellery] protested two or three times, but the king did not listen to these protests.

The Executive of the Department of State Affairs of Silla,[63] Ch'oe Ch'iwŏn, was posthumously granted the position of Minister of the Ministry of Royal Secretaries, and was enshrined in the temple of former worthies.

Ninth month. The king held a banquet for the officials in Kwan'in Hall.

The king went to Hyŏnhwa-sa where he personally struck the newly cast temple bell; after this he made all the officials strike it, and everyone donated clothing, goods, and silk.

---

63 Chipsa-sŏng 執事省: highest policy organ in the Silla period.

This year the king sent Ch'oe Chean to Khitan to congratulate the emperor on the Thousand-year festival [ie his birthday]. Kim Maeng was sent to Song.

Hyŏnjong Twelfth year [1021]

Fifth year of the Tianli era of Song, first year of the Daping era of Khitan

Spring, first month. The Black Water Malgal Chief Adut'abuk and others came to offer horses, bows, and arrows.

Second month. The Khitan Censor-in-chief Yao Juxin came to visit bearing gifts.

The people of Anju[64] received two years' exemption from tax, [which amounts to] a remittance of half of all taxes paid since the *kyŏngsul* year [1010].

Two thousand houses outside the Insu Gate [of the capital] burned down.

The Eastern Jurchen general "Embraced by Koryŏ"[65] Majŏgae leading his people came to court.

The king bestowed wine, food, tea, medicine, cloth and silk according to rank on all the men and women of the capital who were over ninety.

Third month. Yu Pang was made Executive Chief of the Ministry of the Royal Secretaries, and Chu Tŏngmyŏng Junior Vice-director of the Department of Ministries.

The Western Jurchen Moilla, Naholla and others came to offer horses and sable skins.

Ch'ŏlli country sent an envoy to request to reattach itself to Koryŏ as

---

64 Anju 安州: modern Chaeryŏng-ŭp in Hwanghae-do, roughly halfway between Kaesŏng and P'yŏngyang. According to the Geography Treatise of the *Koryŏsa*, a defense commissioner was installed in 995 but abolished in the beginning of Hyŏnjong's reign, after which it was attached [to another prefecture]. KRS 58.10b-11a.

65 *Hoehwa changgun* 懷化將軍: from here on such honorary military titles bestowed by Koryŏ on Jurchen warriors start to appear frequently. Literally meaning "Embracing transformation," since the transformative influence was supposed to come from Koryŏ I translated like this.

before.

The envoy from the Eastern Capital of Khitan, the Policy Advisor Zhang Chengyue came bearing gifts.

Summer, fifth month. The king ordered the Senior Assistant Director of the Department of Ministries, Yi Kado, to go to Kyŏngju and retrieve the gold brocade kasaya and Buddha's skull from Kosŏn-sa and the Buddha's tooth from Ch'angnim-sa and place them in the palace halls.

Sixth month. The Censorate requested that monks and nuns from all temples should be forbidden from drinking wine and making merry.

Chang Yŏng was made Vice-director of the Department of Ministries and concurrently Chief of the Ministry of the Royal Secretaries, Supreme Pillar of State—and then was made to retire. Chu Chŏ was made Hallim Academician Recipient of Edicts, Merit Subject Worshiping Letters and Supporting the State, Left Policy Advisor and Supreme Pillar of State.

Han Cho was sent to Song to proffer thanks.

Autumn, seventh month, *kapsul*, first day. There was a solar eclipse.

T'amna offered local products.

The Eastern Jurchen [and?] Black Water [Malgal] chief Kŏulmadugae came.

The ban on monasteries brewing wine was reissued.

Eighth month. Kim Inwi was made Junior Vice-director of the Department of Ministries, and then made to retire.

The king went to Hyŏnhwa-sa to witness the erection of its stele.[66] He personally wrote the title cartouche in seal-script. Earlier he had ordered the Hallim Academician Chu Chŏ to compose the stele inscription.

The king bestowed on his son Hŭm the title of State-protecting merit subject. Ch'oe Sawi was made Acting Grand Preceptor and Acting Director of the Chancellery; Ch'oe Hang was made Acting Grand Mentor and Acting

---

66 The stele and its inscription still exist. It documents the reburial of Hyŏnjong's parents near the temple, which was located north of the capital, and the attending rituals and miracles. See Vermeersch, "Royal Ancestor Worship and Buddhist Politics: The Hyŏnhwa-sa Stele and the Origins of the First Tripitaka," *The Journal of Korean Studies* 18:1 (2013): 115 –146.

Executive Chief [of the Chancellery] and Executive Chief of the Ministry of the Royal Secretaries.

Cho P'ae and six others passed the composition test of the civil service examination, and four people passed the classics examination.

The Eastern Jurchen Silbin and Arigo came to court.

Ninth month. Yi Kong was appointed Commissioner of the Security Council.

The Black Water Malgal Somulgae and Kojimun came to offer local products.

The king dispatched Commissioner of the Security Council Yi Kong and Executive at the Ministry of War Yu Chong to Khitan to offer felicitations on the reception of investiture.

Winter, tenth month. Yi Chuhŏn was appointed Vice-director of the Department of Ministries and Assistant Executive in Political Affairs, Pillar of State.

The Eastern and Western Jurchen chiefs Arodae and Agae and others came to court.

Eleventh month. The Administrator of the Security Council Kang Minch'ŏm died. Kang Minch'ŏm hailed from Chingang County in Chinju. From the beginning he was versed in books, and was not good at archery or horse riding. Yet he was strong-willed and firm, and in the end gained frequent merit in battle.

Twelfth month. The Commissioner of the Security Council Yun Chinggo died. Yun Chinggo hailed from Suan County in Suju. He was ponderous and severe of character, but he was handsome and good at regular calligraphy. After passing the examination he served at the Censorate several times. He was fair and truthful when passing judgment, and never mentioned people's shortcomings; therefore everybody respected and loved him. As soon as he heard of his passing, the king said "Would that there be another one like him in this world! Whom can I rely on now!" and sighed in regret several times in a row. He posthumously made him Vice-director of the Department of Ministries and granted him the title Changgyŏng.

The Director of the Chancellery Ch'oe Sawi presented a memorial that discussed the achievements and mistakes of government, and the king made officials discuss these and put them into effect.

Hyŏnjong Thirteenth year [1022]

First year of the Qianxing era of Song, second year of the Daping era of Khitan

Spring, first month. The Black Water [Malgal] chiefs Sailla and Mant'ubul came to court.

The king posthumously bestowed the title of Marquis of Hongyu [Spreading Confucianism] on Sŏl Ch'ong, and co-enshrined him in the Temple of Former Sages.

Second month. The Western Jurchen Chŏlla came to offer local products.

The Ministry of Revenue petitioned: "Saju is the land where the royal ancestor hails from;[67] formerly people's land (*minjŏn* 民田) was taken and attached to the palace estates. Hence people no longer have the means to pay taxes. We humbly request that the area of public land (*kongjŏn* 公田) within the jurisdiction of Saju be measured (*simnyang* 審量) so that the people can be compensated according to the amount of land [transferred to the palace estate]." The king gave his approval.

T'amna offered local producs.

The king dispatched the Deputy Director of the Arsenals Kim Inyu to offer newyear's greetings [lit. greetings for the spring season].

The Khitan Meng Liu, Yanju and others, four people altogether, fled to Koryŏ.

The king dispatched the Assistant Executive in Political Affairs Pak Ch'ungsuk and the Supervisor of Education Yi Kyŏng to Khitan.

Third month. Yi Kado was concurrently appointed Associate

67 P'ungp'ae 豐沛: literally, "fertile marshes." Here however the characters refer to the hometown of Emperor Gaozu of the Former Han, Feng township in Xinpei county. Hence it is probably a reference to Hyŏnjong's father Anjong, who was exiled to Saju.

Administrator of the Security Council.

Junior Vice-director of the Department of Ministries Yi Chuhŏn died. Originally a minor local functionary, he gradually rose thanks to his diligence and capability. King Sŏngjong used to call him "the piece of metal with the clearest ring."

Summer, fourth month. The Khitan sent the Censor-in-chief Xiao Huaili and others to invest the king as Commander Unequalled in Honor, and made him Acting Director of the Department of Ministries, Supreme Pillar of State, King of Koryŏ, with a stipend village of 10,000 households, and an actual emolument of 1,000 households. They also granted carts, clothing, and ceremonial implements. Henceforth the Khitan era names were used again.

Ch'oe Sawi petitioned: "The names for the senior functionaries in the various prefectures and counties are confusing and not standardized. Henceforth, [the leaders of] administrations of the rank of prefecture or county should be called village head [*hojang* 戶長], whereas those of *hyang*, *pugok*,[68] ferry ports, postal stations and hostels should be called simply head (*chang* 長)." The king followed this advice.

Ch'ae Ch'ungsun was appointed Executive Chief of the Ministry of the Royal Secretaries, and adjoint Resident Governor of the Western Capital.

Fifth month. Han Cho returned from Song. The emperor had bestowed on him books entitled *Sheng hui fang* 聖惠方 and *Yinyang erzhai* 陰陽二宅, as well as the Qianxing [era] calendar and a set of the Buddhist scriptures.

The king's eldest son, the Yŏn'gyŏng Prince, Hŭm, was invested as heir apparent.

The Black Water Malgal Soŭi and others, more than thirty people altogether, came to court.

Sixth month. The king's son Hyŏng was invested as Prince of P'yŏngyang, while Sŏ was invested as Prince of Nangnang.

Yu Pang was appointed Executive Chief of the Chancellery.

---

[68] *Hyang* 鄕 (township) and *pugok* 部曲 (borough) refers to settlements of low status groups in specialized professions, usually indentured laborers or even slaves.

Officials for the Eastern Palace [the heir apparent's palace] were installed.

Mujin [30th] day. The Yŏndŏk princess, née Kim, died. She was given the title of Wŏndŏk, and buried in the Hoe-nŭng tomb.

Autumn, seventh month. The Capital Military Command requested to resettle the Usan People who had been displaced by barbarian invaders in Yeju, and make them permanent householders of that place. The king approved.

Aradae and others of the Eastern and Western Jurchen came, offering local products.

Eight month. The envoy in charge of ritual from the Eastern Capital of the Khitan, Li Kefang, came and said: "From now on the spring and summer courtesy envoys should be combined into one visit, and should also travel together with the envoys of congratulation for the Thousand Year festival and the spring festival. Likewise the autumn and winter courtesy envoys should be combined and also travel with the envoy for congratulating the empress dowager on her birthday."

Chen Xiangzhong, from Fuzhou in Song and others came to offer local products.

The chief of Ch'ŏlli country, Nasa, dispatched the Black Water [Malgal] Abugan to offer local products.

The king took the daughter of the Master of Sacrificial Wines at the National Academy, Sŏ Nul, as a first-ranked consort.[69]

Ninth month. The king granted all men and women of the capital who were eighty or over, as well as those who were seriously ill, wine, food, tea, and cloth according to rank.

The envoy of the Eastern Capital of Khitan, Wang Shourong, came.

The king dispatched the Office Chief at the Slave Agency,[70] Yun Chongwŏn, to Khitan to offer congratulations on the birthday of the queen dowager.

---

69 Sukpi 淑妃: said to be a senior-first rank for women in the office for palace women (Naemyŏng-bu 內命婦); likely a concubine.

70 Togwan nangjung 都官郎中.

The king dispatched Senior Policy Advisor Kwak Wŏn and Aide at the Department of Ministries Wang Sŏ to Khitan.[71]

The Khitan Shouyumei and Wuyuyi and others, nineteen people altogether, came to submit.

Winter, tenth month. The king invested the Yŏn'gyŏng princess née Kim as queen.

Sŏ Nul was made Commissioner of the Security Council and Junior Policy Advisor; Yi Kado was made Commissioner of the Security Council and Master of Sacrificial Wines at the National Academy; Chu Chŏ was made Vice-minister at the Ministry of Rites; and Yi Chag'in was made Chief Censor.[72]

Eleventh month. The Censorate impeached Director of the Chancellery Ch'oe Sawi and Vice-director of the Department of Ministries Pak Ch'ungsuk because they had been dancing drunkenly during a gathering at the polo court, acting disrespectfully [towards the throne]. The king did not allow the matter to be pursued further.

The envoy from the Eastern Capital of Khitan, Gao Zhangyin, came.

Twelfth month. The Khitan Foda and others, eleven altogether, came to submit.

The Western Jurchen Ŏnijŏ came and asked: "My paternal aunt once followed [someone called] Maena who naturalized, and came to reside in the capital. This happened a few years back, but she keeps thinking about her homeland. I would like to redeem her for these local horses." The king ordered that she be allowed to return immediately, and also returned the horses.

The Eastern Jurchen chief Sabin came to offer horses, bows, and arrows.

---

71 Presumably for the autumn and winter courtesies; as per the request of Khitan transmitted in the eighth month of this year, these envoys departed together with the birthday envoy mentioned in the previous entry.

72 Sahŏndaebu 司憲大夫.

Hyŏnjong Fourteenth year [1023]

First year of the Tiansheng era of Emperor Renzong of Song, third year of the Daping era of Khitan

Spring, first month. The king held a banquet for the state councilors in the palace halls.

Ch'ae Ch'ungsun was made Junior Preceptor to the Crown Prince; Sŏ Nul was made Assistant Executive in Political Affairs; Kwak Wŏn was made Commissioner of the Security Council; Yu Pang was made Commissioner of General Command for the Northwestern field army.

The Khitan Jiaofu and others, eleven households altogether, came to submit.

Chin Hamjo and Chu Tŏngmyŏng were appointed Vice-director and Junior Vice-director of the Department of Ministries.

The Black Water Malgal Osabul and others, eighty people altogether, came to offer local products. They were each granted cloth and silk.

Second month. Yi Kong was appointed Resident Governor of the Western Capital.

Ch'oe Ch'iwŏn was posthumously bestowed the title of Munch'ang [splendor of letters] Marquis.

The Eastern Jurchen chief Arobul and the Western Jurchen Naalgae came to court.

Third month. The king dispatched the Director of the Office of Royal Archives Yu Chingp'il to Khitan.

Fourth month. The Khitan sent the Senior Policy Critic Wubai Yelükegong to come and invest the Heir Apparent Hŭm as Supreme General Assisting the State, Acting Grand Preceptor and Acting Grand Guardian, concurrently Director of the Chancellery, Duke of Koryŏ.

The Jurchen Malgal Kundu and others, more than seventy people altogether, came to offer horses.

Fifth month, *ŭlhae* [13th] day. There was an earthquake in Kŭmju.

The Khitan Mahŏjŏ and others, thirteen households altogether, came to submit.

The Censorate petitioned: "During court meetings, some of the officials are kneeling but talking about private affairs; some bow once and then get up, messing up the order of the files. All this impinges on the decorum of the court meetings, so we request to clamp down on this behavior strictly." The king approved.

The king gave a banquet for the higher-ranking civil and military officials in Ch'ŏnbok Hall and gave everyone a horse.

The Khitan Dashinu and Qihuana and others, eight people altogether, came to submit.

The Jurchen chief Iubul came to court.

Sixth month. Because of the drought prisoners were released.

Chang Kyo and three others passed the composition test of the civil service examination, and two people passed the classics examination.

Seventh month. The Khitan sent the Grand Guardian Huang Xin to congratulate the king on his birthday.

The Ministry of Personnel petitioned: "The former *taesang chaerang*[73] Kim Ŏn wore his mourning clothes for his mother's funeral after the designated period [because circumstances prevented him from wearing them during the normal mourning period]; because of his reputation for filiality, we request that he be promoted to the next highest offices so as to encourage others." The king approved.

Ninth month. The Malgal leader Aryŏngju came to court.

Intercalary month. The Khitan envoy Lishouchang came bearing presents.

The envoy of the Eastern Capital of Khitan, Gao Renshou, came.

The king instructed, "the righteous granaries in the various prefectures and counties are meant to offer relief in emergencies, they should not be abused [for other purposes]."

Winter, eleventh month. The Black Water Malgal chief Yahilla and others

---

73 Taesang chaerang 大常齋郎: according to the treatise on economy in the *Koryŏsa*, this was the lowest-ranking office (18th) in the land-rank system (*chŏnsikwa*) promulgated by Mokchong in 998. *Koryŏsa* 78.10b. (大常司儀齋郎) Most likely an official in the Office for Sacrifices (太常府). Spelled T'aesang chaerang 太常齋郎 in the *Koryŏsa* entry for that year.

came to court.

Chen Yi from Quanzhou in Song came to submit.

Twelfth month. The king held a banquet for the state councilors and supreme generals in Kŏndŏk Hall.

Yu Pang was appointed Grand Guardian to the Heir Apparent; Yi Kong was made Executive Chief of the Ministry of the Royal Secretaries and supervisor of the compilation of state history; and Yi Wŏn was made acting Grand Guardian to the Heir Apparent.

Hyŏnjong Fifteenth year [1024]

Second year of the Tiansheng era of Song, fourth year of the Daping era of Khitan

Spring, first month. The Khitan Mashidao and others, three altogether, came to submit.

The Capital Military Command petitioned to recruit more than 100 households from Haŭn *pugok* in the precinct of the Western Capital and transfer them to the military supply fields (*tunjŏn* 屯田) south of Kaju as tenant farmers (*chŏnjak* 佃作).

The king invested the Princess of the Kyŏnghŭng Court, nee Kim, as "Virtuous consort" (Tŏkpi 德妃).

Third month. Yi Chayŏn and eight others passed the composition test of the civil service examination, and ten people passed the classics examination.

The Western Jurchen Koduro and the Eastern Jurchen Sŭlbuldal and others, ninety people altogether, came to submit.

Summer, fourth month. The Black Water Malgal Kodomae and others came to offer local products.

The king bestowed on Yang Kyu and Kim Sukhŭng the title of Enshrined Post-Sam-Han Meritorious Subject.

Fifth month, *chŏnghae*, first day. Although there should have been a solar eclipse there was none.

There were some among the people who banded together and cried to heaven to pray for rain. When the king heard their voices, he refrained from eating, cleansed himself completely, and burnt incense. Standing in the palace courtyard he looked up to heaven and made the following pledge: "If this insignificant person has transgressed, please punish him immediately; if the people have transgressed, please still punish him. I beg you to send down plentiful rain to save everyone." After he spoke, it rained heavily.

The Eastern Jurchen general "Embraced by Koryŏ" Aalla came to court.

The Vice-minister of the Ministry of Ritual Chu Chŏ died. Chu Chŏ was modest and respectful by nature, and excelled at composition. When he first came [from China], it was the academician Ch'ae Ch'ungsun who spotted his talent and secretly requested the king to make him stay. After only a few months he was entrusted with composing the appointment certificates for high officials. When the king fled south, he followed him, thus establishing merit; for this he was awarded the title of merit subject. As a result he rose to prominence, and most of the diplomatic correspondence between the two courts [i.e. Koryŏ and Song] came from his pen. The favor and benefice he received from the king was without compare.

Sixth month. The Executive Chief of the Chancellery Ch'oe Hang died. Ch'oe Hang was the grandson of Ch'oe Ŏnwi. He was intelligent and quiet by nature; he didn't speak much but he always made the right judgment. He passed the examination when still a youth, and twice supervised the examinations himself. All those selected under his watch later became famous scholars. Schooled in Confucianism through the generations, he upheld the family through uprightness. Although he held important positions for a long time, he never took even the smallest [gift] from others. He even counted the months when requesting his salary, and hence his family could not even save a picul of grain in their storage jars. Yet he did not enjoy the life of an official, and even before he turned seventy, he requested to retire. Even though he was appointed several times, he never took up the appointments. However, he was a devout follower of Buddhism, so when he was requested to repair the pagoda of Hwangnyong-sa, he personally went there to oversee the work. This caused considerable damage to farming. Also, in his private residence he stored many sūtras and placed many images; in the end he bequeathed his house to turn it into a temple. When he fell ill, the king personally went to visit him and to comfort him appointed his son Ch'oe Yubu as Gentleman Collating Books in the Palace Library,[74] and granted his son-in-law Yi Chakch'ung [the right to] wear official garb. When the king received the news of his passing, he was deeply saddened, and gave 300 bolts of silk, 500 bolts of cloth, and 1,000 *sŏk* each of rice and barley as bereavement money, but on account of his father's deathbed instructions, Ch'oe Yubu firmly refused these. He was granted the title Chŏrŭi, and was later coenshrined with the king.

Autumn, seventh month. Khitan dispatched the Acting Minister of Education Gao Shou to offer congratulations on the king's birthday.

The Western Jurchen chief Tora and the Eastern Jurchen Noŭlgyŏn and others came to present horses.

Sŏ Nul was appointed commander-in-chief of the Northwestern army camp, and Kwak Wŏn was appointed his deputy.

The T'amna chief Chumul and his son Komol were given military prestige titles of rank 3B, equivalent to supreme general.

Ninth month. Kim Inwi was made vice-director of the Department of Ministries and assistant executive in political affairs, and then made to retire.

The Black Water Malgal Arigo came.

Yueluoci and others, 100 people altogether from the Abbasid kingdom[75] in the Western Regions came to offer local products.

Winter, tenth month. Khitan dispatched the acting vice-director of the Department of Ministries Li Zhenglun.

Eleventh month, *ŭlyu*, first day of the month. There ought to have been a solar eclipse but there was none.

Yi Kong was made vice-director of the Department of Ministries and

---

74 *Pisŏ-sŏng kyosŏrang* 秘書省校書郎.

75 Taesik-kuk 大食國: conventional term in Tang China for people from the Islamic caliphate or Arabs in general.

executive chief of the Ministry of the Royal Secretaries.

On the *kiyu* [25th] day there was an earthquake in Sangju.

This year the five districts of the capital as well as wards and hamlets were determined.

Hyŏnjong Sixteenth year [1025]

Third year of the Tiansheng era of Song, fifth year of the Daping era of Khitan

Spring, first month. The Jurchen general "Embraced by Koryŏ" Yagoga and the general "Seeking Refuge in Virtue" Agolt'aro and others came to court. The king bestowed court ranks and also robes and presents.

Yu Pang was appointed Minister of the Ministry of Defense and Ch'ae Ch'ungsun was appointed Minister of the Ministry of Rites.

The king summoned six people including P'i Wijong and restored their rank titles. Earlier, when P'i Wijong was Office Chief at the Ministry of War, while on patrol outside the border, he spotted the Khitan general Yelü Chege, who was out hunting. Together with the registrar[76] Chŏng Minŭi and others, five people altogether, he galloped toward him and cut of his head; he then returned expecting to receive reward. The relevant authority, because he had arrogated military authority and crossed the border [without authorization] exiled him to a faraway place. Only now was he released.

The Jurchen chief Moilla came to court. Because he had established merit at the border, the king granted him the rank-title of *taegwang*, and bestowed on him as a special favor robes and presents.

Second month. Since it was the Cold Food festival, the king gave a banquet to high-ranking civil and military officials in the palace halls.

Third month. All construction work was halted and farmers were allowed to go [to their land].

---

76 *Chubu* 注簿: according to Hucker (1413) a *zhubu* 主簿 was either a recorder, a low-ranking official at various agencies, or "an assistant magistrate on the staff of various units of territorial administration." In Koryŏ it corresponded to the former meaning.

Summer, fourth month. On account of the drought the king avoided the main palace, reduced the number of dishes, forbade the slaughter of animals, and stopped the performance of music. The king also ordered the investigation of wrongful convictions and offered prayers at various mountains.

The Ministry of Rites said, "Now the Censorate has new regulations to the effect that all officials of the two branches [civil and military] should follow the private form of greeting during court meetings or when meeting in public places. Those who prostrate will immediately be reported and punished. Respectfully we point out that according to the *Book of Rites*, when the gentleman observes rites, he does not seek to change [standards according to occasion]. If we commonly practice according to the Censorate's regulations, how can we distinguish between high and low, or between young and old? We request that only outside the ritual conventions of court meetings and shrine gatherings is it allowed to perform private greetings as one wishes." The king agreed.

Sinmi [20th] day. There was an earthquake in ten counties of Yŏngnam Province.

Fifth month. A royal instruction read: "Chŏng'an County in Haeyang Province has again presented a coral tree; it should be used to upgrade sacrifices to the Dragon spirit of the southern sea as a reward for his secret merit."

Sixth month. A royal instruction read: "Only after one has modelled oneself on Heaven and followed the seasons can one keep disasters at bay and achieve an era of peace. Now what the Ministry of the Royal Secretaries and all the other offices have petitioned, when putting this into practice everyone should exert their minds to follow the 'Monthly Ordinances' and accord with my intentions."

A royal instruction read: "Kang Minch'ŏm and Ha Kongjin's merit was considerable yet their reward was not special; grant each man's sons a higher office."

Autumn, seventh month. The Khitan sent the General-in-chief of the

Palace Gate Guard, Han Chun, to congratulate the king on his birthday.

Chŏnghae [7th] day. There was an earthquake in Kyŏngsang,[77] Ch'ŏngju, Andong, and Milsŏng.

Ninth month. Hasŏllaja and others, from the Abbassid Kingdom, 100 people altogether, came to offer local products.

It was forbidden for ordinary people from the capital and the regions to use patterns of dragons or phoenixes for their clothing or utensils.

Winter, eleventh month, *kab'in* day, first day of the month. The grand astrologer had reported there would be a solar eclipse but there was none; all the officials offered congratulations to the king.

Posŏng Prefecture presented two coral trees.

Twelfth month. A royal instruction read: "All those who committed crimes but had official rank land, should be pardoned and the land returned; exempted from this are genuine thieves; those who forged official or private documents; those who obfuscated the law to receive wealth; those who have enriched themselves while in office, and those who committed treason or disloyal acts through fawning and cunning."

This year Sang'ŭm County was fortified.

Hyŏnjong Seventeenth year [1026]

Fourth year of the Tiansheng era of Song, sixth year of the Daping era of Khitan

Spring, first month. Yi Sŏ was appointed Censor-in-chief.

The Eastern Jurchen general "Seeking Refuge in Virtue" Kŏryŏul and others arrived.

Second month. Khitan sent the Grand Mentor Li Zhishun with gifts.

Sundŏk was fortified.

Third month. Ch'oe Hwang and ten others passed the composition

77 Probably Kyŏngju and Sangju, per the Korean translation on the db.history.go.kr website of the National Institute of Korean History. I.e. the precursor of the name Kyŏngsang Province, which was not yet used as such in early Koryŏ.

test of the civil service examination, and one person passed the classics examination.

Summer, fourth month. Chi Ch'aemun was made Junior Vice-director of the Department of Ministries.

Intercalary [fifth] month. The chiefs of the Eastern and Western Jurchen, each taking their people, sons, and brothers, came to present horses, bows, and catapults.

Khitan sent the Administrative Assistant at the Court Ceremonial Institute[78] Yelü Guda to request safe passage to go to the north-eastern Jurchen. This was not given.

Sixth month. Yi Tan took charge of the Security Council, and Hwangbo Yuŭi was made Censor-in-chief.

Autumn, seventh month. Khitan dispatched General-in-chief of the Palace Gate Guard, Wang Wenjian, to congratulate the king on his birthday.

Chŏngmi [4th] day. It rained heavily, and many houses of people in the capital either floated away or collapsed.

Eighth month. Li Wentong from Guangnan in Song and others came to present local products.

Ninth month, *kiyu* [7th] day. There was flooding in the Western Capital, and more than 80 houses were washed away or destroyed.

Kapcha [22nd] day. The king went to Singwang-sa in Haeju.

Winter, tenth month, *kyeyu* day, first day of the month. There was a solar eclipse.

Imo [10th] day. The king returned from Haeju.

Hyŏnjong Eighteenth year [1027]

Fifth year of the Tiansheng era of Song, seventh year of the Daping era of Khitan

Spring, first month. Ch'oe Sawi was made Grant Tutor to the Heir Apparent; Ch'ae Ch'ungsun and Yi Kong were both made Executive Chief of the

78 *Yuyuan panguan* 御院判官: this term does not occur in Hucker; it is a tentative translation.

Chancellery; Sŏ Nul was made Executive Chief of the Ministry of the Royal Secretaries; Kwak Wŏn and Yi Kado were both made Assistant Executive in Political Affairs; Yi Tan and Kim Maeng were both made Security Councilor; and Yang Chŏk was made Vice-director of the Department of Ministries.

The Eastern Jurchen chief Ch'angbu and others came to offer local products.

Executive Chief of the Chancellery Yu Pang requested to retire on account of his age. The king allowed him to retire, and made him Specially Presented Director of the Chancellery.

The Khitan envoy Li Zhengyun arrived.

Second month. The Ancestral Shrine was restored, and the spirit tablets were re-enshrined in it.

The Black Water Malgal Supreme General "Seeking Refuge in Virtue" Agoraga came to present horses and various implements.

Hyŏndŏk Garrison was fortified.

Third month. The Jurchen leader Sŭlbuldal and others, 100 people altogether, came to court.

Summer, fourth month. The king personally went to the Ancestral Shrine to perform sacrifices, and bestowed higher posthumous titles. A pardon was declared.

Fifth month. Because of drought, the king avoided the main hall of the palace and reduced the number of dishes. [He also urged that] those who were imprisoned would be tried with lenience.

There was frost in Kongju, killing the rice sprouts.

The Heir Apparent Hyŏng was given the honorary title Commander Unequalled in Honor and was made acting Grand Preceptor and Minister of the Royal Secretaries; [prince] Sŏ was given the honorary title Commander Unequalled in Honor and was made acting Grand Mentor and Director of the Department of Ministries.

Sixth month. Yangju reported that the monks of temples in Changŭi, Samch'ŏn, and Ch'ŏngyŏn had violated the ban on brewing alcohol, using more than 360 *sŏk* [of grain] in the process. Yangju requested that they be tried according to the rules. The king agreed.

A royal instruction read: “The Executive at the Ministry of Works Yu P’umnyŏm and others, 143 people altogether, although they fomerly perpetrated the crime of treason or disloyal acts through fawning and cunning, since they have received several pardons, their cimes should be wiped off the records and their names put on the list for official appointments.”

T’amna offered local products.

The Eastern Jurchen chief Moilla and others, more than twenty people altogether, came to court.

Autumn, seventh month. Khitan dispatched Grand Mentor Yi Kuangyi and Yelü Hudougun to offer congratulations on the king’s birthday.

Yŏnggwang Prefecture presented a coral tree that was eight feet high.

Eighth month. The envoy from the Eastern Capital of Khitan, Gao Yan, came.

Li Wentong and others from Jiangnan in Song came to offer 597 fascicles of books.

It was forbidden for monks to wear white shirts, trousers tucked in socks, silk cords, outer robes, leather shoes, colored hats, bamboo rain hats, or hat tassels.

Ninth month. The king ordered construction of Hyeil and Chunggwang temples, and the drafting of laborers and craftsmen. Court officials and remonstrance officials protested, saying that this was a waste of people’s labor, and that this workforce should not be raised. Only senior transmitter Yi Koe petitioned: “To construct temples for Buddha is a work of boundless merit. What could be the harm in making the people work for this?” At the time everyone ridiculed him for this.

Hyŏnjong Nineteenth year [1028]

Sixth year of the Tiansheng era of Song, eighth year of the Daping era of Khitan

Spring, first month. The Jurchen General "Seeking Refuge in Virtue" Mandu and others, more than seventy people, came to court. Kolbu, leading a village of 500 housholds, came to attach himself to Koryŏ.

Second month. The king dispatched Assistant Office Chief at the Ministry of Ritual Kim Ka to the Eastern Capital of Khitan.

A royal instruction read: "Monks and nuns are enticing foolish people to amass wealth, which they transport using the horses from postal stations. There is no harm bigger than this! Make sure that the authorities crack down severely on this."

The king dispatched the Chamberlain for the Palace Treasury[79] Kim Chakpin to Khitan.

Third month Chŏng Chaewŏn and nine others passed the composition test of the civil service examination, and one person passed the classics examination.

Khitan sent General Yelü Su and others with presents.

The Eastern Jurchen General "Seeking Refuge in Virtue" Agol came.

Summer, fifth month. The Jurchen attacked P'yŏnghae Prefecture but could not take it, and retreated. They were pursued and four of the pirate ships were taken; they were all killed.

Intercalary [sixth] month. The Northern Jurchen chief Ahol and others, fifty-seven people altogether, came to attach themselves [to Koryŏ].

Autumn, seventh month. Khitan dispatched the Prefect of Shenzhou, Xiao Qiong, to congratulate the king on his birthday.

The Eastern Jurchen K'oebal's village of more than 300 households came to attach themselves to Koryŏ.

Ŭlmyo [22nd] day. The king's consort Queen Kim died. She was given the title of Queen Wŏnsŏng and she was buried in Myŏng-nŭng.

The Eastern and Western Jurchen chiefs Niobul and Turogae together with more than 200 people came to offer local products.

Eighth month. There were locusts in the nortwest border circuit.

---

79 *Taebu-gyŏng* 大府卿: see Hucker 5940: *ta-fu*, "Chamberlain for the Palace Bursary." See also 6159 *t'ai-fu*.

Ninth month. Li Zhan and others from Quanzhou in Song, more than thirty people altogether, came to offer local products.

The king dispatched First Office Chief of the Department of Ministries Im Pok to Khitan to offer congratulations on the queen dowager's birthday.

The southern part of Ponghwa-san was fortified, so as to move [people] to Koju.

Winter, tenth month. The king dispatched Aide at the Department of Ministries Chŏng Chang to Khitan to show gratitude for favors bestowed.

Fifteen Eastern Jurchen pirate ships raided Kosŏng and invaded Yongjin Garrison. They took prisoner more than seventy people including Junior Colonel Pak Hŭng'ŏn.

Eleventh month. The king dispatched Chamberlain for the Royal Stud[80] Wang Hŭigŏl and Palace Censor Yu Yuryang to Khitan to offer congratulations on the emperor's birthday.

Twelfth month. The Eastern Jurchen Sailla and others came to present horses.

Hyŏnjong Twentieth year [1029]

Seventh year of the Tiansheng era of Song, ninth year of the Daping era of Khitan

Spring, first month, *kyesa* [3rd] day. Empress Dowager Ch'ŏnch'u, née Hwangbo-ssi, passed away. She was buried in Yu-nŭng.

Second month. To avoid confusion with the [sound of the] king's given name [Sun 詢], those surnamed Sun 荀 changed to Son 孫.

Intercalary [second] month. For the first time, the king ordered all those civil officials below grade four who were not yet sixty to practice archery in the eastern or western suburbs whenever they had a free day.

More than thirty Jurchen pirate ships attacked the eastern border. The administrative assistant at the Local Navy Command, Cho Yunjŏng, drove them away.

80 *T'aebok-kyŏng* 太僕卿.

It was forbidden for military personnel from the capital or from the regions to request others to take over their regular corvée duty.

The Eastern and Western Jurchen Ahol, Sailla, and Kolkae and others more than 100 people altogether, came to offer horses and military equipment. They were given a promotion in rank.

Third month. Ten Eastern Jurchen pirate ships raided Myŏngju, but the Executive to the Military Commissioner,[81] Kim Hu, defeated them.

Summer, fourth month. A Tripitaka Assembly was held in the Hoegyŏng Hall, and 10,000 monks were fed on the polo court.

Khitan sent Supreme General Yelü Yanning and others with presents.

The Khitan Cao Wu together with his family fled to Koryŏ.

The high officials debated whether the ritual utensils at the Ancestral Shrine should be augmented, but the Ministry of Rites cited the 'Royal Commands' [of the *Book of Rites*] passage saying that the principle of "In good years no luxury, in bad years no frugality" should be upheld. This put an end to the discussion.

Fifth month. More than 400 Eastern Jurchen raided Tongsan County.

The king addressed his councilors of state: "The Jurchen have repeatedly breached our borders and are causing severe damage. We should summon their leaders and give them more lavish rewards and titles; this is what is called 'embracing people through virtue.'" But Assistant Executive in Political Affairs Kwak Wŏn objected: "The Jurchen have the face of humans but the mind of animals. Rather than embracing them with favors, we should awe them with our might." The king approved.

Sixth month. The T'amna crown prince Ko'ono came to court. He was granted the title of "Naval Attack" general and given a set of robes.

Bandits formed in the mountains of Kwangju, so officers of the Dragon-Tiger Army were dispatched to apprehend them.

Monks with spouses were drafted to be used as corvée labor for the construction of Chunggwang-sa.

---

81 *Pyŏngma p'angwan* 兵馬判官: executive of a military commission according to Shulz; here I take the 'pyŏngma' to stand for Pyŏngmasa, a military commissioner.

Autumn, seventh month. Khitan dispatched General Yelü Guanning and others to offer congratulations on the king's birthday.

T'amna presented local products.

Nineteen counties in Tŭngju and Myŏngju in Sakpang Circuit were raided by foreign bandits; they were given tax relief.

The T'amna person Chŏng'il and others were returned from Japan. Originally he was part of a crew of twenty-one, who were cast adrift in a storm and reached a far-flung island in the farthest southeast. The people of that island were very tall and their bodies were covered in hair; their language was totally different [from ours]. They were detained but after seven months seven people including Chŏng'il stole a boat and sailed northeast where they reached Nasa in Japan,[82] and were returned alive.

Eighth month, *chŏnghae* day, first day of the month. There was a solar eclipse.

The Jurchen *taesang* K'oebal, leading 300 households of his people, came to submit. They were granted territory around an old Parhae fortresses to settle.

Zhuang Wenbao and others, eighty people altogether, from Guangnan in Song, came to present local products.

Kyemyo [17th] day. The king went on an inspection tour to the west.

The king ordered the Assistant Executive in Political Affairs Yi Kado, the Vice-director of the Department of Ministries I Ŭngbo, Censor-in-chief Hwangbo Yuŭi, and the Senior Aide at the Department of Ministries Hwang Churyang to raise 238,938 able adult workers and 8450 craftsmen to construct the outer walls of Kaegyŏng. Originally Executive [Chief of the Royal Secretariat-Chancellery] Kang Kamch'an had requested construction since the capital had no walls. To determine the base of the wall, Yi Kado first ordered people to hold up parasols and encircle the city. He then went up a high place and instructed them how to move so as to make sure that it was evenly distributed. It measured 10,660 paces in circumference and was twenty-seven feet high; there were 4,910 bays of wooden structures on top.

---

82 Nasa-bu 那沙府: probably Nagasaki.

Ninth month. The general of the Eastern Capital of Khitan, Da Yanlin [Tae Yŏllim], dispatched Aide to the Palace Bursary Gao Jide to announce the founding of [his] dynasty and at the same time to request assistance. Da Yanlin was seventh-generation descendant of Da Zuoying [Tae Choyŏng], the founder of Parhae. He rebelled against Khitan and called his country Xingliao, and used Tianxing as his era name.

Kapcha [9th] day. On the road to Yŏmju, the king composed a poem called "Serenading the Chrysantemems on the ninth day [of the ninth month]." He showed the poem to the Hallim academician and his staff, and ordered them to compose matching poems. *Chŏngmyo* [12th] day. The king proceeded to Haeju, and pledged to reduce taxes by half for the people of Yŏmju and Haeju. Also, to the elderly and those gravely ill in the counties and prefectures they passed through he gave wine, food, and cloth according to rank.

A Royal Instruction read: "Recently I heard that corvée labor for the households attached to palace estates is extremely burdensome, making it difficult for the people to survive. Have the Office of Royal Clan Affairs[83] investigate and ensure the people's livelihood."

The king gave a banquet for the high officials of the civil and military branches who had accompanied him, and gave them presents according to rank.

Winter, tenth month, *kab'o* [9th] day. The king returned from Haeju.

Eleventh month. The king promoted the officials of the commissions for the completion of the city walls of Kaegyŏng and of Chunggwang-sa by one rank.

The king made Chief of the Chancellery Sŏ Nul take charge as Resident Governor of the Western Capital; he also made Vice-director of the Department of Ministries Yi Tan Commissioner to the Resident Governor.

Yi Kado was promoted to Acting Defender-in-chief, Merit Subject who Loyally and Luxuriously Constructed Palace Halls. He also bestowed the surname Wang and granted an estate in Kaesŏng County.

---

83 Chŏnjung-sŏng 殿中省: While Hucker [6561] translates this as "Palace Administration," as the name of this office was eventually changed (in 1310) to Chongbu-si 宗簿寺, it seems to have been in charge of the royal genealogy. However, judging from the context it may have had other responsibilities as well.

Assistant Executive in Political Affairs Kwak Wŏn died. Kwak Wŏn was a man of integrity, who excelled in composition. He passed through all positions in the three main departments, and although he was praised for his administrative abilities he always remained cautious. He was very generous and close to Yi Chag'in, for which he was ridiculed. When Xingliao rebelled, he secretly counseled the king that this was a good opportunity to take back the fortresses occupied by Khitan on the eastern side of the Amnok River, but Ch'oe Sawi, Sŏ Nul, and Kim Maeng all advised the king not to do this. Stubbornly Kwak Wŏn sent troops to attack them but failed to take the forts. Deeply ashamed of this failure he fell ill and died.

The Eastern Jurchen Kudu and others, more than thirty people altogether, came to court.

Twelfth month. The Grand Preceptor of the Xingliao State, Da Yanding [Tae Yŏnjŏng], induced the northeastern Jurchen to attack Khitan, and dispatched an envoy to request aid [from Koryŏ]. The king deliberated this with his state councilors. Director of the Chancellery Ch'oe Sawi and Chief of the Chancellery Ch'ae Ch'ungsun advised: "War is a dangerous affair, one cannot but be extremely cautious. When they are fighting among themselves, who knows, this might be advantageous for us? All we can do is repair the walls and moats and vigilantly watch the beacon fires to see how the situation evolves." The king followed this advice, and henceforth all the roads to Khitan were blocked.

The king recalled the military administrator for the north-western frontier province, Yu So, from mourning and sent him to staff the garrisons. At the time Xingliao had requested help but this had been denied, so he was sent there to prepare for all eventualities.

Hyŏnjong Twenty-first year [1030]

Eighth year of the Tiansheng era of Song, tenth year of the Daping era of Khitan

Spring, first month. The Eastern Jurchen Oŭlla and others, fifty people altogether, came to present horses.

Xingliao dispatched the Assistant Office Chief at the Ministry of Waterways Gao Jide to present a memorial requesting troops.

Second month. Ch'ae Ch'ungsun was put in charge of the position of Resident Governor of the Western Capital; Yi Chag'in was made Assistant Executive in Political Affairs; and Yu So Commissioner of the Security Council.

The Eastern Jurchen Moilla came to present horses.

Inju was fortified.

Summer, fourth month. A royal instruction read: "According to the Song calendar, the twelfth month of last year was a month with 30 days, but according to the calendar presenter by our grand astrologer, it was a month with 29 days.[84] Furthermore, he reported that the 15th day of the first month of this year there would be a lunar eclipse, but there wasn't. This certainly implies that our astronomers are not meticulous. Have the Censorate investigate this matter and report to me."

The Eastern Jurchen Mant'u and others, more than sixty people altogether, came to present light arrows and four halberd ships.

Ch'oe Yusŏn and seventeen others passed the composition test of the civil service examination; the king composed a poem and granted it to them, as a special encouragement.

The chief of Ch'ŏlli Country, Nasa, sent the Jurchen Ch'imt'ahan and others to present marten skins; they requested a calendar, and this was granted.

Fifth month. The Eastern Jurchen Supreme General "Serving the Country" Soholgae and others came to present horses, light arrows, military equipment, and three halberd ships.

The Khitan navy commander and tiger cavalry commandant Da Dao and Li Xiang and others, six people altogether, came to submit. From this time onwards many Khitan and Parhae people came to attach themselves [to Koryŏ].

---

84 *Taejin* 大盡: probably meaning 'completely exhausted' i.e. the maximum number of days in a month; *sojin* 小盡 would then mean a month with a lesser number of days.

Kang Kamch'an was promoted to Director of the Chancellery.

Sixth month. An amnesty was declared. The cloth tax for corvée laborers in the capital was reduced. Outstanding taxes for all prefectures and counties were remitted up until the *mujin* year [1028].

Autumn, seventh month. Liu Chongzheng of the Chief Administration Office of the field army of Xingliao dispatched the Ningzhou prefect Da Qinghan with a memorial requesting aid.

Lu Zun from Quanzhou in Song and others came to offer local products.

Vice-chancellor of the Ministry of the Royal Secretaries Chin Hamjo died. He was an expert in divining arts; whenever the country was in crisis there was a sudden need for prognostication arts, and he was often employed for this. His contemporaries however looked down on him.

Eighth month. Wang Kado was made Vice-chancellor of the Ministry of the Royal Secretaries, and also put in charge of the Finance Commission.

Ninth month. T'amna presented local products.

The prefect of Yingzhou in Xingliao, Li Kuanglu, came to inform that the situation in Xingliao was precarious. Shortly after he heard that the country had perished, so he stayed [in Koryŏ] and did not return.

The king dispatched Kim Ka to Khitan to offer congratulations on the recovery of the Eastern Capital.

Khitan dispatched the General of the Thousand Bull division Luohannu with the following decree: "Recently we have not exchanged envoys, probably because the roads were blocked. Now the one who arrogated the title of ruler of Parhae has been completely surrounded and has eventually capitulated. You should send officials with haste to our country, there is no need to think this over."

Yŏngdŏk Garrison was fortified.

Winter, tenth month. Han Cho was put in charge of the position of resident governor of the Western Capital.

The Khitan Xige and more than 500 people from Parhae came to submit. They were resettled in the prefectures of Kangnam.

Eleventh month. The Western Jurchen Mandu and others, twenty-seven households altogether, came to attach themselves; they were resettled in the Eastern Border Region.

The Censor of Miscelleaneous Affairs[85] Ch'oe Yŏnsu impeached the Assistant Executive in Political Affairs Yi Chag'in for falsely claiming to be a descendent of a merit subject of T'aejo and giving his son a protected appointment. He was relieved of office.

Twelfth month. Executive Chief of the Chancellery Ch'ae Ch'ungsun requested to be relieved of his office on account of illness, but this was not granted.

Sŏ Nul was made Chief of the Chancellery equivalent to Executive Chief, and also put in charge of the Ministry of Personnel.

Commissioner of the Security Council Kim Maeng died.

Director of the Chancellery Ch'oe Sawi requested retirement on account of his old age, but this was refused. Instead he was allowed to come to court once every five days.

Ch'oe Chean was made Commissioner of the Security Council and Hwang Churyang Vice-commissioner.

The Eastern Jurchen General "Keeping the Frontier Tranquil" Moksa Agol, the General "Mollifying those Afar" Alla, and the General "Seeking Recourse in Virtue" Agaeju came to present horses, armor, and light arrows.

Hyŏnjong Twenty-second year [1031]

Ninth year of the Tiansheng era of Song, first year of the Jingfu era of Xingzong of Khitan

Spring, first month. The Eastern Jurchen Iubul came to offer horses and military material.

The king ploughed the first furrow and declared an amnesty.

Executive Chief of the Chancellery Ch'ae Ch'ungsun renounced his office because of illness.

Second month. The king held a banquet for all high officials of the civil

---

85 *Ŏsa chaptan* 御史雜端.

and military branches in the Mundŏk Hall.

All those civil officials who had mastered military skills were to be given military offices.

More than eighty Eastern and Western Jurchen came to offer local products.

Third month. The Jurchen Sailla and others, more than forty people altogether, came to offer horses.

More than forty Khitan and Parhae people came to submit.

Summer, fourth month, *ŭlsa* [28th] day. The king was feeling indisposed.

Yi Tan was made Assistant Executive in Political Affairs.

Fifth month. Yu So was appointed Vice-minister of the Ministry of Rites and Assistant Executive in Political Affairs. Hwangbo Yuŭi was made Commissioner of the Security Council.

Ch'oe Sawi was made Minister of the Department of Royal Secretaries and then retired. Yi Kong was made Vice-director of the Department of Ministries and [honorary] Minister of Works;[86] he was also put in charge of the resident governor of the Eastern Capital.

There was an amnesty for public crimes punished with labor or lower sentences. Also, for loans to the people, only the original amount would have to be returned, not the interest.

On the *sinmi* [25th] day the king's illness grew worse. He summoned the heir apparent, Hŭm, and entrusted him with all affairs; then suddenly he died in Chunggwang Hall. He was given the posthumous title "Primordial Culture" and the temple name Hyŏnjong. The crown prince was enthroned but he stayed in the side room [of the funerary room] where he mourned mornings and evenings next to the coffin.

The historian Ch'oe Ch'ung wrote: "As is written in the *[Zuo] Tradition*, 'If Heaven is about to elevate him, then who can deny him?'[87] Queen Dowager

---

86 Sagong 司空: see Hucker 5687, probably a prestige title, although in some cases used for an official entrusted with construction works.

87 From the *Zuo zhuan*, 23rd year of Lord Xi [637 BC]. Durrant, Li, and Schaberg, *Zuo Tradition*, vol. 1, 371.

Ch'ŏnch'u maneuvered through illicit relations so as to take power, but Mokchong understood the people's wishes and removed Ch'ŏnch'u's clique from power, sending a missive from afar [to Hyŏnjong] to take over the throne and keep the royal line intact. Thus, how can one but believe the phrase 'If Heaven is about to elevate him, then who can stop him?' However, because of the machinations of his aunt, armed officials were plotting revolt, and a strong neighbor took advantage of this situation. The capital laid waste, the king escaped in the royal palanquin, enduring untold hardship. After everything had returned to normal and peace had been concluded with the barbarians, the cultivation of culture was revived, taxes reduced and labor shortened. The virtuous and wise were promoted, and politics was carried out in a fair and balanced way. The capital and the outer regions were at peace, and there were bumper harvests. This can be called a ruler who revived the dynasty!

Yi Chehyŏn wrote: "What Ch'oe Ch'ung is talking about is what is commonly called 'the mandate to rule.' Goujian tasted bile so that he could wipe out the shame of Huaiji;[88] Xiaobai forgot about his time in Ju and thereby had a disastrous legacy for Qi.[89] If a ruler believes he has the Heavenly Mandate and then behaves impudently and breaks the law, even though he may have obtained the mandate he is certain to lose it. Therefore the superior man will be mindful of chaos when times are orderly, and will think of danger in times of peace. He will be as careful about the end as about the beginning; like this he will be at ease with Heaven. As for Hyŏnjong, this is called 'someone in whom I cannot find fault.'"[90]

---

88 Goujian (r. 496–464 BC) was the ruler of the state of Yue in the Warring States Period. Embroiled in a feud with the neighboring kingdom of Wu, at one time Wu captured Yue's capital at Kuaiji and kept him prisoner for three years; after his return Goujian reputedly forced himself to eat bile in order not to forget this humiliation and take vengeance.

89 Kang Xiaobai was the personal name of Duke Huan of Qi (r. 685–643 BC). Following a coup in Qi, he fled with his tutor to Ju, waiting for the right time to take power in Qi. What calamity Yi Chehyŏn is referring to is however not clear to me.

90 From *Analects* 8.21.

Kapsul [28th] day. The king [i.e. Tŏkchong] led his officials in wearing mourning clothes; the ordinary people wore black caps and white clothes.

Sixth month. Sŏ Nul was appointed Acting Grand Mentor. Kang Kamch'an was exceptionally promoted to Acting Grand Mentor and Director of the Chancellery, founding meritorious subject and marquis of Ch'ŏnsu Prefecture.

The Western Jurchen General "Pacifying the Frontier" Ajidae and others twenty-seven people, came to offer horses.

The king ordered relevant offices to change the format of the congratulatory addresses at the Ancestral Shrine and the Three Tombs.

The Eastern Jurchen Generals Taewan and Sailla and others, fifty-eight people altogether, came to present horses.

The chief of Ch'ŏlli Country, Munasa, dispatched Yag'oja and others to present marten fur.

Pyongsin [20th] day. [Hyŏnjong] was buried in Sŏl-lŭng tomb; officials were exempted from duty.

Musul [22nd] day. The king removed his mourning clothes.

The king went to the Kyŏngnyŏng shrine[91] to report his accession, and declared an amnesty.

Autumn, seventh month. The king bestowed on his councilors of state the horses that had been presented by the circuits.

Yu So was appointed Inspecting Marshal for the Military Commissioner of the Central Army.

The Envoy for Reporting Bereavement, Office Chief at the Ministry of Works Nan Chengyan, came to report that Emperor Shengzong had passed away. The decree [informing Koryŏ of Shengzong's passing] was transmitted in the hall where Hyŏnjong's spirit tablet was kept.[92] The king led the Bereavement Envoy to the palace to express his grief.

---

91 Kyŏngnyŏng-jŏn 景靈殿: Hall in the palace where the portraits of deceased kings were enshrined.

92 Panhondang 返魂堂: before being enshrined in the Ancestral Shrine, the spirit tablet was kept here for three years during the mourning period.

The Parhae Palace Gate Guard Tae Tohaengnang[93] and others, fourteen people altogether, the Administrative Assistant for the various armies Ko Chinsang, and the Clerk for all Purposes[94] Wang Kwangnok came to submit.

The Khitan envoys to congratulate the former king on his birthday, Yelü Wende and Zhao Xiangxuan, came to transmit an imperial missive in the hall for Hyŏnjong's spirit tablet.

Eighth month. The Eastern Jurchen General Koŏbu and others, thirty people altogether, came to offer local products.

A royal decree read: "The Jurchen General Adugan together with 340 households came to submit. They were detained in the territory of Kaju and Ch'ŏlchu; yet originally Adugan belongs to the clan of Cha Hangsa of Tongbŏn 東蕃, so they should be sent to resettle in Tongbŏn."

Wang Kado requested permission to present a queen in marriage to the king.

Yi Tan was appointed vice-director at the Department of Ministries and Assistant Executive in Political Affairs.

Kang Kamch'an, who had retired as Director of the Chancellery, died. Kang hailed from Kŭmju; his character was pure and upright, and he was not interested in trade or production. From a young age he loved learning and devising extraordinary plans. He was short of stature and always wore shabby clothes, so that his disheveled looks were no different from commoners. But in court meetings his countenance was stern and composed, and whenever the country was confronted by a crisis he decided on the main strategy, thus acting like a steadfast pillar to the country. When he turned seventy he was granted a cane and cushion and allowed to attend court every three days; eventually he retired from his duties altogether and lived in a villa south of the city walls. He died at the age of eighty-four; the king grieved deeply and bestowed lavish mourning gifts. His posthumous title was Inhŏn 仁憲 and all officials were ordered to attend the funeral. He

---

93 Tae Tohaengnang 大道行郎: although this looks like a title rather than a name, I could not find it in any glossary; as Tae is a common Parhae surname, I provisionally interpreted it as a name.

94 *Kongmok* 孔目: Hucker 3503, literally the clerk "for every hole and item."

was co-enshrined with Hyŏnjong in the Ancestral Shrine.

The historian comments: "It is truly impressive, how Heaven's benevolence is lavished on these people! When the country was facing catastrophic defeat, it should naturally manifest a worthy who stands out among his generation. During the crises of the *kiyu* [1009] and *kyŏngsul* [1010] years, treacherous officials fomented revolt, and a powerful enemy invaded, so there was revolution internally and violence externally. Thus when the country was lurching towards a grave crisis, if there would not have been someone like Duke Kang at this time, who knows what would have happened to this country! He himself took charge of the planning during court consultations, and then went out himself to attack the enemy and quell the chaos, thus keeping the Three Han safe, and establishing himself as an eternal support for preserving the dynasty and keeping the people alive. If there were not someone like him, given birth to by Heaven to help the people in their hour of need, then who could have accomplished this. How tragic [his death], yet how rewarding [his life]!"

According to a popular tradition, there once was an envoy who passed through Sihŭng County at night, when he saw a big star fall into a family's home. He sent out a clerk to inspect, and right at that moment the lady of the house gave birth to a son. The envoy found this remarkable, and took the son with him to raise him. This was none other than Kang Kamch'an. Later an envoy from Song China saw him and unconsciously bowed down to him saying 'I have not seen the Mun'gok star[95] for a long time, but now it is actually here.' Although this appears to be a ridiculous legend, how would Kang's case be different from that of Fu Yue receiving the energy of the Ji

95 *Mun'gok sŏng* 文曲星: one of the stars of the big dipper; also used for an eminent literatus.

and Wei stars,[96] or of Shen Bo and Fu Hou subduing Songyue?"[97]

Ninth month. The king went to Oejesŏg-wŏn.

The Eastern Jurchen General "Embraced by Koryŏ" Oŏna Kaero and others, sixty-seven people altogether, came to offer local products.

A Royal Instruction read: "The former Assistant Executives in Political Affairs Kwak Wŏn and Kim Maeng, and the Commissioner of the Security Council Yun Chinggo all established merit that should not be forgotten. Therefore I cherish Kwak Wŏn's son Kwak Chŭng, Kim Maeng's son Kim Tŏkpu, and Yung Chinggo's son Hŭidan; they should all be recruited and given an official position."

Winter, tenth month. Sŏ Nul was appointed Director of the Chancellery, and Wang Kado and Yu So were both appointed Executive Chief of the Chancellery and concurrently Executive Chief of the Ministry of Royal Secretaries.

The Khitan Wang Shounan and others, nineteen people altogether, came to submit; they were resettled in the south.

The councilors of state requested that normal dishes were restored at court; the king approved.

The king gave a banquet for the elderly and retired officials on the polo court; the musicians were present but did not play [because of mourning etiquette].

The king took Wang Kado's daughter as a queen.

The king dispatched the Office Chief at the Ministry of Works, Yu Kyo, to Khitan to assist in the funeral [of Emperor Shengzong] and Kim Haenggong to offer congratulations at the enthronement [of the new emperor, Xingzong, 1031–1035]. Wang Kado then made the following proposal: "Khitan is now

---

96 Fu Yue 傅說: legendary figure from the Shang Dynasty. King Wu Ding had a dream in which he was introduced to a wise man in heaven; after waking he made a drawing of that wise man and had his officials search for him. This turned out to be Fu Yue. Ji – Wei: 箕尾: sagittarrus and scorpio.

97 Shen Bo was a wise minister at the court of King Xuan of Zhou (and also his maternal uncle); the reference to Songyue 崧岳 might be because of the title of an Ode in the *Book of Odes* (Song Gao 崧高) that refers to the story of Shen Bo's settlement of a southern state.

faithfully conducting relations with us, yet they still have the ambition of annexing us. Now their ruler has passed away, and the emperor's son-in-law Piti is revolting in the Eastern Capital. We should use this opportunity to request them to destroy the fortresses and bridge on the Amnok and return those of our people they are still detaining. If they do not honor this request, then we will cut off relations." A memorial with this request was then entrusted with the envoys.

The Eastern Jurchen *wŏnbo* Kaero and others, forty-six people altogether, came to court. They were promoted in rank and given presents.

The Censorate petitioned: "Yi Kong, who is now in charge as Resident Governor of the Eastern Capital, has appropriated assets for himself and makes his house slaves ride the official horses from the postal stations. We request that this be dealt with according to the law." The king followed this advice.

The king went to the polo court to feed 30,000 monks.

Vice-director of the Department of Ministries I Ŭngbo was additionally appointed Acting Minister of Education, and Junior Vice-director at the Department of Ministries Kim Yŏt'ak was additionally appointed Acting Minister of Works.

Intercalary month. An examination was held at the National Academy, and Chŏng Kongji and others, sixty people altogether were selected. They were tested on rhyme-prose poems, 6-stanza and 10-stanza poems. This was the beginning of the National Academy Test.

Executive Chief of the Chancellery Yi Kado was ill and had to skip the court deliberations.

Eleventh month. Commissioner to the Resident Governor of the Eastern Capital, the Vice-minister of the Ministry of Taxation Yi Chag'in, died.

The king ordered relevant offices to give clothes and padding to people from various countries who had come to submit.

The Eastern Jurchen General Moira came to present horses. Furthermore, he said "since I come from a faraway border region, I could not make it to the funeral [of Hyŏnjong]. Please allow me to pay my respects at the tomb."

The king gave permission.

The Eastern Jurchen Odunae and others, more than forty people altogether, came to present local products.

A Royal Instruction read: "The former Vice-director of the Department of Ministries Chi Ch'aemun followed King Hyŏnjong on his journey south; this is merit of the first class, so his merit rank should be recorded [as such] to encourage future generations."

Kim Haenggong returned from Khitan and reported that they would not honor what Koryŏ had requested. Executive Chief of the Chancellery and twenty-eight other officials argued that since the request had not been granted it was fitting to stop sending envoys. However, Commissioner of the Security Council Hwangbo Yuŭi and thirty-two others argued that if relations were broken off, the ordinary people would be the ones to suffer, so it would be better to continue exchanging envoys to give the people a break. The king agreed with this counsel. Sŏ Nul and Wang Kado then argued that they should stop sending envoys for newyear's congratulations and continue using the Daping era name of Shengzong.

Twelfth month. The king ordered Ch'oe Sawi, who had retired as Director of the Chancellery, to come to court once every five days to enter the Departments and inspect affairs.

4. Tŏkchong, Chŏngjong, Munjong (I)

Tŏkchong , Great King of Respectful Vigour

His given name was Hŭm 欽 and his courtesy name Wŏllyang 元良. He was the oldest son of Hyŏnjong, and his mother was Queen Wŏnsŏng 元成, née Lady Kim. He was born on the *ŭlsa* day of the fifth month of the seventh *pyŏngjin* year of Hyŏnjong [1016]. His character was strong and decisive. He was on the throne for three years and lived to the age of nineteen.

Tŏkchong First year [1032]

First year of the Mingdao era of Song, first year of the Chongxi era of Khitan

Spring, first month. The Censorate impeached Chamberlain for the Palace Treasury Wang Hŭigŏl, Second Office Chief Yu Paeg'in, Office Chief at the Board of Rites Ch'oe Pokkyu, and Assistant Office Chief Yi Ŭngnyŏn. When they were assigned to serve in the Western Capital, they obtained fields and prospered; the Censorate requested them to be removed from office, and the king complied.

Khitan dispatched a resident envoy to come [to Koryŏ], but when he reached Naewŏn-sŏng, he was not received. Then Sakchu, Yŏng'in Garrison, P'ach'ŏn and other counties were fortified in preparation.

The king went to Naejesŏg-wŏn.

The name of the king's birthday was changed from "Humane Longevity" to "Responding to Heaven" (*Ŭngch'ŏn* 應天) festival.

The Western Jurchen Chagon and others, eight people altogether, and the Parhae Saji Myŏngdong and others, twenty-nine people altogether, came to submit.

Second month. The "Awe Inspiring" Vice-lieutenant[1] of T'ongju, the Headman Kim Kŏ, was promoted to Junior Colonel; the Sub-colonel Sugyŏn was promoted to Junior Colonel. Kim Kŏ and others had, during the Khitan invasions, strengthened the walls and guarded them well; moreover they had established merit by capturing the Grand Master Ma Shou.

Sat'ong of Parhae and others, seventeen people altogether, came to submit.

Ch'ŏlli Country dispatched an envoy to cultivate good relations.

Hwangbo Yuŭi was made Assistant Executive in Political Affairs, and Hwang Churyang was made Commissioner of the Security Council.

Third month. Paek Kai and eight others passed the composition test of the civil service examination, while four people passed by royal fiat.

The Khitan palace eunuch Gao Shanwu and the palace guard Gao Zhencheng and others, fifteen people altogether; Capital Township Supervisor of the Left[2] Daguang; the naturalized Administrative Assistant for Military Affairs in Baozhou Ch'oe Unbu; and the Prefecturally nominated Presented Scholar Li Yunheng and others fled to Koryŏ.

Chief Steward of the Accommodations Office Pak Wŏnjak requested that relevant offices be ordered to produce leather carts, exquisitely made arbalests, and thunderbolt catapults.[3] The king approved.

Wang Kado was put in charge of compiling the state history; Yi Tan was appointed Secretary *cum* Executive Chief of the Ministry of Royal Secretaries; Hwang Churyang was to assist in the compilation of state

---

1 *Chinwi puwi* 振威副尉: tentative translation. This is a local title, not to be confused with central military offices.

2 *Zuoxiang duzhihuishi* 左厢都指揮使: inferred meaning.

3 There is unfortunately no way to determine what exactly these weapons were.

history; and Yu Chingp'il was made Vice-director of the Department of Ministries.

The court deliberated on the merit of those who had died in battle since the *kyŏngsul* year [1010]. Pan Hŭiak was posthumously appointed Director of the Directorate of Royal Workshops, Kim Yŏn'gyŏng Director of the Directorate of Weaponry,[4] Chŏn Inyŏng Deputy Director of the Foreign Relations Office,[5] Yu Paekpu Deputy Director of the Office of Regalia,[6] Kim Yangjwa Deputy-director of the Directorate of Royal Workshops, and Yang Paek Assistant at the Office of Royal Clan Affairs.[7]

Because of the drought, the corvée laborers for the construction of Pongŭn and Chunggwang temples were released from duty.

Summer, fourth month. The king avoided the main palace halls and had the number of dishes reduced. The slaughter of animals was forbidden and those imprisoned for minor crimes were released.

The Eastern Jurchen *wŏnyun* Koduro and others, came to offer local products.

The Khitan Neiyigu from the Xijia tribe and others, twenty-seven people altogether, came to submit.

The king personally made a sacrifice to the heavenly bodies to pray for rain on the polo court.

Fifth month. The Parhae man Sarodŏk and others, fifteen people altogether, came to submit.

Sixth month. The Western Jurchen "Embraced by Koryŏ" General Idong and others, eight altogether, came to court, and were promoted by one rank.

The Parhae people Urŭm, Yag'i, and others, twelve people altogether, and Soŭlsa and others, seventeen people altogether, came to submit.

The Eastern Jurchen general "Seeking Refuge in Virtue" Yaŏp'o and others, eight people altogether, came to offer local products.

The king received the bodhisattva precepts in the Ŭnggŏn Hall of the

4 *Kungi-gam* 軍器監.

5 *Yebin sogyŏng* 禮賓少卿.

6 *Wiwi sogyŏng* 衛尉少卿.

7 *Chŏnjung-sŭng* 殿中丞

palace.

Autumn, seventh month. Yi Yegyun and others, eight people altogether, had been detained by the Khitan while they were on an embassy; the king granted their spouses and children presents according to rank.

The Western Jurchen *taesang* Yaban and others, twenty-five people altogether, and the Eastern Jurchen *chŏngjo* Kairo and others, ninety-one people altogether came to present local products.

The Parhae person Ko Sŏng and others, twenty people altogether, came to submit.

Eighth month. The *taesang* Chuo beat his mother; [after execution his body] was displayed in the market place.

The Eastern Jurchen *chŏngbo* Tuŏbo and others, twenty people altogether, came to present local products.

Yi Tan was made Chief of the Chancellery, and Hwangbo Yuŭi vice-minister of the Board of Personnel and assistant executive in political affairs. According to the old system, a "proclamation on hemp"[8] was to be delivered in the officials' houses, but this time all officials were gathered for the proclamation in Kŏndŏk Hall.

The Eastern Jurchen *poyun* Taeyu and others, thirty people altogether, came to court.

Ninth month. The Eastern Jurchen *taesang* Yaŭlhan and others, thirty people altogether, and the Grand General "Upholding the Country" Yoŭllae and others, fifty people altogether, came to court.

All those punished to do labor or lighter punishments were pardoned.

Winter, tenth month. The Parhae Headquarters Clerk Yi Namsong and others, ten people altogether, fled to Koryŏ.

Pak Wŏnjak requested to install twenty-four "eight-ox-arbalests" in the border fortresses. The king approved.

There was an earthquake across ten counties in Sangju circuit.

The Khitan Liu Xinsi and others, fifteen people in total, fled to Koryŏ.

---

8 *Sŏnma* 宣麻: this refers to the king's symbolic gift of walking stick and table to aged officials, usually marking their retirement.

Eleventh month. The king dispatched envoys to the nine provinces to select soldiers.

The castle lord of Urŭng sent his son Puŏing tarang to present local products.

The Western Jurchen *chŏngjo* Taep'ogo's retainers, fourteen people altogether, came to present local products.

Twelfth month. The Khitan Luogu and others, ten people altogether, came to submit.

Tŏkchong Second year [1033]

Second year of the Mingdao era of Song, second year of the Chongxi era of Khitan

Spring, first month. The Eastern Jurchen General Kaedagan and others, twenty-five people in total, came to court.

Ch'ŏlli Country dispatched an envoy to present horses and marten skins. In return, the king bestowed very lavish gifts.

Liu Shouquan from Song together with others, fourteen people altogether, fled [to Koryŏ].

Hwang Churyang was put in charge of the Censorate.

The Eastern Jurchen General Pogiaŏnae and others, 113 people in total, came to present local products.

The Khitan Qiunai and others, eighteen people altogether, fled [to Koryŏ].

The lieutenants of the Left-Right Division and Ferocious Army O Haeng, Yi Hwang, and Sin Sŏllip, were rewarded with one grade for having caught seven Khitan soldiers.

Second month. The Western Jurchen seal-holder Koŭmp'a and the Khitan grand preceptor Gu Shenghuan and others, eleven people altogether, came to present local products and weapons.

The Eastern Jurchen General "Embraced by Koryŏ" Kŏŏul and others, forty-nine people altogether, came to court.

Third month. A royal instruction read: "Recently officials have debated the issue and requested to stop the practice of proclaiming and sending off new appointments. However, I am afraid that this will lead to the gradual deterioration of ritual propriety. From now on, for all the military and civil ranks above senior rank three, and for all appointments to the Security Council, have people dispatched to the appointee's house to proclaim the edict of appointment."

The Western Jurchen General Iulbul came to present local products.

Pirates raided Paeksŏk harbor in Kansŏng County and took with them fifty people.

Ch'oe Hŭimok and seven others passed the composition test of the civil service examination, two people passed the classics examination, and two passed by the king's grace.

The Khitan of the Xijia tribe Guyao and others, eleven people altogether, came to submit; they were settled in Kangnam.

Summer, fourth month. The Parhae person Suŭlbun and others, eighteen people altogether, and Kasu and others, three people altogether, came to submit.

The Eastern Jurchen General "Seeking Refuge in Virtue" Koŏbu and others, twenty-six people in total, came to present local products.

Pirates raided Samch'ŏk County and captured more than forty people.

Fifth month. The Western Jurchen *chŏngwi* Saŏha and others, three people in total, came to court.

Sixth month. The Parhae person Sŏnsong and others, seven people altogether, came to submit.

Im'in [9th] day. An earthquake struck Andong District and Hapchu.

The Western Jurchen Grand General "Embraced by Koryŏ" Kŏira and others, twenty-four people altogether, came to court; the *chungyun* Kosa and others, six people altogether, came to submit; Komohan and others, twenty-five people in total, came to present local products.

Shen Liu and others, twenty people altogether from Song, fled to Koryŏ.

The Eastern Jurchen *taesang* Kojimun and others, forty-one people in total, came to court.

Autumn, seventh month. The Eastern Jurchen *chwayun* Ap'o and others, forty-three people altogether, came to present local products.

Eighth month. The traders from Quanzhou in Song, Dou Gang and Lin Ai and others, fifty-five people altogether, came to present local products.

Hyŏnjong was enshrined in the Royal Ancestor Shrine.

The king ordered the Chief of the Chancellery Yu So to construct a defensive perimeter along the northern border. It was to start from near old Kungnaesŏng on the Western Sea shore where the Amnok empties into the sea, and eastwards straddling the following thirteen places: Wiwŏn Garrison, Hŭnghwa Garrison, Chŏngju, Yŏnghae Garrison, Yŏngdŏk Garrison, Yŏngsak Garrison, Unju, Ansu Garrison, Ch'ŏngsae Garrison, P'yŏngno Garrison, Yŏngwŏn Garrison, Chŏngyung Garrison, Maengju, and Sakchu. Then passing Yodŏk Garrison, Chŏngbyŏn Garrison, and Hwaju, it would reach the eastern sea. It was to be a stone-built wall stretching for more than 1,000 leagues, with a height and width equal to twenty-five feet.

Winter, tenth month. The Eastern Jurchen General "Seeking refuge in virtue" Yobin and others, thirty-seven people altogether; the *wŏnbo* Oduna and others, sixty-three people altogether; the Western Jurchen Grand Preceptor Agakp'al and others, fourteen people altogether, came to court.

The rank titles of merit subjects of previous generations were increased.

The Khitan invaded Chŏngju.

A letter of instruction read: "Undeservedly we were chosen to continue our ancestors' task of governing the Three Han, so our mind has been firmly set on governing the country and our heart is devoted with filial thoughts to the ancestors. This year the tri-annual royal ancestor ritual[9] takes place, and now that is upon us to personally prepare for the ritual, we would like to extend the special favor of rejoicing with all, whether at the center or in the provinces. There should be a grand amnesty in the country, except for disloyalty, unfiliality, extortion, and treason; those with punishments below banishments should be pardoned, those sentenced to decapitation

---

9 Hyŏphyang 祫享: ancestor ritual in which all tablets of kings are gathered in the shrine for T'aejo.

or strangulation should have their sentences commuted to banishment to inhabited islands, while those banished before should be relocated to less remote places. Those who have accepted money to commute sentences should be released."

Chŏngju, Anyung Garrison, and Kansong County were fortified.

Eleventh month. Because the Western Jurchen Uhwa and others, 156 people altogether, had merit in the preparation of the border wall, they were promoted by one rank.

Twelfth month. The Western Jurchen *poyun* Posil and others, thirty-nine people altogether, came to present local products.

The ritual of greeting when meeting on the roads for civil and military officials of all grades was determined.

The Parhae person Kijilhwa and others, eleven people altogether, came to submit. They were resettled in the south.

Tŏkchong Third year [1034]

First year of the Jingyou era of Song, third year of the Chongxi era of Khitan

Spring, first month. A royal instruction read: "Frugality and using only what one needs is the way of the people. For dyeing the royal robes, the Bureau of Royal Clothing should only stock one year's provision of smartweed,[10] and not budget for anything more than that. The *yangban*[11] normally wear purple robes when they are in their offices, but there is no point in doing so. If they are not with the king, let them wear informal black robes."

The Eastern Jurchen *chŏngjo* Tarogan and others, fifty-eight people, came to present local products.

Hwang Churyang was made assistant executive in letters and supervisor of the Hallim Academy.

---

10 Hongjich'o 葒芝草:

11 *Yangban* 兩班: a term designating the civil and military branches of the government, eventually used as a generic term for all officials.

Second month. The Eastern Jurchen Grand General "Mollified from afar" Chudal and others, thirty-six people, and the *chwayun* Adogan and others, forty-two people, came to offer local products.

The king took a daughter of Hyŏnjong as his queen.

Third month. Chang Kŭngmaeng was made junior vice-director of the Department of Ministries, and Yi Chakch'ung Chief Censor and was also put in charge of the Hallim Academy.

The Eastern Jurchen General "Upholding the Country" Adogan and others, thirty-two people, came to present local products.

A royal instruction read: "Agriculture and sericulture are the basis for clothing and food; all the officials in the provinces, prefectures, and counties should observe the royal instructions and not interfere with the three seasons [for agriculture, i.e. spring, summer and autumn], to ensure that the ordinary people are at ease."

The king gave a banquet for his officials in Mundŏk Hall in honor of Yu So and others for their merit in constructing the border wall. He conferred on Yu So the title of Merit Subject Promoting Loyalty through Border Works.

Summer, fourth month. Joint Security Councilor Ch'oe Ch'ung petitioned: "During the time of King Sŏngjong, it was mandated that the text of the 'Six correct ways and six deviant ways' from the *Garden of Persuasions*[12] was to be written on the walls of all government bureaus, in the center as in the provinces, together with the 'Six Criteria for the Regional Inspector'.[13] Since this is already a long time ago, please have them written and displayed again, so that those in office will know where to exert themselves and where to restrain." The king approved.

The field and woodland rank system for *yangban* and military reservists[14]

---

12 *Shuo yuan* 說苑: A text that collects important disquisitions by scholar-officials of the past, usually in the form of dialogues between ruler and minister. Authored by Liu Xiang (79–8 or 77–6 BCE) of the Former Han Dynasty,

13 *Cishi liutiao* 刺史六條: also devised during the Former Han Dynasty; mainly designed to avoid abuse of power by regional administrators. See http://www.chinaknowledge.de/History/Terms/cishi.html

14 *Han'in* 閑人: soldiers selected from local magnate families to augment regular troops.

was changed.

The Eastern Jurchen General "Embraced by Koryŏ" Ira and others, twenty-five people, came to present local products.

Fifth month. The Eastern Jurchen General "Seeking Refuge in Virtue" Kolbo and others, twenty-seven people, came to present local products.

Executive Chief of the Chancellery Wang Kado died. Before, he had requested to retire to his hometown Ch'ŏngju to nurse his illness. When he died, the local government office took care of the funeral. He was given the posthumous title Yŏngsuk, and he was co-enshrined with King Hyŏnjong in the National Shrine.

Hallim Academician Pak Yuin was made instructor to the Prince of P'yŏngyang, while the proctor in the Security Council Chin Hyŏnsŏl was appointed instructor to the Prince of Nangnang.

Sixth month. The Eastern Jurchen General "Pacifying the Borders" Igudo and others, thirty people in all, came to present local products.

All the princes[15] were instructed to attend court deliberations once every five days.

Autumn, seventh month. The Western Jurchen *wŏnyun* Mo'o and others, twenty-two people in all, came to present local products.

Yi Tan was appointed Executive Chief of the Chancellery, Min Kagŏ and Yu Chingp'il junior vice-director and vice-director of the Department of Ministries, Hwangbo Yuŭi vice-chancellor of the Ministry of the Royal Secretaries and joint executive chief of the Ministry of the Royal Secretaries, and Ch'oe Ch'ung vice-minister of the Board of Punishment and Councilor on the Security Council.

A royal instruction read: "I have reflected on what the Board of Punishment reported on its deliberations regarding the letter of the law regarding capital punishment. Even though the law may prescribe the death penalty, if there is doubt regarding the crime it is better to regard it as light as possible, and be lenient in meting out punishment. These are the statutes of previous kings. For those who have beaten up the head of a

---

15 *Chewang* 諸王: literally "all the kings" but likely referring to the princes.

family, planned murder, committed murder, or committed violent robbery, after caning they should be sent to an uninhabited island. Even if they have committed violent robbery and harmed people holding a stick, or less grave offenses, they should be sent to inhabited islands." After this, sixty-nine people avoided the death penalty in capital prisons.

Ninth month, *kyemyo* [17th] day. The king was struck down with illness and transferred the throne to his younger brother the Prince of P'yŏngyang, Wang Hyŏng. He then died in the Yŏnyŏng Hall of the Palace. The same day the Prince of P'yŏngyang ascended the throne, and bestowed the title Kyŏnggang 敬康, and the temple name Tŏkchong.

Winter, tenth month, *kyŏng'o* [14th] day. Tŏkchong was buried in Suknŭng tomb.

Yi Chehyŏn's eulogy: "In the reign of King Ch'ungnyŏl, Yi Sŭnghyu, also known as the man from Mt. Tut'a, presented his *Chewang un'gi* 帝王韻紀 [rhymed chronicle of emperors and kings] to the throne. In it he wrote 'How could Tŏkchong reign for only four years, when the phoenix had come as an auspicious sign?' But checking with the veritable records, there is no mention of such a thing. There is merely a vulgar tradition that says 'A phoenix came to the Wibong [Glorious phoenix] Gate and paraded around; but a group of crows came and cawed at him, so it flew away.' The people therefore hated crows and young and old alike took their bows and shot them. Thus throughout Tŏkchong's reign there were no crows in the capital.' Now the phoenix is the leader of all the feathered animals; if a group of crows were able to chase it away, how could it be called a phoenix! The *Chewang un'gi* has simply not examined the facts. Tŏkchong in observing the mourning for his father showed utmost filiality, and in government did not change the way of his father. He employed his father's old officials, people such as Sŏ Nul, Wang Kado, Ch'oe Ch'ung, and Hwang Churyang. Thus at court there was no cheating or hiding, and the people were at ease. Even if there was no phoenix, his temple name was 'Tŏk' [virtue], which is fitting."

Eleventh month. The king went to Sinbong Pavilion, and declared a general amnesty.

The P'algwanhoe was organized, and the king went to the Sinbong Pavilion and gave a banquet for all his officials; he then went to Pŏbwang-sa. The next day was the main celebration of the P'alghwanhoe, and the king again gave a banquet and then watched music and performances. From the center and from the provinces memorials were offered in celebration. Song traders, Eastern and Western Tribesmen,[16] and T'amna all offered local products. The king bestowed them seats to observed the rituals; afterwards this became a regular practice.

Twelfth month. The king's younger brother Wang Sŏ was made acting grand preceptor and joint minister of the Ministry of the Royal Secretaries; Wang Ki was made Acting Grand Guardian; Hwang Churyang was appointed Vice-minister of the Ministry of Rites and Assistant Executive in Political Affairs; and Ch'oe Chean was made Vice-minister of the Ministry of Personnel.

Chŏngjong, Great King of Gracious Countenance

The king's given name was Hyŏng 亨 and his courtesy name Sinjo 申炤, and he was a younger brother of Tŏkchong. He was born on the *muin* day[17] of the seventh month of the ninth year of Hyŏnjong (1018). He was benevolent and filial, magnanimous yet sharp and decisive, and did not get distracted by details of etiquette. He was on the throne for twelve years and lived to the age of thirty-two.

---

16 *Pŏn* 蕃: this word has many meanings, among which "fence" and "barbarian" are probably closest to the intended meaning, although it is also possible that it refers to a specific ethnic group. As a proper noun (place name or family name) it is pronounced P'i rather than Pŏn. Although it has a condescending meaning, given the fact that this people were clearly considered allies to Koryŏ tribesman seems to be a better choice than barbarian. In case of military confrontations however I translated it as "barbarian."

17 According to the entry for his birth in the annals for King Hyŏnjong, it was a *chŏngch'uk* day.

Chŏngjong First year [1035]

Second year of the Jingyou era of Song, fourth year of the Chongxi era of Khitan

Spring, first month. Ch'oe Ch'ung was appointed Security Councilor and Vice-minister at the Ministry of Punishments.

The Eastern Jurchen General "Embraced by Koryŏ" Moira and others, fifty-seven people altogether, came to court. They were granted presents according to rank.

Second month. The wife of the civilian Tŭgyŏm from Chinju gave birth to three sons. According to the old customs she was granted the "three son's rent" of forty *sŏk* each.

The Western Jurchen chief Kaago and the Eastern Jurchen General "Upholding the country" Kojimun and others, forty-seven people altogether, came to court.

Third month. Yi Tan was appointed Executive Chief of the Chancellery and Chief of the Ministry of the Royal Secretaries; Hwangbo Yuŭi was appointed Executive of the Ministry of the Royal Secretaries and Overseer of Affairs at the Ministry of Personnel.

Kim Much'e and thirteen others passed the composition test of the civil service examination, and one passed the classics examination.

The king invested the Yŏnhŭng Princess née Han as consort Hye and declared an amnesty.

Summer, fourth month. The king personally bestowed a banquet for the national elders of eighty or over on the polo court.

It was forbidden to gather firewood in the illustrious mountains of the capital, where trees were planted all around.

Fifth month. The Khitan Naewŏn-sŏng notified Hŭnghwa Garrison as follows: "We venture to submit the following: Your country was originally our vassal, and previous [Khitan] emperors without fail bestowed their largesse on you. Over the course of many years, they never tired of sending embassies across mountains and seas. Recently, because of the punishment of the criminals, the ritual of sending an embassy to our court was blocked. Since the traitorous elements have now been eliminated, it is fitting that you proceed with the tribute missions, how come for several years you have not resumed the friendly relations of old? [Instead] you build walls and obstruct the roads, erect wooden palisades and keep out our mounted warriors. Yet don't you know that to the country of Shu the stone bull provided a shortcut?[18] If you keep acting like this, later you will invite ridicule. Now our present emperor [Xingzong], building on the foundations of previous emperors, has consolidated the borders in the eight directions. In the south, the Xia emperors have chosen the righteous path and pledged eternal harmony; to the west various kings have followed suit and pay tribute. Only the eastern territory has not yet grasped the respect due to the pole star; if [the emperor] strikes you down with lightning in a fit of anger, then how will you keep your people secure? Quickly decide whether you are going to comply or not."

Sixth month, *pyŏngjin* [4th] day. An earthquake shook the capital.

The Eastern Jurchen Oŏgo and others, twenty-seven people in total, came to court.

Yŏngdŏk Garrison sent a reply to the notification from the Khitan in Naewŏn-sŏng: "In your letter you said 'Recently, because of the punishment of the criminals, the ritual of sending an embassy to our court was blocked. Since the traitorous elements have now been eliminated, it is fitting that you proceed with the tribute missions.' Respectfully we submit that it was at the beginning of the [Da] Yanlin [Tae Yŏllim] revolt in your country when you, the suzerain country, raised an army, that the roads became treacherous and blocked, holding up the people. After this the Drafting Advisor of the Department of Royal Secretariat, Kim Ka, gave felicitations upon the recovery of the Eastern Capital. When the Executive at the Ministry of Taxation Yi Suhwa was on his way to present local tribute,

---

18 This probably refers to a story from the Warring States Period. The ruler of Shu, a fertile land surrounded by impenetrable mountains, was famed for his greed. King Hye of Qin then came up with the plan to make a huge stone bull and cover his behind with gold, spreading the rumor that it could poo gold. The covetous ruler of Shu then carved a path through the mountains to get the bull, thus opening the path for the Qin troops to attack and subjugate Shu.

the previous great king [i.e. Hyŏnjong] passed away.[19] Commissioner for Audience Ceremonies Ch'ae Ch'ŭnghyŏn then went to relay the news of the king's death, but then the previous emperor [Shengzong] passed away [in 1031]. Thus Senior Assistant Director at the Department of Ministries Yo Kyo hurried to assist in the funeral [of the emperor]. This was when the current emperor succeeded to the throne, and Reviewing Policy Advisor Kim Haenggong followed to transmit congratulations. Thus since the pacification of the [Xing]liao, mourning days followed one after the other. How can this be called 'blocking the ritual of sending an embassy to court!' Furthermore you claim, 'you build walls and obstruct the roads, erect wooden palisades and keep out our mounted warriors.' Now as per Fu Xi's hexagrams (i.e. the *Yijing*) establishing earthen [fortifications] in dangerous places is a perpetual rule. The State of Lu closed the gates and the people passing through were more on their guard than ever. Thus by setting up walls and blocks we are marking our territory, with the aim of giving repose to and settling the border people, but not with the intention of blocking the imperial transformation. Furthermore you also write 'Only the eastern territory has not yet grasped the respect due to the pole star.' But formerly among the envoys who travelled to and fro, six of our envoys have been detained in your country; and the two cities of Sŏnju and Chŏngju, which have been constructed within our borders have not yet been returned to us. Thus we will continue to pray wholeheartedly for a good outcome on this. His highness the king has just started his reign and is getting to know the people to make a new start. Heaven's munificence reaches far and wide; as we have stated in repeated memorials, please return our people and our territory; so far this request has not yet been granted. If this had already been sincerely realized, how could we be indolent in the tribute ritual? It all rests on a gracious order, why go to the trouble of blaming? Furthermore you also write 'if [the emperor] strikes you down with lightning in a fit of

---

19 Although this might also refer to Tŏkchong, given the context Hyŏnjong seems to be more likely. Contacts were basically interrupted in early 1032 when Koryŏ refused entry to the Khitan "resident envoy" (*liushi* 留使).

anger, then how will you keep your people secure?' Respectfully we submit that the present emperor cherishes even the insignificant, and listens to the unworthy with magnanimous heart. Looking after this tribute territory he will bestow his grace on it, so how would he be enraged by those who have no guilt? Having read your letter carefully, it seems that you have spoken to us in jest."

Autumn, seventh month. The Ministry of Personnel petitioned, "The former Vice Director of the Department of Ministries Yi Kong once committed the offense of sullying and insulting [his position], but since he has been repeatedly pardoned, please restore him to his original position. The king followed this advice. The Censorate disputed this, and shortly after he was dismissed.

Hwangbo Yŏng was made Security Councilor and concurrently Chief Censor.

The king's birthday was designated the Changnyŏng Festival.

An edict read: "As I have not laid off the mourning clothes for the previous king, for offenses punishable by decapitation, [the penalty should be commuted to] caning and banishment to an uninhabited island; for offenses punishable by hanging, [the penalty should be commuted to] caning and banishment to an inhabited island."

Eighth month, *sinmi* [20th] day. The capital was struck by an earthquake.

The Western Jurchen Grand General Iubul and others, forty-four people altogether, and the Eastern Jurchen *taewan* 大完[20] Kaedahan and others, fifty-two people altogether, came to court.

Ninth month. The Eastern Barbarian General "Seeking Refuge in Virtue" Oda and others, twenty-three people altogether, came to court.

Kyemyo [23rd] day. An earthquake struck nineteen prefectures including Kyŏngju.

The long wall was constructed in the northwest circuit from the Song pass eastward so as to stop clashes with border bandits. Also, Chaejŏn was fortified, resettled with people, and renamed Ch'angju.

---

20 This looks like a regional office title, but is only attested three times in the annals.

Winter, tenth month. The Eastern Jurchen leader Ŏbullo and others, sixty people in total, came to court.

Eleventh month. The Eastern Jurchen chief Arogan and others, sixty-five people in total, came to court.

Twelfth month. The Eastern Tribesman *taewan* Kodohwa and others, thirty people in total, came to court.

Chŏngjong Second year [1036]

Third year of the Jingyou era of Song, fifth year of the Chongxi era of Khitan

Spring, first month. The Eastern Jurchen General "Embraced by Koryŏ" Sara and others, eighty-two people in total, came to court.

The Censorate stated: "The outer officials[21] of the provinces use the people at times when they should not do so, thereby impeding agricultural work. Please dispatch officials to investigate, and have them dismiss or promote the officials [based on an assessment of their actions]." The king agreed.

Those who have committed offenses on official duty punishable by banishment or less, and those who have committed private offenses punishable by beating or less, and those who have to redeem for crimes, were pardoned.[22]

Second month. The king went to the main palace hall to inspect the court assembly and bestowed emolument badges on all officials.

Yu So was made Executive Chief of the Chancellery and concurrently Executive of the Royal Secretary. Ch'oe Chean was made Vice-director of the Department of Ministries and Security Councilor; Yi Chakch'ung was appointed Vice-minister of the Ministry of Personnel, Hallim Academician, and Recipient of Edicts. The same day a decree was issued: "The retired

21 *Oegwan* 外官: officials sent from the center to provincial or prefectural posts.

22 Normally this kind of decision would be in the form of a royal instruction (*kyowal* 敎曰), which seems to be much less used after Hyŏnjong. (instead *chewal* 制曰 used here)

Defender-in-chief and Vice-director of the Department of Ministries I Ŭngbo retired on account of his age. However, his merit to the earth and grain deities is clear, and I shall not forget it. Please consider granting those of his sons and grandsons who are without office their first appointment."

The Eastern Jurchen leader Taesin and others came to offer camels. General "Pacifying the border region" Agol and others, 135 people in total, came to court. General Kaero and others, seventy-one people altogether, came to offer horses.

Eastern Jurchen pirate ships raided Samch'ŏk County and Tongjin Camp, taking local people. The resident commander[23] set an ambush in the reeds, and when the bandits were returning, he banged the drum and launched a surprise attack. He captured or beheaded more than forty bandits.

Third month. Hwangbo Yuŭi was appointed Executive Chief of the Chancellery and concurrently Executive of the Royal Secretariat, taking charge of affairs at the Ministry of Taxation. Yu Chingp'il was made Assistant Executive in Political Affairs and jointly commissioner to the resident governor of the Western Capital.

Summer, fourth month. At the beginning of summer festival, ice was to be presented. An edict read: "This year heat has not come early, so let us wait till the fifth month to present the ice."[24] An official memorialized: "When the sun is in the northern territories[25] the ice is stored; when it is in the west it is taken out, a lamb is offered and it is offered for use. In storing things, this is the universal rule; when it is universally applied there will not be any unseasonable events or other calamities. Therefore the way of using ice is from the vernal equinox till the beginning of spring, when it has to be completely consumed. When it is presented in the fifth month, the old laws are violated, and yin and yang will not be in harmony. Please present the ice at the beginning of summer." The king followed this advice.

The Eastern Jurchen chief Obuga and others, eighty-six people altogether,

---

23 *Sujang* 守將.

24 What is meant here is presumably the first use of ice that has been stored in winter.

25 *Pungnyuk* 北陸: not certain what is meant here.

and the northeastern Jurchen leader *t'aesa* Adogan and others, fifty-nine people altogether, came to court. An official said "*t'aesa* 太史 is a Khitan office title. Since Adogan has now turned his allegiance [to Koryŏ], please change this title to *chŏngbo*." The king followed this.

The retired Executive Chief of the Chancellery Ch'ae Ch'ungsun died. He was granted the posthumous title Chŏnggan.

A decree read: "The former Vice Director of the Department of Ministries Yi Kong, even though he was impeached a second time, as a state councilor of former kings who was often entrusted with the writing of important documents, I request that he be reinstated in his old office, and then retired."

Fifth month. It was forbidden to gather firewood from famous mountains in the capital and in the countryside.

An official petitioned: "Since spring it has rained little. Please follow the customs of old and review cases of possible misconviction, provide relief for the poor and bury the corpses that are abandoned in the fields. First pray for the intercession of mountain and sea spirits[26] at those mountains and streams near the capital that can generate clouds and rain. Next pray at the Ancestral Shrine once every seven days. If it does not rain, then go back to the beginning and perform the mountain stream prayers again. If the drought is severe, hold a rain-praying ceremony, move the markets, stop using parasols and fans, forbid the slaughter of animals, and do not feed grains to the horses of officials." The king followed this advice, and also avoided the main throne hall and reduced the number of his dishes.

Sixth month. The Finance Commission said, "Last year, Noesan *pugok* and other places,[27] three altogether, within the jurisdiction of Milsŏng, were stricken by floods, which damaged fields and carried away crops. Please remit land rents and other taxes for a year." The king followed this advice.

The king personally performed a sacrificial rite and it rained.

---

26 *Akchin haedok* 岳鎭海瀆:

27 *Pugok* 部曲: as seen, a special administrative unit where base people or slaves lived, often specializing in particular professions. The word that I have here translated as "places," *so* 所, could in this context also designate an administrative unit settled by a specialized labor force, usually engaging in mining or metallurgy or other crafts.

The state councilors addressed a letter to the king, saying: "Even the wise emperors and enlightened kings of antiquity could not avoid natural disasters, all they could do was to cultivate virtue in their practice of government, and turn the disasters into blessings. This year from spring onwards there has been an increasingly severe drought, and your majesty [responded by] avoiding the main palace halls and reducing the dishes. You exerted yourself from before dawn to late evening, reproaching yourself and reflecting on your deeds. At that time the rains responded, and widely moistened the paddies and fields. We can surely expect a bumper harvest! Prostrating ourselves we beg you to return to the palace halls and resume your regular meals, and deal with affairs as before."

The king decreed: "This insignificant person has no virtue, and this brought about the disastrous drought. Although we have now obtained rain, we should still be wary of the future. However, I cannot ignore the request of my great officials." The king then followed their advice [and resumed his usual routines].

Mujin [21st] day. In the capital and the Eastern Capital, and in the administrations of Sangju, Kwangju, and Anbyŏn District there was an earthquake, which destroyed many people's houses.

An official petitioned: "We request that retired Director of the Chancellery Yu Pang and others, seventeen people altogether, be granted ice until the beginning of autumn." The king granted this request.

Autumn, seventh month. The Security Council petitioned: "Respectfully prostrate we have examined your decree, ordering [local administrations] to present 300 *kŭn* of ginseng. The 1,000 *kŭn* that were recently presented suffice for the provision of the royal court. Tribute to the government all comes from the people's toil, and should not be used on a whim. We beg you not to make such orders again." The king was displeased. The Chancellery then also remonstrated: "The emperors and kings of old reduced their selfish desires and tastes and got rid of luxury. They were modest, cultivated themselves and emptied their minds, and accepted remonstrance, so as to nurture the people and establish an era of peace. Recently disasters have been manifold, so it is fitting to purify your mind and reproach yourself, how could you waste resources that do not bring benefit and thereby waste the blood and tears of the people? Please follow what the Security Council[28] petitioned." The king agreed to this.

The Song merchant Chen Liang and others, sixty-seven people altogether, came to offer local products.

An edict read: "Recently heaven and earth have manifested strange signs, and we take this as a warning for a lack of virtue. Every day I try to be more careful, and do not dare to take it easy. All the ministers and officials should not be indolent when doing their work, except when they are on leave or their work at court has finished. Hereby we can stop the disasters and anomalies." Furthermore the king added "Among the officers and soldiers, those whose families are poor and whose personal land[29] is insufficient are many. Now at the border the wars never cease, so we cannot but provide relief for them. Order the Ministry of Taxation to distribute public land to augment their income."

A decree read: "In the *ŭlmyo* year [1015], when the Khitan invaded, Kang Sŭngyŏng was in the vanguard [of the defense], and he died in battle. His merit should be remembered; posthumously appoint him Deputy Director at the Directorate of Weaponry and appoint his son Kang Hwa to his first office."

The country of Japan returned Kyŏmjun and ten others who had been cast adrift.

Kyŏngja [24th] day. Queen Hye of the Han lineage died. She was given the posthumous title Queen Yongsin and buried at Hyŏn-nŭng.

The tribute envoy and memorial envoy, the Aide to the Senior Assistant Director of the Department of Ministries, Kim Wŏnch'ung, suffered shipwreck near Ungjin on the way to Song and returned.

Eighth month. Hwangbo Yŏng was appointed Vice-minister at the

---

28 Here identified as Mirwŏn 密院 rather than the more usual Chungch'u-wŏn 中樞院.

29 *Myŏngjŏn* 名田: literally "name fields," probably meaning the personal share land assigned to every commoner who comes of age.

Ministry of War, Yi Chakch'ung Security Councilor, and Kwak Sin Chief Censor.

Ten thousand monks were fed on the polo court.

A royal decree read: "The other day I perused the report by the Ministry of Punishments on crimes punishable by decapitation and by strangulation. We have till recently been wearing mourning clothes, and have also recently experienced many anomalies. I want to implement the virtue of respecting life to show my mind of saving the people. All those who have committed crimes punishable by decapitation or strangulation shall have that sentence forfeited and will instead be sent to uninhabited islands. For those who have committed these crimes yet show remorse, have them sent to inhabited islands." Those who escaped death numbered 116.

Mujin [23rd] day. An earthquake shook the prefectures and counties under the jurisdiction of the Eastern Capital as well as Kŭmju and Milsŏng.

Ninth month. The Eastern Jurchen General Agol and others, 135 people in total, came to present horses.

Winter, tenth month. The Eastern Jurchen General "Upholding the Country" Yoya and others, seventy-four people in total, came to court.

Eleventh month. The Eastern Jurchen General Oŭlya and others, seventy-eight people altogether, came to court.

The Eastern Court of Great Charity (Tong Taebi-wŏn 東大悲院) was repaired to shelter the cold, hungry, sick, and destitute, and clothe and feed them.

Twelfth month. The Eastern Jurchen Grand General "Upholding the Country" Yoŭldo and others, seventy-four people in total, came to court.

Tŏkchong was enshrined in the Royal Ancestor Shrine. Initially the king had asked about the *zhao-mu* principle[30] to his state councilors, and Sŏ Nul, Hwang Churyang, and others answered: "When Hyŏnjong was enshrined, based on what is written about brothers being placed in the same *zhao* or

---

30 *Zhao-mu* 昭穆: principle governing the placement of tablets in the shrine relative to that of the dynastic founder-apical ancestor, who is placed at the center. Outlined in the "Royal Regulations" chapter of the *Li ji*.

mu line, Hyejong, Chŏngjong and Kwangjong were placed in the same *zhao* group, while Kyŏngjong and Sŏngjong were in the same *mu* line. Mokchong was again in the *zhao* line, and Hyŏnjong was enshrined in a *mu* chamber. This gives two *zhao* and two *mu* [shrines], which together with T'aejo's chamber makes five. Now with Tŏkchong's enshrinement the number has surpassed five shrines.[31] Please move Hyejong, Chŏngjong, and Kwangjong so that they can be enshrined on the western wall of T'aejo's shrine. The tablet for Taejong, who was conferred a title of ruler posthumously, should be moved to his grave, where it can be offered to. This would be proper."

Yu Chingp'il responded as follows: "T'aejo is now in the position of great-grandfather [to the present ruler], so the maximum number of ancestors that should be offered to [five] has not been reached. Therefore Hyejong, Chŏngjong, and Kwangjong do not need to be moved. Just move Taejong to his tomb and enshrine Tŏkchong in the next chamber, this would be proper."

Hwang Churyang and others responded: "The meaning of Yu Chingp'il's discussing the '[number of] generations [to offer to] has not been exhausted' lies in the fact that is difficult to move or destroy four shrines at the same time. Now I have heard that in the ancient classics it is said 'if the generation exceeds the great-great-grandfather then their shrine is destroyed.' Seen from this perspective, it is not a question of whether or not the generation is exhausted when the father, grandfather, great-grandfather and great-great-grandfather [level] is reached, but rather that the collateral generations should not be taken into account. Hyejong, Chŏngjong, and Kwangjong were brothers to your majesty's grandfather, so they cannot be considered in the same line as your grandfather. Formerly, Zhong Ya of Jin memorialized Emperor Jing:[32] 'You should not offer to your great-uncle, his name should be removed [from the shrine].' The court followed this proposal. This clearly means that brothers of your grandfather should not

31 Only the Son of Heaven was allowed to have seven shrines, a lesser ruler or vassal was only allowed five.

32 Emperor Jing: not a reigning emperor, but an ancestor of the founder of the Jin Dynasty (265-316); Zhong Ya: not certain from which source the story is derived.

enter the shrine. Hyejong, Chŏngjong, Kwangjong and Taejong should all be removed and destroyed."

After this, the king was perturbed by the thought of having to remove four spirit tablets at the same time, and thus wanted to follow the advice of Yu Chingp'il. Thus Hwang Churyang said again: "[Now] T'aejo takes up one shrine, Hyejong, Chŏngjong, Kwangjong and Taejong one *zhao* shrine, Kyŏngjong and Sŏngjong one *mu* shrine, Mokchong one *zhao*, and Hyŏnjong one *mu*, thus completing the required five shrines. But if we discuss it from the viewpoint of the sequences of various family branches, Hyŏnjong is an uncle to Mokchong. If he would have taken the throne before Mokchong, he could have been in the same level as Kyŏngjong and Sŏngjong. However, since he succeeded Mokchong, Hyŏnjong was enshrined in the second *mu* shrine below Mokchong. Now if we enshrine Tŏkchong, then the four tablets of Hyejong, Chŏngjong, Kwangjong and Taejong can be removed and destroyed. Yu Chingp'il only discussed the problems involved in removing the four shrines, he did not discuss the number of *zhao* and *mu* shrines. Rituals for the Ancestral Shrine are a major state affair, they cannot be decided on the basis of subjective feelings. If we put Tŏkchong in a *zhao* shrine then there will be three *zhao* and *two* mu shrines, which together with T'aejo's makes six, which is not according to the ancient regulations. If we discuss it from the viewpoint of the sequences of various family branches, then Hyŏnjong will be the first *mu* shrine, followed by Kyŏngjong and Sŏngjong, and Mokchong will be below him. It is what is addressed in the Gongyang Commentary of the *Zuo zhuan*: 'The sequence of sacrifices for Lord Xi and Lord Min has been reversed.'"[33]

Sŏ Nul said: "What Hwang Churyang reported conforms with the ancient regulations. But in the state of Lu, besides the *zhao-mu* sequence for the lords, there was also the case of the temples for the descendants of King Mu and King Wen.[34] Therefore the tablets of Hyejong, Chŏngjong and Kwangjong need not be removed." The king followed this.

---

33 See the *Gongyang zhuan* 公羊傳, second year of Lord Wen.

34 See *Li ji*, "Ming Tang Wei" 明堂位.

An official petitioned: "In the counties and prefectures under Kŭmju there was heavy rain, causing the embankments to break, thus destroying houses and damaging fields. It would be fitting to reduce or remit taxes for this year; please dispatch a messenger to comfort the people." The king followed this.

Chŏngjong Third year [1037]

Fourth year of the Jingyou era of Song, sixth year of the Chongxi era of Khitan

Spring, first month. More than 860 houses of people in the capital city were destroyed by fire.

Second month. Retired Executive Chief of the Chancellery Pak Ch'ungsuk died.

On the *kyeyu* [30th] day five comets emerged; each of them was five to six feet long.

Third month. No Chŏngp'ae and eleven others passed the composition test of the civil service examination and two people passed the classics examination.

A woman in Sangju gave birth to triplets. [Each of the] sons was granted thirty *sŏk* of millet; this became a regular custom.

Summer, fourth month. The king personally made sacrifices at the Ancestral Shrine, and declared an amnesty.

The Western Jurchen Chief Saon and others came to present local products.

Intercalary fourth month. The Eastern Jurchen *chŏngbo* Adogan and others, fifty-three people altogether, came to court.

Fifth month. The Eastern Jurchen General "Seeking Refuge in Virtue" Igudu and others, were each granted an official rank.

Sixth month. Since the king had personally sacrificed and procured the grace of his ancestors, he personally held a banquet for all the state elders on the polo court.

Autumn, seventh month. On the memorial day for Queen Dowager Wŏnsŏng, all the officials went to Kŏndŏk Hall and offered memorials of condolence to the king, a custom that started here.

The king went to Kŏndŏk Hall to bestow cane and table [on retiring officials]. He made Yu Chingp'il Executive Chief of the Royal Secretariat and concurrently Executive of the Royal Secretariat-Chancellery. Hwang Churyang was [likewise] made Executive Chief of the Royal Secretariat and concurrently Executive of the Royal Secretariat-Chancellery, and put in charge of affairs at the Ministry of Rites. Ch'oe Chean was made Vice-director at the Department of Ministries and Assistant Executive in Political Affairs and Security Councilor. Ch'oe Ch'ung was made Assistant Executive in Political Affairs and State Historiographer.

Eighth month. The king invested his younger brother, the Prince of Nangnang, Wang Sŏ, as Acting Grand Preceptor and concurrently Royal Secretary. He also invested the Duke of State of Kaesŏng, Wang Ki, as Acting Grand Guardian.

The Song merchant Lin Bin and others came to offer local products.

Ninth month, *kiyu* [10th] day. There was an earthquake in Kwiju, Sakchu, Pakchu, and T'aeju.

The king went to Poje-sa.

The Khitan of Naewŏn-sŏng received an imperial missive and informed Yŏngdŏk Garrison [of its contents]: "The country of Koryŏ has from early on tasked itself with sending us tribute, but recently there is no news or [if there is news] we observe many deficiencies. If you want to cultivate the tribute relationship, it is fitting that you first send a memorial. Once we can verify its sincerity and truthfulness, we will then issue a separate edict." The king ordered Director of the Chancellery Sŏ Nul and thirteen others to discuss this. They advised the king "It would be right to send an envoy with a memorial."

Winter, tenth month. The Eastern Jurchen General Ayudae and others, fifty-nine people altogether, came to court.

The Khitan infiltrated the Amnok River with military ships.

Twelfth month. The king dispatched Deputy-Director at the Office of Royal Clan Affairs Ch'oe Yŏnha to Khitan with the following memorial: "This country respectfully submits that since the former imperial dowager and Emperor Shengzong bestowed investiture and an edict that announced the opening of tribute relations and the allotment of respective roles, this Eastern Territory has looked up [to the Emperor] as if directing itself to the northern dipper, and each year without fail one king after the other exerted themselves in performing this duty. Recently when your former vassal my deceased older brother [Tŏkchong] succeeded the throne to continue the dynastic line, he pledged allegiance to the august throne. Then he learnt that a virtuous sovereign had come to the throne and newly promulgated his reign. He was ready to present the two official missions[35] to the august throne, but did not receive the edict that gave gracious permission to do so. Thus filled with doubts he kept delaying these missions. But from recent years to the present, the years and seasons have passed, and we have stopped the tribute relations already for a good while. Recently we received an indirect missive which we gladly embraced in our shallow mind. Respectfully we would like to honor the legacy of the empress dowager and become a firm protective border. Polishing the rustic customs of our country, we will strive to honor the imperial court; following your cultural model even more strongly and sincerely, we will send missions across sea and land forever after."

Chŏngjong Fourth year [1038]

First year of the Baoyuan era of Song, seventh year of the Chongxi era of Khitan

Spring, first month. The Khitan dispatched Ma Baoye to court.

The Eastern Jurchen General "Seeking Refuge in Virtue" Kojimun came to court; his title was changed to General "Embraced by Koryŏ" and those accompanying him all received office titles.

35 I.e. one of condolence on the death of Shengzong and one of congratulations for the accession of Xingzong in 1031.

Second month. In the central precinct [of Kaesŏng] 860 houses burnt.

Third month. Ch'oe Yŏnha returned from Khitan. The decree [he brought with him] read: "The small countries serving the great, this is the universal rule governing all countries; to reject the old and strive after the new is the correct instruction for all the liege barons. You, sirs, have through the generations received instructions and the calendar, and have sent annual missions. However, the previous lord of your country after receiving the throne, stopped with the tribute missions that were his task. The seasons passed, and our celestial court failed to keep track of the situation. Recently we perused your memorial, and perceive its sincerity. If you want to master the practice of the great bow, you should [first] refer to Chen's ceremony of the Sushen arrow.[36] If your mind is sincere then trust will be repaid with love. Besides the answer granting permission, there are many other things that are praiseworthy. You should strive to think of a permanent plan, and do not neglect to report on your office."

The Eastern Jurchen General "Seeking Refuge in Virtue" Kujira and others, sixty-two people altogether, came to court.

Summer, fourth month. Executive [of the Chancellery] Yu So died. He was bestowed the title Yang'ŭi and co-enshrined with King Tŏkchong.

The king dispatched the Senior Aide at the Department of Ministries Kim Wŏnch'ung to Khitan in a mission of gratitude for the beneficence shown, and also to request the era name.

Fifth month. The Military Commander of the Eastern Border Circuit reported that the Jurchen Kudun and Kodohwa from Wigyeju had a conflict with their commanding officer Kaero over precious goods. Taking advantage of Kaero's inebriation they beat him to death.

The king ordered the lower councilors to consult with Director of the Chancellery Sŏ Nul and others, who argued: "Although the Jurchen are of a different kind, however since they have naturalized, their names are

---

36 This refers to a story from the *Shuo yuan* (Garden of Persuasions), in which Confucius explains to the ruler of Chen how the Sushen became vassal after presenting a kind of arrow.

registered in the official records, so they are the same as ordinary people and thus they should absolutely follow the laws of the leading country. Now they have killed their superior because of a fight over wealth, and this crime cannot be forgiven; please deal with them according to the law."

Then the Executive Chief of the Royal Secretariat Hwang Churyang and others argued: "These people, although they have naturalized and have become our buffer, yet they have people's faces but the mind of animals. Thus they do not know about the principle of things, and have never adapted to civilized ways. Thus the criminal law should not be applied to them. Moreover, according to the letter of the law, 'all those naturalized foreigners, if they have committed crimes against those of their kind, each should be tried according to their original customary law.' In fact, the elders of their neighboring village have already applied their customary law: the wealth of the families of the two perpetrators has been taken as indemnity for the house of Kaero. So what more is there to discuss and decide?" The king followed Hwang Churyang's arguments.

Sixth month. Director of the Chancellery Yu Pang died.

Autumn, seventh month. The Ministry of Punishments at the Department of Ministries reported as follows: "In the capital and the provinces those sentenced to beheading and strangulation number 103." The king decreed "The punishment should be lowered: those sentenced to beheading should be beaten and sent to uninhabited islands, while those sentenced to strangulation should be beaten and sent to inhabited islands."

Eighth month. For the first time the Khitan era names were adopted.

Floods damaged the crops, so the recruitment of autumn corvée labor was halted.

The Eastern Jurchen General "Embraced by Koryŏ" Adu and others, forty-nine people altogether, came to court.

The king dispatched Audience Usher Kim Hwaŏn to the Eastern Capital of Khitan as an envoy for ritual affairs.

The Northwestern Jurchen General "Seeking Refuge in Virtue" Yaban and others, twenty-six people altogether, came to court.

The Song merchant Chen Liang and others, 147 people altogether, came to offer local products.

Winter, tenth month. Khitan dispatched the Grand General of the Left Thousand Bull Division, Ma Baoye, to deliver the following decree: "You, Sire, have responded to human feeling and have been allotted the authority to administer your country. Recently you hurriedly dispatched a memorial which reached the palace from afar, stating how you had been blocked [from performing tribute relations] but declaring your eagerness to resume the sending of tribute. Even though I have already approved your request, it is fitting to make a point of displaying this intent to put you at ease, and to record the profoundness of our thoughts. Do not forget this intention. Now I am sending an envoy to comfort you and put you at ease."

Eleventh month. Hwang Churyang was appointed Executive Chief of the Chancellery, and Yi Chakch'ung Assistant Executive in Political Affairs, Pillar of State.

The Khitan Envoy to Return the Courtesy from the Eastern Capital, the General Commander of the Valiant Army,[37] Kang Dening, arrived.

The king dispatched Ch'oe Ch'unggong to Khitan to congratulate [the emperor] on the Yongshou festival, and also to congratulate on the newyear.

Twelfth month. The Eastern Jurchen General "Seeking Refuge in Virtue" Kojimun and others, fifty people altogether, came to court.

The Department of the Royal Secretariat-Chancellery petitioned the king: "The cranes, geese, ducks, and goats of the Eastern Pond every day are fed rice and grains, causing a great deal of expense. We request that they be released on sea islands." The king followed this.

Chŏngjong Fifth year [1039]

Second year of the Baoyuan era of Song, eighth year of the Chongxi era of Khitan

---

37 *Yongjun duzhihui* 勇軍都指揮: a term that I could not find in reference works; tentative translation.

Second month. The king dispatched Director at the Office of Royal Clan Affairs Yi Sŏnggong to Khitan to present local products, and the Office Chief at the Ministry of Taxation Yu Sŏn to offer thanks for the mission of comfort. Director of the Chancellery and Official in Charge of the Capital Military Command Sŏ Nul petitioned the king: "In recent years the Khitan wanted to build more fortresses on the eastern bank of the Amnok. Now that they have resumed amicable relations, we can use Yu Sŏn's mission to add an additional memorial requesting to put a stop to this." The king followed this.

Hwang Hangji and seventeen others passed the composition test of the civil service examination, and two people passed the classics examination; the king also passed one person by royal grace.

Third month. The king decreed that since the people from the counties and prefectures in the southeastern maritime province were suffering from hunger, the righteous granaries should be opened to provide famine relief.

Summer, fourth month. Yu Sŏn returned from Khitan with the following edict: "I took note of and reflected on what you reported regarding the apparent obstruction of agriculture by the fortifications east of the Amnok River. Looking back on the connected fortresses established since the time of my ancestors, they are simply the usual provisions for an outpost in the border region. What harm would they do to the border area? It is my task to uphold the existing norms, so at this time this is something that is difficult to change. My previous vassal Wang Hŭm [Tŏkchong] once took the trouble of sending a memorial reporting that the road to transport tribute was blocked. Since you succeeded to his rank, your tribute for the first time reached me together with a memorial stating your wish that we should honor precedents. Know that if you strive more in diligent respect, this will be the beginning of an eternal plan that I will wholeheartedly accord with. Only cultivate to reclaim [what was lost] and do not contemplate making any disturbances."

Khitan dispatched Chief Minister at the Court of Judicial Review Han Baoheng to invest the king as Commander Unequalled in Honor, Acting Grand Guardian and jointly Director [of the Chancellery], Supreme Pillar of State, King of the Country of Koryŏ with a stipend village of 7,000 households and an actual emolument of 1,000 households. Also he was bestowed the title of Merit Subject of Utmost Loyalty, Protecting Integrity and Upholding the Suzerain.

The king decreed: "As for the prefectures in the northeastern circuit, since last year floods destroyed the harvests, the people are destitute. Have the Agricultural Inducement Envoys of the circuit distribute grain and salt from the granaries to relieve them."

Fifth month. Twenty-six people from Japan came to submit.

Sixth month. A decree said: "Since the previous king the weapons have been stored and the letters cultivated; this has already lasted a good number of years. But although all around everything is peaceful, the war should not be forgotten. Dispatch envoys to the two [other] capitals and the various prefectures of the two circuits, summarily select valiant men and instruct them in archery and horse riding."

It rained heavily in the northwestern circuit, and the Amnok River overflowed, taking with it more than seventy war ships.

Autumn, seventh month. Khitan dispatched Director of Imperial Manufactories Chen Mai to congratulate the king on his birthday.

The king dispatched Policy Advisor of the Right [i.e. the Chancellery] Im Yugan to Khitan to offer thanks for the investiture.

Eighth month. The Song merchant Wei Ji and others, fifty people in total, came to present local products.

Ninth month. Vice-commander of the Capital Military Pak Sŏnggŏl petitioned: "Chŏngbyŏn Garrison in the Eastern Circuit is a place often targeted by barbarian bandits. Please have it fortified." The king agreed.

Winter, eleventh month. Sukchu was fortified.

Twelfth month. The king dispatched Executive at the Ministry for Taxation Song Yung to Khitan to offer congratulations on the Yongshou festival and also on the new year.

A decree read: "It is the period of Great Cold, with snow storms and heavy frost, so I am concerned lest the poor freeze or starve to death. Among the group of more than eighty foreigners who naturalized and those who returned after being taken by the tribesmen, have officials identify the old and young and grant each cotton paddings."

Intercalary [twelfth] month. The Khitan returning the courtesy envoy from the Eastern Capital, Da Jianji [Tae Kyŏnje] arrived.

Chŏngjong Sixth year [1040]

First year of the Kangding era of Song, ninth year of the Chongxi era of Khitan

Spring, first month, *pyŏngjin* day, first day of the month. There was a solar eclipse.

The Eastern Jurchen Grand General "Upholding the Country" Yoŏ and others, fifty people altogether, came to present local products. The General "Soothing from Afar" P'agŏl and others, forty people altogether, came to present horses.

The king dispatched Policy Advisor of the Right T'ae Hyŏnsŏk to Khitan to present local products.

The Northwestern Jurchen General "Seeking Refuge in Virtue" Kodu and others, forty-six people altogether, came to present local products.

Second month. The king bestowed on soldiers from the two capitals who had achieved merit on the border clothing according to rank.

Several hundred bays of the corridors around Sŭngp'yŏng Gate caught fire, and the fire spread to the Censorate.

There was famine in Yŏnggwang Prefecture and Imp'i County. The Righteous Granary was opened to provide relief.

The Eastern Jurchen General "Embraced by Koryŏ" Yodu and others, forty-eight people altogether, came to present horses.

The king ordered his officials to determine the system of weights and to equalize the system of measuring contents.

The king invested the consort Yŏ, née Han-ssi, as his queen.

Kimhae District was fortified.

Third month. The Eastern Jurchen General "Upholding the Country"

Agol and others, thirty-three people altogether, came to offer horses. The Northwestern Jurchen General "Pacifying the Border" Ingbo, and others, fifty-one people in total, came to offer local products.

A decree read: "Executive of the Royal Secretary Yu Chingp'il comes from a family that has established its merit across the generations, and with his literary talent he has assisted several kings; his merit is worthy of being recorded." Then the king granted his son Yu Chak the position of Clerical Scribe in the Ministry of Works.

Summer, fourth month. Wu Zhijie, a Khitan from the Eastern Capital, and more than twenty others came to submit; they were settled in the Yŏngnam area.

The Khitan informal envoy,[38] the Qinzhou Defense Commissioner Ma Shichang, arrived.

The Northwestern Jurchen General "Upholding the Country" Aihua and others, twenty-seven people in total, came to offer local products.

Sixth month. The king dispatched the Junior Assistant Director at the Department of Ministries Yu Paeg'in to Khitan to proffer thanks.

The Eastern Jurchen General "Pacifying the Border" Moira and others, fifty people altogether, came to offer local products.

Lieutenant Pyŏn Yu was promoted by more than one rank to senior colonel. Before, when Yu So was fortifying the Amnok fortresses, the Khitan came to attack, and Pyŏn Yu broke ranks to fight them first so as to raise the spirits of the troops. For this reason the king gave this order.

Autumn, seventh month. The king appointed Yang Taech'un as Vice-commissioner to the Anbuk Protectorate. Vice-director of the Department of Ministries Ch'oe Ch'ung petitioned: "Yang Taech'un is of superior resolve, and is resourceful and outstanding in military strategy. If there is trouble at the border, apart from him there is nobody we can send. Thus, it is not appropriate to send him to a local position." The king then did not grant [his petition].

Khitan dispatched the Xiazhou Surveillance Commissioner Zhao Anren to

---

38 *Hoengsŏnsa* 橫宣使.

offer congratulations on the king's birthday.

A decree read: "Since last year there have been numerous droughts and floods, and the people have been stricken. The paddies and fields are void of agricultural activity, and privately people have exhausted all their resources. This is caused by this insignificant person's lack of virtue, I am deeply aggrieved by this. Let the granaries be opened to provide relief."

Eighth month. Vice-minister at the Ministry of Punishment and caretaker of affairs at the Censorate Yi Chujwa died. Yi hailed from the Eastern Capital, but though his family had been poor for generations, as a youth he was clever and bright, so the resident governor, Yi Sŏnggong, appraised him in one glance. When his tenure was finished, he took him [Chujwa] to the capital and enrolled him in the national academy. He passed the civil service examination and served in various positions in the Censorate and Departments under successive kings for more than forty years. He was out of the ordinary in terms of talent and capacity for work, and he was called a great statesman of his age. When he died the king grieved and posthumously appointed him Minister of Works, and exceptionally ordered all officials to assist in the funeral.

The king dispatched Executive at the Ministry of Works Yu Ch'ang to Khitan to offer congratulations on the empress's birthday.

The Eastern Jurchen Kododal and others, fifty-three people in total, came to offer local products.

Ninth month. The Northwestern Jurchen General Yaban and others came to offer horses.

Yi Chayŏn was put in charge of the Security Council, and Wang Ch'ongji was appointed Senior Transmitter at the Security Council.

The Khitan Envoy to Return the Courtesy from the Eastern Capital, the General Commander Gao Weihan, arrived.

The Northern Jurchen General Iuhwagolbo came to submit. He was granted fields and a house to settle in the capital region.

Winter, tenth month. The Northwestern Jurchen Inghwaro and others, thirteen people altogether, came to submit. The *chŏngjo* Pugŏ and others, more than one hundred people, came to present local products.

Commissioner for the Directorate-General of the Western Military Command[39] Pak Wŏnjak produced a silk-stringed nine-pronged catapult[40] that he presented to the throne; it was very skillful, and the king rewarded him lavishly. He also ordered that more be produced and placed in the eastern and western border garrisons.

The Eastern Jurchen General Saira and the Northwestern Jurchen General Tonghwaro and others, more than 400 people, came to offer local products.

Eleventh month. A merchant from the Abbasid Kingdom called Ponahap together with others arrived, and offered local products. The king ordered his officials to put them up in an official hostel and provide them generously. When they returned they were granted gold and silk.

The king dispatched Executive at the Ministry of Works Yi Injŏng to Khitan to offer congratulations on the Yongshou festival and also on the new year.

Twelfth month. The Eastern Jurchen *wŏnyun* Adugan and others, fifty people altogether, came to present horses.

Twenty commoner households from the Eastern Capital of Khitan came to submit.

Chŏngjong Seventh year [1041]

First year of the Qingli era of Song, tenth year of the Chongxi era of Khitan

Spring, first month. The Western Jurchen *taesŭng* Kojiji and others, fifteen people altogether, came to present horses.

The Ministry of Taxation petitioned: "In Chungmo County under the jurisdiction of Sangju, in Yusŏng Prefecture under the jurisdiction of Hongju, and in Imjin, Im'gang and other counties under the jurisdiction of Changdan County, the amount of land people have and its quality is very

---

39 *Sŏmyŏn pyŏngma togamsa* 西面兵馬都監使. Tentative translation.

40 *Sujil kugungno* 繡質九弓弩. It is not possible to determine what this device looked like.

unevenly distributed, please dispatch a commissioner to measure the land and equalize the food [tax] and corvée [distribution].” The king approved.

The Chancellery petitioned: “According to the old laws, all those who have committed a crime should not receive land held in perpetuity (*yŏng'ŏpchŏn*). Supreme General Yi Hongsuk once committed a crime against the constitution (*hŏnjang* 憲章) and was exiled to Yŏngnam. So his wife, sons and grandsons ought not to receive land prebends.” The king ruled: “Once Yi Hongsuk, when the Khitan troops attacked T'ongju and although the city had nearly fallen, defended it firmly and in the end it did not fall. Thus he established a merit that is undying, and should be rewarded through the generations as a motivation for the future. Thus the prebends should stand.”

Second month. The Chancellery petitioned: “In recent years, prefectures and counties have suffered bad harvests and people have difficulty feeding themselves. In truth this is due to the fact that the administration by local officials does not take into account people's feelings, and the punishments do not accord with Heaven's design, leading to harm in the harmonious energy and a situation such as this one. Please promulgate a command that attenuates the punishments and exhorts agriculture so as to save the people from their distress.” The king followed this advice.

Yu Ch'ang and four others passed the composition test of the civil service examination and five people passed the classics examination.

The Western Jurchen General “Upholding the Country” Iudae and others, eighteen people altogether, came to present horses.

Third month. The Eastern Jurchen *chungyun* Yasaro and others came to court.

Summer, fourth month. The Chancellery petitioned: “Yŏngju and others of the thirty-three greater prefectures in the northern circuit, and Kohwa and other greater prefectures in the eastern circuit all border the area of the tribesmen, and because of defensive duties have never before been levied taxes. In the *kimyo* year [1039] officials petitioned to impose tax quotas, so the said prefectures and garrisons in the two circuits each year had to contribute 50,290 bolts of cloth, and the equivalent of[41] 14,049 *kok*[42] of dried grains. Because of this the border people are unhappy, so please exclude them from the tax registers." The king followed this advice.

A regular Tripitaka Assembly for the spring season was first held in Hoegyŏng Hall. This assembly became regularly held in spring and autumn, with the spring assembly lasting six days and the autumn assembly seven days.

The Eastern Jurchen chief, the *taesang* Igae and others, came to court.

Fifth month. The king went to the two tombs of Hyŏn-nŭng and Sŏn-nŭng and decreed: "When our sagacious ancestor unified the Three Han, there were loyal officials who assisted him; among their descendants some have ended up becoming slaves or commoners. Of those who never held office, summon officials to test them on literary and military skills, and allow all to attain office."

The king bestowed cane and table on Director of the Chancellery Sŏ Nul.

Sixth month. The Eastern Jurchen *chŏngbo* Obu and others, twenty-six people in total, came to court.

Autumn, seventh month. The Western Jurchen General "Seeking Refuge in Virtue" Sojira and others came to court.

Khitan dispatched Deputy Minister of the Court of Imperial Regalia Geng Zhijun to offer congratulations on the king's birthday.

Eighth month. The king ordered the Supervisor for Military Affairs in the Northwestern Circuit, Vice-director of the Department of Ministries Ch'oe Ch'ung, to go to the border. The king personally went to his private quarters to bestow clothes and send him on his way.

The Eastern Jurchen "Mollified from Afar" General P'aŭldal and others, fifty people in total, came to court.

Comets were observed in the eastern sector for more than twenty days before they disappeared.

---

41 *Chŏllap* 折納: the dictionary definition of this term is "pay tax in kind exceptionally in money."

42 *Kok* 斛: unit of volume equal to half a *sŏk*. See table of weights and measures.

Ninth month. The Ministry of War petitioned: "The Special Directorate for Selecting Soldiers is selecting the sons and brothers of military and civil officials of rank seven and above. They fill up the military divisions apart from those specializing in letters who apply for the examination. Although this is in consideration of the maxim 'do not forget times of danger even in times of peace,' they are all descendants of generations of meritorious subjects of old; hence since the time of our founding ancestor they do not provide corvée labor. Moreover in the *kapcha* [964] and *pyŏngja* [976] years there was already a decree forbidding this. This is not only a matter of forgetting the merit of previous generations, it is also against the old edicts. Please forbid them from filling up the military divisions." The king followed this advice.

The two garrisons of Yŏngwŏn and P'yŏngno were fortified.

Winter, tenth month. The king travelled to Hogyŏng [P'yŏngyang].

Comets were again observed in the eastern sky for more than ten days.

On the *sinsa* [5th] day the royal carriage reached the Taedong River. The Resident Governor [of the Western Capital], Assistant Executive in Political Affairs Hwangbo Yŏng, received the king at the ferry of the river. The king boarded the royal boat and bestowed a banquet for his state councilors. He then ordered General Sŭnggae and others to practice archery. But Junior Policy Monitor Kim Sangbin remonstrated, and the king desisted. He then entered Sŏn'ŭn Hostel.

Ch'oe Ch'ung was appointed Executive Chief of the Royal Secretariat and Hwangbo Yŏng Acting Minister of Works and Vice-director of the Department of Ministries.

Eleventh month, *pyŏng'o* day, first day of the month. The king returned from Hogyŏng.

The Song merchant Wang Nuo and others came to offer local products.

The Eastern Jurchen General "Mollified from Afar" Saira and the General "Pacifying the Border" Yaŏgae and others, sixty-two people in total, came to present horses.

Twelfth month. The king inspected archery skills at Kwiryŏng Pavilion on the Eastern Pond.

The Eastern Jurchen General "Upholding the Country" Agaju and others, fifty-five people in total, came to present local products.

Walls were constructed for Hwan'ga County in the Eastern Circuit.

The king dispatched Hallim Academician Recipient of Edicts Pak Yuin and Assistant Executive of the Right Yi Yuryang to Khitan to offer congratulations for the ritual of investiture. Supervisor of the Chamberlain of the Court of the Royal Regalia Yu Ch'am presented tribute goods.

Chŏngjong Eighth year [1042]

Second year of the Qingli era of Song, eleventh year of the Chongxi era of Khitan

Spring, first month. Director of the Chancellery Sŏ Nul again requested to retire, but the king did not grant his request.

The Eastern Jurchen leader Kondu and others came to present horses; General "Seeking Refuge in Virtue" Adogan and others, forty-nine people in all, came to present local products.

The Military Commissioner for the Northwestern Circuit reported on the registration of barbarian households east of the Amnok River up to Ch'ŏngsae Garrison.

Second month. The Eastern Jurchen General "Mollified from Afar" Kojimun and others, thirty-six people in total, came to offer local products. They were granted offices according to rank.

The Western Jurchen chief Kojiji and others, twelve people in all, came to present local products. The Foreign Relations Office petitioned: "in recent years, Kojiji and others were very helpful in the construction of P'yŏngno and Yŏngwŏn fortress, so please bestow lavish presents on them." The king followed this advice.

The Vice-resident Governor of the Eastern Capital Ch'oe Ho and others carried out the royal command to carve the printing blocks for the *History of the Former Han* and the *History of the Later Han*, as well as for the *History of the Tang*, and presented the [printed books] to the throne.

Third month. The Department of the Royal Secretariat requested that on the days the king held court meetings in his private quarters, the officials may reply themselves to royal questions. The king agreed.

The Ministry of Rites petitioned: "This year in the fourth month your majesty should hold the ancestral sacrifices, yet the directorate for the investiture of the queen is to hold the ceremony of investiture [for the queen] on the twenty-first [of the fourth month]. We request that the sacrifice be held on the same day." The Department of the Royal Secretariat-Chancellery petitioned: "The king's sacrifices are a rite that has a fixed date, whereas the rite of investiture can be held when it is convenient. Please hold the sacrifice first." The king followed this advice.

The Northwestern Jurchen General "Pacifying the Border" Yaŏgae, General Iubul, and others, forty-seven people in all, came to offer local products.

Summer, fourth month. The Eastern Jurchen *taesang* Oŏdal requested oxen for ploughing. The king bestowed ten oxen from the military fields in the Eastern Circuit.

Sixth month. A decree read: "The most important agricultural period is about to begin yet the rains have stalled. Officials should send petitions on any possible means through which the drought can be relieved."

Royal Secretary Sŏ Nul died. He was the son of Sŏ Hŭi. At first Sŏ Nul took ill and went to Chijang-sa. The king sent the Right Transmitter of Edicts Kim Chŏngjun to inquire after his health, and then also bestowed two royal robes, 1,000 *sŏk* of grain, and two horses on the temple to pray for blessings. When the illness grew worse the king went to see him in person, and elevated him by royal decree to the position of *Samjung taegwang* Royal Secretary. He also bestowed land held in perpetuity (*yŏng'ŏpchŏn*) to his sons and grandsons. Sŏ Nul then died. The king went to Chunggwang Hall and mourned below the corridors. Posthumously he bestowed the title of Wŏnjae, and he was later co-enshrined with the king.

The Capital Military Command petitioned: "In Yŏngp'a-su in Yŏlsan County in the Eastern Circuit, Sub-lieutenant Kanhong fought with the enemies, but vastly outnumbered and with all arrows shot and his forces depleted, he died. Please promote him posthumously and grant him a reward." The king followed this.

The Eastern Jurchen General "Seeking Refuge in Virtue" Yaibul and others, twenty-five people in total, came to court.

Executive Chief of the Royal Secretariat Yu Chingp'il died.

Autumn, seventh month. Khitan dispatched Office Chief at the Ministry of Personnel Feng Li to come and offer congratulations on the king's birthday.

Eighth month. The Eastern Jurchen General "Mollified from Afar" Saira and others, sixty-eight people altogether, came to offer local products.

Ninth month. The Eastern Jurchen General "Seeking Refuge in Virtue" Agae and others, fifty-eight people; the Northwestern Jurchen General "Mollified from Afar" Koduro and others, came to present local products.

Winter, eleventh month. Khitan dispatched the Acting Vice-minister of the Ministry of Rites Wang Yongyan with the following edict: "Since the ten counties south of the pass belong to our country since ancient times, I was planning to raise an army to discuss the recovery of our ancient territories. Song then sent several urgent messengers to indicate their willingness to make important decisions: they decided to send, besides the annual tribute of 300,000 *yang* of silver and 300,000 bolts of silk, a separate annual present of gold and silk in lieu of the taxes due [from the ten counties]. Thus the treaty [of Chanyuan] was renegotiated and eternal cordiality was established. We gave special tax and corvée remissions to the military across the various provinces, and moreover sent them back to their original divisions. Who would have thought that this insignificant person would achieved this beautiful result! All the military and civil officials repeatedly thrust illustrious names and titles on me and despite firm refusal was forced to acquiesce to these requests and selected the third day of the eleventh month to hold the great ritual [to confer the titles] in both palaces. You sire, as a self-designated foreign vassal who decided to pledge loyalty to your suzerain nation, would undoubtedly rejoice upon hearing this news, and thus we send envoys to inform you of it."

The Eastern Jurchen General "Pacifying the Border" Tongbul and others came to present horses.

Twelfth month. The retired Executive Chief of the Chancellery Hwangbo Yuŭi died.

Chŏngjong Ninth year [1043]

Third year of the Qingli era of Song, twelfth year of the Chongxi era of Khitan

Spring, first month. Hwang Churyang was exceptionally promoted to Acting Grand Guardian, Director of the Chancellery, Supervisor of the Ministry of Personnel.

The Western Jurchen General "Seeking Refuge in Virtue" Kolgae and others, thirty-six people in total, came to offer local products.

Second month. Ch'oe Chean was appointed Executive Chief of the Chancellery and concurrently Executive Chief of the Royal Secretariat; Ch'oe Ch'ung was made Acting Minister of Works and State Historiographer, Supreme Pillar of State; Hwangbo Yŏng and Yi Chakch'ung were both appointed Executive of the Royal Secretariat and Executive of the Department of the Royal Secretariat-Chancellery.

Third month. The Western Jurchen chief Koduro and others, forty people altogether, came to offer local products.

An Assembly of the Hundred Seats was held in the Hoegyŏng Hall and 10,000 monks were fed.

The Eastern Jurchen General Kaero and others, forty people in all, came to present horses.

Summer, fourth month. The military commander of the Northeastern Circuit petitioned: "The Jurchen General 'Mollified from Afar' Saira through a ruse brought the sea and land bandit leader Nabul and others, 494 people in total, into Hwaju Hostel." The king asked the ministers to deliberate this and they advised: "This lot have the faces of humans but the hearts of beasts. Order the military commander to reduce the numbers and divide them in groups to send to court in succession." The king followed this.

A decree read: "The rains that should have come are late, this is worrisome for agriculture. Surely the punishments have been partial and the people harbor resentment. Have the authorities examine all cases with sentences lower than banishment and release them."

The Eastern Jurchen General Idabul arrived at court.

A ban was issued for the capital and the rest of the country on wearing clothes made of gauze with patterns of brocade golden dragons or phoenixes.

Fifth month, *chŏngmyo* day, first day of the month. There was a solar eclipse.

An edict read: "It is my lack of virtue that has led to this drought and has caused successive calamities. We should order the Bureau of Royal Diet to disband its hawk-hunting division and to ban catching fish with bamboo traps."

The king declared an amnesty, and avoided the main throne hall.

On the *ŭlmi* [29th] day there was rain. The officials went to Kŏndŏk Hall to offer congratulations.

Sixth month. The Eastern Jurchen chief Yubuldal and others, twenty-five people in total, came to court.

The military commander of the Northeastern Circuit petitioned: "Administrative Assistant for the Seaboard across various Provinces Hwangbo Kyŏng alone commanded war ships far into the ocean to attack pirates, capturing or killing very many. We requested that he be given a special reward." The king followed this advice.

Autumn, seventh month. Khitan dispatched Attendant Censor Tao Jushan to offer congratulations on the king's birthday.

The Eastern Jurchen Chief Adugan and others, sixty-six people in total, came to court.

Eighth month. As the death sentences for the capital and the regions were carried out, the king avoided the main palace halls, ate fewer dishes, and stopped the playing of music.

Ninth month. Officials petitioned: "Commissioner at the Directorate for the Construction of Chunggwang-sa Chŏng Chang together with the local bureau clerk Sŭng Chŏk stole goods from the directorate. We request that they be punished by beatings followed by banishment as the law prescribes." An edict said: "Follow the lighter [punishment] prescribed in the law books." The Censorate complained: "We request that this be settled according to the law statutes," and the king gave permission for this.

The Eastern Jurchen General "Pacifying the Borders" Tongbullo and the General "Mollified from Afar" Saira and others, taking with them eighty-eight Jurchen who had not yet been civilized [by Koryŏ] came and reported: "These non-civilized people used to embrace violence and raided the border lands. Through [our] edification they have suddenly rectified their mistakes. Today we have brought the leaders of sea and land [tribes] to the palace to declare their wish of becoming border residents. From now on every time a neighboring bandit [group] makes a movement we will report it." The king praised them and exceptionally bestowed gold and silk and raised their rank.

The garrisons of Yŏngsak and Sudŏk were fortified.

Winter, tenth month. The Eastern Jurchen General "Pacifying the Borders" Yasagae and others, eighty people in all, came to present local products.

Eleventh month. The Returning-the-courtesy envoy from the Eastern Capital [of Khitan], the Acting Vice-director of the Department of Ministries Zhang Changling, arrived.

Khitan dispatched General of the Palace Gate Guard Xiao Shenwei and Executive at the Ministry of Rites Han Shaowen to invest the king as Acting Grand Mentor, conjointly Royal Secretary, granted a stipend village of 3,000 households, of which 300 were effective. They also bestowed on him the title of merit subject "Equalizing Virtue and Establishing Principle." Prestige titles and merit ranks remained the same as before. At the same time a carriage, robes, hats, sword, and seal, together with the state letter goods were bestowed. The king established a dais to receive the edict.

Eastern tribesmen pirates used eight ships to attack Sŏgok County, taking more than forty people captive before they left. The military leader and soldiers were punished for neglecting defensive duties.

Twelfth month. The star-leader[43] of T'angna Country, General "Naval Strike" Kari petitioned: "Since the prince Tura recently died, we request that Hoing be the next prince." As before local products were presented. T'angna is the same as T'amna.

Chŏngjong Tenth year [1044]

Fourth year of the Qingli era of Song, thirteenth year of the Chongxi era of Khitan

Spring, second month. With 180 battle ships from the Yesŏng River, military provisions were transported to fill the granaries of the prefectures and garrisons of the Northwestern Border Circuit.

Summer, fourth month. 1,415 Eastern Jurchen carrying gifts came to request an alliance. Each was granted clothes and silver utensils.

Kim Wŏnhyŏn and fifteen others passed the composition test of the civil service examination, and two passed the classics examination. The king also qualified two people by royal grace.

Fifth month. The Eastern Jurchen General Kura and others, twenty-five people in all, came to offer local products.

Sixth month. The king received the bodhisattva precepts in Kŏndŏk Hall.

Autumn, seventh month. Khitan dispatched Acting Grand Guardian Liu Congzheng to offer congratulations on the king's birthday.

The king dispatched Junior Vice-director of the Department of Ministries Yi Koe and Chief Steward of the Accommodations Service Ch'oe Hŭijŏng to Khitan to proffer thanks for the investiture.

The king ruled that all the central and local officials who sent in grain were allowed to measure it themselves.

Eighth month. The Eastern Jurchen General Adogan and others, forty-six people in total, came to offer local products.

Ninth month. The Eastern Jurchen General Saira and others, 125 people in total; Kunido and others twenty-six people in total; the Western Jurchen

---

43 *Sŏngju* 星主: title for leaders of T'amna country (Cheju).

Grand General Koduro and others, twenty-seven people in total, came to offer local products.

Winter, tenth month. Changju, Chŏngju, and Wŏnhŭng Garrison were fortified.

Eleventh month. The Military Commander for the Northeast Kim Yŏnggi petitioned: "Now the construction of the three fortifications is almost finished; it would be fitting for all the local officials and clerks involved in overseeing the labor for the project to receive rank and reward. Moreover, the territory where the three fortresses are being built was originally a bandit's lair, so we can expect invasions to occur. To prevent this troops were stationed in strategic spots to prevent the bandits from approaching. These soldiers also deserve reward. During the construction period, Vice-minister of the Ministry of War Ko Yŏl and others achieved merit, so they also deserve reward so as to encourage those who come after." The king followed this.

The Eastern Jurchen General Oŭldal and others, 144 people in all, came to offer horses, and petitioned: "We live in the border region of your country, and looking forward to your edification became subjects some years ago. However, every time we worry about the incursions of the hideous caitiffs, so we could not yet manage to settle down. Now thanks to the construction of the three fortresses, the path is blocked for the bandits, so we came to court to give thanks." The king gave lavish presents and sent them back.

Sŏndŏk Garrison was fortified.

The king decreed: "For all those who have borrowed public or private grain and die [before returning the loan], do not seek to recover the loan."

Chŏngjong Eleventh year [1045]

Fifth year of the Qingli era of Song, fourteenth year of the Chongxi era of Khitan

Spring, first month. The Eastern Jurchen General "Seeking Refuge in Virtue" Aduju and others, fifty people in total, came to offer local products.

Second month. The king bestowed on Kwagyo Hostel on the Imjin River the title Chaje-sa. Previously this ford did not have a ferry or a bridge, so people struggled to get across and many ended up drowning. The king was vexed by this and ordered officials to construct a pontoon bridge. From then on people and horses [crossed the river] as if they were treading land.

A decree read: "All those civilian and military officials whose parents live more than 300 *li* away, will receive one period of thirty days' leave every three years to visit their parents; those whose parents are no longer alive will be granted one term of fifteen days' leave every five years to clean the graves, regardless of the distance to the tombs. Those of rank five and above should report to me [before leaving]; for those of rank six and below relevant officials will approve the leave. As for those who have passed the examination [but do not hold office yet], the extent of leave for visiting parents or sweeping graves is as above.

The Eastern Jurchen General "Mollified from Afar" P'aŭldal and others, sixty-five people in total, came to present horses.

Third month. The Eastern Jurchen General "Embraced from Afar" Yŏmhan and others, seventy-five people in all, came to court.

Summer, fourth month, *chŏnghae* day, first day of the month. The grand astrologer reported: "There should be a solar eclipse, but because of the cloud cover it cannot be observed." The assembled officials proffered congratulations.

The Eastern Jurchen leader General Saŏdu, Yoŏra and others, 105 people in all, came to offer horses. General "Pacifying the Borders" Kodohwa and others, seventy people in total, came to offer local products.

The Administrative Assistant to the Military Commissioner for the Western Circuit, Investigating Censor Yi Ch'un, petitioned: "More than a hundred barbarian bandits invaded Yŏngwŏn Garrison and Changp'yŏng Camp,[44] taking hostage more than thirty soldiers; I request that the officers[45]

---

44 Changp'yŏng-su 長平戍: 'su' refers to a defensive position or field camp, barracks; it is likely a permanent settlement but smaller than a garrison (-chin). In an entry for the fourth month of 1054 it is referred to as Changp'yŏng Garrison, perhaps implying that it had been fortified.

45 Changgyo 將校: "officers" is the modern meaning of the term, its exact meaning for Koryŏ

in charge be punished because of their incompetence in guarding the fortress." The king agreed.

The Palace Library presented the newly printed "Correct Meaning" of the *Book of Rites* in seventy volumes, and the "Correct Meaning" of the Mao [commentary on the *Book of Poetry*] in forty volumes. The king ordered one copy each to be stored in the royal collection and donated the rest to his ministers.

Fifth month. The king decreed: "Since the 'Minor Heat' date is approaching, judge all heavy crimes leniently and release those who have committed minor offenses."

The merchant Lin Xi from Quanzhou in Song and others came to present local products.

Soldiers in the Eastern Circuit fought with barbarian bandits.[46] The victors received a horse from the royal stable.

Intercalary [fifth] month. Since it had been raining hard for a long time, those in prison [for major crimes] had their sentences reviewed and those who had received minor sentences were released.

Sixth month. The Khitan informal envoy, Acting Grand Mentor Yelü Xuan, arrived.

Autumn, seventh month. Khitan dispatched the Acting Junior Vice-director of the Department of Ministries Gao Weiji to offer congratulations on the king's birthday.

Ninth month. The Eastern Jurchen General Kojimon and others, forty-five people in total, came to court.

Winter, tenth month. A ban was again issued on the wearing of short daggers.

Eleventh month. Since the period of severe cold had started, those incarcerated for light offenses were released and corvée labor was halted.

The Eastern Jurchen Koch'a and others, thirty-six people in total, came to present local products.

---

is obscure but likely it is a contraction of various leading military officials.

46 This sounds like a competition rather than an actual battle.

Chŏngjong Twelfth year [1046]

Sixth year of the Qingli era of Song, fifteenth year of the Chongxi era of Khitan

Spring, second month. The king decreed "For everyone who wants to establish as a legitimate heir a secondary son according to the law, if the secondary son dies through accident, then the grandson can be established [as the legitimate heir].[47] If there is no grandson, then a half-brother[48] may be designated; if there is no half-brother then a grandson through a concubine's son[49] may be designated. If there are no male grandchildren then a female grandchild may be established."

Yŏnghŭng Garrison was fortified.

Third month, *sinsa* day, first day of the month. There was a solar eclipse.

Yi Injŏng and sixteen others passed the composition test of the civil service examination, and one passed the classics examination.

The king ordered Director of the Chancellery Ch'oe Chean to go to the polo court and offer incense for the start of the street scripture parade. For the parade the streets of the capital were divided into three paths; in each of them the *Prajñāpāramitā sūtra* was carried in colorfully decorated palanquins. In front marched monks in full dharma robes, walking and chanting at the same time. The Supervisor of Militia, wearing his official dress, also followed and inspected. This street parade was intended to pray for blessings on behalf of the people, and was called "scripture procession" (*kyŏnghaeng* 經行). From this year it became a regular event.

Summer, fourth month, *chŏngmyo* [17th] day. The king felt indisposed. On the *pyŏngsul* day[50] the officials prayed for him in Buddhist temples.

---

47 *Chŏk* 嫡: A term that is well known through Chosŏn era debates where it means "secondary sons," i.e. sons born to anyone but the primary wife (i.e. a secondary wife, or a new wife after the primary wife died; not the son obtained through a relation with someone from a lower status group or concubine). What exactly it embraced in Koryŏ is however not altogether clear. "Grandson" here refers to the grandson through the secondary son.

48 *Tongmoje* 同母弟: this would then imply a son obtained from the wife's prior marriage.

49 *Sŏson* 庶孫.

50 Since a *pyŏngsul* day comes nineteen days after a *chŏngmyo* day, this would correspond to the sixth day of the following month, or the seventh day in case the fourth month was a 29-day month. Based on the table with all the first days of the months throughout Koryŏ

Fifth month. The Ministry of Personnel petitioned: "Director of the Office of Regalia and also supervisor in charge of the Bureau of Astrology Sŏ Ung has taken sick leave already 180 days ago. According to the law, any serving official who takes more than 100 days' leave will be relieved from office. We request that Sŏ Ung be dismissed from office." The king decreed: "Sŏ Ung excels at his work, he is the foremost of all astrologers. We exceptionally grant him 200 days' leave."

Chŏngyu [18th] day. The king's disease remained serious. He summoned his younger brother the Prince of Nangnang, Wang Hwi, to the bedchamber. He ordered him to take charge of all state affairs, and died the same day. The Nangnang Prince then took the throne in front of the coffin. The king [i.e. Munjong] bestowed on him the posthumous title Yonghye 容惠, and the temple name Chŏngjong. He was buried in Chu-nŭng tomb. In accordance with the king's last will, the officials followed the custom of Emperor Wen of the Han, and kept the scale of the tomb small and frugal.

Yi Chehyŏn's eulogy went: "T'aejo already warned us that the Khitan are greedy and violent, and cannot be trusted. Yet to dismiss the old entente on the pretext of one disastrous event was not part of the plan. In very difficult circumstances Hyŏnjong managed a return to normality, but then ran out of time to solve this issue. Tŏkchong never managed to gain full maturity of age, thus he had to be careful not to provoke any conflict. Wang Kado's argument to cut off friendly relations was not as good as Hwangbo Yuŭi's plan to sustain the people by maintaining cordial relations. In the third year of succeeding to the throne, Chŏngjong sent our great man Ch'oe Yŏnha to Khitan, and in the fourth year Khitan sent its envoy Ma Baoye. From this time onwards the friendly alliance was resumed. Moving them [to resume the relation] was not achieved merely through utmost sincerity. What was needed was an exquisite plan, and the scholar-gentleman to comprehend it

in Chang Tong'ik's *Koryŏsa yŏn'gu ŭi kich'o* (P'aju: Kyŏngin muhwasa, 2016), p. 134, it corresponds to the seventh day of the fifth month. In any case the big gap between the two events is rather strange.

and put it into practice so as to safeguard the country."

The king [Munjong] decreed: "In the previous reign, the royal chairs, beds, and accessories were all inlaid with gold and silver, and seat cushions were made of fine silk textile interwoven with gold or silver thread. Have the officials replace them by copper, iron, and ordinary silk."

In accordance with Chŏngjong's last will, Yŏnch'ang Palace was bestowed on consort Lady No. Originally, Chŏngjong had heard of Lady No's extraordinary beauty, secretly betrothed her, and showed her great favor. The Chancellery and the Censorate remonstrated: "The previous king did not betroth Lady No in accordance with ritual. Moreover the order was made in a time of confusion, and hence should not be followed." The king did not allow to overturn the order.

Sixth month. The king dispatched Office Chief at the Ministry of Works Ch'oe Wŏnjun to Khitan to announce that they were in mourning.

Kimi [10th] day. The king personally made a sacrifice to the stars.[51] Originally there was an order to have the king make this sacrifice in person every year on this day.

The king went to the Sinbong Pavilion and declared a general amnesty. All those with an official position were raised by one rank.

The king dispatched Office Chief at the Ministry of War Kim Kyŏng to construct fortresses and agricultural estates along the coast from the East Sea to the South Sea so as to stop conflicts with pirates.

Autumn, seventh month. The king decreed: "The navy soldier Ŭnjil of P'arŭm-do and the navy soldiers Kwanghyŏp, Kwangdal, and Yŏnggil of Yang-do all have merit in catching pirates." At the same they were granted the rank of *chungyun*.

The king decreed: "In the thirteenth year of Chongxi [1044], the Eastern Pirates besieged Chŏngbyŏn Garrison. Sub-colonel Chŏng Kwangsun fought bravely to drive back the enemy but died on the battlefield. His merit was great, so let him be posthumously promoted to Junior Colonel of the

---

51 *Ch'oje* 醮祭: the dictionary definition of this term is "to make a sacrifice to the stars."

Golden Bird Division."

Eighth month. The king went to Sŏnjŏng Hall and summoned Director of the Chancellery Ch'oe Chean and Executive Chief of the Chancellery Ch'oe Ch'ung and others to discuss successes and failures of the current administration.

Ninth month. Because of their age, the king granted retired Vice-director of the Department of Ministries Ch'oe Pusŏng, Junior Vice-minister of the Department of Ministries Cho U, Supreme Generals I Ŭngbo and Kim Honggwang and others wine, food, and robes.

A Hundred Seat Assembly [to recite] the *Humane Kings sūtra* was held within the palace for three days.

The king personally gave a banquet on the polo court for officials aged eighty or above, as well as the following categories of common citizens, male and female: filial sons and grandsons, righteous husbands and chaste wives, elderly without spouse or children and orphans, and those with terminal disease; he also granted presents according to rank.

Winter, tenth month. Director of the Chancellery Ch'oe Chean and others petitioned: "According to the military classics, 'An army of ten thousand selects three thousand as crack troops, and an army of one thousand selects 300 crack troops.' We request that the generals of each of the Six Armies is ordered to select 200 vanguard troops." The king agreed.

Officials petitioned: "Those of the palace halls, gates, temples or offices whose titles contain your majesty's personal name should all be changed."

An Assembly to Dispel Calamities was held in the Hoegyŏng Hall.

Eleventh month. The kind decreed: "In the third year of the Dazhong xiangfu era [1010] the Khitan army invaded and raided the northwestern area. Military Inspector Yang Kyu, second in command Kim Sukhŭng and others took the lead and put their bodies on the line to fight the enemy in successive battles, defeating them; but the arrows came down as dense as the quills on a hedgehog, and in the end they died in battle. In the eleventh year of the Dazhong xiangfu era [1018], as the Khitan army rushed in, Vice-minister at the Ministry of War and managing affairs at the Security Council

Kang Minch'ŏm was appointed supreme commander. Spurring the army on, he attacked and defeated the Khitan at the plateau of Pan-yŏng pass. The Khitan army ran towards the north, throwing away their weapons and armor, which blocked the road. Kang Minch'ŏm took prisoner or killed 10,000 Khitan. To commemorate his merit, and to reward him at the same time, it would be fitting to include his portrait in the Hall of Merit Subjects. This would encourage future generations."

Director of the Chancellery Ch'oe Chean died. When the "Sincerely Written Injunctions" by T'aejo were lost in the military turmoil, he obtained the "injunctions" in the house of Ch'oe Hang, and stored them so as to present them to the king. Thanks to this they were transmitted to the next generation.

Twelfth month. All officials went to Kŏndŏk Hall to congratulate [the king] on the Sŏngp'yŏng festival. The king feasted the state councilors and court officials from junior four and above in the Sŏnjŏng Hall. The Sŏngp'yŏng Festival is the king's birthday. The Monastic Registry petitioned: "let the country henceforth organize an Assembly to Pray for Blessings every year as a regular custom for this festival at the Oejesŏg-wŏn for seven days. The officials should celebrate at Hŭngguk temple, and the [officials of] the Western and Eastern Capitals, the four protectorates and eight departments (*sadoho p'almok* 四都護八牧) in the Buddhist temples of their jurisdictions." The king approved.

Khitan dispatched Royal Recorder Zhou Zongbai to convey condolences.

Munjong, Great King of Benevolence and Piety, part 1

His given name was Hwi 徽 and his courtesy name Ch'ogyu 燭幽; originally his given name was Sŏ 緒. He was the third son of Hyŏnjong, and his mother was Queen Wŏnhye 元惠, née Lady Kim. He was born on the *kyemi* day of the twelfth month of the tenth *kimi* year of Hyŏnjong [1019]. From youth he was clever and bright, and when he grew up he loved learning and was a good archer. He had a good grasp of the bigger picture, and was magnanimous, embracing all people alike. Everything that was reported to him or that was decided he always remembered. He was on the throne for thirty-seven years and lived to the age of sixty-five.

Munjong First year [1047]

Seventh year of the Qingli era of Song, sixteenth year of the Chongxi era of Khitan

Spring, first month. The king decreed: "Recently, in the *kapsin* year [1044], bandits raided the Northeastern Circuit; the soldiers Yi Sŏmhan and others, forty people in all, acting as a vanguard, declared victory [over the invaders]. They should all be rewarded with office according to rank."

The king decreed: "The deceased Security Councilor Im Yugan was loyal and steadfast, and on numerous occasions rendered valuable service. It would be fitting to give special treatment. May his son Im Yanggae be granted an office of the eighth rank."

The king decreed: "In the various prefectures and counties of all administrative levels, year after year lavish sutra-turning gatherings are held. We surmise that local clerks rely on this to gather what they desire, thus causing trouble and breaking the law; they certainly do not have the intention of producing blessings. Henceforth it is forbidden to become drunk, overeat, or have entertainment at these gatherings."

The king decreed that military guard stations (*kunsu* 軍戍) should be established in the two counties of Sang'ŭm and Hakp'o along the coast to thwart raids by barbarian pirates.

Second month. Military Commissioner for the Northwestern Circuit Yang Taech'un petitioned: "The local leaders and clerks, soldiers and civilians of the Yŏnju defense, more than 800 people, reported that vice-defense commissioner Sohyŏn from the moment he arrived encouraged agriculture and sericulture, assisted and helped the people and had many administrative achievements. As a matter of principle, I report this to the throne." The king decreed that the Ministry of Personnel should evaluate him according to the regulations and employ him.

Khitan dispatched the Military Governor of the Loyal and Obedient Army, Xiao Shenwei, Acting Vice-director of the Office of Royal Clan Affairs Kang Huacheng and others to make sacrifices before Chŏngjong's tablet at the palace morgue room. The king personally went to observe the ritual.

The Capital Military Command petitioned: "The Eastern Barbarian chief Adugan, since he attached himself to us has received many favors and rewards, yet now he has betrayed us and gone over to the Khitan. There is no crime greater than this! The leader of his clique Kojimun and others are now in their territory. We request to secretly dispatch troops to seize him and bring him back within our borders, interrogate him with torture to extract the reasons for his behavior and then sentence him according to the law." The king approved.

Sixty-thousand arrows for the crossbow and 30,000 arrows for the arrow cart were sent to the Northwestern Circuit.

The king went to Naejesŏg-wŏn and from then on frequently traveled to temples.

Third month, *ŭlhae*, first day of the month, there was a solar eclipse. The Censorate petitioned: "According to the old statutes, if there is even a slight solar or lunar eclipse, the Board of Astrology is to report this in advance, and then the king should report this across the country. A drum will be struck at the Altar of the Earth Deities, and your highness should wear a white robe and avoid the main palace halls; the officials should also don white robes and each should guard their office, and with clasped hands should stand facing the sun until it gets bright again. Now the Director of the Spring Office Yu P'aeng and the Aide to the Grand Astrologer Yu Tŭkso were confused about the heavenly bodies and did not report this in advance. We request that they be dismissed from office."

The king decreed: "Forgive them."

The Censorate remonstrated: "As for solar and lunar eclipses, they are regular occurrences based on Yin and Yang [movement]. If there is no mistake in calculating the calendar, then these phenomena can be proven. But if an office does not have the right people, then those people should lose their position. How can you be lenient in the law for the sake of convenience? Please follow our original request and have them punished." The king acquiesced.

The Eastern Jurchen General "Upholding the Country" Saira and others came to present local products. He was promoted to Grand General "Seeking Refuge in Virtue."

Executive Chief of the Chancellery Hwangbo Yŏng submitted a letter to the king: "Your subject does not have [male] progeny, so I humbly request that my daughter's son Kim Noksung be made my descendent." The king approved.

The Eastern Jurchen General Yaŏhae and others, six people, each leading their people, pledged their territories. The king granted fields and houses and settled them in the interior.

Summer, fourth month. The king went to Sŏnjŏng Hall and summoned his state councilors and censors to discuss the successes and failures of the current administration.

Ch'oe Ch'ung was appointed Director of the Chancellery, Kim Yŏnggi Executive Chief of the Chancellery, Kim Wŏnch'ung Executive Chief of the Royal Secretariat, Pak Yuin Vice-director of the Department of Ministries and Assistant Executive in Political Affairs, and Yi Chayŏn Vice-minister of the Ministry of Personnel and Assistant Executive in Political Affairs. As per the old custom, on the day of presenting the [retirement] cane, one of the councilors would bring a decree table and give it to the one reading the decree. This time as the five councilors were presented with the cane on the same day, the king exceptionally ordered the commissioner for audience ceremonies to bring the table, and this became the new rule.

As it had not rained since spring, the king avoided the palace halls and suspended the regular court meetings. The slaughter of animals was stopped, and the use of dried meats and salted seafood was also stopped. The king also ordered officials across the country to reinvestigate criminal cases.

A Hundred Seat Assembly was organized at Hoegyŏng Hall, and 10,000 monks were fed on the polo court.

Kim Chŏngsin and sixteen others passed the composition test of the civil service examination, and three people passed the classics examination.

The Eastern Jurchen Agaju and others came to offer local products, and he was granted the title of Grand General "Pacified from Afar."

Fifth month. The Eastern Jurchen General Oŏnae and the *taesang* Obulch'a and others came to court.

The king decreed: "Last year there was drought for a long time, and the people on the border are suffering from hunger. Open the righteous granaries to offer relief."

Sixth month. A decree read: "Law serves as precedent for determining punishment. If it is clear then there will be no mistakes or excesses; if is not clear then there is no distinction possible between grave and light crimes. The laws that are now in effect are sometimes erroneous, and this grieves me deeply. Now I have ordered Director of the Chancellery Ch'oe Ch'ung to gather law officials to carefully emend the laws and make them accord with correct principles. At the same time the wording and calculations will also be carefully revised."

The king called Ch'oe Ch'ung and others to Mundŏk Hall for a meeting; he asked them about military affairs and various other affairs.

The Eastern Jurchen General "Pacifying the Borders" Nodo and others came to offer local products. Saibul and others came to court. The Khitan Gao Wuzhu and others came to submit.

Autumn, seventh month. A decree read: "The acting Minister of Education and Vice-director at the Department of Ministries Chang Kŭngmaeng has established merit for a long time at the border, but while serving the country neglected his family. It is fitting to extend special favor to show my deep feelings of respect. [Even though] his sons and grandsons are excluded from the habitual protected appointment, exceptionally one of his sons should be granted office."

A civilian from Changyŏn County called Mun Han pretended that he was possessed by spirits and descended into madness killing his father, mother, sister, and little niece. He was executed and his body exposed on the market place. The Ministry of Punishments petitioned: "The county magistrate Ch'oe Tŏg'wŏn and the county marshal Ch'oe Sungmang failed to deliver good administration and edification of the people, leading to this inauspicious affair. Moreover they were late in reporting this affair, so they should be dismissed from office." The king agreed.

The king summoned his state councilors for a meeting in Mundŏk Hall to ask them about achievements and failures of current policies.

The king decreed that the patrolling officer and the local censor of the Western Capital should select ten regiments for the Ferocious Army and the Navy following the example of the supreme capital, namely to select 300 elite troops among every thousand men under the leadership of a junior colonel. They would still fall under the jurisdiction of the local military command.[52]

A decree read: "According to the old regulations, to settle affairs in the border regions, councilors of the two bureaus [Chancellery and Security Council] are ordered to send someone specializing in military affairs, called the Great Military Commissioner for the Lieges (Taebŏn pyŏngma 大蕃兵馬). But the name and its function do not match, which is why it should be changed to Military Commissioner for the Expedition Corps (Haengyŏng pyŏngmasa 行營兵馬使)." After this the king made Security Commissioner Wang Ch'ongji commissioner for the Central Army of the Northeastern sector and concurrently Military Commissioner for the Expedition Corps.

The Chancellery petitioned: "respectfully we submit: according to the old books, the halberd is made like a spear but with two branches in which knives are inserted. On the tips of the halberds used by his gatekeepers the Emperor Wu of Wei used to have a toad head from which a pennant hung; the halberds were twelve feet long, and decorated with blue and yellow

52 Chwabu 左府 (also chwayŏng 左營 according to some sources): probably the local military command of P'yŏngyang.

colors. Now the halberds used in the palace halls and at the Ancestral Shrine use a demon's head, which is really something without justification. We request that they are changed to the old model and painted with a toad's head." The king followed this.

Eighth month. A decree read: "The purpose of the Office of Merit Evaluation is to evaluate merit among the myriad officials. Now they only rely on clerical skills to determine this, which is not right. From now on, when evaluating all officials from the center or the regions, their evaluation report should be consulted and entrusted to the relevant bureau for deliberation."

The Censorate petitioned: "Respectfully we submit: recently we witnessed the appointment of Yi Hŭiro and Hong Tŏg'wi as investigating censors. Yi Hŭiro has a quick temper; he filled various positions at the center and in the regions, yet never achieved anything of note. This year Hong Tŏg'wi, while the mourning for Chŏngjong had not yet ended was seen inebriated and making merry on the eve of the Lantern Festival together with Registrar of the Guards Sŏ Kyŏngŭi, completely disregarding the decorum expected of a subject. They are unfit for the Censorate, so please dismiss them." The king did not allow this, upon which the Censorate remonstrated; this time the king followed their advice.

The Ministry of Punishments again requested that the death penalty be carried out, but the king said: "People's lives are extremely precious, since they cannot be born again. This insignificant person, whenever he hears on those condemned to death waits till the third plea and then still worries about getting it wrong. If there has been an injustice carried out, then even if one wants to appeal there is no longer any way: swallowing the resentment and the cries of despair, is not this painful! Be extremely careful in your investigations!"

The Eastern Jurchen General "Mollified from Afar" Muiro, Adu and others came to present local products. The liege chiefs of Maengnago village, Yanggwaji village and others, thirty tribes in all, leading their people attached themselves [to Koryŏ].

Ninth month. The Song merchant Lin Ji and others came to offer local products.

Khitan dispatched the Royal Inspector of Fuzhou Song Lin to invest the king as Commander Unequalled in Honor, Acting Grand Guardian, concurrently Director [of the Chancellery], Supreme Pillar of State, King of Koryŏ with a stipend village of 7,000 households, and a true stipend investiture of 1,000 households. At the same time he was granted the title of Merit Subject Assisting Timeliness, Establishing Principle and Infinite Loyalty.

Winter, tenth month. Retired Executive Chief of the Chancellery Hwangbo Yŏng died.

The Eastern Jurchen General Kododal and others, forty people in total, came to present local products. Komujŏ of Maengna village and others, 312 households in total, came to attach themselves to Koryŏ.

The Departmental Commissioner for Chinju, Ch'oe Pokkyu, settled more than 10,000 households of displaced people and gave them a livelihood. The king was greatly pleased and rewarded him.

Eleventh month. The Eastern Jurchen General Majigosa and others, forty-six people, came to present horses.

The king summoned his state councilors to Mundŏk Hall to discuss achievements and mistakes of current policies.

The Ministry of Personnel petitioned: "Respectfully, we follow your edict to reduce one staff member of all the government offices, large and small, in the capital and beyond. Only the offices in charge of patrolling the border remain as before. Now we venture to observe that in the prefectures and departments of P'aesŏ and Sannam Provinces the workload is severe yet staff is short, thus many affairs are piling up. This is most unfortunate. We request to keep staff numbers in the mountain prefectures and departments as before, and make this a permanent rule." The king decreed his approval.

Twelfth month. Retired Executive Chief of the Chancellery Yi Tan died.

The king decreed that one son of former Director of the Chancellery Ch'oe Chean, even though he was not of the age to hold office, should be granted an office of Level Eight.

A prince called Hyu was born; later his name was changed to Hun.

The Ministry of Personnel petitioned: "According to the old custom, all officials of all offices, if they have not yet requested retirement due to age, when they reach the age of sixty-nine they are relieved of their office during the biannual roster check of officials. Now the Vice-director of the Grand Physicians at the Bureau of Medicine, Kim Ching'ak, has reached the age for retirement so should be relieved of his office."

The king decreed: "Kim Ching'ak is a famous physician who has served the kings, he should be allowed to serve for a few more years."

The Eastern Jurchen Yago and the Western Jurchen Kosa and others came to court.

Munjong Second year [1048]

Eighth year of the Qingli era of Song, seventeenth year of the Chongxi era of Khitan

Spring, first month. The Eastern Jurchen General "Embraced by Koryŏ" Kuramaribul and others, forty people altogether, came to present horses. The king bestowed presents according to rank.

The king decreed: "For all those who committed crimes and have been banished to the countryside, if they have aged parents they are allowed to remain and care for them. If they die, they have to return to their place of banishment."

Intercalary [first] month. The Eastern Jurchen General "Seeking Refuge in Virtue" Saira and others, thirty-five people in total, came to present horses. The General "Embraced by Koryŏ" Doguna and others, thirty-eight people; the Western Jurchen General "Pacifying the Borders" Kojiji and others, twenty-four people in all, came to present local products.

Khitan dispatched Grand General of the Thousand Bull Division Wang Ze and others to Koryŏ.

Third month. The Censorate petitioned: "The sowing of the seeds has already started, yet the seasonal rains have not yet started. Now the labor for the construction of Taeun and Taean temples will soon be raised, and those of service age will abandon agriculture. If even one man does not plow, there will be those who go hungry. How could the tasks of the three agricultural seasons be abandoned? Moreover you once issued a pardon letter saying that corvée for all building projects would be limited to three years. The whole country rejoiced, and was moved by those virtuous words. But in the end it was not implemented. Trust is the great treasure of the country and cannot be abandoned. We fear that the slanderous blame for changing one's word will start with this. Respectfully we submit that the work on both temples be suspended until the fallow season." The king approved.

Summer, fourth month. The king went to Oejesŏg-wŏn to listen to sūtra recitation from the railings. Of old he had the habit when returning from a trip to the mountains to stop the carriage at this place, and ordering a monk to mount the phoenix carriage and expound the dharma from the railings [of the carriage]. This became a regular custom.

The king decreed: "All offices should start work at the beginning of the snake hour (9 AM) and stop work at the beginning of the chicken hour [5 PM]. This has been an established rule. However, throughout the four seasons the time of daylight can be short or long, but it is never the same. From now on, when the days are long work should start at the beginning of the dragon hour [7 AM] and when the days are short at the beginning of the snake hour."

Sixth month. The Eastern Jurchen chief Osa and others, twenty-six people in all, came to court.

Autumn, seventh month. The king decreed that henceforward all officials, whether high or low, would be granted two days of leave for each of the four mid-season sacrifices.

Eighth month. Chŏngjong was enshrined in the Ancestral Shrine.

Ninth month. The Eastern Jurchen General "Seeking Refuge in Virtue" Adu and others, thirty-six people in total, came to court.

A Hundred Seat Assembly [for the Humane Kings Sūtra] was held in

Hoegyŏng Hall for three days, and 10,000 monks were given food in the polo court, and 20,000 more in famous temples of the provinces.

Winter, tenth month. The king personally sacrificed at the Ancestral Shrine and declared an amnesty.

Eleventh month. To encourage loyalty, the king raised the rank of those officials from the Chancellery and Security Council and others who take part in court deliberations who had taken charge of the sacrifices [at the Ancestral Shrine].

Khitan dispatched Vice-director of the Court for Imperial Entertainments Xing Pengnian to offer congratulations on the king's birthday.

Khitan's Returning the Courtesy Envoy from the Eastern Capital, the Prefect of Dizhou Gao Qingshan, arrived.

Twelfth month, *kab'o* day, last day of the month. There was a solar eclipse.

Munjong Third year [1049]

First year of the Huangyou era of Song, eighteenth year of the Chongxi era of Khitan

Spring, first month. The Eastern Jurchen Agol and others, thirty-two people altogether, came to offer horses.

Khitan dispatched Supreme General of the Thousand Bull Division Xiao Weide and Censor-in-chief Wang Shoudao to invest the king as Acting Grand Mentor, conjointly Royal Secretary, King of Koryŏ. He was also bestowed a stipend village of 3,000 households, and an effective grant of a stipend village of 300 households. He was also granted the merit subject title of "assisting loyalty, upholding the great." His rank titles were as before. At the same time he was bestowed a carriage, robe, cap, sword, seal, and seal cord; and the following presents: clothing, belts, silk, saddles, and other things. The king received his investiture at the southern outskirts [of the capital].

Second month. Ch'oe Ch'ung was appointed Acting Grand Guardian, Yi

Chayŏn Acting Minister of Education, Wang Ch'ongji Acting Minister of Works and Supreme Pillar of State, and Chŏng Kŏl Jointly in charge of the Security Council.

The king invested his younger brother the Prince of P'yŏngyang, Wang Ki, as Acting Grand Preceptor, and concurrently Royal Secretary.

Third month. The commissioner for supervising granaries in the Northeast Circuit petitioned: "The Administrative Assistant for the Defense of Kyoju, Yi Yubaek, has successfully managed fortifications and moats, and in repairing and providing implements is the first among all the prefectures. Also, the clerks and people of Yŏnsŏng and Changyang which are part of [Kyoju] say that since Yi Yubaek was appointed, he has encouraged agriculture and assisted the people. Even if his term of duty is completed, they want to keep him on." The king praised this and passed on the memorial to the Ministry of Personnel.

The king gave a banquet to the state elders who had reached the age of eighty at the palace gate: Junior Vice-director of the Department of Ministries Ch'oe Posŏng, Director of the Court of Royal Entertainments Cho Ong, and Supervisor of the Household of the Heir Apparent Yi T'aeksŏng. The king personally went up to them to serve them wine, and then bestowed on Ch'oe Posŏng and Cho Ong one official robe each and two winged caps, as well as thirty measures of Noewŏn tea. He bestowed one official robe on Yi T'aeksŏng. They were also allowed to ride their horses from the gate of the palace building to exit through the main gate, but the three elders firmly refused this. The next day the king gave a banquet for the elderly commoner men and women as well as righteous husbands, chaste wives, filial sons, obedient grandsons, widows and widowers without offspring, orphans, and the terminally ill or injured on the polo court. Seats were allocated based on status in the Left and Right Tongnak Pavilion and its galleries; the king also bestowed presents according to rank.

The Eastern Jurchen Marihae and others, twenty people in all, came to present horses.

Yi Injŏng was appointed Vice-director of the Department of Ministries,

Pillar of State; Kim Chŏngjun was appointed Commissioner of the Security Council and Supervisor of the Censorate.

Summer, fourth month. The king decreed: "Last year the monsoon rains destroyed crops and the people do not have enough to eat. Send out commissioners to provide relief and make sure that everyone survives."

The Western Jurchen Pugŏ and others, twenty people, and the Eastern Jurchen General "Upholding the Country" Saira and others, seventy-nine people, came to present horses.

Fifth month. Pak Insu and fourteen others passed the composition test of the civil service examination], one person passed by royal grace, and four people passed the classics examination.

The "merit and protected farmland and woodland" (*Kong'ŭm chŏnsi pŏp* 功蔭田柴法) act was promulgated.

Sixth month. Pirates of the Eastern Barbarians raided Imdo County and kidnapped seventeen people.

The Military Commissioner for the Northeast Circuit reported: "Yugo, chief of the Shock Troop Brigade in Unam County and others, eleven people in all, went on a night patrol and reached Ch'ŏnjŏng camp. Suddenly more than forty Barbarian bandits entered the camp and all soldiers fled or hid themselves. Yugo however took the lead in fighting the bandits, who subsequently dispersed. We request that he be given an office commensurate with his merit."

The king ordered that the sick and hungry be gathered in Tongsŏ Taebiwŏn [Universal Mercy convent] to be aided and looked after.

The king decreed that every year from the sixth month till the onset of autumn ice should be distributed to retired state councilors once every three days; [next], to officials from vice-directors and vice-ministers at the Department of Ministries, directors of various institutions, and grand generals upwards once every seven days, and that this should be a permanent rule.

Autumn, seventh month. The Eastern Barbarian pirates raided Kŭmyang County and took twenty people hostage.

Eighth month. The Song merchant Xu Chan and others, 133 people, came and presented precious objects.

Ninth month. The king decreed that those among the local clerks whose brother or sister died, if they reside in a faraway administration, need not request leave from capital officials, but should directly request leave to the locally posted officials. For the mourning of their wife's parents, regardless of whether it is a first or later wife, leave should be granted.

The king's son Chŭng was born. Later his name was changed to Ki, and later it was changed again to Un.

Winter, eleventh month. The "awe-inspiring" Lieutenant Puŭring and others, seventy-seven people from T'amna country, and the Northern Jurchen chief Pugŏ and others, twenty people, came to offer local products.

An official from Tsushima in Japan dispatched the chief Myŏngim 明任 and others to return twenty of our fellow countrymen who had been cast adrift. The king bestowed presents on Myŏngim and the others according to rank.

Twelfth month. Khitan dispatched Vice-director of the Palace Administration Ma You to congratulate the king on his birthday.

More than 320 soldiers from Yŏnghŭng Garrison in the Northeastern circuit reported that "Garrison Commander Chŏng Chagyŏm had promoted agriculture and sericulture, equally distributed corvée labor, repaired fortifications, and prepared military equipment. Moreover, on land full of gravel and rocks that was not cultivated he recommended sowing various grains, thus annually harvesting more than 200 *kok*. His merit and achievements are outstanding, and even though his term has already ended, we request that he be allowed to remain in office." The king sighed in admiration and allowed this.

Munjong Fourth year [1050]

Second year of the Huangyou era of Song, nineteenth year of the Chongxi era of Khitan

Spring, first month. The military commissioner for the Northeast, Pak Sŏnggŏl, reported: "Last year in the tenth month pirates snatched two warships from Chinmyŏng [County] and left. Recording Officer to the Military Commissioner Mun Yangnyŏl immediately led some warships and together with the Administrative Assistant at the Local Navy Command of Wŏnhŭng, Song Chehan, he went in pursuit. Reaching the pirates' lair, they burnt their straw huts and killed twenty of them. Their merit is worthy of reward." The king ordered that this be passed on to the Capital Military Command.

Director of the Chancellery Ch'oe Ch'ung was given [the prestige title of] Commander Unequalled in Honor and was made Acting Grand Mentor. He was also bestowed the title of merit subject "Promoting Loyalty and Praising the Way." Kim Wŏnch'ung was appointed Executive Chief of the Chancellery and Minister of the Ministry of Punishments. Yi Chayŏn was appointed Executive Chief of the Royal Secretariat; Chŏng Kŏl was appointed Commissioner of the Security Council and Hallim Academician, Receiver of Edicts.

Second Month. The commissioner for supervising the granaries of Hŭnghwa-do in the northwest reported: "Previously in the *muja* year [1048] there was a locust infestation in Ch'angju within our province. For those among the people who had already paid their taxes that year, we request that, depending on how much they lost, in accordance with the law reduce or exempt their taxes." The king agreed.

Third month. Yŏngsak Garrison was fortified to stop incursions by barbarian bandits.

The Eastern Jurchen General "Pacifying the Borders" Yŏmhan and others, ninety people, came to present horses and marten skins. They were granted presents according to rank. Fifteen people including Yŏmhan, because of border aggressions in the past, were detained.

Summer, fourth month. The king went to Hyŏn-nŭng and Sŏl-lŭng[53] and declared an amnesty.

---

53 The tombs of T'aejo and Hyŏnjong, respectively.

The Parhae person Kaeho and others came to submit.

The Department of the Royal Secretariat petitioned as follows: "The prefectures and counties in the west of Kwannae-do[54] last year had a bad harvest, and the people suffer from hunger. We request that the grain be used from the official granaries of public institutions to enable plowing and planting. For those who are so poor that they cannot subsist by themselves, please provide grain from the Righteous Granaries to help them." The king agreed.

The king ordered officials to determine the borders of Taegŏlla and Sogŏlla villages of the Eastern Jurchen to prepare against attacks.

Sixth month. Eastern Barbarian pirates raided Yŏngp'a Camp in Yŏlsan County and abducted eighteen men and women.

The king decreed: Soldiers in the fortresses along the northeastern seaboard have not managed to obtain stable livelihoods. To embrace those who are far from us, there is nothing better than carefully considering their leader. We should appoint Vice-minister of the Ministry of War Yang Kam as this autumn and winters' military commissioner for barbarian matters.

Autumn, seventh month. Eastern Barbarian pirates raided P'ach'ŏn County.

The Eastern Jurchen chief Kollagae and others came to present local products. They also returned four people who had been kidnapped against payment, thus the king bestowed gold and silk.

Ninth month. The Khitan returning the courtesy envoy from the Eastern Capital, the Commander-in-chief of the Loyal and Valiant Army, Gao Chang'an, arrived.

The military commissioner for the Northeast reported: "When pirates raided Yŏlsan County, we sent Recording Officer to the Military Commissioner Mun Yangnyŏl in pursuit with twenty-three warships. He pursued them to Ch'oja island and defeated them after a fierce battle. Nine bandits were executed and more than thirty of their villages were burned. He also destroyed eight of their ships and seized more than 100 weapons. We

54 Kwannae-do 關內道: roughly corresponding to modern Ch'ungch'ŏng provinces.

request that he be rewarded for his merit." The king followed this advice.

Winter, tenth month. Capital Military Command Commissioner, Vice-minister at the Ministry of Personnel Wang Ch'ongji, petitioned: "According to the *Zuo zhuan*, 'During times of peace, do not forget the crises.' Also, it is said, 'Do not believe that the enemy will not come; believe that you should prepare.' Therefore every year in the mid-autumn period the country summons all officials of the eastern and southern orders[55] together at the city outskirts to drill them in archery and horseriding. All the more so for the soldiers of the various armies and divisions, who are the country's fangs and claws. During the agricultural off season they should be drilled in [receiving orders with] drums, use of pennants, and formations. Moreover the cavalry does not practice. I request to first select an elite cavalry vanguard, and for each division provide ten sets of horse armor so as to train them in galloping and pursuit. Also make the Censorate, the Ministry of War and the Six Armies take charge of training and inspection." The king agreed.

Eleventh month. The Capital Military Command Commissioner, Director of the Chancellery Ch'oe Ch'ung and others, made the following petition to the king. "Because of last year's crop failure, in the prefectures and garrisons of the northwest the people are destitute. The men are worn down by corvée labor, and the women are exhausted from paying back loans. How could they manage? We request that aside from the repair of walls and moats, all corvée labor be suspended." The king agreed.

In Chinmyŏng County Vice-commissioner at the Bureau of Royal Inspectors Kim Kyŏngŭng led his ships in an attack on three pirate ships at Uyŏl-do. He defeated them and executed several dozen pirates. Numerous [pirates] drowned.

Intercalary month. Khitan dispatched as informal envoy Military Governor of the Kuangyi 匡義 Army Xiao Zhi.

Cao Yi, a Han Chinese from Khitan, came to submit.

Twelfth month. Khitan dispatched the Royal Inspector from Gaozhou

---

55 I.e. the Tongban 東班 and Namban 南班, specialized officials lower in hierarchy than the civil officials.

Xiao Yu to congratulate the king on his birthday.

Ch'oe Ch'ung petitioned: "The Eastern Jurchen chief Yŏmhan and others, eighty-five of them, because of their frequent border raids in which they kidnapped border people, have been detained in the capital for some time now. However, the barbarians have the face of people but the minds of animals. They cannot be punished with criminal laws, and they cannot be educated through humanity and righteousness. If they are detained for too long, they will get angry and harbor resentment. Their feelings of attachment for their homeland is also very strong. Moreover the cost of detaining them is considerable. Please have them released and returned." The king agreed.

Munjong Fifth year [1051]

Third year of the Huangyou era of Song, twentieth year of the Chongxi era of Khitan

Spring, second month. There was a fire at the Capital Markets Bureau, which spread to 120 adjacent homes. The king ordered officials to grant them timber and tiles.

Because of hunger among the people, the king ordered the granaries to be opened to provide relief.

Third month. Vice-director of the Department of Ministries Yi Suhwa died.

Summer, fourth month. Ch'oe Sŏk and eighteen others passed the composition test of the civil service examination, and three passed the classics examination.

The king decreed that the Eastern Jurchen bandit leader Agol and others, seventy-seven people, who had been detained in the Kwangin Hostel, be released and returned.

The Department of the Royal Secretariat-Chancellery[56] petitioned: "To construct or repair Chonghŭng-sa, Taean-sa, Taeun-sa and others, corvée labor has been mobilized for the engineering work. Among all the projects

[56] Here identified as Naesa Munha-sŏng 內史門下[省].

you manage, it is neither urgent nor important. The artisans and workers are worn down day and night, while wives and children exert themselves running back and forth to deliver and prepare food. Since spring and summer they have hardly rested, and moreover last year was a year of bad harvests and the people are short of food, so they will not have enough energy to endure this. Corvée labor should be raised when the circumstances allow it, so we request that you wait until there is no agricultural work." The king agreed.

Fifth month. Because of the drought the king declared an amnesty.

Autumn, seventh month. Tsushima Island in Japan dispatched an envoy to demand the extradition of three fugitive criminals including Yanghan 良漢.

Officials reported: "In the capital there is a filial son called Sŏk Chu. Orphaned at a young age, having nowhere to go to he shaved his head and became a monk. He carved effigies of his parents and then painted and dressed them. He treated them with proper ritual as if they were alive, greeting them and enquiring after their health." The king responded: "Even Ding Lan's[57] piety does not surpass this!" He then ordered the officials to reward him lavishly.

The Eastern Jurchen *wŏnbo* Kosa and others, twenty-six people in total, came to offer local products.

Eighth month. The king personally bestowed a banquet for those over eighty as well as the terminally ill, filial sons and obedient grandsons, and chaste wives, on the polo court. He also bestowed presents according to rank.

The Eastern General "Seeking Refuge in Virtue" Tuyabul and others, thirty-one people in total, came to present local products.

Ninth month. The Jurchen raided the Northeastern circuit. Vice Military Commissioner [for the Northeast] Kim Hwasung attacked them and killed fifty-nine of them. The king bestowed robes, silk, and silver utensils. To the military clerks he bestowed presents according to rank.

The Jurchen raided the Northwestern circuit. Military Commissioner [for the Northwest] Pak Chongdo attacked them and killed more than ten of

---

57 One of the twenty-four paragons of filial piety from China, who also served wooden statues of his parents.

them. He also obtained twenty war horses and an incalculable number of armor and arms. The king praised him highly.

Winter, tenth month. The Jurchen raided the Northeastern circuit. The military commissioner [for the Northeast] dispatched troops to pursue them, killing more than twenty.

The Returning the Courtesy Envoy of the Khitan Eastern Capital, Acting Vice-minister of the Ministry of Works Yelü Xiuxing arrived.

Eleventh month. Because of the failed harvest in Sukchu, T'onghae and other counties of Unjung Province, were exempted from this year's land tax.

Twelfth month. Khitan dispatched the Prefect of Enzhou, Liu Congbei, to offer congratulations on the king's birthday.

Munjong Sixth year [1052]

Fourth year of the Huangyou era of Song, twenty-first year of the Chongxi era of Khitan

Spring, first month. The Eastern Jurchen General "Embraced by Koryŏ" P'ogaju and the General "Seeking Refuge in Virtue" Taro; the Western Jurchen General "Pacifying the Border" Kobanji and others came to present horses.

The Eastern Jurchen *chŏngbo* Map'a and others, forty-eight people requested to enter Chŏngju and be entered into the household registers as people from outside the pass. The king granted fields and houses and settled them in the interior.

Second month. The princess of the Yŏndŏk Palace, Lady Yi, was invested as royal consort.

The Eastern Jurchen *wŏnbo* Arin and others, twenty-nine people, came to present horses.

The Altar for the Earth and Grain Gods (Sajik-tan 社稷壇) was newly constructed to the west of the imperial city. The king went there to personally sacrifice. He conferred on his servants and staff one honorary rank. To the soldiers who accompanied his carriage he bestowed presents according to rank, and to the staff who had constructed the altar he bestowed one honorary rank.

Because there was hunger in the two provinces of Kwansŏ and Anbuk, the king ordered that granaries be opened to provide relief.

Third month. Kim Wŏnsuk was appointed censor-in-chief.

The king ordered the Grand Astrologer Kim Sŏngt'aek to compile the "Ten Essences Calendar;" Yi Inhyŏn to compile the "Seven Heavenly Bodies Calendar,"[58] Han Wihaeng to compile the "Observing the Movements Calendar,"[59] Yang Wŏnho to compile the "Calendar of Disappearances," and Kim Chŏng the "Supreme One Calendar."

A decree read: "Soldiers from the prefectures, garrisons, and camps of the Northeastern Circuit because of successive droughts are suffering from hunger. Give orders to provide relief." The king also bestowed clothing and uniforms.

Because there was hunger in the capital, the king ordered officials to gather more than 30,000 starving people to give them rice, millet, salt, and fermented soybeans.

Summer, fourth month. Officials reported: "In the four counties of Ssangbu, Man'gyŏng, Okku, and Isŏng there has been drought since last year and the crops failed. The people are starving, so please exempt them from land rent and taxes." The king followed this.

Eight thousand *sŏk* of millet was transported from the Yongmun granary to Yŏmju and Paekchu to give to farmers.

Fifth month. In Samsal village in the Northern Circuit, the bandit leader Koin led his barbarian soldiers in a siege of Ch'idam station. Recording Officer for the Military Commissioner Kim Ch'unggan and Administrative Assistant for the Defense of Chaju Chang Ipsin led their troops in an attack on the bandits, routing and pursuing them. More than fifty of the captured

---

58 *Ch'iryoryŏk* 七曜曆; i.e. sun, moon, and the five planets visible from earth.

59 Kyŏnhaengnyŏk 見行曆: tentative translation; nothing else is known about these calendars, so all we know is what can be inferred from the titles.

bandits were executed.

On account of the drought the king avoided the main palace hall and reduced the amount of dishes served. He also ordered all convictions of the capital and the regions to be reinvestigated.

The Eastern Jurchen chief Kojimun and others, twenty-five people in all, came to offer local products.

An edict read: "Recently during the Tonghe era (983–1011) when the Khitan troops invaded the country, our august father Hyŏnjong took refuge south of the mountains. Junior Vice-director of the Department of Ministries Pak Sŏm accompanied the king on horseback throughout, withstanding all hardship until the capital was recovered, he remained loyally by the king's side so that the Altar of the Earth and Grain Deities remained intact. His likeness should be painted on the halls [of the Altar] as an example to those who come after."

The king ordered civil and military officials who regularly attended audiences as well as retired statesmen to submit a letter stating the achievements and failures of the current administration.

An edict read: "The Acting Grand Preceptor and Royal Secretary Ch'oe Sawi during the reign of my august father on many occasions saved King Hyŏnjong from crises with his loyalty and uprightness, thus not only safeguarding the dynasty and its shrines, but also restoring it. He should be enshrined in the Ancestral Shrine [together with Hyŏnjong]. Those of his nephews who have not yet gained office should be given a post of rank eight. First Office Chief at the Department of Ministries Ha Kongjin in the 28th year of the Tonghe era [1010] faced the invading Khitan army without concern for his own body. Sticking out his three-inch tongue he managed to overcome a great army. His portrait should be drawn in the halls [of the Ancestral Shrine]. His son Ha Ch'ikch'ung should be promoted to an office of the fifth rank."

Sixth month. The presented scholar Zhang Ting from Song China arrived. He was given the post of Editor in the Palace Library, and the king also bestowed on him robes, a belt, colored silk, and silver.

The Eastern Jurchen Kojimun and others crossed the sea to attack Samch'ŏk County. The Defending General of Imwŏn Military Camp, Ha Churyŏ, led his troops out of the fortress gates, and turning towards them said: "They are many and we are few; if every man fights his own war without regard for his body, victory is ours!" Then he grasped his shield and sword and charged. Just at that time it so happened that the Administrative Assistant to the Regional Military Commander of Anbyŏn, Kim Sungjŏng, was on a tour of inspection of the military camps under his jurisdiction. When he reached the border of the jurisdiction, the bandits heard their horns sounding and thought they were relief troops that were about to arrive. Startled, they were in disarray, and Ha Churyŏ profited from this to defeat them, capturing or beheading more than ten; the remaining bandits fled.

Autumn, eighth month. An edict read: "Since Han Sik, Mun Chil, U Kiri, and Kim Yŏl followed my august deceased father on his flight south and thus established their merit, we posthumously bestow on them the post of Supreme General of the Left-Right Division. Because Ha Kongjin has merit in protecting the shrine of the earth gods, we posthumously confer on him the post of Executive at the Ministry of Works.

A decree read: "The Altar for the Earth [and Grain] Gods enshrines Kuryong-ssi 勾龍氏 as the Lord of the Earth (Hut'o 后土). However, it is not appropriate to call him by name on title boards or congratulatory addresses, so replace 'Kuryong-ssi' with 'Lord of the Earth'."

The Song merchant Lin Xing and others, thirty-five people in all, came to offer local products.

Ninth month. The Song merchant Zhao Shou and others, sixty-six people in all, came to offer local products.

The Eastern Jurchen General Sasiha and others, forty people in all, came to present horses.

A Hundred Seat Assembly was held for three days in the Hoegyŏng Hall and 30,000 monks were fed on the polo court and various famous temples.

Winter, tenth month. The king invested his nephew Wang Kyŏng as Acting Grand Guardian cum Director of the Department of Ministries,

Prince of Nangnang, and Wang Kae as Acting Grand Marshal cum Director of the Department of Ministries, Prince of Kaesŏng.

An edict read: "Pae Hyŏn'gyŏng and the other six merit subjects who assisted our T'aejo in establishing the dynasty had merit worthy of being inscribed on bells and cauldrons. Give official posts to those of their descendants who do not have any; those who have an official post, raise them by one rank."

Eleventh month. The king went to the Sŏnjŏng Hall. The Censorate had requested to debate the achievements and failures of the current administration.

Twelfth month. Khitan dispatched the Prefect of Yongzhou, Yelü Shiqing, to offer congratulations on the king's birthday.

The retired Executive Chief of the Chancellery Kim Yŏnggi died.

Munjong Seventh year [1053]

Fifth year of the Huangyou era of Song, twenty-second year of the Chongxi era of Khitan

Spring, second month, *ŭlsa* [5th] day. A comet emerged from the Arsenal Constellation[60] and entered the Wing Star;[61] it was about ten feet long.

The Eastern Jurchen Abuhan and others, thirty-three people altogether, came to present horses. They were also indemnified for six people who had been taken hostage, being granted office titles and awards according to rank.

The crown prince of T'amna Country, Suunna, sent his son, Lieutenant aide-de-camp[62] Komul to present local products. The king bestowed on the crown prince the title of Middle Tiger General, and also bestowed official robes, a silver belt, silk, and medicine.

Third month. U Sang and twenty others passed the composition test of the civil service examination, and two people passed the classics examination.

---

60 *Koru* 庫樓: corresponding to the Zeta Centauri system.

61 *Iksŏng* 翼星: 27th of the 28 traditional constellations; as far as I can ascertain there is no clear correspondence with a constellation from the Western tradition.

62 *Paeyung kyowi* 陪戎校尉: military rank title, ninth rank.

Summer, sixth month. The Finance Commission petitioned: "According to the old regulations, for every *sŏk* of rice [harvested], one *sŭng* was set aside to cover wastage in storage;[63] today the rice from twelve granaries is transported to the capital granaries. Since it is transported across water and land repeatedly, so in effect this surplus amount does not suffice to cover actual wastage. The transporters now have to cover the deficiency. We request that for every *kok* of rice an increased amount of seven *sŭng* be levied." The king agreed.

Autumn, seventh month. The Ministry of Rites submitted a petition: "Respectfully [we submit]: according to the *Tang shu*, in the eighth year of Kaibao of Emperor Xuanzong [749] on the *kyŏng'in* day of the intercalary sixth month, the emperor personally went to the Daqing palace and presided in Hanyuan Hall where he received the investiture documents submitted[64] by the officials. We request that your majesty follow this precedent and on the first day of every intercalary month go to your private quarters for audiences." The king approved.

Yi Chayŏn and Wang Ch'ongji were appointed Executive Chief of the Chancellery. Kim Chŏngjun and Pak Sŏnggŏl were made Assistant Executive in Political Affairs.

The Eastern Jurchen General "Embraced by Koryŏ" Kododal and others, thirty people altogether, came to present horses, and also to return hostages. They were given presents and higher ranks.

Intercalary [seventh] month. There was flooding in Munju and Yongju in the Northeastern Circuit, and more than 100 homes were carried away by the water. The king dispatched an envoy to convey his sympathy.

Ninth month. The Censorate petitioned: "In the various ministries outside the palace walls officials are in attendance day and night, yet there are no dormitories for them. As we happened to observe for the case of China, all

---

63 *Momi* 耗米: According to the dictionary definition of this term, when claiming the interest on grain loaned from the state granaries, an extra amount was demanded to cover the wastage estimated to occur during storage.

64 *Sangch'aek* 上冊: since this is an unusual expression, it is not clear exactly what is meant here.

officials are gathered together in a dormitory complex. Now as for all the officials involved in the drafting of edicts, please have them overnight in the Hallim Academy." The king agreed.

On the *pyŏngsul* [20th] day, the king went to the Western Capital.

Winter, tenth month, *pyŏngsin* day, first day of the month. There was a solar eclipse.

On the *kyŏngja* [5th] day, the royal carriage reached the Taedong River. The king entered a boat with viewing tower and gave a banquet to the princes and state councilors.

The king went to Hŭngbok-sa and then returned to the boat with viewing tower on the Taedong River and feasted his supreme generals and other high officials.

The king gave a banquet for the filial sons and grandsons, righteous husbands and chaste wives, lonely elderly people and orphans. He granted presents according to rank.

The king feasted those officials who took part in the court audiences in Changnak Hall and conferred silk according to rank.

On the *ŭlmyo* [20th] day the king mounted his carriage and left the Western Capital. Reaching the boat with viewing tower on the Taedong River, he ordered General Chŏng Sŭp and others, eight people in all, to practice archery. Junior Colonel Yu Hyŏn's arrow crossed the river. The king praised and rewarded him, and next gave a banquet for the princes, state councilors, and his officials in attendance.

The envoy to the Resident Governor [of P'yŏngyang], Wang Ibo, came to the Saengyang postal station to bid farewell. Each [of his party] was granted one set of official robes.

On the *chŏngsa* [22nd] day the king reached Chabi Pass, and in the Mirŭk-wŏn offered incense and donated clothing. When the royal retinue passed the highest point of the pass there was a woman carrying two infants. The king took pity and gave rice.

On the *sinyu* [26th] day the king returned from the Western Capital.

Twelfth month. Khitan dispatched the prefect of Lizhou, Xiao Su, to congratulate the king on his birthday.

A decree read: "Director of the Chancellery Ch'oe Ch'ung has served as the fountainhead of Confucianism for several generations [of kings], and his virtue is outstanding among the Three Han. Although we cannot honor his request to retire on account of his age, have the relevant office inspect the old canons and bestow a cane and table for managing his work."

Munjong Eighth year [1054]

First year of the Zhihe era of Song, twenty-third year of the Chongxi era of Khitan

Spring, first month. The Eastern Jurchen *chungyun* Yŏngson and others, eighteen people in all, came to present horses.

Second month. The king invested his son Wang Hun as crown prince, and declared an amnesty. He also raised the rank of all those in office by one grade.

The king gave a banquet for all officials in Kŏndŏk Hall and bestowed silk according to rank.

Third month. A decree read: "All land grades [are determined as follows]: the highest category is land that never lies fallow, the middle category is land that lies fallow once, and the lowest category land that lies fallow twice.[65] One *kyŏl* of mountain fields that never lies fallow equals one *kyŏl* of flatland fields; for [mountain fields] that lie fallow once, they equal two *kyŏl* [of flatland fields], and [mountain fields] that lie fallow twice, they equal three *kyŏl* [of flatland fields].

Summer, fourth month. Last year Munju, Yongju, Tŭngju, Chinmyŏng County, and Changp'yŏng Garrison all suffered from flooding, so the Righteous Granary was opened to provide relief. Furthermore, grain from

65 Although the first category (不易田) clearly refers to land that can be cultivated every year (or throughout the year?), in the case of the second category (一易田), it is not clear over what interval it lies uncultivated, but likely it means that it can be cultivated only once every other year, whereas the third category (再易田) would then be open for cultivation only once every three years.

the Ch'unju, Kyoju, Tongju, and other granaries was transported to provide seeds and food.

Yi Chayŏn was promoted to Grand Mentor.

The Northern Jurchen General "Pacifying the Border" Koch'a and others, thirty-nine people in all, came to present horses.

Yu Sŏnnyŏ and twenty-four others passed the composition test of the civil service examination, and two passed the classics examination.

The king dispatched Reviewing Policy Advisor Kim Yangji to Khitan to announce the investiture of the crown prince.

Fifth month. The spirits of famous mountains and great rivers were additionally honored by the addition of the two characters "Ch'ongjŏng" [Bright and upright] to their merit titles.

T'amna sent an envoy congratulating the king on investing the crown prince.

On the *ŭlyu* day [22nd], lightning struck Hoegyŏng Hall.

The king decreed that since people across all provinces, prefectures, and counties were suffering from hunger, many were wandering around without any occupations; therefore local clerks of the *t'ongp'an* rank upwards should inspect and inquire about local needs, and open the granaries if necessary.

Autumn, seventh month. The Song merchant Zhao Shou and others, sixty-nine people in all, came to present rhinoceros horn and ivory.

A son was born to the king; he was named Hŭi, which was later changed to Ong.[66]

Khitan for the first time established the Gongkou-men palisade[67] in the fields east of Baozhou city.

Eighth month. The Military Commissioner for the Eastern Circuit petitioned: "Changju is located in a high and treacherous terrain, and within its walls there are no wells. We request to install a palisade on the flat terrain

66 He would later become King Sukchong (r. 1095–1105).

67 Gongkou-men lan 弓口門欄: It is not certain if the first part is a proper noun or simply a description of the structure. Since Baozhou/P'oju was located on the eastern side of the Amnok River, this fence was clearly intended as a defense against Koryŏ.

outside the south gate and move people there; in case of an emergency they can be moved back inside the walls." The king agreed.

Ninth month. A record was made of the merit of defeating bandits at Ch'idam station in the *imjin* year [1052]. Soldiers were rewarded with offices commensurate with their previous offices and were given very generous presents.

Winter, tenth month. The Eastern Jurchen General "Mollified from Afar" Idabul and others, twenty-eight people in total, came to present horses and return three of our people who had been taken captive, Singŭm, Wibong, and Sŏmnye. Moreover they also related the following: "The tribesmen Silbin, Yŏmhan, Pidan, and Maribul have previously received offices from the Khitan, but when they heard that the king [of Koryŏ] was favorable towards people from other territories, they wished to see him, so we took the liberty of taking them with us." The king granted Idabul, Silbin, Yŏmhan, Pidan, and Maribul office or promoted them, and gave presents to the others according to rank.

The Khitan informal envoy, Yizhou prefect Yelü Fang, arrived.

Eleventh month. The Military Commissioner for the Northeastern Circuit petitioned: "Munju and Yongju were afflicted by floods for two years running, which severely damaged the crops. We request that tax and corvée duties be reduced." The king agreed.

The Khitan Pacification Commissioner, Yizhou prefect Yelü Gan, arrived.[68]

Twelfth month. Khitan dispatched the Fuzhou prefect Yelü Xin to congratulate the king on his birthday.

Officials requested to posthumously accord 3200 of T'aejo's merit subjects including *taegwang* Ch'ŏnmyŏng sequence offices.[69] The king agreed.

The king ordered officials to select twenty people who were either grandsons of grade three officials or sons of grade five or above officials as

---

68 Sic. Note the very close similarity in title and name with the entry before the previous one.

69 *Ch'ajejik* 次第職: not clear what this entails.

personal guard pages of the crown prince, and ten people who were either grandsons of grade five officials or sons of grade seven or above officials as personal guard attendants. This was to be a permanent rule.

Munjong Ninth year [1055]

Second year of the Zhihe era of Song, first year of the Qingning era of Emperor Daozong of Khitan

Spring, second month. The Eastern Jurchen General "Upholding the Country" Idabul and others, twenty-seven people in all, came to present local products.

Summer, fifth month. Khitan dispatched Military Governor of the Kuangyi Army Yelü Ge and Chief Minister of the Court of Imperial Entertainments Chen Yi to invest the king as Acting Grand Preceptor, and granted an additional 5,000 households as stipend village, with 500 effective. Also were bestowed: carriages, caps, official robes, mace, swords, and other presents. The king received the investiture in the southern suburbs. Also, Khitan dispatched the Lizhou Prefect, Xiao Lu, to invest the heir apparent as Duke of State-Crown Prince of the Three Han. The heir apparent received the appointment in the courtyard of the Office for Audience Ceremonies.

Autumn, seventh month. The Capital Military Command petitioned: "Previous emperors and empress dowagers of Khitan decreed that the territory east of the Amnok River belongs to us. However, meanwhile they have either constructed fortresses and bridges or a palisade, thus slowly encroaching on the old border, this is what is called 'reckless behavior.' Moreover now they have constructed a postal pavilion, further gobbling up our territory. According to the *History of Lu*,[70] 'Do not allow gradual seeping in, otherwise it will be too late for plans.' We should send a state

---

70 *Lu shi* 魯史: refers to the Spring and Autumn Annals (*Chunqiu* 春秋), a chronicle of the state of Lu between 770 and 479 BC. This passage is actually from the Zuo Commentary on the text. In the translation of Durrant, Li, and Schaberg: "Do not encourage creeping vines to spread! Once they spread, they are difficult to control." *Zuo Tradition*, Vol. 1, 9.

letter to the resident governor of the Eastern Capital [of Khitan], explaining that this is unacceptable. If he does not listen, then we should dispatch an envoy to report to the emperor."

Thereupon the following letter was drafted to the resident governor of the Eastern Capital: "This country is the successor to the country founded by Kija, which bordered on the Amnok. Moreover the previous Empress Dowager and Emperor have bestowed jade letters on us, benevolently granting the same border. Recently, our suzerain country has entered our borders to construct a bridge and fortresses. Crossing mountains and seas we have diligently paid obeisance to your emperor, and also presented a memorial requesting the return of our old territory, all to no avail. Earnestly we pray for a reply to our request. Recently soldiers from Naewŏn fortress approached our fortresses and moved the palisade [closer to us]. Furthermore in order to build more residences the stone and wood have already been prepared. People living in the border area are surprised and anxious about this, and do not know what to make of it. Prostrate, we hope that the great king will consider carefully his close neighbors, cherish them from afar and bestow benevolence, and report faithfully to the emperor, so that he can return the land once given to us, and destroy the bridges, palisades, and residences that have been built there."

Ch'oe Ch'ung was made Royal Secretary, and allowed to retire. Yi Chayŏn was appointed Director of the Chancellery and caretaker of the Ministry of Personnel. Kim Chŏngjun was made Executive Chief of the Royal Secretariat, and so was Pak Sŏnggŏl; the latter was also made Supreme Pillar of State. Kim Wŏnjŏng was Vice-director of the Department of Ministries and Assistant Executive in Political Affairs, and concurrently Junior Guardian to the Crown Prince.

The Khitan Kang Qingzun and others, fifteen people in all, came to submit to Koryŏ and returned fifty-three people who had been taken captive.

The Eastern Jurchen Chief Yasiro and others, twenty-six people in all, came to present local products. They were given office titles and rewards according to rank.

A decree read: "The younger sister of the former Queen Dowager, my deceased mother, protected us and King Tŏkchong when we were young, and we would like to invest her with an elevated noble rank and stipend village[71] in reward for previous merit. The Security Council should be ordered to ratify this decree and implement it."

Eighth month. The Ministry of Personnel petitioned: "Acting Vice-director of the Bureau of Construction and Maintenance Yu Kongŭi is the great-grandson of *taegwang* Yu Kŭmp'il. Previously he committed an offence, and as a result languished in nominal appointments [i.e. prestige titles]. Previously a royal decree ruled that the scions of merit subjects co-enshrined with T'aejo, even though they committed a crime, should be employed. Therefore we now would like to appoint Yu Kongŭi as Defense Commissioner for Sukchu."

The Chancellery replied: "Yu Kongŭi once committed the crime of deceitful flattery and his name remains in the criminal records. Therefore we cannot employ him." The king agreed.

Director of the Chancellery Yi Chayŏn petitioned: "Disasters or blessings of heaven and earth are always a response to the criminal justice getting it right or wrong. Therefore in rewarding and punishing we cannot be but extremely cautious. Prostrate, I observe that the Ministry of Personnel and the Ministry of Punishments in adjudicating important affairs, leave more and more things unattended, so that there are many unresolved cases. I submit that personnel of the two ministries be carefully vetted on the performance of their key duties, and that the diligent be rewarded and the idle be punished. This will accord with your majesty's diligent administration and compassionate punishments, and signs of heaven and earth's blessings will be forthcoming." The king agreed.

Ninth month. The envoy to convey the news of Khitan emperor Xingzong's passing, Vice-minister at the Court of State Ceremonial Zhang Sifu, came. When the king heard that he had crossed the Amnok River, he ordered that dishes be reduced and music stopped; the slaughter of animals

---

71 *Sungjak ŭpsu* 崇爵邑酬.

was forbidden, as was hunting. The Ministry of Rites petitioned: "In the *[Book of] Rites*, the heir to the throne does not wear mourning for the son of Heaven; furthermore children do not wear the fine hempen mourning cloth.[72] We request that, based on these ritual precepts, the crown prince and the Marquises of Nangnang, Kaesŏng, and Kugwŏn do not wear mourning clothes. For the Duke of P'yŏngyang and those below and civil and military officials who took part in audiences, wear mourning clothes." The king followed this.

The king, wearing a plain white shirt, at the head of all his officials, left Ch'angdŏk Gate to receive the edict. Deeply in mourning and attired in mourning clothes, court audiences and markets were suspended for three days.

The Capital Military Command, following old decrees, requested that in the ninth month commissioners be dispatched to drill troops in the capital and beyond. The king agreed.

The Song chief merchant[73] Huang Xin stated: "Your subject has brought his sons Puan and Shian to submit; however I have an eighty-two-year old mother in my home country who is sad and misses her family. Please let me send back my oldest son Puan to take care of her." This was allowed.

The king dispatched the administrator of the Security Council, Ch'oe Yusŏn, and the Executive at the Ministry of Works Yi Tŭngno to Khitan to offer condolences and assist in the funeral.

Winter, tenth month. A decree read: "The kings and emperors of old esteemed the Buddhist teachings, this can be ascertained in the records. Furthermore since the time of our august progenitor [T'aejo] all kings have constructed Buddhist temples to procure blessings. Since this insignificant person inherited the throne, I have not managed to cultivate virtuous government, leading to various disasters. I hope that through the power of dharma, blessings and benefit can be brought to the country. Have officials

---

72 *Sima* 緦麻: hemp woven with a fine thread; for mourning distant relatives (shortest mourning period of three months).

73 *Togang* 都綱: a term for the representative of a group of foreign traders in Koryŏ.

select a spot to construct a temple."

The Chancellery petitioned: "From ancient times, sage emperors and enlightened kings did not build temples or raise pagodas in order to achieve an era of great peace. All they did was to esteem the dharma and exercise caution and restraint in government, and avoid harming the people's vitality; thereby of itself the dynasty and the shrines prospered continuously. Formerly Bodhidharma told Emperor Wu [of Liang] that there was not the slightest merit in constructing temples and pagodas. This means that he worshiped the merit of non-action [*wuwei* 無爲], and did not esteem the merit of action. Moreover as for the reasons the august progenitor built temples, first this was to reward for the dedications and vows for unification; second, to suppress the wayward elements of the geomantic configuration. Now the wish to build new temples will put strain on the people who have to perform corvée labor that is not urgent. Resentment and enmity will grow, and the veins of energy of the land will be damaged. Disasters will surely arise, and humans and spirits alike will be resentful. This is not the way of establishing an era of great peace." The king did not acknowledge [the petition].

Eleventh month. The king went to the Eastern Pond. Acting Vice-director of the Office of Regalia Ch'oe Sŏngjŏl without reason entered [the area] and reached the king's tent. The king was startled and ordered him to be put in prison. The Court of Justice opined that someone who forced his entry into the king's residence should be executed, but the king said: "Even though the law has a clause explicitly stating that this punishment should be meted out, this would be a cruel application of government. Furthermore he can be useful for literature and calligraphy, so he should be forgiven." The Chancellery remonstrated, but the king did not acknowledge their petition.[74]

The Returning the Courtesy Envoy of the Khitan Eastern Capital, Acting Vice-minister of the Ministry of Works Yelü Dao arrived.

Twelfth month. Khitan dispatched the prefect of Jinzhou, Yelü

---

74 *Pullap* 不納: the king's opposition to policy proposals occurs very rarely, yet here it is noted twice in succession.

Changzheng, to congratulate the king on his birthday.

Munjong Tenth year [1056]

First year of the Jiayou era of Song, second year of the Qingning era of Khitan

Spring, first month. An official from the Ministry of Rites reported: "The ritual implements in the Ancestral Shrine are old and worn out, and are no longer fit to be displayed [during sacrifices]. According to the 'Summary of the Rules of Propriety,' 'When sacrificial robes are worn out, they should be burnt; when sacrificial vessels are worn out, they should be buried.'[75] As for the *bian* 籩 basket, the *fei* 篚 basket, black robes, and red shoes, order the Censorate to either burn or bury them." The king agreed.

The Eastern Jurchen General "Upholding the Country" Agaju and others, fifty people in all, came to present horses.

The name of Yŏngdŏk Garrison 寧德鎮 was changed to Yŏngdŏk Fortress 寧德城 in order not to violate the taboo on the temple name of the Xingzong emperor of the Northern Dynasty: Zhen 鎮 "garrison" is pronounced the same as Zhen 眞 "true."

Second month. An official petitioned: "Yŏm Kach'ing, who was taken by barbarians, is the grandson of Samhan merit subject Yŏm Hyŏngmyŏng. In the *kyŏngsul* year [1010] Khitan troops forced their way into the capital and Kach'ing helped his parents evade the troops, but meeting with bandits he was taken prisoner. In the first month of the first year of the Qingning era [1055] he fled to us with his son. The land and estate held in perpetuity by his father and grandfather ought to be returned to him." The king agreed.

Construction on Hŭngwang-sa was started in Tŏksu County, which was moved to Yangch'ŏn. Administrator of the Security Council Ch'oe Yusŏn remonstrated: "Formerly Emperor Taizong of Tang was of divine sagacity and unsurpassed military valor, to the point that no other ruler can compare with him. Yet he did not allow people to ordain as monks, and did not allow

---

75 *Liji* 禮記, "Quli"曲禮 I.72

the construction of Buddhist or Daoist temples so as to honor Gaozu's intent. Histories and records all praise him for this. Our T'aejo's injunctions state: 'State Preceptor Tosŏn surveyed the mountains and rivers of our country for their suitability. Every place where a temple could be built, there is none where one has not been built. Those who later succeed to the throne as well as nobility and eminent in-laws, queens and officials, none would be allowed to vie with each other to construct votive shrines that could damage the virtue of the earth.' Now your highness has succeeded to a line of kings that has built a strong base, and you ascended during a long period of peace. It is fitting that you are frugal in expenses and spare the people so as to fully protect this endeavor and transmit it to the next generation. So how can you extract the people's wealth and deplete their energy for a project that is not urgent? Do you want to endanger the country's foundation? This is what I am deeply confused about." The king replied to him with due concern. Another day when he went to the king and they had a casual conversation, the king comforted and praised him in a relaxed and informal manner: "Remonstrating and arguing are a sign of loyalty, following and praising are deceitful flattery." Ch'oe Yusŏn replied: "Founding the dynasty and transmitting are easy, protecting and completing it are difficult."

T'amna presented tribute.

Third month. The king invested his son Chŭng as Marquis of Kugwŏn.

Intercalary [third] month. Acting Minister of Works, retired as Junior Vice-director of the Department of Ministries Ko Yŏl died. He was a Black Water [Malgal], good at archery, who at various occasions established merit in battle. He was a famous general of his generation, and those who heard about his passing all felt it a great loss.

Summer, fourth month. Yi Kanbang and twelve others passed the composition test of the civil service examinations, two people passed by royal grace, and four passed the classics examination.

Fifth month. Floods in sixteen counties of Ch'angnyŏng Prefecture under the jurisdiction of Milsŏng Prefecture damaged crops.

Sixth month. A decree read: "Now that the grains have to ripen the rains show no sign of abating. We should be worried about the future. Give orders to pray for clear skies at all shrines."

The Ministry of Rites petitioned: "For the heir apparent's processions, the regalia and music should be reduced to half those of big processions. Please order the Office of Regalia to divide them and assign to the Household of the Heir Apparent." The king agreed.

Autumn, seventh month. Because the Eastern Tribesmen frequently raided the border the king dispatched the Eastern Circuit Cavalry Deputy Commander,[76] the Attendant Censor Kim Tan, to subjugate them. Kim Tan swore in front of his troops "In the face of the enemy forget your family, sacrificing your body for the country is your lot. Our fate will be sealed today." The three armies were stirred by this speech and fought with double courage. More than twenty of their camps and settlements were destroyed, and the enemy was routed. They seized innumerable weapons, sheep, and horses.

Eighth month. Because death penalties were carried out, the king avoided the main palace halls, ate simple food, and did not listen to music.

The resident governor of the Western Capital petitioned: "The books needed for the candidate presented scholars and classics exam takers of the [Western] Capital are all copied by hand, so many characters have been mistakenly transcribed. Please distribute the Nine Classics, Histories of the Han, Jin, and Tang, the *Analects*, *Classic of Filial Piety*, philosophical and historical works of various schools, collected works, medical works, divination and geomantic works, law treatises, and mathematical works from the Palace Library to the various academies." The king ordered officials to print one copy of each work and send them [to the Western Capital].

Food was given to 30,000 monks.

Ninth month. A decree read: "To assess the quality and honesty of the administration of governors, prefects, controller-generals, magistrates, and county marshals, and of resident local officials; and also to assess

---

76 *Pyŏngma isa* 兵馬貳師: tentative translation, since this is the only occurrence of this term.

the financial state and happiness of the people, commissioners should be dispatched." The bureau in charge however requested that this be stopped, on account of the excessive stress this would put on the post station officials who would have to look after the commissioners. The king replied, "To our knowledge, my predecessors frequently sent out commissioners to find out people's problems, and therefore in all provinces those who governed the people were honest and upright and made the people feel at ease. Recently however norms and standards have deteriorated, but there is no attempt being made at redressing these issues, and there is laxity in carrying out official duties; everyone is merely thinking of personal profit and associations with the powerful. In alleys of villages, a lot is being carried off in bags, while in the fields there is little encouragement for cultivating mulberry [for silkworks] or hemp. In some areas there is produce such as fish or salt, and goods such as woods or lacquer; some families have stored their harvest: these are all targeted by them. If there is anyone who is reluctant to let go of their possessions, then they are punished heavily on a pretext and beaten to the point their life is endangered. Though the people harbor resentment and pain, nobody dares to raise a complaint. Even if there is someone who tries to rectify this, in the end thanks to their powerful contacts this comes to naught. The harm to the people gets worse day by day, so if officials and resident local officials act like this, how can the ordinary people live at peace? Night and day I toil away at trying to resolve this abuse, yet those in important positions and with power do not think it possible [to do something about it] and merely chat away; how is this possible? Now I appoint the concurrent Attendant Censor and Assistant Office Chief at the Ministry of Punishments Yi Yujŏk as Commissioner to enquire after the people's wellbeing for the three provinces south-east of the mountain, i.e. Ch'ungju, Kyŏngju, and Sangju; concurrent Censor of Miscellaneous Affairs and Office Chief at the Ministry of War Kim Yakchin and Office Chief at the Ministry of Rites Ch'oe Sang as Commissioners to enquire after the people's wellbeing for the seven provinces south of the mountain, i.e. Chinju, Naju, Chŏnju, Ch'ŏngju, Kwangju, Kongju, and Hongju; concurrent Investigating Censor and Probationary Intendant-Secretary at the Department of Royal Clan Affairs An Minbo Commissioner to enquire after the people's wellbeing for the three provinces of Kwansŏ, Kwanbuk, and Kwannae; Investigating Censor Min Ch'angsu as Commissioner to enquire after the people's wellbeing for Kwannae East Province. They are to be dispatched separately by province; let there be no delay."

The king ordered the heir apparent and all princes to organize a reception at the pavilion on the Eastern Pond, and to summon the "flowering talents" Ch'oe Ŭng and Yi Sŏ, together with the royal kinsman Wang Ch'ung, and to compose poems. Each was given silk by the king.

A decree read: "Recently I perused what the astronomers reported, namely the frequent occurrence of strange natural phenomena. This must be the consequence of our inferior virtue and lack of unity in our political decisions. Trembling with fear, night and day I remain restless. From this month onwards I will avoid the main palace, reduce the number of dishes, and in various other ways respond to Heaven's censure. All the officials on all levels should each carefully reflect from their respective positions, and tell me straight up if I have erred, without hiding anything."

A decree read: "When Śakyamuni proclaimed his teachings, he emphasized purity as primordial: he kept as far away from impurity as possible and removed all cravings. Nowadays there are those disciples who take on the name 'monk' to avoid corvée labor, but in fact they amass goods for profit, engage in agriculture or trade as their main occupation. Actively they break the letter of the Vinaya, passively they have no sense of purity. The cassock draped over the shoulder is used to hide a jar of wine, and the place for chanting sutras is abused as a field for growing leeks and garlic. They intermingle with merchants and get drunk and make merry when receiving guests, shouting over the Avataṃsaka court and despoiling the Ullambana [ritual]. They wear secular caps and clothing, and on the pretext of repairing their temples, they go out in the streets with flags, drumming, chanting, and piping [to raise money]. Bumping into people on the market place they fight with people until the blood starts flowing. We aim to distinguish good from bad and establish clear codes and examples. It is now necessary to sift through all the temples, be it in the capital or in the regions; all those [monks] who practice the precepts should remain in peace, but those who break the precepts should be dealt with according to the law."

Winter, tenth month. The Japanese envoy, the top ranking official[77] Kwŏnye Tŭngwŏn 權隷藤原[78] and the court minister Noech'ung 賴忠 and others, thirty people in total, arrived. They were given a hostel in Kŭmju.

The heir apparent went to the Ancestral Shrine.

The king personally sacrificed in the Ancestral Shrine and gave more prestigious titles to nine kings. He then declared an amnesty.

Eleventh month. The Song merchant Huang Zheng and others, twenty-nine people, came to offer local products.

The Eastern Jurchen Yasaro and others, fifty people in all, came to present local products.

Director of the Chancellery Yi Chayŏn petitioned the king: "Recently because of the construction of Hŭngwang-sa, Tŏksu County was transferred to Yangch'ŏn. Because of this the people have had to build their houses and have had no respite. With the men carrying and the women dragging [their belongings] they form a long line on the roads. The poor fear ending up in a ditch, while the rich have no place to safeguard their possessions. Please exempt one year's taxes and corveé labor [for the people of Tŏksu]." The king decreed a special exemption for two years.

Twelfth month. Khitan sent the Yongzhou prefect Xiao Weixin to congratulate the king on his birthday.

Central and local [officials] raised a toast to congratulate the heir apparent on the Ever-flourishing festival.[79]

The Eastern Jurchen General "Mollified from Afar" Sajiha and one other person were executed. They had taken people and goods from Sakchu.

---

77 *Chŏngsangwi* 正上位: probably a reference to his rank in the embassy.

78 The second part corresponds to the Fujiwara clan, but it is not clear how the first part ought to be read in Japanese.

79 *Changhŭng-jŏl* 長興節: probably the prince's birthday.

Changwŏn Pavilion was established to the south of Pyŏng-ak 餠嶽 on the Western River. Tosŏn in his *Song-ak Myŏngdang-ki* 松嶽明堂記 had written "On the banks of the Western River there is a prime geomantic spot where a gentleman rides his horse. One-hundred and twenty years after *pyŏngsin* year [936] when T'aejo unified the country, if a construction is built on this spot, the dynasty will be extended." Thus the king ordered the Grand Astrologer Kim Chongyun and others to examine the land and build [this construction].

5. Munjong (II), Sunjong, Sŏnjong

Munjong (II)

Munjong Eleventh year [1057]

Second year of the Jiayou era of Song, third year of the Qingning era of Khitan

Spring, first month. Ko Yu was appointed Junior Policy Monitor. The Royal Secretariat petitioned: "Ko Yu is of T'amna lineage, and is not suited to remonstrating.[1] If you cherish his talents, please appoint him to another office." The king agreed.

Ŭlmi [18th] day. A meteorite fell over Hwangju, with the sound of crashing thunder. Hwangju sent the stone to the capital, where the Ministry of Rites reported: "Previously in the Song dynasty there were also cases of meteorites falling, and in the Qin there was a falling star. From the Jin and Tang onwards this was attested frequently, so it is a common occurrence, and has no relation to misfortune or good fortune. Now the fact that it was reported as a strange occurrence is in fact a misleading report; please punish the officials involved." A royal decree expressed approval, and after this the stone was sent back.

---

1 Kan-sŏng 諫省: Literally, the "remonstrating Department." This appears to be another name for the Department of Royal Secretariat (Chungsŏ-sŏng).

Third month. Khitan dispatched Military Governor of the Heavenly Virtue Army Xiao Jicong and Grand General of the Left Thousand Bull Guard Wang Shouzhuo to invest the king as Concurrent Director of the Department of Ministries, and granted an additional 5,000 households as a stipend village, with 200 effective households. The emperor also bestowed cap and gown, carriage, silver utensils, silk, saddle, bow and arrows, and other presents. The king, at the head of all his officials, received the investiture in the southern suburbs. [Khitan] also dispatched the Imperial Inspector for Lizhou, Xiao Su, and Chief Minister of the Court of the National Granaries Chai Dezi to invest the heir apparent as Military Governor of the Obedient Righteousness Army (Sunŭi-gun 順義軍) and appoint him Surveillance and Supervisory Commissioner for Sakchu, Tŭngju, and other prefectures, Grand Master for Splendid Happiness,[2] Acting Grand Marshal and Associate Executive Chief of the Royal Secretariat and concurrently, Roving Prefect of Sakchu Commissioned with Extraordinary Powers for all Military Affairs in Sakchu, Supreme Pillar of State, Duke of State of the Three Han with a stipend village of 3,000 households, including 500 effective households. The heir apparent at the head of all officials went to the southern suburbs to receive the investiture. The king secretly went to observe the ceremony.

The great-grandson of Director of the Chancellery Ch'oe Suk, Ch'oe Mu, was employed additionally to a post equivalent to Scribe to the Director of the Ministry of Taxation.[3]

I Yuch'ung was made Associate Administrator of the Security Council, Im Chong'il Junior Vice-director of the Department of Ministries, and Wang Musung Censor-in-chief.

Summer, fourth month. A decree read: "Last year we dispatched an

---

2 *Chonglu daifu* 忠祿大夫: prestige title of rank 2b from Tang onwards. Note that the normal title is *Gwanglu daifu* 光祿大夫, but due a taboo Liao changed it to *Chonglu daifu*. Hucker 1666, 3349.

3 祿…加戶部令史同正: a puzzling title, given all the hedging that is taking place; mention of the great-grandfather suggests it is a protected appointed, while the "additional" and "equivalent to" suggest it is only an honorary appointment. "Tongjŏng" is a term occurring only in Korean bureaucracy for an appointment with no actual duties normally expected of someone with this title.

envoy [to Khitan] to request that the postal pavilion outside the palisade be destroyed. Not only was it not destroyed, to the northeast of the Song Pass more and more fields have been opened up for cultivation, and hermitages have been established where people have been stationed and goods stored. This is clearly with the intent of invading our territory. We have to make an utmost request for stopping this."

The Department of the Royal Secretariat argued: "Their court has not actually violated the border, and moreover after the new emperor took the throne they sent an additional decree of investiture. We have not yet sent a return embassy to express gratitude, so to raise the matter of the border first would seem to be inappropriate."

The king replied: "When they have already established a fortification, then not only is it a case of locking the stable door after the horse has bolted, it also shows per force that they are ignoring us. We should send an envoy at the time of the Mid-Autumn festival to proffer thanks for the investiture and after that proceed with submitting our request."

An edict[4] read, "Because a chief and deputy envoy for two separate investiture missions came simultaneously [from Khitan], clerks and people in the capital and the regions alike are exhausted on account of receiving and housing them. Those detained because of [protocol?] mistakes committed should be released. As for the counties and prefectures through which the missions passed, land rents and taxes should be cut in half. As for the officials who assisted when we received the investiture, and those who accompanied us on the dais, officials of the ranks who take part in audiences shall be promoted in rank; local functionaries should be given an additional 'equivalent to' position. Functionaries who work for the heir apparent, prognosticators, calligraphers, and the standard bearers in the royal retinue should all be allowed to enter officialdom. As for the other soldiers, please distribute presents according to rank."

---

4 This is one of the rare occasions where *cho* 詔 is used rather than *che* 制 for a royal proclamation. Both can be translated as 'edicts' (Wilkinson, *A Manual*, 533). For the latter Wilkinson adds that it is used for "important pronouncements." Whether or not there is an important distinction between the terms is not clear.

Yi Chun and thirteen others passed the composition test of the civil service examination, and four people passed the classics test.

Fifth month. Assistant Executive in Political Affairs Kim Wŏnjŏng memorialized: "Now the Ministry of War has requested the dispatch of soldiers to prepare defenses in the Western and Eastern Border Circuits. Recently however soldiers and people alike have suffered due to the reception of the investiture envoys, and those drafted to work on Hŭngwang-sa also had no time to recuperate. Furthermore, salaries are insufficient; we request that following the precedent of the soldiers who took part in the investiture ceremony, presents be given [to the soldiers drafted] according to rank." The king consented.

The Eastern Jurchen General "Embraced by Koryŏ" Kododal and others, twenty-five people in all, came to present local products.

The consort of the Hŭngsŏng Palace[5] died. The king decreed: "Give orders so that a royal tomb be built and households assigned. Attending functionaries should offer sacrifices at the appropriate times." The Department of the Royal Secretariat objected: "According to the Rites, 'if the father's concubine (*sŏmo* 庶母) has a son, fine hemp [mourning clothes] should be worn for three months.' Now the consort of the Hŭngsŏng Palace has no progeny, so your highness does not wear mourning. Please remove the tomb title and the seasonal sacrifices." The king agreed.

Sixth month. The Khitan Returning the Courtesy Envoy from the Eastern Capital, Acting Vice-minister of the Ministry of Works Yelü Kexing arrived.

The Eastern Jurchen General "Mollified from Afar" Yoŏnae and others, twenty-five people in all, came to present local products.

Autumn, seventh month. The king ordered his officials to test the skills of the nationalized Song person Zhang Wan, namely on the "way of three miraculous transformations" and the "prognostication of the six *im*-stems"[6]

---

5 Hŭngsŏng-kung pi 興盛宮妃: probably refers to a secondary consort or concubine of his father, Hyŏnjong.

6 *Yug'im chŏm* 六壬占: probably refers to the six combinations containing the ninth heavenly stem, 壬 with successive earthly branches in the sexagenary cycle. There is also a work with that title attributed to one Zhu Mi 祝泌 of the Song.

and then appoint him Astronomical Observer at the Bureau of Astrology.

The king gave a banquet for men and women aged eighty or over as well as filial sons and grandsons, righteous husbands and faithful wives, the widowed, orphans and those with fatal illnesses on the polo court, and bestowed presents according to rank.

The king went to the Sŏnjŏng Hall to adjudicate on serious crimes from across the country deserving heavy punishment.

Eighth month. The Song merchant Ye Delong and others, twenty-five people in all, came to present local products.

The king bestowed robes, silver utensils, saddle, cloth, silk, and rice on Director of the Chancellery Yi Chayŏn.

The king put Proofreader in the Palace Library Kyŏng Chŏngsang provisionally in charge of the Hallim Academy. The Department of the Royal Secretariat objected: "Kyŏng Chŏngsang is the descendant of metal artisans. He is not fit for a position of purity and importance. Please remove him."

The king replied: " 'When we gather the mustard plant and earth melons, we do not reject them because of their roots.'[7] In other words, we cherish those that can be employed. Kyŏng Chŏngsang's talents and knowledge are such that he deserves being picked, how can it be appropriate to bring up his lineage?" The king did not allow [the decision to be overturned].

The Song merchant Guo Man and others, thirty-three people in all, came to present local products.

On the *sinmi* [27th] day the king went to the Western Capital.

Ninth month. The king dispatched Wang Ibo and Ch'oe Wŏnjun to Khitan to give thanks for the edict of investiture.

Winter, tenth month. The Khitan informal envoy, Taizhou Prefect Yelü Hong, arrived.

Eleventh month, *pyŏngja* [4th] day. The king returned from the Western Capital.

Kim Chŏngjun was appointed Executive Chief of the Chancellery and

---

7 From the *Book of Poetry*, Gu Feng chapter in the Odes of Bei.

also of the Department of the Royal Secretariat.

Twelfth month. Khitan dispatched Junior Policy Critic Wang Zongliang to congratulate the king on his birthday.

The king dispatched Executive at the Ministry of Taxation An Minbo to Khitan to congratulate the empress dowager on her birthday and Executive at the Ministry of Works Ch'oe Kyeyu to offer congratulates on the Heavenly Peace Festival (Tianan jie 天安節).

Vice-director of the Department of Ministries Chi Maeng requested to retire from office on account of his age. The king especially issued an edict that refused this request. The Department of the Royal Secretariat petitioned: "To retire at seventy is a matter of propriety. Please allow it."

The king decreed: "Previously on account of the fact that Chi Maeng's ancestors established merit for the dynasty, before his request for retirement on account of old age, for several years already I allowed him to personally assist in court audiences,[8] and later also bestowed cane and table. Now if on account of what you request I suddenly change my previous words, I fear that Chi Maeng will think that I am just fooling around with him."

The Department of Royal Secretariat again petitioned: "According to the instructions of the *Rites*, all those aged officials who 'know the affairs of Heaven and Earth' can be granted a cane and table. Now Chi Maeng is recorded as having received office through a protected appointment, so he is not one who 'knows the affairs of Heaven and Earth' nor has he established merit in battle. For the rest, even in political affairs he has not given any essential counsel to your majesty. If you have in mind the exploits of his ancestor, in that case granting a personal participation in audiences for one year suffices. If you however extend this to several years, and moreover grant cane and table, we fear that this is excessive partiality. Please retract your earlier order." The king agreed.

Kim Wŏnjŏng was appointed Executive and Executive Chief of the Department of Royal Secretariat; Kim Hyŏn was made Vice-director of the

---

8 *Sijo* 侍朝: literally, to assist the king in person; interpreted in Korean translations as the right to stand during court audiences [rather than to kneel].

Department of Ministries and Assistant Executive in Political Affairs; Han Kongsŏ was made Junior Vice-director of the Department of Ministries. The Censorate objected: "According to official regulations, there can be only one vice-director and one junior vice-director at the Department of Ministries. Now Im Chong has already been appointed junior vice-director, and now Hang Kongsŏ has been given the same post. This is not in accordance with the old regulations, please rescind the order." The king did not allow this.

Munjong Twelfth year [1058]

Third year of the Jiayou era of Song, fourth year of the Qingning era of Khitan

Spring, second month. The Capital Military Command petitioned: "The metal tribute tax from the circuits inside Ansŏ Military Command used to suffice for armaments. Recently the construction of Hŭngwang-sa led to increased taxes, which have become unbearable for the people. Please reduce the military armament metal tribute for Yŏmju, Haeju, and Anhu that is exclusively used for Hŭngwang-sa for two years so as to reduce the excessive labor." The king agreed.

The Drafting Advisor of the Royal Secretariat, Ch'oe Sang, petitioned: "Recently I accompanied the Khitan envoy Wang Zongliang to send him off. When we reached Kŭmgyo station at night, Wang Zongliang, noticing the row of torches, said 'to send me off with wine in the suburbs, the night is encroached by lighting torches. Now the clothes of the servants and slaves [carrying the torches] are short and they look pitiable. Henceforth we should wait till dawn to continue the journey. I have heard that to receive guests and envoys, your country encourages them to drink into the night. Now observing that the rituals and music [of Koryŏ] uniformly resemble those of China, I cannot help but admire this. However, on three occasions I went to the royal palace for a banquet, and every time lamps were placed there. In our dynasty, candles are only allowed at nightfall. If ordinary people or officials have to meet a guest, even if it is deep into the night, they are not allowed to light candles.' Your servant concurs that the royal way is to rule facing the light, and hence [the king] should receive guests in broad daylight. Furthermore, lamps and candles are ultimately made through the sweat and toil of the people, and if they are overused, I fear that it will impact on the virtue of frugality. In ancient times, when Jingzhong of Chen drank the wine of Lord Huan, he refused the Lord's order to light [the lantern] and continue [drinking], saying: 'your servant has divined about this day but not about this night.'[9] Humbly I submit that from now on banquets or other amicable rituals are held during the day; for rituals of leaving or returning, the time of the court audiences can be used." The king agreed.

Khitan dispatched Acting Junior Vice-director of the Department of Ministries Xiao Xi to announce the passing of the empress dowager. The king received him with black hat and coarse clothing.

Summer, fourth month. The king additionally made Ch'oe Ch'ung Royal Secretary and ordered him to retire. He bestowed as presents robes, a belt, silver utensils, silk, cloth, and a saddle.

Imja [12th] day. There was an earthquake.

The Eastern Jurchen General "Mollified from Afar" Taro and others came to present horses.

The Ministry of Rites petitioned: "Prostrate, we received the ruling saying 'when the king attires for official ceremonies, it should be red or yellow. As for the other colors that can be worn, investigate the former statutes and report.' Now according to laws, calendars, and treatises, yellow is the color of the center, and hence the color of the ruler. According to the *History of the Tang*, 'The son of heaven wears ochre, and hence forbade officials from wearing the three types of yellow for their robes.' It is also said 'The dark-red robes are worn for court audiences on the first day of the month.' The *Ritual Code of the Kaiyuan era* say 'when the emperor prays at the altar of heaven he wears the dark-red robes.' An old history states: 'if it is dyed

---

9 From the *Zuo Commentary on the Spring and Autumn*; see Durrant, Li, and Schaberg, *Zuo Tradition*, Vol. 1, 193.

once it is called bright red,' adding a note that *kang* 絳 means purple or red. Yet the robes of emperors and kings when attending ceremonies are either yellow, ochre, or red. For banquets or minor audiences the ruler can choose what is comfortable. Thus apart from the red and yellow that your majesty is wearing now, no other colors are allowed."

Fifth month. The king decreed that Vice-minister of the Ministry of Works Yu Kyu's son Yu Chunggyŏng should be granted a rank and office through protected appointment.

Director of the Chancellery Yi Chayŏn and others protested, saying "The mother of Yu Chunggyŏng was born from the adulterous relationship between Executive Chief of the Chancellery Yi Kong and a daughter of his older brother. He is not fit to stand amongst the ranks of officials."

Executive Chief of the Chancellery Kim Wŏnjŏng and others argued "This is Yi Kong's crime, not something that either Yu Chunggyŏng or his father have committed. Moreover they are the descendants of merit subject Yu Kŭmp'il, so it is not appropriate to block their path to officialdom. I request that following precedent you bestow a protected appointment on him." The king followed what Kim Wŏnjŏng and others argued for.

Yi Chayŏn again spoke up: "Kang Sahu took the civil service examination ten times yet failed to pass; relying on the pardon of the *kabo* year [1054], he was allowed to wear the official robes for the first time. Yet Kang Sahu is the great-grandson of the Gentleman-Confucian Hall Usher Kang Sanggwi. 'Hall usher' is an office belonging to the express couriers.[10] In a decree of the *Muja* year [1048] it is specified that 'the sons and grandsons of lightning clerks, locators, dinner servants, curtain attendants, express couriers, and gate attendants[11] who have taken and passed the civil service examination, classics examination, law test, calligraphy test, accounting test, medicine test, divination test, and geomancy test, or have established great merit in military affairs, are allowed to enter the ranks of officialdom.' Furthermore,

---

10 These are tentative translations of low-ranking offices that receive little exposure in the sources. The original terms are *tang'in* 堂引: hall usher, *kusa* 驅史: express courier.

11 *Chŏlli* 電吏, *soyu* 所由, *chusŏn* 注膳, *maksa* 幕士, *kusa* 驅史, *munbok* 門僕: tentative translations of various non-ranking clerical offices belonging to various departments.

according to a special decree of the *pyŏngsin* year [1056], 'those sons and grandsons of the above-mentioned people who have become official through special grace, will be given office similar to the official career of their father or grandfather.' Hence Kang Sahu should not become an official."[12]

Assistant Executive in Political Affairs Kim Hyŏn and others argued "Although the office of Kang Sahu's great-grandfather Kang Sanggwi was [merely] hall usher, he was also gentleman-Confucian. His father Kang Sŏ also took the examination ten times and eventually entered officialdom. The ten years of arduous study in dire circumstances by Kang Sahu should also be taken into consideration. Prostrate, we hope that he will be allowed to enter officialdom." The king sided with Yi Chayŏn's arguments.

The Eastern Jurchen General "Seeking Recourse in Virtue" Sanggon and others, thirty-three people altogether, came to present horses. The king bestowed on them robes and utensils according to rank.

Because of the drought, those imprisoned for light offenses were released.

Sixth month. Khitan dispatched Supreme General of the Left Palace Guard Xiao Kan to give goods bequeathed by the Dowager Empress.

The Chancellery petitioned: "Your majesty decreed that 'since the observations of the signs for wind, clouds, floods, and droughts made by Astronomical Observer Yi Sinhwang are always correct, he should be given the eighth rank straight away [skipping the ninth].' We do not know anything about Yi Sinhwang's origins, moreover when he first came to court his conduct led to several complaints. Furthermore, to observe and investigate [the heavenly signs] is his job, so it is not appropriate to skip one rank."

The king decreed "Nobody is as proficient in his work as Yi Sinhwang, so my earlier decree should be honored."

The Eastern Jurchen *chŏngjo* Pundae and others, twenty-three people,

---

12 The reasoning of the first edict quoted should be sufficiently clear; for the second one, Yi Chayŏn appears to be saying that in those precedents the descendants obtained office as a special favor of the king, not automatically because of their forebear's office. At first I thought that Kang Sahu's case was brought up in connection with Yu Chungggyŏng, but this appears to be simply another case.

came to present local products. The king bestowed on them presents according to rank.

Autumn, seventh month. The Chancellery petitioned: "Now that the agricultural land and woodland belonging to Kyŏngch'ang-wŏn has been transferred to Hŭngwang-sa, its fishermen, boat people, and slaves have all been returned to officialdom. Now regarding Kyŏngch'ang-wŏn, it emerged out of previous kings' concern to provide for their progeny by donating fields and cultivators, to be passed on through the generations so that nobody would be lacking. Now the royal family has become ever more expansive, if everyone would be given a palace estate there would not be enough. And then to take an existing palace estate and attach it to a Buddhist temple! We request that that the fields and cultivators, fishermen and boat people all be restituted."

The king decreed "The fields and woodlands have already been donated to the Three Jewels, so it is difficult for them to be returned. The same amount of public land should be given [to the palace estate] and for the rest it should be done as you propose."[13]

A decree read: "For several years now there has been either too much rainfall or too little, and there have been several disasters. This is all due to the fact that punishments have been made in error, and mounting resentment and anger have provoked these calamities. If we want to respond to Heaven's chastisement and comfort the people, we should forgive crimes and be lenient in punishment, reflect on ourselves and cultivate virtue. Among civil and military officials, specialized offices, and functionaries of the two capitals, if there are those who have been demoted or expelled; and among leading civil and military functionaries of the various prefectures and garrisons, if there are those who are guilty, have their superiors investigate the gravity of their misdemeanor and reinstate them [in case the misdemeanor was light]. As for those who committed crimes connected with flattery or treason, and repeated offenders of private crimes, they are excluded from this revision. Those official crimes with punishment lower

---

13 I.e., the slaves, fishers and boat people should be attached to the newly donated public land.

than labor, and private crimes with punishment lower than caning, should be pardoned."

Eighth month. The Song merchant Huang Wenjing and others came to present local products.

The king wished to cut trees in T'amna and Yŏngam in order to build big ships that could travel to Song China. The Department of the Royal Secretary protested saying "The country has established cordial relations with the northern dynasty, and the border is now secure and the people enjoy their lives; this is the utmost way of protecting the country. Formerly in the *kyŏngsul* year [1010], Khitan sent a letter of reprobation saying 'in the east you associated with the Jurchen, and in the west you had exchanges with the Song, so what are you planning on?' Furthermore, when Vice-minister Yu Ch'am went there as envoy, the resident governor of the Eastern Capital asked him about the fact that we exchange envoys with the southern dynasty, which suggests that he had suspicions. If something like this leaks out, it would lead to discord. Moreover, the territory of T'amna is small and the people poor, they merely rely on trading marine products by shipping it on rafts for their livelihood. Last fall, trees were cut and transported across the sea for the construction of a new temple, which caused much hardship. Now cutting more trees would increase their hardship and might lead to revolts. Moreover our country is already replete with cultural goods, rites, and music, and merchant ships frequent us, bringing precious goods on a daily basis. In truth there is nothing that we can obtain from China, Unless we want to cut relations with Khitan forever, it is better not to send envoy ships to Song." The king agreed.

Ninth month. The Khitan Returning the Courtesy Envoy of the Eastern Capital, Acting Senior Policy Advisor Yelü Yanning, arrived.

Winter, tenth month. The king bestowed clothing on the soldiers stationed at the border in the Eastern Circuit.

Twelfth month. Khitan dispatched the Prefect of Yanzhou, Guo Zaigui, to congratulate the king on his birthday.

The Eastern Jurchen General "Embraced by Koryŏ" Idonghwa and others, twenty-six people in all, came to present local products. Each of them was raised in rank and granted presents commensurate with rank.

Intercalary [twelfth] month. The Eastern Jurchen General "Pacifying the Border" Kododal and others, fifty people in all, came to present horses.

On the *pyŏngsin* day, the last day of the month, there was a solar eclipse.

Munjong Thirteenth year [1059]

Fourth year of the Jiayou year of Song, fifth year of the Qingning era of Khitan

Spring, first year. The king feasted all princes and state councilors until late at night, and granted each a horse from the royal stables.

The Eastern Jurchen *chŏngwi* Morŏgŭm and others, fifty-three people, came to present horses.

Second month. The Ministry of Taxation petitioned: "Kyŏnju within Yangju circuit established a town office already 105 years ago, but after successive floods and droughts fertile and barren fields are no longer equally distributed. Please dispatch a commissioner to re-equalize the fields." The king decreed his permission.[14]

The Eastern Jurchen *chŏngbo* Osa and others, twenty people in all, came to present horses. General "Pacifying the Borders" Kŏdabul came to present local products.

The king dispatched as memorial envoy the Assistant Office Chief at the Ministry of Works Ch'oe Sŏkchin to Khitan.

Yang Sillin and sixteen others passed the composition test of the civil service examination], four passed the classics examination passers, and four passed by royal favor.

Third month. The king ordered officials to drill the palace guards.

---

14 The system of local administration of Koryŏ is still poorly understood. The passage suggests that the establishment of a town office—the text has *ŭp* 邑, which I interpret entails the establishing of an *ŭpsa* 邑司, the local administrative office, staffed by the local elites—also entailed the redistribution of land for taxation purposes. This happened in 954, apparently, but is not attested in the entries for that year.

The Military Commissioner for the Northeastern circuit petitioned: "In Anbuk protectorate and Kuju, T'aeji, Yŏngju, and Wiju, for the counties that border on the sea, the land was allotted to people a long time ago, leading to an unequal spread of fertile and barren land. Please dispatch a commissioner to equalize the distribution." The king agreed.

Summer, fourth month. The king personally sacrificed at the Ancestral Shrine and declared a pardon.

Fifth month. Thieves entered the tomb chamber of Hyŏn-nŭng. The Supreme General of the tomb guards, Ŭnjŏng, and others were punished by imprisonment.

The king decreed that the woodland of officials of the two capitals should not go beyond the Masu Pass.[15] Signs forbidding this were to be erected, and offenders to be painfully punished.

Autumn, eighth month. The merchants Huang Wenjing and Xiao Zongming from Quanzhou in Song, and the physician Jiang Chaodong, were about to return when the king decreed that three people including Xiao Zongming and Jiang Chaodong were allowed to remain.

The king gave a banquet for the Vice-minister of the Department of Works, Hong Kae, and Supreme General Ha Hŭnghyu, who were over eighty, at the Office for Audience Ceremonies. The king personally offered the flower wine and feasted with them the whole day, and then he bestowed robes. Furthermore the king also gave a banquet for the elderly, those seriously and terminally ill, filial sons and daughters, chaste wives and righteous husbands, 1,280 people altogether, in the galleries of the polo court. On the same day similar banquets were also given in the Western Capital and all prefectural seats.

The Song merchant Fu Nan and others came to offer local products.

The king decreed that in the two capitals as well as the prefectures and counties of the southeast, those families with three sons were allowed to have one son aged fifteen to take the tonsure and become a monk.

---

15 Masu-ryŏng 馬樹嶺: a pass in South Hamgyŏng Province. Also known as Masik-nyŏng 馬息嶺 after Yi Sŏnggye rested his horse there.

Ninth month. The Khitan Returning the Courtesy Envoy of the Eastern Capital, Acting Senior Policy Advisor Yelü Yanning, arrived.

The king bestowed winter clothing on the soldiers stationed along the northeastern border.

Winter, tenth month. Soldiers of various royal guards were drilled on the eastern outskirts of the city.

The Khitan Duoyuyi and one other person came to submit.

Eleventh month. The Eastern Jurchen General "Seeking Refuge in Virtue" Moha and others, forty-seven people, came to present horses.

Twelfth month. On the *sinyu* day, the first day of the month, there was a solar eclipse.

Khitan dispatched Acting Minister of Education Yelü De to congratulate the king on his birthday.

Munjong Fourteenth year [1060]

Fifth year of the Jiayou year of Song, sixth year of the Qingning era of Khitan

Spring, second month. The king went to Changwŏn Pavilion.

Third month. The Department of the Royal Secretariat-Chancellery petitioned: "Now Director of the Court of Royal Entertainment Ch'oe Yubu has been appointed vice-resident governor of the Western Capital. His father Ch'oe Hang through his integrity and high morals was a mainstay of the country, and to commemorate his merit previously a foundation was set up at Hyŏnhwa-sa to hold memorial services. Every year Ch'oe Yubu was sent there to offer incense. Now his younger brother Ch'oe Yŏngbu is serving as governor of Ch'ŏnan District, and his term is not yet completed. Now if Ch'oe Yubu also leaves [the capital] to serve as [vice] governor of [the Western] Capital, we are deeply concerned that during the sacrificial rites at the tomb no one will be present. We request that Ch'oe Yubu be given a rank three appointment and is not made to serve outside the capital." The king agreed.

Autumn, seventh month. The Song merchant Huang Zhu and others, thirty-six people, came to offer local products.

Tsushima returned our castaways.

Eighth month. Because the monsoon rains did not stop, criminal cases were reinvestigated.

The Song merchant Xu Yi and others, eighty-eight people, came to present local products.

Ninth month. The Eastern Jurchen General "Embraced by Koryŏ" Arin and others, nineteen people, came to present local products.

Because the Song presented scholar Lu Yan had literary talent, he was appointed Editor of the Palace Library.

I Yuch'ung was appointed Commissioner of the Security Council.

Winter, eleventh month. The Khitan Gift Transmitting Envoy,[16] the Royal Inspector for the jurisdiction of Gaozhou Xiao Ao, arrived.

The Eastern Jurchen Grand General "Seeking Refuge in Virtue" Agaju and others, thirty-seven people, came to present local products.

Twelfth month. Khitan dispatched the Imperial Inspector for the Jurisdiction of Yongzhou Yelü Lie to congratulate the king on his birthday.

The Department of the Royal Secretariat-Chancellery caught fire, and it spread to the southeastern corridors of the Hoegyŏng Hall.

Munjong Fifteenth year [1061]

Sixth year of the Jiayou year of Song, seventh year of the Qingning era of Khitan

Spring, first month. The Appeasing and Investigating Commissioner for P'aesŏ Province, Han Chŏng'ik, petitioned: "Yongch'ŏn station within my jurisdiction was previously afflicted by floods, and both the offices and people's houses were washed away. Only now have they moved back and reconstructed the offices and houses, but the people's energy has been

16 Sŏnsasa 宣賜使: Literally, "Envoy to announce what is bestowed." Due to a lack of context it is not possible to construe its function.

depleted. We request the reduction of this year's and next year's land rents and taxes." The king agreed.

Second month. The Royal Inspector of the Western Seaboard petitioned: "Hwangju and Pongju last year suffered from floods, which destroyed the fields. The people residing there are suffering from hunger, so we request that the Righteous Granaries be opened to provide relief." The king agreed.

Im Chong'il was appointed Vice-director of the Department of Ministries and Commissioner of the Security Council.

Because Ch'angnyŏng and eight other prefectures within the jurisdiction of Milsŏng last year suffered from flash floods that damaged the crops, this year's summer taxes were reduced.

The king decreed: "If the king's rule prioritizes punishment, when it is applied strictly the people will suffer, but if it is applied leniently they will become indolent. If punishment is evenhanded [however], yin and yang will be in harmony and wind and rain will be in due measure. If the law loses its sense of proportion, feelings of resentment will accumulate and produce disasters. There will always be cruel ministers and callous functionaries in this world. We always strive to pursue further training, and take utmost caution in applying precedent in punishing, yet every time I am worried that officials or functionaries will be callous and partial. Henceforth the functionaries of the Ministry of Punishments should be carefully selected and commissioned, so that there are no longer any wrongful punishments."

Third month. Na Kyeham and nineteen others passed the civil service examination, and two people passed the classics examination.

Summer, fourth month. The Khitan Returning the Courtesy Envoy from the Eastern Capital, Vice-minister at the Ministry of Works Xiao Shuosi, arrived.

Sixth month. The king went to Pong'ŭn-sa and after that to the National Academy. He told his attendant officials: "Confucius is the teacher of all kings, how can I not pay my respects?" and bowed twice.

The name of the Department of Royal Secretariat-Chancellery was changed from Naesa Munha-sŏng 內史門下省 to Chungsŏ Munha-sŏng

中書門下省.

The Song presented scholar Chen Wei was appointed Editor at the Palace Library, Xiao Ding and Xiao Qian were made Recipients of Edicts before the Gates and Ye Sheng Recipient of Edicts before the Throne. Chen Wei was talented in letters, and the other three were good in tones and rhyme.

Autumn, eighth month. The Military Commissioner for the Eastern Circuit petitioned: "The Sub-colonel Kyŏngbo of Chŏngju at the head of more than twenty soldiers was scouting for bandits when he suddenly ran into the bandit chief Ahabi and more than 200 bandits. He fought them and defeated them, killing more than ten. We request that he be rewarded for his merit." The king agreed.

The Song merchant Guo Man and others came to present local products.

Ninth month. Officials petitioned: "Last year floods damaged crops, and now people in the capital are suffering from hunger. Please open the granaries to relieve them." The king agreed.

The Capital Military Command petitioned: "The bandit leader Arabul and others have raided the border, kidnapping people. Recording Officer for the Military Commissioner at P'yŏngno Garrison Kang Yŏng and Recording Officer for the Military Commissioner of the Northwestern Circuit Ko Kyŏng'in leading their troops pursued them to Hangma Garrison[17] and defeated them, executing several tens of them and obtaining many weapons. It would be fitting to manifest reward." The king agreed.

Im Chong'il was made Assistant Executive in Political Affairs, and Wang Musung was put in charge of the Security Council.

Winter, tenth month. Han Kongsŏ was made Acting Minister of Works and probationary Vice-director of the Department of Ministries.

Eleventh month. Ch'oe Yusŏn was made Assistant Executive in Political Affairs, and was also provisionally put in charge of the Hallim Academy.

Twelfth month. Khitan dispatched Acting Grand Mentor Xiao Shu to congratulate the king on his birthday.

---

17 Hangma-jin 降魔鎭: Literally, devil-subduing garrison, a term that is often associated with monastic troops, particularly of the Jurchen.

Wang Ch'ongji was made Director of the Chancellery and also appointed to take charge of the Ministry of Personnel; Kim Wŏnjŏng was made Executive of the Chancellery and concurrently of the Department of Royal Secretariat-Chancellery; Ch'oe Yusŏn was made Executive of the Department of Royal Secretariat and concurrently of the Department of Royal Secretariat-Chancellery, and provisionally put in charge of the Ministry of Personnel; I Yuch'ung was made Assistant Executive in Political Affairs; Kim Wŏnhwang Commissioner of the Security Council; Kim Ŭijin Senior Policy Advisor and concurrently manager of the Security Council; and Kim Yangji was appointed Censor-in-chief.

Xiao Zongming, originally from Song, was provisionally made Audience Usher.

Munjong Sixteenth year [1062]

Seventh year of the Jiayou era of Song, eighth year of the Qingning era of Khitan

Spring, first month. The Liao Returning the Courtesy Envoy from the Eastern Capital, Acting Junior Vice-director of the Department of Ministries Yelü Zhang arrived.

Kim Wŏnjŏng was barred from leaving for the Western Capital as its resident governor. Before the king had made him manage affairs at the Western Capital from afar, but in his reports he went against the king's instructions.

Second month. The king's son Wang To was invested as Acting Director of the Department of Ministries, Probationary Minister of Education, and Marquis of Chosŏn.

Koyŏp and others from T'amna came to present local products.

A decree read: "As for the administration of punishment, the life of the people depends on it. Wise kings of old regarded punishment only from the viewpoint of compassion. Trying to learn from old examples, I was fastidious in the selection of judiciary staff, yet still fear that I did not select the right people and that injustices will take place. Henceforth at least three people should be present before interrogation of the prisoner can take place. This should be the established procedure."

Third month. Supervisor of Education Hwang Hangji had examined the students at the National Academy, but in assessing the grades was very partial. At the time this provoked fierce discussion, so the king ordered Drafting Advisor of the Royal Secretariat Chŏng Yusan to reexamine them. Chŏng Yusan requested that the method of sealed envelopes[18] be used. Using sealed envelopes at examination places started from this.

Summer, fifth month. Crimson weeds were growing in the courtyard of the Chunggwang Hall, so the king ordered officials in charge of composition to compose prose poems and poems [on this topic].

Sixth month. The Eastern Jurchen General "Seeking Refuge in Virtue" Pundae and others came to court.

Autumn, seventh month. The Eastern Jurchen Monae and others came to court.

Eighth month The Eastern Jurchen Nŭgŏ, Ŭru, and Monae came to court.

The king went to Hŭngwang-sa and decreed: "This project has brought together our best resources for a long time, and now the construction is about to be completed. Now that I am personally able to observe the merit that went into this, I wish to extend several special recompenses. All the heavy punishments of the capital and beyond will be commuted to banishment. For public crimes punished with labor or lighter, and for private crimes punished with caning or lower, these will all be pardoned. For the functionaries in charge of corvée labor, ranks and rewards should be granted."

Winter, tenth month. The star-leader of T'amna, Koil, came to present local products.

The Eastern Jurchen Grand General "Seeking Refuge in Virtue" Marihae and Agaju came to court.

---

18 *Pongmibŏp* 封彌法: presumably so that the answer sheets could not be tampered with after the candidate had composed the answers.

Twelfth month. Khitan dispatched the Imperial Inspector for the Taizhou jurisdiction, Gao Shouzheng, to offer congratulations on the king's birthday.

Munjong Seventeenth year [1063]

Eighth year of the Jiayou era of Song, ninth year of the Qingning era of Khitan

Spring, first year. The king feasted his officials in the Kŏndŏk Hall and bestowed silk according to rank.

Second month. The Eastern Jurchen General "Seeking Refuge in Virtue" Hoehwa and Sanggon[19] came to present horses.

Third month. Khitan sent the Great Collection of Buddhist Scriptures; the king prepared a dharma carriage to welcome it in the western suburbs.

The star-leader of T'amna, Turyang, came to court. The king especially conferred on him the title of General "Bright Authority."

Summer, fourth month. The king conferred on the heir apparent the nine classics from the Palace Library as well as histories, biographies, and treatises of various schools.

Fifth month. Hong Ki and twenty-nine others passed the civil service examination, one person passed the classics test, and five were passed by royal favor.

Autumn, seventh month. Kim Wŏnjŏng was appointed Probationary Grand Marshal and Director of the Chancellery, and subsequently passed away.

Eighth month. A decree read: "Recently many students at the National Academy are neglecting their studies, and the instruction does not reach them. The blame for this rests with the academic officials. Henceforth they should dedicate themselves to the encouragement of study. By the end of the year the good and the bad shall be separated, and hence who can stay and who should leave. Those among the Confucian scholars who have

---

19 *Hoehwa sanggon* 懷化霜昆: since the first part is normally used for the title General "Embraced by Koryŏ," I suspect this passage may have been garbled.

been there nine years, and the law scholars who have been there six years, if they are still ignorant and without accomplishment, they should all be dismissed."

Ninth month. A decree read: "This year the rainfall was insufficient, so we cannot count on the fall harvest. Instruct all the prefectures to prepare for relief activities.

The Song merchant Guo Man and others came to offer local products.

Pak Sŏnggŏl was promoted to probationary Grand Marshal and Director of the Chancellery; Im Chong'il was made Executive Chief of the Department of Royal Secretariat and Pillar of State, and then retired.

Winter, tenth month. The Song merchant Lin Ning and others came to present local products.

The king went to Changwŏn Pavilion.

Eleventh month. Khitan dispatched the Prefect of Yizhou, Xiao Ge, as envoy.

The Eastern Jurchen General "Seeking Refuge in Virtue" Marihae and others came to court.

Twelfth month. Khitan dispatched Junior Policy Critic Li Risu to congratulate the king on his birthday.

Munjong Eighteenth year [1064]

First year of the Zhiping era of Yingzong of Song, tenth year of the Qingning era of Khitan

Spring, first month. The military commissioner for the Northwestern circuit petitioned: "Recently in the *Imin* year [1062] in Maengp'o, village bandits were planning to invade our border and enter P'yŏngno Garrison. The tribesman chief Che Chunna came to warn the garrison commander about this, so we hid our troops under cover of the grass and reeds and waited for them. The bandits indeed showed up, and our troops collectively attacked them, taking prisoner or killing a great many. We request that Che Chunna be rewarded with gold and silk." The king followed this.

Second month. A decree read: "For the spring and autumn sacrifices to the mountains outside the capital commissioners are appointed to more than ten provinces, but the appointment process is cumbersome and the roads and stations are not in a good state. Order the commissioners for supervising granaries in the Northern and Eastern Border Circuits, and the royal inspector for P'aesŏ Province take on the role of officiant in the mountain sacrifices. As for the provinces south of the mountain, as before dispatch commissioners. This is to become a regular procedure."

One-hundred-and-seven ships from the Yesŏng River were sent six times a year to transport grain from Yongmun Granary to Inju, Yongju, Ch'ŏlchu, Sŏnju, and Kwakchu as well as Wiwŏn Garrison to stock up military grain rations.

Third month. A decree read: "Last year excessive rains caused floods and damaged the autumn crops. I am worried about the ordinary people who urgently need relief. Order Chamberlain of the Royal Stud Min Ch'angsu to organize from this month to the fifth month a food bank to the south of Kaeguk-sa to give to poor people."

A Humane Kings Assembly was held in the Hoegyŏng Hall for three days, and 10,000 monks were fed on the polo court.

Summer, fourth month. The king ruled that since the public land provided for Taeun-sa, constructed first by the previous king to provide blessings for the country, was small and the tax income low, it was insufficient to provide for the Buddhist services, so additionally 100 *kyŏng* of good quality land was to be bestowed.

Because of the continuing drought, markets were moved and the use of parasols and fans forbidden.

The king ruled that from the fifteenth of the fifth month to the fifteenth of the seventh month a porridge and vegetable [stall] was to be organized in Pot'ong-wŏn on the Imjin River for people on the road.

Fifth month. The king gave a banquet for the Western Jurchen general "Pacified from Afar" Kojiji and others, thirteen people altogether, at the Foreign Relations Office, and gave the customary presents.

Intercalary [fifth] month. The Eastern Jurchen bandit leader Mach'igae and others, more than 100 people, crossed the sea in ships and raided Namp'o in P'yŏnghae Prefecture, burning people's houses and kidnapping nine people. Because the border-guarding functionaries failed to pursue and apprehend them, they were punished.

The Ministry of War petitioned: "It has been a long time since the registers for military families have been compiled. Many are damaged because of insects or rot, and as a result the size of the military is not clear. We request that new registers be made following the old method." The king agreed.

Sixth month. The commissioner for the palace walls petitioned: "Please dismiss those among the palace guards who do not wear purple robes or do not have weapons." The king agreed.

Autumn, seventh month. Because Hwanga County in the Northeastern circuit had been invaded numerous times by Eastern Tribesman pirates, it was moved to Yangch'on.

The Song merchant Chen Gong and others came to present local products.

Eighth month. The Song merchant Lin Ning and others arrived, presenting precious treasures.

One thousand cotton-padded jackets and trousers, and one thousand fur hats were given to the poorest soldiers guarding the northwestern border.

Winter, tenth month. Khitan dispatched the acting Junior Policy Advisor Yelü Dou to announce that the king would receive an investiture.

Eleventh month. The Ministry of Taxation petitioned: "Kwangju experienced a long drought, stretching from winter to autumn, but repeatedly suffered from hail so that in the end nothing could be harvested. As for Pongju, in the *kyŏngja* year [1060] a great flood destroyed houses and crops, so that most of the people do not have a place to live. We request that for both jurisdictions the dispatch of commissioners to measure the land be halted." The king agreed.

Twelfth month. Khitan dispatched Chamberlain for the National Treasury Hu Zhong to congratulate the king on his birthday.

The Khitan Gaonu and others, three people, and the Black Water [Malgal]

Baoqi and others, eight people, came to submit.

The king ordered that padded jackets and trousers, fur hats, and shoes be taken from the Storage of Battle Dresses and given to the poorest soldiers on the border.

Munjong Nineteenth year [1065]

Second year of the Zhiping era of Song, first year of the Xianyong era of Khitan

Spring, first month. The Eastern Jurchen Ijidal and others, sixteen people altogether, came to present horses.

Second month. The Eastern Jurchen leader Sanggon and others, twenty-two people in all, came to present local products; General Abuhan and others, twenty-six people, came to present horses.

The king invested his son Wang Hŭi as Probationary Minister of Works, cum Director of the Department of Ministries, Marquis of Kyerim.

Summer, fourth month. Khitan dispatched the Ningyan Army Military Governor Yelü Ning and the Imperial Inspector for the Yizhou jurisdiction Ding Wentong to invest the king as Merit Subject with the title "Guarding the Just and Protecting Righteousness," with a stipend village of 3,000 households, including 300 effective. They also conferred on him the nine-tasseled crown and the nine-pattern robes,[20] a jade mace, jade book, ivory cart, a set of robes, silk, bow and arrows, saddle, and other presents. The king received the investiture in the southern suburbs. They also dispatched the Imperial Inspector for the Lizhou jurisdiction Yelü Di and Director of the Office of Imperial Regalia Ma Anru to invest the heir apparent as conjoint Director of the Chancellery and also to augment his privileges. They also conferred on him the nine-tasseled crown and the nine-pattern robes, an ivory insignia, a bamboo book, leather carriage, a set of robes, silk, saddle,

20 *Kuryugwan* 九旒冠, *kujangbok* 九章服: while the Chinese emperor was allowed to wear a crown with twelve tassels and robes with twelve types of decoration, a liege of the emperor was only allowed nine.

bow and arrow, wine, and other presents. The heir apparent received the investiture in the southern suburbs.

Sixth month. The king went to Mundŏk Hall to re-examine the presented scholars. Attendant censor No Tan reported on this in a way that went against the royal purport. The king was enraged and ordered people to drag him away; after removing his robes, he was about to be tied up. Then Executive Ch'oe Yusŏn stepped up and addressed the king: "If an official has committed a crime, he should be handed over to the Judicial Commission." The king's anger then somewhat abated, but eventually the examination was called off, and only those who had taken the examination ten times or more without passing were selected. Yi Wŏnjang and others, five in total, were selected by royal grace and appointed to their first office. Two people were also selected from the classics examination. The next day No Tan was demoted to assistant office chief in the Slave Agency.

The Eastern Jurchen General "Embraced by Koryŏ" Ingwi and others, seventeen people, came to present horses.

Autumn, seventh month. The king went to the dragon boat on the Eastern Pond and entertained the heir apparent and the royal kin group; the banquet lasted till deep in the night.

Eighth month. The king dispatched Junior Vice-director of the Department of Ministries Kim Yangji and Deputy Director of the Office for Royal Clan Affairs Sŏ Chŏng to Khitan to express gratitude for the edict of investiture.

Ninth month. The Song merchants Guo Man, Huang Zong, and others came to present local products.

The king dispatched Vice-minister of the Ministry of Rites Ch'oe Sang and Vice-director of the Bureau for Maintenance and Construction Kim Sŏngjŏm to Khitan to express gratitude for the edict of investiture for the heir apparent.

Winter, twelfth month. Khitan dispatched Senior Policy Critic Fu Ping to congratulate the king on his birthday.

Munjong Twentieth year [1066]

Third year of the Zhiping era of Song, second year of the Xianyong era of Liao

Spring, first month. A decree read: "Henceforth but for no longer than three years, it is forbidden throughout the country to slaughter animals."

Second month. The Finance Commission petitioned: "Already four years have passed since the death of Director of the Chancellery Kim Wŏnjŏng, but any statement of condolence is still lacking. We request that a bereavement donation be made." The king decreed that 130 *sŏk* of grains be bestowed [on his family].

Unhŭng Granary burnt down. A decree read "At the Unhŭng Granary fire the officials in charge neglected to protect it. Thus what has been accumulated in the course of years was lost in one night's disaster. How painful is this! Henceforth all granaries and other storage facilities should be patrolled by fire wardens. The Censorate should regularly inspect them, and if there is someone who is not on his post that day, regardless of his rank he shall first be imprisoned and then reported to me."

Third month, *chŏngch'uk* [23rd] day. A star appeared in the northwestern sky that was as big as the moon; suddenly it changed into a comet.

The resident governor of the Eastern Capital of Khitan reported that their country's name was again "Great Liao."

Summer, fourth month, *kyŏngin* [7th] day. An earthquake hit the capital.

The king decreed that close officials would act as special commissioners for the Left and Right Granaries of the capital as well as the Yongmun and Unhŭng Granaries.

Ko Chungsin and thirteen others passed the composition test of the civil service examinations and two people passed the classics examination.

A decree read: "The *Book of Documents* says 'Eating should only be done when it is time.' When one man does not till the earth, there will certainly one who goes hungry. As for the office of prefect, agriculture is the most urgent task. All the senior locally posted officials should take with them commissioners for encouraging agriculture."

Director of the Court of Royal Entertainment Ko Pokch'ang was dispatched to Liao to offer congratulations on changing the name of the country.

Autumn, seventh month. An edict read: "The seventh month is the time when all the crops ripen, but the effect of the remaining Yang energy is still strong, and the drought still severe. This must have been caused by an unjust sentence that has brought punishment to the innocent. We have been pondering this day and night, yet have not found peace. All the officials, be it at the center or in the countryside should investigate sentence records and inspect prisons to make sure there are no innocent people there or exaggerated sentences."

The king decreed "Regarding those among the officials who have caused people to die of fright when putting those returning to the countryside in the registers of commoners, in their case the death sentence would be an injustice and should therefore be removed [as punishment]."[21]

Winter, eleventh month. The Liao informal envoy, the Guizhou prefect Yelü Jia, arrived.

Twelfth month. Liao dispatched Director of the Court for Imperial Entertainment Wang Quhuo to congratulate the king on his birthday.

Munjong Twenty-first year [1067]

Fourth year of the Zhiping era of Song, third year of the Xianyong era of Liao

Spring, first month. Hŭngwang-sa was completed. It measured 2,800 bays and took twelve years to complete. The king wanted to hold a maigre feast to celebrate the completion, and gathered monks from all over the country. He ordered them to select 1,000 monks who upheld the precepts and send them to the ceremony, and then ordered them to reside permanently in the temple. A special Grand Lantern Festival was held that lasted five days and

---

21 What exactly is meant with this decree is not clear. Especially who "those who returned to the countryside" (*kwihyangja* 歸鄕者) refers to, and why this was an issue, is not clear. "Causing people to die of fright" (*inoegu chisa* 因畏懼致死) is an equally baffling phrase.

nights. Then he ordered all officials together with Ansŏ Military Command, the five prefectures of Kwangju, Suju, Yangju, Tongju and Suju, and the two counties of Kanghwa and Changsŏ to make colored ribbons and garlands that should be hung from the palace courtyard to the gates of the temple, closely connected like the scales of a fish. On both sides of the road taken by the royal carriage lamps and torches lighted the way as if it was day. For this day the king prepared escorts for his carriage, and led the officials in offering incense and donating wealth and clothes to the Buddha. A Buddhist event of such lavishness had never been seen before.

The king went to Ch'ang-nŭng and granted his servant officials one rank title each, and bestowed presents on the guards according to rank.

Intercalary [first] month. The Eastern Jurchen General "Embraced by Koryŏ" Ingwi and others, twenty-two people altogether, came to present local products.

Second month. On account of the completion of Hŭngwang-sa an amnesty was declared.

The king decreed that henceforth the prefectures and counties no longer had to send dried fish as tribute.

Third month. Wang Ch'ongji, who retired as Royal Secretary, died.

The king decreed: "The deceased Directors of the Chancellery Ch'oe Hang and Kang Kamch'an, and Assistant Executive in Political Affairs Kim Maeng, were all upright and loyal officials who established their merit in assisting successive kings in their rule. The fact that all around the people live in peace and good health is thanks to the influence of these gentlemen. Therefore Ch'oe Hang and Kang Kamch'an shall be posthumously made probationary Grand Preceptor cum Royal Secretary, and Kim Maeng Grand Preceptor to the Heir Apparent and Director of the Chancellery."

The king went to Changwŏn pavilion.

The king decreed that 49,400 *sŏk* of grains should be transported to the northern prefectures to be distributed to people in the border region.

Summer, fourth month. Because there was famine in Kwannae and P'aesŏ provinces, Allan Granary was opened to provide relief.

Fifth month. The king feasted the state elders in the Office for Audience Ceremonies and bestowed clothes and presents.

Sixth month. The king decreed that the annual tribute of cowhide, sinew, and horn from the various prefectures should be replaced by hemp cloth.

The king decreed that 27,690 *sŏk* of rice should be transported from Allan Granary to the north so as to replenish military provisions.

Autumn, ninth month. The king went to Song'ak Pavilion to give a banquet; he ordered the literary officials to compose poems. Chief of the Chancellery Ch'oe Yusŏn composed a poem that was both clever and sublime. [The king] gave him one horse.

State Preceptor Haerin requested to return to the mountains on account of old age. The king personally attended his goodbye dinner at Hyŏnhwa-sa and bestowed tea, medicine, gold and silver utensils, colored silk, and other treasures.

Winter, twelfth month. Liao dispatched Imperial Inspector for the Ningchuan jurisdiction Hu Ping to congratulate the king on his birthday.

Yangju was designated the Southern Capital (Namgyŏng) and the [newly appointed] resident governor and his staff resettled people there from neighboring prefectures.

Munjong Twenty-second year [1068]

First year of the Xining era of Shenzong of Song, fourth year of the Xianyong era of Liao

Spring, first month, *kapsul* [1st] day. There was a solar eclipse.

The Eastern Jurchen General "Seeking Refuge in Virtue" Sanggon and others came to court.

Ch'oe Yusŏn was appointed Minister of the Ministry of Personnel; Wang Musung was appointed Minister of the Ministry of Punishment; and Kim Ŭijin was appointed Minister of the Ministry of War.

Second month. The T'amna Star-leader, General "Seaborne Strike" Kayaing came to present local products.

The king ruled "All those without progeny who also do not have any nephews can adopt a child of less than three years rejected by others and raise him as if it was their own son. The child also gets their family name and will be recorded in the census as their heir. This is already established as law. [However], those who have their own progeny as well as nephews and still adopt a child of different surname, this is comprehensively forbidden."

Third month. The king ruled "Last years the prefectures and counties north of the capital suffered from bad harvests so there has been a lot of famine among the people. The granaries should be opened to provide relief."

Summer, fourth month. Ch'oe Sang was appointed associate manager of the Security Council.

Ch'oe In and sixteen others passed the composition test of the civil service examination, two people passed the classics examination, and one passed by royal favor

Fifth month. The king ruled: "From spring to summer, the appointed rains failed to arrive on time, and a fierce heat withered the crops on the fields. This punishment is caused by the fact that this insignificant person's virtue is insufficient. Therefore I intend to prostrate myself for this heavenly censure. Henceforth, all those who committed various crimes across the country who received punishments lower than banishment for official crimes or labor for private crimes, will be pardoned."

Sixth month. The Eastern Jurchen General "Seeking Refuge in Virtue" An'gŏ and others came to court.

The Administrative Assistant to the Military Commander for the Eastern Border Circuit, Im Hŭiyŏl, and others while patrolling Ch'o Island encountered ten pirate ships. Following a battle the pirates were defeated, and seven ships were obtained; the number of pirates killed or taken prisoner was very high. The king praised him and bestowed robes and belt on Im Hŭiyŏl and others. All those with merit were given higher reward titles.[22]

---

22 *Ka chaksang* 加爵賞: this could also mean "given augmented titles and rewards."

The king ruled that it was forbidden to adopt from the generation of one's father's brothers or their sons and grandsons.[23]

Autumn, seventh month. Huang Shen arrived from Song. Earlier, the Song emperor had summoned the Supply Commissioner-in-chief of Huainan, Jiangnan, Liangzhe, and Xinghu North and South Circuits Luo Zheng, and told him: "From old Koryŏ has been called 'a country of gentlemen.' From the generation of our founding ancestors they have diligently paid their dues. Afterwards they were blocked from doing so for a long time. Now I heard that their ruler is a sage king. People should be dispatched to instruct him." Luo Zheng then proposed to send Huang Shen and others to transmit the son-of-Heaven's will. The king was pleased and received them very generously.

The Song merchant Lin Ning and others came to present local products.

The Administrative Assistant to the Military Commander for the Eastern Border Circuit, Im Hŭiyŏl, and others again patrolled Ch'o Island by night. Reaching Yŏmna harbor they encountered eight pirate ships. Three were destroyed, and the crew of the remaining ships landed on shore and fled. They were pursued, and more than thirty were killed. The king generously granted higher reward titles.

Eighth month. The king ordered the heir apparent to summon the Song presented scholar Huang Shen and compose poems together with Chin Chamgo, Chŏ Wŏnbin and others in Okch'ok Pavilion.

Kang Wŏn'gwang was appointed censor-in-chief.

Ninth month. Ch'oe Ch'ung, who had retired as Probationary Grand Preceptor and Royal Secretary, died. He hailed from Taenyŏng Prefecture in Haeju. He was of imposing stature and demeanor, and his character was stubborn and upright. From a young age he loved to learn and was good at composition. During the reign of Mokchong he came first in the civil service examination, and served four kings in either military or civilian

23 Presumably the implication of this is that only the children of one's brothers can be adopted, not the progeny of one's father's siblings. However, I am not certain that this is the correct reading of this ruling.

capacity as needed. When he reached the age of seventy, he requested to retire, but the king several times went against his wishes. [Finally] he gave special permission, but kept consulting him on important military and state affairs. He received successive merit subject titles.[24] During the revival under Hyŏnjong the weapons had barely come to rest, but there had as yet not been any opportunity for literary education. Ch'oe Ch'ung received a royal a summons and after that embarked on a tireless project of education. The students overflowed from his house into the gates and the street, and thus he divided [his residence] into nine studies which he named Naksŏng, Taejung, Sŏngmyŏng, Kyŏngŏp, Chodo, Solsŏng, Chindŏk, Taehwa, and Taebin. They were called "The disciples of Director [of the Chancellery] Ch'oe." All those who wanted to take the civil service examination first had to become one of his disciples and study there. Every year in the summer months he borrowed a monk's room at Kwibŏp-sa for summer lectures. He selected those among his disciples who had passed the civil service examination and whose study was outstanding but who had not yet secured office as tutors. The curriculum for instruction consisted of the nine classics and three histories. Sometimes there was a senior scholar who passed by; in that case he held a poetry competition. Displaying the roster of names in sequence he called forth the names and then they entered. A small wine party was prepared; uncapped and capped students were divided in rows to the left and right. Holding their cups and plates, everybody moved up [to receive the drinks] and back with propriety, old and young in sequence. Poems were declaimed back and forth throughout the day; those who witnessed this could not suppress sighs of admiration.

When he died the king dispatched Director of Medicine Yi Yŏm with a decree of condolence bestowing the posthumous title Munhŏn 文憲. He was co-enshrined in King Chŏngjong's chamber in the Ancestral Shrine. After this the scholars applying for the examination all listed their name in the registers of one of the nine studies, and they were called the disciples

24 Since the concatenation of titles is too long to translate, I have left it out here. The full title is 推忠贊道佐理同德弘文懿儒保定康濟功臣.

of Duke Munhŏn. Besides him there were eleven Confucian scholars who established their disciples; they were thus referred to by people as the "Twelve [schools of] disciples." Among these Ch'oe Ch'ung's disciples were the most flourishing, representing the beginning of the flowering of schools in the Eastern Country. Therefore contemporaries called him the Confucius of the Eastern Country.

Winter, tenth month. The Eastern Jurchen General "Embraced by Koryŏ" Arin and others came to court.

Twelfth month. Liao dispatched the Imperial Inspector for the Yizhou jurisdiction Wei Cheng to offer congratulations on the king's birthday.

Vice-director at the Department of Ministries Wang Hyŏn three times sent a letter requesting [retirement on account of] old age; the king gave his permission.

A new palace was built in the Southern Capital.

Munjong Twenty-third year [1069]

Second year of the Xining era of Song, fifth year of the Xianyong era of Liao

Spring, first month. The Eastern Jurchen General "Embraced by Koryŏ" Saŏga came to court.

Summer, fourth month. There was a drought.

Fifth month. The king went to Changwŏn Pavilion and obtained a stone with a propitious writing. He ordered his literary officials to present songs and poems.

Sixth month. The Song merchant Yang Congsheng and others came to present local products.

Autumn, seventh month *ŭlch'uk* day, first day of the month. There was a solar eclipse.

The Song merchant Wang Ning came to present local products.

Winter, tenth month. [The king supervised] practice in shooting the silk-stringed nine-pronged catapult in the northern suburbs.[25]

---

25 See chapter 5, 10th month of 1040.

Intercalary eleventh month. The king's younger brother Wang Ki, the Duke of P'yŏngyang, died.

Twelfth month. Liao dispatched Vice Censor-in-chief Gao Song to congratulate the king on his birthday.

The Returning-the-courtesy envoy of the Eastern Capital of Liao, Acting Junior Vice-director of the Department of Ministries Yelü Jilige, arrived.

Munjong Twenty-fourth year [1070]

Third year of the Xining era of Song, sixth year of the Xianyong era of Liao

Summer, fourth month. Ch'oe Iksin and nineteen others passed the composition test of the civil service examination, two people passed by royal favor, and one person passed the classics examination.

Sixth month. Hŭngwang-sa was fortified.

Autumn, eighth month. Kim Ŭijin, who retired as Executive of the Chancellery, died.

Censor-in-chief Kang Wŏn'gwang died.

The Supply Commissioner of Hunan, Xinghu, and Liangzhe in Song, Luo Zheng, again dispatched Huang Shen.

The king ruled: "The Western Jurchen chief Hoedŏk should be given the title of General 'Upholding the country'." His father Iubul had performed meritorious deeds on the border since the time of the former king. That is why the king gave this order.

Ninth month. The king gave a banquet at Sangch'un Pavilion and ordered his close officials to compose poems. The party ended deep into the night.

Winter, eleventh month. Storages to keep charcoal and iron were established on all sides of the capital.

Twelfth month. Liao dispatched Director of the Office of Regalia He Xu to congratulate the king on his birthday.

Munjong Twenty-fifth year [1071]

Fourth year of the Xining era of Song, seventh year of the Xianyong era of Liao

Spring, first month. Kim Haenggyŏng was appointed Vice-director of the Department of Ministries and Minister of the Ministry of Punishments; Ch'oe Yubu was appointed Junior Vice-director of the Department of Ministries.

The king appointed his son Wang Su as acting Director of the Department of Ministries, Probationary Minister of Works, Marquis of P'yŏngyang; Ch'oe Yusŏn was made Probationary Minister of Education, and I Yuch'ung was made Specially Advanced Probationary Minister of Works.

Kim Haenggyŏng was made Assistant Executive in Political Affairs.

The Western Jurchen General "Embraced by Koryŏ" Punt'ae and others came to present local products.

Third month. The king dispatched Executive at the Ministry for Taxation Kim Che with a memorial to Song. Initially, Huang Shen upon his return had sent a missive to Fujian so that [Koryŏ] would be invited to present tribute with due ceremony. Thus the king dispatched Kim Che via Dengzhou to present tribute.[26]

The Eastern Jurchen General "Seeking Refuge in Virtue" Sanggon and others, twenty-two people, returned our captured people for ransom.

Summer, fourth month. The Western Jurchen chief Noudal and others, ten people in all, came to present local products. Each was granted an office title. Mahodal and others, eighteen people in total, came to present local products; he was promoted to General "Seeking Refuge in Virtue" and granted the prescribed presents.

Fifth month. Wang Musung was appointed Executive of the Royal Secretariat and also of the Chancellery, as well as Minister of the Ministry of War.

---

26 The intention of having the invitation sent via Fujian was likely that Koryŏ envoys should enter Song through a Fujian harbor; Ningbo (then called Mingzhou) in particular was a key port for embassy ships. Yet Koryŏ evidently chose to send a ship to Dengzhou on the Shandong peninsula, which was much closer to Liao territory and hence more dangerous.

The Western Jurchen Yoyŏn came to court, and he was generously granted a reward title.

The Judicial Commission petitioned: "The Registrar at the Foreign Relations Office, the Song native Zhou Hang, was hired on account of his talent for writing. Now he is guilty of accepting bribes; we request that his office land be rescinded and that he be sent back [to Song]." The king decreed his approval.

Sixth month. A decree read: "Recently it has come to our attention that many soldiers of various armies have deserted. This is due to the fact that the division of tasks is not fair. Those with wealth or power use this influence to shirk their tasks, while those who are poor have to do all the work. Moreover they lack food and clothing, and have no time to rest. Even though on numerous occasions I issued a benevolent edict that reduced their burdens, officials did not put this into effect. In recent years soldiers have started to harbor resentment and blame the king for his lack of compassion. From now on, all non-urgent corvée labor should be eliminated, and the number of soldiers used for patrolling and inspection should be cut back to half the original number. The offices they resort under or the generals that command them are not allowed to use them for their own ends. Those who go against this should be punished. Order the Ministry of War and the Special Commission for Selecting Soldiers to implement this ruling."

The saddle maker Song Yuna, since he is the great-great-grandson of the Sam Han merit subject and Grand Mentor So Kyŏktal, was given special exemption of corvée and was allowed to enter officialdom.

Autumn, eighth month. The Eastern Jurchen General "Seeking Refuge in Virtue" Kosa and others, fifteen people, came to present local products. General "Embraced by Koryŏ" Saŏga and others, twenty people, came to present horses,

The Song merchant Guo Man and others, thirty-three people, came to present local products.

Ninth month. The Song merchant Yuan Ji and others, thirty six people, and [the Song merchant] Wang Hua and others, thirty people in all, came to present local products.

Because of the "Double Nine" festival, the king went to Sangch'un Pavilion to give a banquet for the heir apparent, the Marquis of Kyerim, the Marquis of P'yŏngyang, and the state councilors I Yuch'ung and Wang Musung; each was granted one horse.

Winter, tenth month. The Song merchant Xu Man and others, sixty-one people, came to preset local products.

Eleventh month. The Western Jurchen chief Mandubul and others, leading their flock, came to submit. Each was granted a reward title according to rank.

The Western Jurchen chief Yuju and others, ten people; the Eastern Jurchen chiefs Tarogon, Sanggon, and others, fifty-eight people, came to present local products.

Probationary Minister of Education Yu Koman died.

Twelfth month. Liao dispatched Yizhou prefect Gao Yuanji to congratulate the king on his birthday.

Five-hundred *sŏk* of rice from Hyŏndŏk Palace was released to prepare food for poor people at Sŏ Pot'ong-wŏn.

Munjong Twenty-sixth year [1072]

Fifth year of the Xining era of Song, eighth year of the Xianyong era of Liao

Spring, second month. The king decreed that the Ministry of Rites should reform the system of ritual dress.

The Eastern Jurchen Maduhan and others, twenty-five people altogether, came to submit.

Third month. Kim Tŏkpu was appointed junior vice-director of the Department of Ministries.

Pak Yugak and twenty-one others passed the composition test of the civil service examination and two people passed the classics examination.

Summer, fourth month. Executive Chief of the Royal Secretariat I Yuch'ung died.

Fifth month. The Western Jurchen General "Seeking Refuge in Virtue" Masanae and others came to present local products.

Sixth month. Song dispatched medical officials Wang Yu and Xu Xian to Koryŏ.

Kim Che returned from Song. The emperor bestowed on the king robes, belt, gold brocade, silver utensils, and other presents.

Autumn, seventh month. The soldier Chang Sŏn alerted the king to an insurrection; he reported that Lieutenant Kŏsin and a party of more than 1,000 was planning to depose the king and instead enthrone his younger brother, the Duke of P'yŏngyang, Wang Ki. The king ordered their arrest. Kŏsin was executed and his whole family was exterminated. Wang Ki had already died, so his son Wang Chin was exiled to Namhae County and Wang Chŏng to Andong District. Both died soon after. The youngest son, Wang Yŏng, on account of his young age, was spared. The king promoted Chang Sŏn to general, and bestowed on his brothers, sons, and grandsons an honorary title.

Intercalary [seventh] month. Executive of the Chancellery Wang Musung was banished to Andong District, Princess Yi of the Changnyŏng Palace and the master of the Suan House of Yi were banished to Kokchu; all of them had been implicated in Kŏsin's plot.

Ch'oe Yubu was made Minister of the Ministry of Punishment.

Ninth month. The Eastern Jurchen Sanggon and others came to present horses.

Winter, eleventh month. Liao dispatched the prefect Yongzhou, Yelü Zhi, to Koryŏ,

Twelfth month. Liao dispatched Acting Grand Marshal Zhang Rihua to congratulate the king on his birthday.

The Eastern Jurchen Saŏha and others came to present local products.

Munjong Twenty-seventy year [1073]

Sixth year of the Xining era of Song, ninth year of the Xianyong era of Liao

Spring, first month, *ŭlsa* day, first day of the month. There was an earthquake.

An official petitioned: "Respectfully, according to the law statutes, families of artisans and traders use their skills to serve those above; solely versed in their craft, they cannot enter officialdom to stand on a par with scholar-officials. Registrar of military equipment Ch'oe Ch'unghaeng and Equivalent to Director of the Bureau of Beverage Supervision Yang Un have an artisan as their maternal grandfather, while Sub-colonel Narye and Sub-lieutenant Yesun have artisans as their paternal grandfather. Looking up to the ranks of scholars, they reject their vocation and have already entered the court ranks. Thus they cannot return to being artisans. I request that each will be restricted to his current office, and not be allowed to transferred or reappointed."

The king decreed: "Based on the precedent of Junior Colonel Ch'ungmaeng being restricted to Grand General, I allow them to be employed as officials."

The Department of Royal Secretariat refuted this, saying: "Ch'oe Ch'unghaeng and others do not have any great merit, they have obfuscated their descent to illegally enter the class of officials. It is not appropriate to compare with Ch'ungmaeng, who established merit on the border."

The king decreed: "Apart from essential functions or positions governing people, everything should proceed as per my previous decree."

Second month. The Eastern Jurchen commandant of a prefecture loyal to Koryŏ, Kodohwa, leading his people, requested that his place would become part of Koryŏ proper and be integrated in the system of local administration. The king bestowed on Kodohwa the name Son Posae,[27] and also conferred the title of Grand General "Embraced by Koryŏ." The others were all granted names and titles.

---

27 孫保塞: Literally, Son "Guarding the Frontiers."

The Commandant of Sŏngju, Grand General "Upholding the Country" Sodŏk and others, fourteen people, came to present horses.

Third month. The king went to Honghwa-sa, and then to Hyŏnhwa-sa, where he held a drinking party in Pongnae Pavilion. Late at night he returned.

Summer, fourth month, *kapsul* day, first day of the month. There was a solar eclipse.

The king decreed: "Tribesmen from outside the fifteen border prefectures are one after the other attaching themselves to us, wishing to establish local administrative units; even as we speak this is continuing. This is truly the numinous power of the Ancestral Shrine and the Earth and Grain Deities Shrine. First make sure that the state councilors are appraised, and then wait till all, near and far, have sincerely and wholeheartedly submitted, before determining the prefectures and counties. After that I will personally show my respects. As to the ritual of this and the heir apparent's role in the ceremonies, please discuss the details and report to me."

The king went to Kwisan-sa and held a drinking party on the Turtle Platform (Kwidae 龜臺). The heir apparent, princes, and state councilors all took part in the party. Late at night the king returned.

The military commissioner for the Northwestern circuit reported: "Outside of the Long Wall, 11,494 *kyŏng* of land has been brought into cultivation. We request to keep it until the fall harvest so as to augment military provisions." The king decreed approval.

Fifth month. The military commissioner for the northwestern sector reported: "The Western Jurchen chief Mandubul and others request that their territory receive administrative divisions like the Eastern Tribesmen. The tribesman chief General "Mollified from Afar" Korŏbu and Yogyŏl from Mihae village, both near the P'yŏngno border garrison, also want to be included in our census registers, to serve as an eternal border screen. Upon inspection, it was found that this includes thirty-five household comprising 252 people. We request that they be attached to our territory."[28] The king

28 *P'ando* 版圖: the dictionary definition of this term is "territory," but P'ando-sa is also a

approved.

The same military commissioner also requested: "The Koryŏ-allied[29] tribesman commander Taŏhae and others, because the Samsan village bandits kill and kidnap people and steal goods, teamed up with Junior Colonel Munsŏn from Chŏngju and attacked them; Because of this merit, please impart royal grace rewards."

Director of the Chancellery Ch'oe Yusŏn and others argued: "The bandits from Samsan village are originally not raiders of the border. Now the barbarian army did this to settle personal scores, not on account of our purport. If we bestow rewards, this will engender further enmity and resentment. Please do not give rewards." The king followed this advice.

Sixth month. The military commissioner for the Northeastern sector reported: "The chiefs of Samsan, Taeran, Chijŭl and other villages have come here with the request to enter their 1,238 households on our census registers. We request that officials be ordered to report on the names for the [new] prefectures, and also to bestow a sealed document." This was followed.

The military commissioner for the Eastern Circuit reported: "The tribesmen leaders of the Eastern Barbarian communities of Taeje, Chago, Hasa, and others wish to become part of our administrative system. The place where these tribes live is remote, and in the past they never came to court. Now they all want to submit. We request to wait until all the tribes outside the pass have come to request integration into our system, and after that determine the border." This was allowed.

The military commissioner reported: "Eastern Tribesmen pirates have raided P'ajam *pugok* and have kidnapped people. The military commander of Wŏnhŭng Garrison went to fight them on Ch'o Island with several tens of war ships, killing twelve and taking prisoner sixteen." The king was pleased and bestowed on the manager of military affairs, Director of the

---

term for the Ministry of Taxation, so it might also meant that they were inscribed on the tax rolls.

29 Naebu 內附: lit. 'internally attached.' It is not clear what the various grades of affiliation were among the Jurchen and other groups who pledged loyalty to Koryŏ.

Palace Library Yi Sŏngmi, and military commander at the Bureau of Royal Inspectors, General Yŏm Han, and others, silver medicine boxes. Other military clerks were given reward office according to rank.

Autumn, seventh month. The chiefs of Chijŭl village and other Northeastern Jurchen communities requested affiliation with Koryŏ and offered a tribute of local products.

A decree read: "The Black Water [Malgal] interpreter Kogasŏro persuaded the Eastern Tribesmen to join our prefectures and counties. Because of this merit he should be granted the title of Executive Captain in the Capital Gate Division, and granted the name 'Maeng.'"

The Local Navy Command for the Southeastern seaboard reported: "The Japanese Wangch'ikchŏng 王則貞 and Songyŏngnyŏn 松永年 and others, forty-two people, came to request [permission] to present local products. The local representative[30] of Iki island dispatched Tŭngjŏng Anguk 藤井安國 and others, thirty-three people, also requesting permission to present local products." The king decreed that they should be sent via sea to the capital.

Eighth month. The king dispatched Chamberlain for the Royal Stud Kim Yanggam and Drafting Advisor of the Royal Secretariat No Tan to Song to proffer thanks for their generosity and to offer tribute goods.

Ninth month. The Hallim Academy reported: "As for the eleven Eastern Jurchen villages including Taeran that allied themselves with Koryŏ,[31] we request to turn them into the eleven prefectures named Pinju, Iju, Pokchu, Hangju, Sŏju, Sŭpchu, Minju, Taeju, Kyŏngju, Puju, and Wanju, and also to confer on them sealed letters; they too ought to resort under Kwisun-ju." The king agreed.

Winter, twelfth month. Liao dispatched Ningzhou prefect Daze to offer congratulations on the king's birthday.

---

30 *Kudanggwan* 句當官: Not certain what kind of office this refers to, perhaps a Japanese title.

31 Here too the term *naebu* 內附 is used

Munjong Twenty-eighth year [1074]

Seventh year of the Xining era of Song, tenth year of the Xianyong era of Liao

Spring, second month. The captain of a Japanese ship, Chungni 重利, and others, thirty-nine people, arrived and presented local products.

Summer, fourth month. Because of the drought, markets were moved.

Yi Ha and twenty-five others passed the composition test of the civil service examination, and two people passed the classics examination.

Sixth month. The Eastern Jurchen General "Embraced by Koryŏ" Choyangin and others came to present horses.

The Assistant Professor in Medicine Ma Shian from Yangzhou in Song and others, eight people in all, arrived.

Autumn, seventh month. Yi Chingmang was appointed Junior Vice-director of the Department of Ministries.

Eighth month. The Eastern Jurchen General "Seeking Refuge in Virtue" Sora and others, twenty-eight people in total, came to present horses. They were granted presents according to rank.

Ninth month. The fifth-generation descendant of the Marquis of Munch'ang Ch'oe Ch'iwŏn, Ch'oe Sŏnji, was appointed as Assistant at the Bureau of Dyeing.

The Western Jurchen General "Seeking Refuge in Virtue" Kosu and others, ten people in all, came to present horses.

Winter, twelfth month. Liao dispatched Director of the Court of Imperial Entertainment Jia Yong to congratulate the king on his birthday.

Munjong Twenty-ninth year [1075]

Eighth year of the Xining era of Song, first year of the Dakang era of Liao

Spring, first year. Director of the Chancellery Ch'oe Yusŏn died. Ch'oe Yusŏn succeeded to previous masters in the Confucian tradition, passing on councillorship as a family vocation. He served two kings. Although he was not regarded as having exceptional merit, everybody valued him. He was posthumously styled Munhwa and was later enshrined with the present king.

Yi Chingmang was appointed Vice-director of the Department of Ministries and manager of the Ministry of War. Chŏng Yusan was appointed assistant executive in political affairs and state historiographer; Yu Hong was made deputy commissioner of the Security Council.

Summer, fourth month. The king dispatched Executive at the Ministry of Punishments Ch'oe Sŏk to Liao to congratulate [the emperor] on his Heavenly Peace Festival, Intendant-Secretary at the Department of Royal Clan Affairs Chŏn Hamjŏng to congratulate [the heir apparent?] on the Earthly Quiescence Festival, Assistant Office Chief at the Slave Agency General Cho Yubu to offer congratulations for the new year, and Palace Censor Hŏ Ch'ung to present tribute goods.

Due to the drought, corvée laborers for various construction projects were released.

Intercalary [fourth] month. The Japanese merchant Taegang 大江 and others, eighteen people in all, came to offer local products.

Fifth month. The Grand Astrologer petitioned: "From Spring to summer it has been very hot and now rain has fallen, so we fear that the crops will suffer. We request that your majesty pray to the hills and streams." The king decreed his approval.

The Song merchant Wang Shunman and others, thirty-nine people in all, came to present local products.

Autumn, seventh month. Fifth-nine Japanese merchants arrived.

The Bureau of Military Commanders and Inspectors[32] from Liao's Eastern Capital transferred a missive requesting to settle the border east of the Amnok River. The king dispatched administrator of the Security Council Yu Hong and Junior Assistant Director of the Department of Ministries Yi Tanggam to investigate with the Liao envoy how to settle the border. However, they returned without having reached an agreement.

32 Bingma dubushu 兵馬都部署: this appears to be a contraction of two functions: military commissioner and Bureau of Imperial Inspectors.

Yi Chŏng was appointed Executive and Executive Chief of Royal Secretariat and Supreme Pillar of State; Chŏng Yusan was made Vice-minister of the Ministry of Personnel; Kim Yakchin was made Vice-minister of the Ministry of Taxation, Assistant Executive in Political Affairs, provisional manager of the Bureau of Taxation and Junior Guardian to the Heir Apparent; and Mun Chŏng was appointed Vice-minister of the Minister of Punishments and administrator of the Security Council.

Eighth month, *kyŏngin* day, first day of the month. There was a solar eclipse.

Winter, tenth month, *pyŏngsin* [eighth] day. A comet was spotted.

Eleventh month. Liao dispatched Imperial Inspector for the Jurisdiction of Yizhou Yelü Fu as informal envoy.

Twelfth month. Liao dispatched Grand Mentor Wu Da to congratulate the king on his birthday.

Yi Chŏng was put in charge of the military commissioners for the northwest, and Kim Yakchin for the military commissioners for the northeast.

Munjong Thirtieth year [1076]

Ninth year of the Xining era of Song, second year of the Dakang era of Liao

Spring, first month. The Eastern Jurchen General "Seeking Refuge in Virtue" Chang Hyang, Kaero, and others, twenty-nine people, came to present horses.

The king ordered officials to provide coats and trousers to those among the soldiers sent out to defend the border who were poor.

Second month, *chŏnghae* day, first day of the month. There was a solar eclipse.

The Eastern Jurchen Kabong and others, twenty people in all, came to offer local products.

Yi Uk and twenty-nine others passed the composition test of the civil service examination, and two people passed the classics examination.

Summer, fourth month. An official petitioned: "Recently, because of flooding, Pongju was moved and the prefecture's residence was reconstructed. However, the people have not yet managed to reestablish their livelihood, so we request an exemption of this year's grain rent, taxes, and corvée labor." The king agreed.

Liao dispatched Imperial Inspector for the Yongzhou jurisdiction Xiao Weikang with an edict announcing the passing of the empress dowager. The king, donning white dress, led his officials to receive the edict, displaying their grief.

The king dispatched Vice-minister of the Ministry of Taxation Wang Sŏk and Executive at the Ministry of Punishment Yi Chawi to Liao to express condolence and assist in the funeral.

Autumn, eighth month. The king dispatched Executive at the Ministry of Works Ch'oe Saryang to Song to express gratitude for their favors and present tribute.

An official petitioned: "The northern dynasty has established hermitages outside the pass of Chŏngyul Garrison. Please send an envoy requesting their destruction." The king followed this.

Ninth month. An official requested that according to former protocol, shooting the silk-stringed nine-pronged catapult ought to be practiced in the southern suburbs. The king agreed.

Winter, tenth month. An official petitioned: "Twenty-five monks and lay people from Japan have arrived in Yŏnggwan Prefecture, informing us that to wish the king a long life they have carved Buddhist statues. We request that they be brought to the capital to present them." The king allowed this.

Eleventh month. A decree read: "Once Yang spreads its energy, the myriad things obtain their life, but during the period of storing their Yang energy we should ensure that they can subsist. Order all administrative divisions to forbid people from hunting or fishing. Those who disobey will be punished."

Liao dispatched Director of the Court of Imperial Entertainments Shi Zonghui to hand over the robes, colored silk, and silver utensils left behind by the empress dowager.

Twelfth month. Liao dispatched Director of the Court of Imperial Entertainments Guo Shanli to congratulate the king on his birthday.

The king ordered that every exam passer, be it composition or classics, from a prefecture or county where for the past thirty or forty-five years [respectively] no one managed to put their name on the list of passers, should be given seventeen *kyŏl* of fields; those from a place where no one passed in the last hundred years should be granted twenty *kyŏl* of fields and one male and one female slave. As for those who passed the various professional examinations, each should be given land according to rank.

The *yangban* field and woodland rank system was changed; also, the system of offices was changed: a [new] hierarchy and salary scale was determined.

Munjong Thirty-first year [1077]

Tenth year of the Xining era of Song, third year of the Dakang era of Liao

Spring, second month. The Eastern Jurchen General "Embraced by Koryŏ" Pangjin and others, twenty people in all, came to present horses.

Third month. The king promoted his sons, the Marquis of Chosŏn Wang To, and the Marquis of Kyerim Wang Hŭi, to the noble rank of duke. Wang Pi was especially promoted to Acting Minister of Works and Marquis of Kŭmgwan, and Wang Ŭm was specially promoted to Acting Minister of Works, Marquis of Pyŏnhan.

The king inspected the northwestern part of the capital and gave a drinking party at West Mountain near Irwŏl-sa; again he inspected the southeastern part and gave drinking party at Gazing at the Sea Mountain.

Summer, fifth month. Yi Chŏng was appointed Probationary Grand Preceptor and Director of the Chancellery, and died on that very day.

Autumn, seventh month. The Song merchant Lin Qing and others, twenty-eight people, came to present local products.

Eighth month. The Sacrificial Rite Commissioner for Naju Province, Vice-director of the Palace Treasury Yi Tanggam, petitioned: "The Chinese envoys are ordered to pass by Koman Island hostel, yet because it is somewhat far from the sea lane, the ships find it inconvenient. We request that a guesthouse be constructed in Chŏnghae County under the jurisdiction of Hongju as a place to receive and send off [the Chinese embassy]." A decree was issued to put this into effect, and [the guesthouse] was called Anhŭng.

Ninth month. The Song merchant Yang Congsheng and others, forty-nine people, came to present local products.

Winter, eleventh month. Chŏng Yusan was made manager of the Ministry of Rites; Kim Haenggyŏng was made manager of the Ministry of War; Mun Chŏng was made assistant executive in political affairs and commissioner to the resident governor of the Western Capital; Ch'oe Yugil was made probationary minister of works and manager of the Finance Commission.

The Eastern Jurchen General "Seeking Refuge in Virtue" Kangsu and others, fifty-eight people, came to present horses.

Twelfth month. Liao dispatched the Acting Grand Mentor Yang Xiangji to congratulate the king on his birthday.

T'amna offered tribute.

Munjong Thirty-second year [1078]

First year of the Yuanfeng era of Song, fourth year of the Dakang era of Liao

Summer, fourth month. U Wŏllyŏng and nineteen others passed the composition test of the civil service examination, and three people passed the classics examination.

A Buddhist maigre ritual was held at Tongnim and Taeun temples to wish the Song emperor a long life on the occasion of his birthday.

The Military Instructor from Mingzhou in Song, Gu Yungong, came with a letter from the Song emperor stating his intention to send an embassy.

The king said: "Being deemed worthy to look forward to an embassy from the Great Dynasty is something that fills me with joy and dread at the same time. May all those in charge [of receiving the embassy] do honor to their office; when receiving them at the guesthouse, let nothing be amiss. Those who work diligently and faithfully ought to be rewarded with a promotion beyond the normal step up; those who are lazy and inattentive, may be liable to demotion."

Sixth month. Song dispatched the Senior Policy Critic An Tao and Royal Recorder Chen Mu with an imperial edict, also bestowing on the king robes, a belt, saddle, silk, musical instruments, and gold and silver objects. The king received the edict; when the ceremony was completed, he told those around him: "How extraordinary that the emperor does not neglect this small country, yet dispatches his great ministers far away. Being the object of such rare grace fills me with pride, and at the same time I cannot hide my feelings of shame." The heir apparent led the officials in expressing congratulations. The Eastern and Western Capital, the military commissioners of the Western and Eastern border circuits, the eight departments and four protectorates all expressed their congratulation. The king ordered the heir apparent to host a banquet for the visiting envoys in Kŏndŏk Hall [of the palace].

Autumn, seventh month. An Tao and the rest of his party were about to return, so the king entrusted them with a memorial of gratitude. Furthermore he also revealed that he suffered from stroke-induced paralysis, and requested medical officials and medicine. At the time relations with Song had been severed for a long time, and when An Tao and the others first came, the king and all the people of the country were joyful. Beyond the customary gifts of clothes, belts, and saddles, gifts of gold, silver, valuables, grains, and various other things were beyond count. When they were about to return, since the ships could not carry everything, they requested to trade the goods they had received for silver, and the king instructed his officials to give permission for this. An Tao and Chen Mu were avaricious by nature, and frequently they requested the number of dishes be reduced and the amount saved be given in silver. At the time people said the following: "After the return of the embassy of Executive Lü Duan, we did not see any envoys from China for a long time. Now when we heard they were coming, we looked forward with sky-high hope. We certainly never expected their actions to be like this."

The golden pagoda of Hŭngwang-sa was finished. Silver was used on the inside and gold on the outside, 427 *kŭn* of silver were used and 144 *kŭn* of gold.

Ninth month. Japan returned Koryŏ and other sailors who had been cast adrift from T'amna, eighteen people altogether.

The Capital Military Command petitioned: "The eight *pugok* of Chuŭm are located on a plain near the sea, and they have been raided numerous times by the pirates from the Eastern circuit. The people are not at ease where they live, so we request that the city be moved." A decree was issued to that effect.

The Jurchen Komasu and others, fourteen people in all, came to submit. They were settled in the prefectures of the Southern Border Circuit.

Winter, tenth month. The Eastern Jurchen Marihae and others, twenty-three people, came to court. The king ordered officials to change their names and bestow official titles on them.

The Capital Military Command petitioned: "The walls of five cities including Chŏngju are big yet their population small; we request to relocate 100 households each from prefectures and counties in the interior to resettle these cities." The king agreed.

It was forbidden for officials and people to wear clothes of any shade of yellow.

Eleventh month. The Liao Gift Transmitting Envoy, Imperial Inspector for the Yizhou jurisdiction Yelü Wen, arrived.

Twelfth month. Liao dispatched Director of the Office of Regalia Lü Shian to congratulate the king on his birthday.

Munjong Thirty-third year [1079]

Second year of the Yuanfeng era of Song, fifth year of the Dakang era of Liao

Spring, second month. Kim Che was appointed Vice-minister of the Ministry of Personnel and Assistant Executive in Political Affairs.

The Eastern Jurchen chief Nura and others came to present horses.

Summer, fourth month. The Eastern Jurchen Yaŭpkan came to submit, saying "My father Arabul and mother Oswae, my older brother Chejuna and other members of my family, six people, in the *chŏngsa* year [1077] came to submit, now I wish to join them." The king said "Even though barbarians are similar to animals, they still have feelings of filial piety. He should be allowed to be with his parents and other family members, and settle in the Yŏngnam area."

The Western Jurchen Suuna and others, six people, came to court and submitted the office titles conferred by the northern court. Instead they were granted the title of *wŏnbo* and the king also bestowed gold and silk.

Fifth month. Northern barbarian bandits were raiding the P'yŏngno Pass. Sub-lieutenants Kanggŭm, Chongbo, and others lay in ambush in the grass waiting for the bandits. When they fired at the two people in the vanguard, the rest dispersed. They were given a reward.

Sixth month, *chŏngyu* day, first day of the month. There was a solar eclipse.

The Western Jurchen General "Seeking Refuge in Virtue" Koran and others, twenty people, came to present camels.

Autumn, seventh month. Song dispatched Secretarial Receptionist at the Office for Audience Ceremonies Wang Shunfeng and Hallim Medical Officials Xing Zao, Zhu Daoneng, Chen Shen, Shao Huaji, and others, eighty-eight people, carrying an imperial decree they came to deliver medicine.

Eighth month. The Song merchant Lin Qing and others, twenty-nine people, came to present local products.

Ninth month. Japan returned our castaways, the merchant An Kwang and others, forty-four people in all.

Winter, eleventh month. The Japanese merchant Tŭngwŏn 藤原 and others came with thirty conch shells and 300 bushels of seaweed to donate to Hŭngwang-sa to wish the king a long life.

Twelfth month. Liao dispatched Royal Recorder Ma Gaojun to congratulate the king on his birthday.

Munjong Thirty-fourth year [1080]

Third year of the Yuanfeng era of Song, sixth year of the Dakang era of Liao

Spring, second month. A decree read: "The late Director of the Chancellery Wang Ch'ongji and Vice-minister of the Ministry of Rites and Commissioner of the Security Council Chŏng Paegŏl were both loyal and upright, and with their uncommon skills they stood out in their times. Although a long time has passed, how can we forget them! It is fitting to bestow special concern so as to clarify how highly I consider such worthies. Wang Ch'ongji should be conferred the title of Probationary Grand Preceptor, Royal Secretary, and Chŏng Paegŏl Probationary Grand Marshal, Director of the Chancellery, Marquis of Kwangyu.

Third month. The king invested his son Wang Su as Acting Minister of Works, Probationary Director of the Department of Ministries, and Marquis of Puyŏ.

The Ministry of Punishments petitioned: "The Ministry of Taxation has appropriated the lands of Hŭngwang-sa and given them to Mallyŏng Hall. We request that they be punished." The king ruled that the position of the officials and clerks at the Ministry of Taxation [who were responsible for this] should be taken away and that the lands and villages be returned.

The Eastern Jurchen General "Embraced by Koryŏ" Yu Sin and others came to court.

The king dispatched vice-minister at the Ministry of Taxation Yu Hong and Executive at the Ministry of Rites Pak Illyang to Song to give thanks for their gift of medicine and also to present tribute.

Summer, fifth month. Kim Sangje and seventeen others passed the composition test of the civil service examination, and three people passed the classics examination.

Sixth month. The outer protective pagoda in stone covering the golden pagoda of Hŭngwang-sa was finished. An amnesty was declared.

Autumn, seventh month. Yu Hong and others returned from Song. The Song emperor had bestowed on the king robes, gold-threaded silk, and silver vessels. Originally, when Yu Hong and his party set sail, a gale suddenly started, nearly overturning the ships. When they took stock after reaching Song, about half of the tribute products had perished. The emperor comforted them and sent them back with an edict urging the king not to punish Yu Hong and the rest of the embassy.

Song dispatched the medical official Ma Shian to Koryŏ.

Ninth month. State Councilor Chŏng Yusan three times submitted a letter requesting to retire on account of his age; the king conferred a cane and table but let him continue his work. Not long after he insisted very strongly to retire, and the king allowed this.

Pyŏngsul [27th] day. The king traveled to the Western Capital.

Intercalary [ninth] month. Satsuma 薩摩 Prefecture in Japan dispatched an envoy to present local products.

Winter, eleventh month, *kich'uk* day, first day of the month. There was a solar eclipse.

Kihae [eleventh] day. The king returned from the Western Capital and declared an amnesty.

Twelfth month. Liao dispatched the imperial inspector of the Shuizhou jurisdiction Gao Si to congratulate the king on his birthday.

Eastern Tribesmen were fomenting insurrection. Executive Chief of Royal Secretariat Mun Chŏng was made commander of the expeditionary force; Ch'oe Sŏk, Associate Manager of Security Council Affairs, and Vice-minister at the Ministry of War Yŏm Han were made Military Commissioners, and Senior Transmitter Yi Ŭi was made Vice-military Commissioner. Leading 30,000 cavalry and infantry troops, they camped outside Chŏngju. At night they divided into three armies of 10,000, and each led them from different routes straight at the bandits' lair. When dawn broke, suddenly the roar of drums shook the earth and the bandits shook with fear. Then they led the troops into the attack, killing 392 bandits and capturing 39 of their leaders. They also obtained more than a hundred horse and cattle while the instruments [weapons] they had thrown away covered the earth in heaps. In all more than ten settlements were destroyed. When night fell they returned in triumph. After reporting their victory, the king dispatched First Assistant Office Chief Pae Wi with a decree to Mun Chŏng and others stating: "Recently one thing after the other caused trouble at the border, keeping me worried from dawn to dusk. Reading what you have reported, thanks to your great plan the tribesmen have been subjugated and a scourge of the people has been removed. This also means that I no longer have to look back over my shoulder to the eastern side and worry. This is solely thanks to your merit."

The king then especially bestowed on Mun Chŏng a silver box with a weight of 100 *yang*, and on Ch'oe Sŏk, Yŏm Han, and Yi Ŭi each one silver box weighing 50 *yang*, which were all filled with incense.

Munjong Thirty-fifth year [1081]

Fourth year of the Yuanfeng era of Song, seventh year of the Dakang era of Liao

Spring, first month. Mun Chŏng was made Merit Subject Promoting Loyalty and Aiding Edification, Crushing the Bandits and Pacifying the Border. He was also specially raised to Supreme Pillar of State, State-building Count of Changyŏn County with a Stipend Village of 1,000 households, 200 effectively enfeoffed. Ch'oe Sŏk was made Acting Minister of Works, Vice-minister of the Ministry of Personnel, and Assistant Executive in Political Affairs, manager of affairs at the Finance Commission, Pillar of State. Kim Yanggam was made Assistant Executive in Political Affairs, Minister of the Ministry of War, and concurrently Resident Governor of the Western Capital,

Pillar of State. Yŏm Han was appointed Vice-minister at the Ministry of War.

The Administrator of Military Affairs in the Northwest Circuit, Wang Chŏ, petitioned: "The Western Tribesman chief Abuhwan and others, nine people in all, have devoted themselves to defending the border. It would be fitting to grant them reward ranks." The king ordered to grant Abuhwan and others, three people in total, the title of general "Mollified from Afar," and Sandu and others, six people in all, the title of general "Embraced by Koryŏ." All were given presents according to rank.

Second month. The Western Jurchen chief Ch'adan and others, six people in all, came to present iron armor and weapons. The king bestowed on them robes, belts, and silk according to rank. He then also decreed "All those among the Eastern or Western Chiefs who want to have an audience, should first report to the Military Commissioner, and only after securing permission are they allowed to come to the palace. This should be a permanent rule."

The Song merchant Lin Qing and others, thirty people in all, came to present local products.

A decree read: "Last winter the barbarian devils in the north-eastern circuit were wiped out in one morning, and the border incursions ceased at once. This is all thanks to the numinous aid of the ancestors above, and the valiant stratagems of the officers below. Now that the troops have returned in triumph, we should report this to the Ancestral Shrine and the Six Tombs. A date should be selected for this event."

Third month. The king went to Changwŏn Pavilion.

Kim Yanggam was provisionally put in charge of affairs at the Security Council.

An edict determined that parents aged more than seventy but less than eighty were to be allocated one attending taxable male;[33] those less than ninety would be allocated two, and those up to the age of ninety five.

Because it was the birthday of the Song emperor, the king gave a banquet at the guesthouse where Ma Shian resided, and also bestowed gifts for this

---

[33] *Chŏng* 丁: generally used for anyone above the age of 16 who becomes liable to tax and corvée duties.

ceremonial occasion.

Summer, fourth month. Mun Chŏng petitioned: "Now is the month for agricultural activities; rain has been plentiful and the people hardly have enough time to till the fields. I request that your highness, embodying heaven and nurturing the people, would cease the corvée labor for the constructions at Hŭngwang-sa as well as the commissioners for inspecting the twelve granaries so as to relieve the people's troubles." The king agreed.

The king dispatched Vice-minister at the Ministry of Rites and Executive at the Ministry of Personnel Yi Chawi to Song to present tribute and to give thanks for the granting of doctors and medicine.

The Foreign Relations Office petitioned: "The Song person Yang Zhen has arrived here in a merchant ship and claims that he is qualified for the civil examination test but has failed repeated tests. On the basis of what was stated please send him back to his country." The king agreed.

Fifth month. The Eastern Jurchen chief Chin Sun and others, twenty-three people in all, came to present horses. The king ruled: "All of the foreign people who come to court should not stay in the capital for more than fifteen days. This should become a permanent rule."

The king dispatched Commissioner of Royal Reception Ko Mongsin to Liao to congratulate the emperor on the Heavenly Peace festival, Junior Reparationer Wi Kang to give thanks for birthday presents bestowed, Office Chief at the Ministry of Taxation Ha Ch'ungje to present tribute, and Audience Usher Ch'oe Chuji to give congratulations for the new year.

Sixth month. Vice-minister at the Ministry for Personnel Ch'oe Sŏk and others petitioned: "Last year's presented scholar No Chun is the son of an illegitimate union of his father with a close relative.[34] Please bar him from officialdom for life."

The king said: "In selecting and employing people one should not always stick to precedent. Like all the other presented officials, he can be given an office and registered on the audience roll."

State Councilor Mun Chŏng and others argued: "Only when the family is

---

[34] *Taegongch'in* 大功親: comprises several relations including first degree cousins.

straightened can the country be governed. No Chun's father failed to have a proper marriage, and thereby muddled and sullied human morals. However, our country reveres Confucian culture, and we urgently need to employ scholars. Please give him a grade and office." The king followed this.

Autumn, seventh month. Yi Chingmang, who had retired as assistant executive in political affairs, died.

Eighth month. The Western Jurchen Mandu and others, seventeen people altogether, came to submit together with their families. The Foreign Relations Office petitioned: "According to the old regulations, apart from those border people of our country who had been taken by barbarian bandits but came because they missed their homeland, and those from Song China who have certain talents, in cases such as Black Water [Malgal] and Jurchen, they would certainly not have been allowed to enter. Now according to these old regulations Mandu and his ilk should be sent back."

But Vice-minister at the Ministry of Rites No Tan argued: "Even though Mandu and those who came with him are ignorant folks, they came here because they admired our righteousness. Thus we cannot refuse them, They should be settled in the counties south of the mountains, and entered into the tax registers." The king followed his advice.

The king ruled: "For a long time the palace in the Western Capital has lain in ruins. We should recruit laborers to repair it. Moreover ten *li* east and west of the [Western] Capital spots should be divined to construct a left and right palace so as to be used as a royal residence during tours of inspection."

The Song merchant Li Yuanxu and others, sixty-eight people, came to present local products.

The Eastern Jurchen General "Seeking Refuge in Virtue" Hogan came to present horses.

Ninth month. The Northeastern barbarian tribesman leader Ahae sent his son Sŏhae and others to court.

Winter, tenth month, *kapcha* [11th] day. The king went to the P'yŏngju hot springs, and returned on the *kyeyu* [20th] day.

The kind declared an amnesty.

The king ordered that all soldiers of the capital and beyond who had parents of seventy or older and no other brothers should be allowed to care for their parents, and start their military service only after their parents had died.

Eleventh month. Yi Chŏnggong was made Assistant Executive in Political Affairs and State Historiographer.

Liao dispatched the Imperial Inspector for the jurisdiction on Lizhou, Yelü Derang, as informal envoy.

Vice-minister at the Ministry of War Yŏm Han addressed a letter to the king requesting retirement on account of old age. The king did not grant his request.

Twelfth month. Liao dispatched Director of the Court of Imperial Entertainments Yang Yixiao to congratulate the king on his birthday.

Manager of affairs at the Bureau of Astrology Yang Kwan'gong petitioned: "Now I have corrected the calendar for the coming year, and it contains no mistakes or questionable passages. Only the Last Day of the year has been settled as a dog day following the Great Song Calendar since the *kimi* year [1079].[35] However, according to books on yin and yang [prognostication], 'the first dragon day (*chin'il* 辰日) that is closest to the Great Cold (Taehan 大寒) day shall be the Last Day.' Our country has been using this day for a long time. Moreover, the old histories say that in the Xia dynasty it was called Jiaping 嘉平, in the Yin [Shang] Dynasty Qingsi 淸祀, in the Zhou Dala 大蜡, and in the Han La 臘. Although the names are all different, it is all about repaying the gods at the end of the year by hunting animals and gathering together a myriad offerings. This should not be randomly changed, so I request that officials be entrusted with working out the details and then put [the calendar] into practice." The king followed this.

Vice-minister at the Ministry of Works Hong Tŏksŏng twice sent a letter

---

35 *Nap'il* 臘日: as explained here, it was often the third dog day [eleventh of the twelve earthly branches, *sul* 戌] after the winter solstice, usually a day of offerings to give thanks for the harvest. Although not exactly the last day of the lunar calendar year, it was one of the last and similar in custom to New Year's Eve.

requesting retirement on account of old age but the king did not allow it.

Munjong Thirty-sixth year [1082]

Fifth year of the Yuanfeng era of Song, eighth year of the Dakang era of Liao

Second month. The Eastern Jurchen Yoŏgo and others came to court.

Summer, fourth month. A commoner from Hongwŏn County found 100 *yang* of gold and 150 *yang* of silver when digging the earth, and presented it to the king. The king said "Heaven bestowed this" and then returned it.

Fifth month. Because of the drought, the king prayed for rain. On the *chŏngmi* [27th] day it rained heavily.

Sixth month. The king declared a pardon and raised the office rank of all officials in the two capitals by one rank.

Autumn, eighth month. The Song merchant Chen Yi and others came to present treasures.

The Eastern Tribesman bandit chief Chang Hyang and others, fourteen people, were allocated land in a remote place south of the mountains.

Ninth month. On the *kyemi* [5th] day the king went south on a tour of inspection. On the *chŏnghae* [9th] day he reached Pongsŏng County, and gave a banquet for the double ninth festival. He ordered officials of the Chancellery and Security Council, as well as his close officials, to compose poetry. On the *ŭlsa* [27th] day they reached Onsu [Hot springs] Prefecture.

Winter, tenth month. The king composed a poem and ordered his close officials to present matching poems, which were then ranked. Senior Policy Advisor Yi Chŏng's poem was the most outstanding, and the king granted him a horse from the royal stables. The others were granted silk according to rank.

Eleventh month. On the *kapsin* [7th] day the king returned to the capital, and decreed that all the mountain and river spirits he traversed on his journey should be given higher titles. The accompanying officials were also to be given higher reward titles. As for the clerks and servants, they were given presents according to rank. The prefectures, counties, and postal stations along the route he had taken were remitted half of their land rents and taxes for this year.

Tsushima sent and envoy to present local products.

Twelfth month. Liao dispatched the Imperial Inspector for the jurisdiction of Shuizhou, Li Kesui, to congratulate the king on his birthday.

Executive Chief of the Royal Secretariat Kim Yakchin died.

Munjong Thirty-sixth year [1083]

Sixth year of the Yuanfeng era of Song, ninth year of the Dakang era of Liao

Spring, first month. The king feasted the elderly on the polo court and bestowed presents according to rank.

Yi Chŏnggong and Ch'oe Sŏk were both appointed Executive and Executive Chief of the Department of Royal Secretariat; Kim Yanggam and Wang Sŏk were appointed Vice-director and Junior Vice-director respectively of the Department of Ministries.

Second month. The Eastern Jurchen General "Seeking Refuge in Virtue" Yobin and others came to present horses; each was granted a reward office.

Third month. Ŭm Chŏng and thirteen others passed the composition test of the civil service examination, three people passed the classics examination, and one passed by royal favor. The old regulations merely provided for one examination administrator to take charge of the examinations, but from now on an associate examination administrator was also installed, and this became a permanent fixture.

Summer, fourth month. A decree read: "From spring to summer is the prime season for agriculture, yet frost and hail have caused destruction. I worry that prisoners have thoughts of resentment that are blocking things up; have all those imprisoned in the capital and beyond tried in a lenient way. All the corvée labor at construction sites should be halted."

Fifth month, *pyŏngja* day, first day of the month. The king felt indisposed.

Autumn, seventh month, *sinyu* [18th] day. The king's illness grew serious, and he bequeathed an edict transmitting the throne to the heir apparent, Wang Hun. He died in Chunggwang Hall. Later that day the heir apparent ascended the throne.

The king dispatched Senior Policy Monitor for Drafting Royal Decrees O Injun to Liao to announce the king's passing.

Eighth month, *kyemi* [10th] day. The king was given the posthumous title Inhyo [Humane and Filial] and the temple name Munjong. On the *kapsin* [11th] day he was buried at Kyŏng-nŭng.

Yi Chehyŏn wrote: "Hyŏnjong, Tŏkchong, Chŏngjong, and Munjong: What the father accomplished, the sons continued, and when the older brother died the younger one arose. Thus from beginning to end a period spanning eighty years was truly flourishing. Munjong himself was diligent and frugal, he promoted men of talent and wisdom, he loved the people and was compassionate in meting out punishment. He esteemed learning and respected the elderly; just as you do not lend famous vessels to criminals, he did not transfer authority to those he was intimate with. Even in the case of close relatives, without merit they would not get any reward. Even in the case of cherished people in his inner circle, if they were guilty, he would punish them. He did not have more than ten eunuchs and servants, and palace attendants had to be selected on the basis of their talent and capacity, and they numbered not much more than twenty. Superfluous offices were removed, other affairs were simplified to save money and enrich the state. The great granaries were replete with the rice of many harvests, families were provided for and people were satisfied. Thus it was called an era of great peace, and the Song dynasty frequently bestowed edicts of praise and reward, while the Liao dynasty annually congratulated the king on his birthday. To the east the Japanese crossed the sea to present treasures, to the north the tribesmen knocked at our gates to receive a place to settle. Therefore, Lin Yuan considered our dynasty one of sagely rule.[36] The only

36 Lin Yuan was originally from Song but became citizen of Koryŏ and served under King

problem is that he changed one county in Kyŏnggi Province into a Buddhist temple, which was more resplendent than the palace, and whose walls were higher than those of the capital. It had a golden pagoda and everything imaginable, making one doubt whether it could not be compared to Emperor Liang of Wu. When one wants to give praise to a person's qualities, it is saddening that one has to bring this up."

The king [Sunjong] went to Sinbong Pavilion and declared an amnesty.

Winter, tenth month. A Buddhist ritual was held at Hoegyŏng Hall for three days, and 30,000 monks were fed.

The king raised his younger brother Wang Un to the position of Probationary Grand Preceptor and Royal Secretary.

The king suffered from a slight illness, but living in a shed and consumed by grief his illness grew worse. On the *ŭlmi* [23rd] day he ordered his younger brother the Duke of Kongwŏn Wang Un to provisionally take charge of state affairs, and bequeathed an edict transferring the throne to him. This day he died in the mourning parlor, at the age of thirty-seven. He was given the posthumous title of Sŏnhye 宣惠 and the temple name Sunjong 順宗.

On the *pyŏngsin* [24th] day the Duke of Kongwŏn, Wang Un [King Sŏnjong], ascended the throne in Sŏnjŏng Hall.

Yi Chehyŏn wrote: "The three-year mourning is a custom observed from the son of heaven down to ordinary people. However, when it comes to those coming from all around to admire one who wears the crudest mourning clothes, eats only gruel, bears the suffering on his face, and wails in grief, such has not been heard of since the time of Duke Wen of Teng. When Sunjong was faced with the death of his father Munjong, he was so overcome with grief that it made him ill and after four months he passed away. Although it surpasses the practices of the sages, the sincerity of his love for his father was utmost."

Injong. See his biography in *Koryŏsa* 98.

The king [Sŏnjong], at the head of all his officials and wearing mourning clothes went to the morgue hall to make sacrifices.

Eleventh month, *kyŏngsin* [19th] day. The king personally opened the mortuary for the funerary cortege and wept with utmost grief. He [Sunjong] was buried in Sŏng-nŭng.

The Hallim Academy petitioned: "If there are any names of prefectures, counties, and other administrative areas throughout the country, or of temples and public and private buildings, and names of officials and lower classes that violate the taboo on the king's personal name or have the same sound, they should be corrected." The king agreed.

The king went to Sinbong pavilion and declared an amnesty. All military and civilian officials were promoted by one rank.

The king dispatched Attendant Censor Yi Chain to Liao to announce the passing [of the two kings]. When Yi Chain arrived, the Liao emperor refused him permission to enter the capital hostel, and interrogated him: "when two rulers die in quick succession, there must be another reason, you should report the real situation."

Yi Chain addressed the emperor: "Our ruler had an illness, which was aggravated by his grief. This gradually got worse and worse, truly there is no other reason. Please detain me here and dispatch special envoys to my country and investigate the officials there. If they find out that I have deceived you, I deserve the heaviest punishment."

His sincere words convinced the emperor who left the city to come to the tent where he met with Yi Chain and comforted him.

Twelfth month. A P'algwan Assembly was organized. The king went to the tent in front of Sinbong pavilion and received congratulations from the assembled officials. He then went to Pŏbwang-sa. The assembly was held this late because of the previous month's national mourning.

Tables

Table 1. Offices and posts in T'aebong and early Koryŏ
(Based on Cho Insŏng, "Hu Samguk ŭi chŏngnip," in *Han'guksa* 11 (Kwach'ŏn: Kuksa p'yŏnch'an wiwŏnhoe, 1993), 150)

Office	Top post	Second	Lower posts
廣評省 State Council	侍中 chancellor	侍郎 vice-chancellor	郎中 director 員外郎 vice-director
內奉省 Dept. Of Administration	令 minister	卿 vice-minister	監 director 理決 assistant director 評察 assistant chief 郎中 office chief
*內議省 Advisory Council			
*禮賓省 [供賓省?] Foreign Relations Office			
*元鳳省 Academy of Letters			
徇軍部 Min. of Police and Provost Marshal			
兵部 Min. of Defense			
倉部 Min. of Finance			
義刑臺 Min. of Justice			
都航司 Min. of the Navy			
物藏省 Min. of Royal Treasures and Crafts			
內泉部 Min. of the Court Treasury			
珍閣省 Dep. of the Royal Treasury			
白書省 Ministry of Education			
內軍 Honor Guard			

Note: the only explicit mention of Kungye's administrative reforms is in *Samguk sagi*, which describes the system implemented in 904, when his Majin state was proclaimed. This is the T'aebong (proclaimed 911) system, which is derived from the appointments issued by Wang Kŏn in the sixth month of his first year (918). Additional early Koryŏ offices found in the *Koryŏsa chŏryo* are marked with an asterisk.

Table 2. Local officials' ranks in early Koryŏ (*hyangp'um* 鄕品)
(Based on Pak Yong'un, "Chungang ŭi chŏngch'i chojik," in *Han'guksa* 13 (Kwach'ŏn: Kuksa p'yŏnch'an wiwŏnhoe, 1993), 127)

Rank (*p'um* 品)	Rank title	Level (*tŭnggŭp* 等級)
1品	*samjungdaegwang* 三重大匡	1
	chungdaegwang 重大匡	2
2品	*taegwang* 大匡	3
	chŏnggwang 正匡	4
3品	*taesŭng* 大丞	5
	chwasŭng 佐丞	6
4品	*taesang* 大相	7
	wŏnbo 元甫	8
5品	*chŏngbo* 正甫	9
6品	*wŏnyun* 元尹	10
	chŏngyun 正尹	11
7品	*chŏngjo* 正朝	12
	chŏngwi 正位	13
8品	*poyun* 甫尹	14
9品	*kunyun* 軍尹	15
	sinyun 中尹	16

Note: in early Koryŏ this system was used for all officials

Table 3. Department of Royal Secretariat – Chancellery (Chungsŏ-Munha-sŏng 中書門下省)

Junior 1	門下侍中 director of the Chancellery	中書令 royal secretary
Senior 2	門下侍郞平章事 executive chief of the Chancellery 門下平章事 executive of the Chancellery	中書侍郞平章事 executive chief of Royal Secretariat 中書平章事 executive of Royal Secretariat
Junior 2	參知政事 assistant executive in political affairs 政堂文學 assistant executive in letters 知門下省事 administrator	
Senior 3	左常侍 senior policy advisor	左常侍 junior policy advisor
Junior 3	直門下 intendant of the Chancellery	
Senior 4	左諫議大夫 senior policy critic (=司議大夫)	右諫議大夫 junior policy critic
Junior 4	給事中 reviewing policy advisor	中書舍人 drafting advisor
Junior 5	起居注 royal recording editor 起居郎 royal recording secretary	起居舍人 royal recorder
Senior 6	左補闕 senior reparationer	右補闕 junior~
Junior 6	左拾遺 senior policy monitor	右拾遺 junior policy monitor
Junior 7	門下錄事 chief registrar of the chancellery	中書注書 chief scribe of the Roy. Sec.
	主事 (6) master scribe (chief clerk) 令史(6) scribe first class 書令史 (6) scribe second class 注寶 (3) keeper of seals 待詔 (2) decree attendant 書藝 (2) calligrapher 試書藝 (2) probationary calligrapher 記官 (20) recorder second class 書手 (26) copyist first class 直省 (8) department custodian 電吏 (180) message bearer 門僕 (10) page	

Note: valid after Munjong's reign (see Pak Yong'un, "Chungang ŭi chŏngch'i chojik," *Han'guksa* 13, 31); one office per person, except were another figure is given

Table 4. Sangsŏ-sŏng 尙書省 Department of Ministries: staff (after Munjong's reign)
(See Pak Yong'un, "Chungang ŭi chŏngch'i chojik," *Han'guksa* 13: 42)

	都省 Department of ministries	6部 Six ministries *	屬司 Subordinate offices
Junior 1	尙書令 director of the Department of Ministries	判…事 (one for each ministry) minister	
Senior 2	左僕射 vice director 左僕射 junior vice-director		
Junior 2	知省事		
Senior 3		尙書 vice minister	
Junior 3	左丞 senior assistant director 右丞 junior assistant director	知部事 administrator	
Senior 4		侍郎 executive	
Junior 4			
Senior 5	左司郎中 first office chief 右司郎中 second office chief	郎中 office chief	郎中
Senior 6	左司員外郎 first assistant office chief 右司員外郎 second assistant office chief	員外郎 assistant office chief	員外郎
Junior 6			
Junior 7			

* Yuk-pu 六部: Ho-bu 戶部 (Ministry of Taxation), I-bu 吏部 (Personnel), Hyŏng-bu 刑部 (Punishments), Kong-bu 工部 (Works), Ye-bu 禮部 (Rites), Pyŏng-bu 兵部 (War)

GLOSSARY

Aekchŏng-guk 掖庭局 Bureau of Royal Stewards
anch'alsa 按察使 royal inspector
anmusa 按撫使 royal commissioner of pacification
allyŏmsa 按廉使 royal inspector of local government

chaebo 宰輔. See *chaesin*
chaech'u 宰樞. See *chaesin*
chaesang 宰相. See *chaesin*
chaesin 宰臣 state councilor; councilor of state. Also *chaech'u* 宰樞, *chaesang* 宰相, *chaebo* 宰輔, *posin* 輔臣
changgo 掌固 functionaries who work for the heir apparent
Changjak-kam (Changjak-wŏn) 將作監 (將作院) Directorate (Bureau) of Construction and Maintenance; *changjak-kam* director of this institute; *changjak sogam* 將作少監 vice-director
changsŏgi 掌書記 supervising recorder
chegosa 祭告使 sacrificial rite commissioner
Chesul ŏp 製述業 composition test of the civil service exam [*chinsa*]
chi 知 … *sa* 事 minister; concurrent appointment of an official to one of the six ministries; or: manager, superintendent of another institute
chigonggŏ 知貢擧 examination administrator
chijusa 知奏事 senior transmitter
-chin 鎮 garrison
chindu 鎮頭 garrison commander
chinjang 鎮將 garrison commander
chinsa 進士 presented scholar
chipsa 執事 office manager; see Hucker 1056: ~侍: office manager, eunuch official rank 6 in the Directorate of Palace Domestic Service
Chŏlch'ung kundae 折衝軍隊 Shock Troop Brigade
chŏltosa 節度使 military governor

ch'ŏmsa 詹事 supervisor of the household of the heir apparent
Ch'ŏmsa-bu 詹事府 Household of the Heir Apparent
chŏnch'oe 殿最 evaluation by royal inspector of local magistrates, which took place twice a year; they were classified in the evaluation report as excellent (*ch'oe*) or fail (*chŏn*).
chŏlli 電吏 lightning clerk
Chonglu-si 崇祿寺 (Ch., Liao) alternate designation for the Guanglu-si (Court of Imperial Entertainments, changed to avoid a name taboo [Hucker 1666])
chŏnjak 佃作 tenant farmer
Chŏnjung 殿中 Office of Royal Clan Affairs; Palace Administration (Liao, Song)
chŏnjung sogam 展中小監 deputy director of the Office of Royal Clan Affairs
Chŏnjung-sŏng 殿中省 Office of Royal Clan Affairs; Palace Administration (Liao, Song)
Chŏnjung naegŭpsa 殿中內給事 intendant-secretary at the Department of Royal Clan Affairs
chŏnjung siŏsa 殿中侍御史 palace censor
chŏnsikwa 田柴科 stipend land system
-chu 州 greater prefecture
chubu 注簿 registrar; recorder
chumok 州牧 governor [of a first-tier prefecture]
Chungch'u-wŏn 中樞院 Security Council
chungch'uwŏnsa 中樞院使 commissioner of the Security Council
chungnangjang 中郎將 senior colonel
Ch'umirwŏn 樞密院 Security Council
ch'ungwanjŏng 春官正 director of the Spring Office
Chwauwi 左右衛 Left-Right Divisions
cishi (Ch.) 刺史: lit. censor, but usually prefect. Also: regional inspector (Han-Sui); regional chief (N-S Div-Song)

haengyŏng pyŏngmasa 行營兵馬使 military commissioner for the Expedition Corps
haengyŏng tot'ong-sa 行營都統使 supreme commander of the field army
Hammun 閤門 Office for Audience Ceremonies
hammun chihu 閤門祗候 see *kangmun chihu*
hammun injinsa 閤門引進使 reception official at the Office for Audience Ceremonies
hammunsa 閤門使 commissioner for Audience Ceremonies
hammun sain 閤門舍人 presenting official at the Office for Audience Ceremonies
hammun sŭngji 閤門承旨 see *kangmun sŭngji*
hammun t'ongsasain 閤門通事舍人 secretarial receptionist at the Office for Audience Ceremonies
hoengsŏnsa 橫宣使 informal envoy
hojang 戶長 village head
Hŏnsa 憲司 judicial commission
hu 侯 marquis
hyang 鄕 township; settlement for lower status groups
hyanggong 鄕貢 rural selectee
-hyŏn 縣 county
hyŏllyŏng 縣令 county magistrate
hyŏnwi 縣尉 county marshal

ilchik 日直 caretaker (usually at the Security Council)
injinsa 引進使 commissioner of royal reception (usually at the Office for Audience Ceremonies)

jiaolianshi (Ch.) 教練使 military instructor

kamgun 監軍 patrolling officer
kamch'al ŏsa 監察御史 investigating censor
kamch'al sahŏn 監察司憲 investigating censor

kamch'angsa 監倉使 commissioner for supervising the granaries
kamhu 監候 astronomical observer
Kammun-wi 監門衛 Capital Gate Division
kangmun chihu 閣門祗候 audience usher
kangmun sŭngji 閣門承旨 memorial reception staff
kojusa 告奏使 memorial envoy
kŏmgyo 檢校 prefix to a title: 'acting' i.e. someone holding a certain position is assigned temporarily/irregularly to another position; sometimes also in the sense of 'honorary,' i.e., not holding any real responsibility
kong 公 duke
konggŏ 貢擧 local examination; tribute examination: selection of local talents to send to the civil service examination
kong'ŭm chŏnsi pŏp 功蔭田柴法 merit and protected farmland and woodland
Kukchagam 國子監 National Academy
kukcha saŏp 國子司業 supervisor of education
kukkong 國公 Duke of State
-kun 郡 prefecture
Kungi-gam 軍器監 Directorate of Weaponry
kŭnsin 近臣 attendant councilor; member of the royal coterie
kusa 驅史 express courier
kwanch'alsa 觀察使 royal inspector
-kye 界 border circuit
Kyŏngsi-sŏ 京市署 Capital Markets Bureau
kyosŏrang 校書郎 editor-collator
kyowi 校尉 lieutenant

lingjun jiangjun (Ch.) 領軍將軍 general of the palace guard

Maeng-gun 猛軍 ferocious army
Milchiksa 密直司 see Ch'umirwŏn

Minkwan 民官 another name for the Ministry of Taxation (ho-bu 戶部; see Table 4)
-mok 牧 department
moksa 牧使 departmental commissioner
mumunsa 撫問使 appeasing and investigating commissioner
-myŏn 面 military district; here mostly translated as "region" (e.g., "military commissioner for the northwest region")

naesaryŏng 內史令 royal secretary (= *chungsŏryŏng* 中書令). Early Koryŏ: Minister of the Department of Royal Secretaries
naesa sirang p'yŏngjangsa 內史侍郎平章事 executive chief of the Royal Secretariat (chungsŏ sirang p'yŏngjangsa 中書侍郎平章事).
naesi 內侍 palace attendant
nangjang 郎將 junior colonel
-no 路 circuit
nobu 鹵簿 cortege, procession of officials holding insignia

oegwan 外官 outer officials; officials posted to local administrative units
Ŏsadae 御史臺 Censorate
ŏsadaebu 御史大夫 censor-in-chief
ŏsajaptan 御史雜端 censor of miscellaneous affairs
ŏsajungsŭng 御史中丞 vice censor-in-chief

paek 伯 count
p'an 判…*sa* 事 manager; supervisor (temporary assignment of an official to another bureau)
p'angwan 判官 administrative assistant
pang'ŏsa 防禦使 defense commissioner
paeyung kyowi 陪戎校尉 "lieutenant aide-de-camp" military rank title, ninth rank.
P'ando-sa 版圖司 Ministry of Taxation
pisŏgam 秘書監 director of the Palace Library

Pisŏ-sŏng 秘書省 Department of the Palace Library; Office of Royal Archives

pisŏ kyosŏrang 秘書校書郞 editor in the Palace Library

pisŏ kyogam 秘書校勘 proofreader in the Palace Library

Pŏpsa 法司 Court of Justice

posin 輔臣 see *chaesin*

-pu 府 district

pugok 部曲 borough; locales where non-free or semi-free people were settled; in China the term originally referred to serfs: "private retainer … a reference to one category of indentured peasants close to the status of serfs or slaves working the agrarian lands of great families who formed the social elite." (Hucker 4776)

punsa ŏsa 分司御史 local censor

pyŏlchang 別將 sub-colonel

pyŏlgam 別監 special commissioner

pyŏngma noksa 兵馬錄事 recording officer for the military commissioner

pyŏngmasa 兵馬使 military commissioner

pyŏngma pusa 兵馬副使 vice military commissioner

sa 史 assistant

Sach'ŏn-dae 司天臺 Bureau of Astronomy

sado 司徒 minister of education (ceremonial title)

sagong 司空 minister of works (ceremonial title); after 1122: refers to the vice-minister of the Ministry of Works (工部尙書)

Sahŏn-bu 司憲府 Censorate

Sajaegyŏng 司宰卿 director of the Court of Royal Entertainment; according to Hucker (no. 5785): originally court in charge of slaughtering; later unofficial reference to Guanglu-si, Court of Imperial Entertainments.

Sajae-sa 司宰寺 Court of Royal Entertainment

Sajik-tan 社稷壇 Altar for the Earth and Grain Gods

sanong 司農, also *sanonggyŏng* 司農卿 chamberlain for the National Treasury

Sam-sa 三司 Finance Commission

sangjanggun 上將軍 supreme general
sangsam[gwan] 常參[官] consultants-in-ordinary (Hucker 272); generic term for officials expected to attend audiences; usually rank five and above
Sangsŏ kogongsa 尚書考功司 Office of Merit Evaluation
sangwan 散官 prestige titles
sanwŏn 散員 executive captain
si- 試 probationary-
sigŭp 食邑 stipend village
siŏsa 侍御史 attendant censor
sobo 少保 junior guardian
So-bu 少府 Directorate of Royal Workshops
Sobu-gam 小府監 Directorate of Royal Workshops
sogyŏng 少卿 vice-director
sojang 小將: minor general
sŏnyusa 宣諭使 pacification commissioner
sŏryŏngsa 書令史 clerical scribe
su- 守 probationary; acting
-su 戍: military camp; guard station
suguksa 修國史 state historiographer
sujang 守將 defending general
sŭngji 承旨 recipient of edicts
sun'gŏmsa 巡檢使 chief military inspector
sŭngsŏn 承宣 transmitter of edicts; works at Security Council
sŭngsŏnsa 承宣使 pacification commissioner

Ta-bang 茶房 Bureau of Medicine
Taebŏn pyŏngma 大番兵馬 military commissioner for barbarian matters (from 1047 *haengwi pyŏngmasa* 行營兵馬使)
Tae-bu 大府 Palace Treasury; for Liao: Chamberlain for the Palace Bursary (Hucker 5940)
Taebu-go 大府庫 Repository of the Palace Treasury.

t'aebokkyŏng 太僕卿 chamberlain for the Royal Stud
taejanggun 大將軍 grand general
taejŏng 隊正 sub-lieutenant
tangin 堂引 hall usher; belongs to the express couriers (*kusa*)
t'aebo 太保 grand guardian
t'aebu 太傅 grand mentor
Taehak paksa 大學博士 Professor of the Taehak College
t'aehu 太后 queen dowager (empress dowager in the case of Liao)
t'aeja 太子 heir apparent
T'aemyo 太廟 (sometimes Taemyo 大廟) Ancestral Shrine
t'aesa 太史 grand astrologer
t'aesa 太師 grand preceptor
t'aesa kamhu 太史監候 see *kamhu*
T'aesaguk 太史局 Bureau of Astrology
t'aesaryŏng 太史令 see *t'aesa* 太史
T'aeŭigam 太醫監 Directorate of Medicine; director of medicine
t'aewi 太尉 grand marshal
-to 道 province
Tobusŏ 都部署 Local Navy Command
Tobyŏngmasa 都兵馬使 Capital Military Command
togang 都綱 chief merchant (representative of foreign traders in Kaesŏng)
Togwan 都官 Slave Agency
Toho 都護 protectorate
Tohobu 都護府 protectorate
tohobusa 都護府使 regional military commander
toho p'angwan 都護判官 administrative assistant to the regional military commander
tong 同 associate, jointly; prefix indicating that an official already serving in one post had been assigned, additionally, to take part in the work of another post [Hucker 7464]
tongjŏng 同正 (suffix): "equivalent to;" a term occurring only in Korean bureaucracy for an appointment with no actual duties normally

expected of someone with this title

tongpan 通判 (Ch.) controller-general [Hucker 7497]. Oversees the work of a prefect

t'ongsa sain 通事舍人 secretarial receptionist

toryŏng 都領 commandant (of specialized corps)

tot'ong 都統: commander-in-chief

tot'ongsa 都統使 commissioner of general command

Toyŏm-sŏ 都染署 Bureau of Dyeing

tunjŏn 屯田 military supply fields

ŭp 邑 town office (*ŭpsa* 邑司)

Wiwi-sa 衛尉寺 Office of Regalia

Yangbu 兩府 Chancellery and Security Council

Yangon-sŏ 良醞署 Bureau of Beverage Supervision

yangonsŏryŏng 良醞署令 director of the Bureau of Beverage Supervision

Yebin-si 禮賓寺 Foreign Relations Office

yebin sogyŏng 禮賓小卿 deputy director of the Foreign Relations Office

Yesa 禮司 Ministry of Rites (= Yejo, Yebu etc.)

yŏkpunjŏn 役分田 merit-reward land

yŏng'ŏpchŏn 永業田 land held in perpetuity

yurimnang 儒林郎 Gentleman-Confucian, prestige title of rank 9a from Sui to Song [Hucker 3074]

yusu 留守 resident governor

Yusu p'angwan 留守判官 administrative assistant to the resident governor

Yukwi 六衛 Six Armies

Weights and Measures

Establishing the modern equivalents of Koryŏ-era weights and measures is very difficult, first of all because there are few material remains that allow us to ascertain what standards were used, and second because those standards fluctuated over time. Moreover, many units existed in different categories: for example, there existed different types of *ch'ŏk* (foot) depending on their area of use.[1] I have relied primarily on the research by Yi Chongbong[2] to compile the below table, whilst also referring to works on Chinese weights and measures, mainly to determine Western equivalent terms.[3] For each unit, the Sino-Korean pronunciation is given, followed by the character, the Korean vernacular equivalent (as far as I was able to establish these), which type of unit it is, a Western translation (often established during the Treaty Port era), its relation to other key units, and finally an approximate equivalent in the metric system (only for the key units).

ch'ŏk 尺, K. *cha*	length; "foot," a standard foot was about 31.5 cm. in early Koryŏ[4]
hap 合, K. *hop*	volume; "cup," ten cups make one *sŭng*
kok 斛 K. *hwi*	volume; "bushel," equal to half a *sŏk* or 7.5 *tu*
kŭn 斤	weight; "pound" (also "catty"), equal to 16 *yang*; 640 grams in early Koryŏ[5]
kyŏl 結	area; defined as "33 square *po*" in early Koryŏ,

1 Yi Chongbong, *Han'guk chungse toryanghyŏngje yŏn'gu* (Seoul: Hyean, 2001), 305.

2 Besides the work mentioned in the previous note, see also Yi Chongbong, *Han'guk toryanghyŏng sa* (Seoul: Somyŏng ch'ulp'an, 2016).

3 See Endymion Wilkinson, *Chinese History: A Manual*. Rev. and enl. ed. (Cambridge, MA: Harvard University Press, 2000), 554–556; http://www.chinaknowledge.de/History/Terms/duliangheng.html

4 Yi Chunbong, *Han'guk toryanghyŏng sa*, 119.

5 Ibid., 161.

	or about 3,840 m^2 (almost one acre);[6] from Munjong's reign onward, land was graded in different categories, hence there were different *kyŏl* measures as well
kyŏng 頃	area; equal to 100 *mu* 畝 (240 *po* 步 "paces" by 1 pace)[7]
li (ri) 里	length; about 500 m.
mu 畝	area; equivalent to 240 *po* 步 "paces" by 1 pace
p'il 匹	length; bolt of cloth. In Silla, one bolt of silk is said to have measured 7 *po* (13 m.)[8]
po 步	length; "pace," six feet[9]
sŏk 石/碩, K. *sŏm*	as a unit of weight, "picul;" equal to 120 *kŭn*, or 76.8 kg.;[10] as a unit of volume "bushel," equal to 15 *tu*,[11] about 51 liters
sŏm 苫	volume; straw sack of rice; also sometimes in the sense of *sŏk* "bushel"
sŭng 升, K. *toe*	volume; "pint," ten cups (*hap*); 0.340 liters in early Koryŏ,[12] 0.585 liters in Song[13]
tu 斗, K. *mal*	volume; "peck," equal to ten *sŭng*
yang 兩, K. *nyang*	weight; "tael" ("ounce"), 1/16th of a *kŭn*

6 Yi Chongbong, *Han'guk chungse toryanghyŏngje*, 238.

7 http://www.chinaknowledge.de/History/Terms/duliangheng.html

8 *Han'guk minjok munhwa taebaekkwasajŏn*. http://encykorea.aks.ac.kr

9 Yi Chongbong, *Han'guk chungse toryanghyŏngje*, 305.

10 Following http://www.chinaknowledge.de/History/Terms/duliangheng.html; there is no clear evidence that it was also a unit of weight in Koryŏ.

11 Note that this is the official system; in common practice the more standard equivalent of 1 *sŏk* = 20 *tu* was used. Yi Chunbong, *Han'guk toryanghyŏng sa*, 131.

12 Yi Chunbong, *Han'guk toryanghyŏng sa*, 138.

13 Ibid., 133.

Index